INHERITANCE MATTERS

This book makes a compelling case for placing the social and legal practices of inheritance centre stage to make sense of fundamental questions of our time.

Drawing on historical, literary, sociological and legal analysis, this rich collection of original, interdisciplinary and international contributions demonstrates how inheritance is and has always been about far more than the set of legal processes for the distribution of wealth and property upon death.

The contributions range from exploring the intractable tensions underlying family disputes and the legal and political debates about taxation, to revisiting literary plots in the past and presenting a contemporary artistic challenge of heirship.

With an introduction that presents a critical mapping of the field of inheritance studies, this collection reveals the complexity of ideas about 'passing on', 'legacies' and 'heirlooms'; troubles some of the enduring consequences of 'charitable bequests', 'family money' and 'estate planning; and deepens our understanding of the intimate and political practices of inheritance.

Inheritance Matters

Kinship, Property, Law

Edited by
Suzanne Lenon
and
Daniel Monk

•HART•
OXFORD • LONDON • NEW YORK • NEW DELHI • SYDNEY

HART PUBLISHING

Bloomsbury Publishing Plc

Kemp House, Chawley Park, Cumnor Hill, Oxford, OX2 9PH, UK

1385 Broadway, New York, NY 10018, USA

29 Earlsfort Terrace, Dublin 2, Ireland

First published in Great Britain 2023

A catalogue record for this book is available from the British Library.

A catalogue record for this book is available from the Library of Congress.

ISBN: HB: 978-1-50996-481-9
ePDF: 978-1-50996-483-3
ePub: 978-1-50996-482-6

Typeset by Compuscript Ltd, Shannon

ACKNOWLEDGEMENTS

Producing an edited collection during an ongoing global pandemic and across multiple time zones was not without its challenges. We are indebted to our authors for their commitment to this project and for their outstanding intellectual contributions to the field of inheritance studies. Thank you also to our editor at Bloomsbury, Kate Whetter for her enthusiastic support for the project; to Verity Stuart for designing a stellar book cover; and to Linda Goss and Vicki Hillyard for their assistance with this book project.

In keeping with the theme and provocations in this collection Daniel would like to acknowledge his three close friends who died in December 2021. Their distinctive and bold queer legacies are immense: Simon Gaunt (1959–2021), Hennie Klein Gunnewiek (1958–2021) and Aveek Sen (1965–2021).

CONTENTS

LIST OF CONTRIBUTORS

Anne Bottomley, Emeritus Reader, Kent Law School.

Rosie Canning, PhD Candidate University of Southampton.

Allison A Cartier, Bachelor of Social Work. Juris Doctor.

Heather Conway, Professor of Property Law and Death Studies, School of Law, Queen's University Belfast.

Martin Dackling, Docent (Associate Professor)/Senior Lecturer, Joint Faculties of Humanities and Theology, Lund University.

Corinne Delmas, Professor of Sociology, Université Gustave Eiffel.

Delyth Edwards, Lecturer in Inclusion Childhood and Youth, School of Education, University of Leeds.

Máiréad Enright, Reader in Feminist Legal Studies, Birmingham Law School.

Sarah Gilmartin, Lecturer in Law and Postgraduate Research, Lancaster University.

Sheena Grattan, Barrister-at-law, TEP.

Lekha N B, Assistant Professor, Department of Sociology, Sree Narayana College.

Antony Palackal, Professor, Department of Sociology, University of Kerala.

Russell Perkins, Artist.

Mélanie Plouviez, Associate Professor, Social & Political Philosophy, Côte d'Azur University.

Rebecca Probert, Professor of Law, School of Law, Exeter University.

Anita Purewal, Lecturer in Law, Lancaster University.

Allison Tait, Associate Dean, Professor of Law, School of Law, University of Richmond.

Danaya C Wright, T Terrell Sessums and Gerald Sohn Professor in Constitutional Law, Professor of Law, University of Florida.

Jolene Zigarovich, Associate Professor, Dept of Languages & Literatures, University of Northern Iowa.

1

Introduction: Why Inheritance?

DANIEL MONK AND SUZANNE LENON

I. Why Inheritance?

Inheritance rarely takes centre stage in academic studies. Wills and probate along with estate planning are, globally, well-established categories within legal practice, and they are supported by vocational courses and professional texts. Yet 'inheritance' rarely, if at all, features in the title of an academic course; it is not a field with associations, conferences and journals. This was our experience while working in different continents and across different disciplines. We 'fell in' to thinking about inheritance through unconnected and circuitous roots. This collection emerges from a shared excitement in finding in inheritance a fresh perspective for thinking about and through fundamental social, economic and political questions. In curating this diverse collection of essays, bringing together international scholars across numerous disciplines, we want to make the case for thinking about inheritance as *foundational*. By this we mean that inheritance is and has always been about far more than the set of legal processes for the distribution of wealth and property upon death. Those processes are of course at the crux of inheritance. It is what inheritance *does*. Indeed, transferring one's property to those who remain after one's death and actually having the testamentary capacity to do so is not inconsequential. And, the chapters in this collection underscore not only what inheritance does in terms of legal processes but also what inheritances can *do to us*, what *we might do* with that which has been left us, even if that includes *refusing* an inheritance. In thinking of inheritance as foundational, we assert that these legal processes are premised on and legitimised by ways of imagining and thinking about intimate and civic relationships. The formal practices of inheritance law such as writing wills and determining intestacy division describes, codifies, reproduces, and potentially transforms the contours of family and kinship by way of property, perhaps best captured in colloquial phrases such as 'family money' and 'dead hands'. Such terms gesture to the intimacies of the social world we inherit and thus to the sociality of inheritance itself: we inherit broader social conditions that are often understood as 'natural'.

The relationships between parents and children is of course key here, and perhaps the one that most frequently comes to people's minds when thinking about inheritance. Generationality is almost implicit in the expression 'passing on', with its evocative mixture of physical and material associations. But examining inheritance laws and practices challenges essentialist assumptions: there is nothing 'natural' about laws' imagination of this relationship. A cursory look immediately brings to the fore the contrasting emphasis in civil and common law traditions between parental obligations and rights, respectively. And not far beneath the surface one comes up against the discriminatory concepts of 'primogeniture' and 'illegitimacy'. Both haunt inheritance law. Reactions against the former were fundamental to the new social orders established after the French Revolution and the US War of Independence. The legacies of the latter are fundamental to the privileging of the marital and the – often religion-inspired – policing of gender roles, sexuality and indeed the institution, if not always the lived experience, of The Family.

Resolving the question Who Will Inherit?, consequently, goes to the heart of both the most intimate aspects of people's lives and, at the same time, the most public and political relationship: that between people and the state. In both contexts the violence of the law is a recurring motif. To talk of 'disappointed heirs' invokes an array of inter-personal emotional and economic complexities. The resolution of these disputes speaks to identity, status, values and, increasingly, the politics of vulnerability and care. But broadening the focus requires acknowledging and examining structural inequalities, and in particular the legacies of racism and colonialism. Legacies here, revealed in paintings, literature and individual wills, as much as through statute and legal doctrine, are both cultural and brutally economic. The realities of widening economic inequalities and the well-documented impact of inheritance is cause alone to dig deeper into the conditions of possibilities of inheritance practices.

In mapping the intimate and political work that inheritance does, the contributors to this interdisciplinary collection draw on a variety of sources: economic statistics, crime fiction, parliamentary debates about taxation, newspapers announcements, real wills from the archives and fictional ones from literature, as well as case law and legislation. Empirical research across generations provides insight into both personal and professional narratives. Diverse theoretical frameworks provide tools to tell stories which look backwards and forwards, taking the long view and digging deep into the present. The collection is far from comprehensive in its coverage of inheritance, and complements detailed legal analysis and emerging literature across disciplines. In its breadth and depth, we hope it will inspire the foregrounding of inheritance as a frame of reference, an analytic tool, or simply a fresh lens across disciplines that offers innovative ways of thinking about our social world.

II. Themes and Narratives of this Collection

Having sketched out the broader aims of the collection we now turn to the specific perspectives offered by contributors. The chapters have intentionally been selected to collectively map the contours of critical scholarship about inheritance, and to demonstrate breadth and possibilities of thinking through inheritance. While each chapter can be read independently of each other we endeavour here to demonstrate not only overlapping concerns between the chapters but also with the existing scholarship about inheritance and with other disciplines.

Part One: Foregrounding Inequalities – Past and Present

Chapter two by Allison Tait is entitled: 'Defining Family Trees and Building Family Fortunes: A Look into Dispossession and Enrichment through Inheritance Laws'. Writing specifically about and from the perspective of the contemporary US, her work, nevertheless, foregrounds a key theme in inheritance studies which traverses temporal and spatial boundaries: the question of inequality. Existing work has identified how inheritance results in the embedding and exacerbating of economic inequalities. There is, of course, nothing new in noting this – it ever was. But it is also increasingly evident that this is the case even though more people than ever before are likely to inherit.[1] How different societies, jurisdictions, and legal and other policies, in particular taxation, respond to this; and indeed the extent to which inequality is perceived as a 'problem' and, if so whether it is one that the state can and should address, has and continues to vary, and comparative research here has thrown considerable light on national and political cultures.[2]

Tait's contribution draws attention to the intersection between legal conceptions of the family and the race and class implications of US inheritance laws and economic policies. She does this by looking at legal doctrines and definitions alongside statistical evidence of wealth, family form, and access to legal services. It is this cross-disciplinary – law/sociology/economics – method that enables her to unmask the empirically stark but, in law at least, invisible impact of rules and policies. Her analysis reveals that:

> Within the ecosystem of kinship, the forest of family trees, legal rules can prevent the accumulation of family money just as they can further it. The myriad definitions of the family written into both state and federal statute books are a crucible in which economic inequality is crafted and tempered.

Key here is not simply the well-documented centrality and privileging of the institution of marriage, but the impact of intestacy laws premised on marriage on poor, non-white and queer people, groups all far less likely to be married. One consequence of intestacy laws in the US is the extent to which they not only

[1] Atkinson (2018); Piketty (2011), (2014).

[2] A key text here is Beckert (2008). See also Cunliffe and Erreygers (2013); Mason and Finch (2000); Piketty (2014).

exclude understandings of kinship beyond the nuclear married form,[3] but also result in the 'fractionalisation' of estates and how this has led to 'considerable land loss among rural African American families'. Curiously, it is the *absence* of fractionalisation that attracts the attention of those concerned about inequality in the UK, where the practice of primogeniture ensures that vast landed states still remain in the hands of very few.[4] Indeed it was these very practices that post-revolutionary America sought to distinguish itself from in its embracement of a more individualistic testamentary freedom.[5] Nevertheless, while assessment of laws are consequently historically and jurisdictionally contingent, what is constant in both these particular contexts is the extent to which laws have served to enable the very rich to protect their wealth across generations. In turning her attention to the very rich in the US, Tait contributes an important dimension to studies of the impact of inheritance on inequality. She demonstrates that in marked contrast to the penalising impact of rigid and narrow definitions of family for the poor in the context of intestacy, for the rich, law offers remarkable flexibility that goes beyond the middle-class nuclear norm enabling immense support to transfers of wealth. Key here are the legal devices of 'family offices' and private family trusts.

In the US and elsewhere these legal devices are described, and advertised, as 'estate planning'; rather like 'family planning', it is an expression that discreetly veils its fundamental underlying aims. In relation to the latter, 'how to have sex without reproduction' and the former, 'how to pass on money without paying tax'. Both become cast as 'neutral' acts of responsible citizenship – unequal access and availability remain hidden. Estate planning devices have also become ever more sophisticated[6] and, as Tait notes, 'escaping the gaze of governance while reaping economic benefit' they serve to hide wealth as much as they help amass it. Tait demonstrates that the inequality resulting from inheritance is not just a product of state inaction or because of weak attempts at wealth redistribution through taxation and other measures, but a reality that is actively enabled by extensive, creative laws. In this way her work challenges the neoliberal logic of economic laissez faire and reveals the 'myth of non-intervention',[7] making clear the importance of studying the methods and tools of wealth protection alongside poverty and inequality.[8]

While Tait's analysis focuses on the contemporary situation in the US, she makes clear the links with the past, and that the law serves to 'compound, rather than ameliorate, historical injustice'. In doing so Tait asks us to consider, indeed to confront, the fact that there are parallels between the refusal of legal family status

[3] Intestacy laws as a site for thinking about kinship and family form is a rich field as the aims of these laws grapple with achieving 'what most people would want to happen' with value judgments of 'what should happen'. See Douglas et al (2011); Cooke (2009).

[4] See for example Jamoussi (2011); Whightman (1997).

[5] Friedman (2009).

[6] Friedman (2009); Leslie (2014); Madoff (2010); Horton (2017); Harrington (2012).

[7] Olsen (1985).

[8] Graetz and Shapiro (2005); Macdonald (2018).

to enslaved people in the past and the effect of current laws which are, on the surface, silent about race. She makes clear how change and continuity go hand in hand, and that the haunting presence of slavery in particular traverses generations and lives on in a very tangible way through the continuing violence of law.[9]

In chapter three, '"My Reputed Children": Legacies of Enslavement in Atlantic-Island Wills', the inherently and explicitly raced nature of inheritance laws and practices are explored directly. Anne Bottomley, a British property and family legal scholar, draws on a close reading of wills, taking us deep into the practices of testamentary freedom. She demonstrates vividly how wills, as archival texts, present an extraordinarily valuable and in many respects still underexplored resource for scholarship. As she notes: 'The will is a threshold: between life and death; past and future; public and private. In this sense, we need to think of the will as a potent document designed to carry (sometimes difficult) messages.' Despite the fact that wills are legal documents (although not necessarily written by lawyers), it is disciplines beyond law that have taken the lead in revealing the rich pickings they offer to academic scholarship. Historians have used them to challenge assumptions about both religious practice[10] and women's lives;[11] the notion of harm-after-death;[12] and social historians and political theorists have used wills and debates about inheritance to address issues of 'nation making' and wealth distribution.[13]

The Wills examined by Bottomley provide an intimate and visceral insight into the lived experiences of slavery and colonialism. At its heart are the status of the children born to white slave owners and black women and the ways in which wills were, sometimes, used as a vehicle for paternal recognition. Of course, these narratives are not representative of the experiences of all children from this background. The 'gift' of recognition, which sometimes included being freed from slavery and indeed a bequest of other slaves, was always in the sole hands of the father; the violence of racism, and especially the marginalisation and marked absence of concern of the mothers, dominates these texts.

Bottomley locates these narratives within a broader theme of 'illegitimacy'; a concern, fear, stigma and categorisation that haunts so much in family and inheritance law and practice (and recurs throughout this collection). There was a spectrum of possibilities in this long history. At the most fortunate end one can point to the lives of some of the illegitimate sons of Charles II (1630–85): publicly

[9] Here, we would draw attention to scholarly work that addresses the inheritance of slavery in inheritance law itself as well on contemporary racial wealth gaps and inequities. For example, see Strand (2010); Clymer (2012); Brophy (2008); Davis (1999); Roberts (2015); Shammas, Salmon and Dahlin (1987).

[10] Goose and Evans (2000); Craig and Litzenberger (1993); Champlin (1991).

[11] See Whittle (2005); Ainsworth (2019); Hodges (2019); Bennett and Whitick (2007); Fellow (1991); Pölönen (2002); Owens (2001); Porter (2015); Hasson (2013); Rønning et al (2017).

[12] Levenbook (1985); Marquis (1985); Bezziina (2019).

[13] Beckert (2008); Friedman (2009); Miller and McNamee (1997); Perry (2015); Weigle (2008); Povinelli (2021).

acknowledged, and awarded dukedoms and vast estates, many still in the hands of their descendants. But in the context Bottomley examines, the possibilities were contingent on the navigation of race both in the colonies in the Caribbean ('on-island') and in Britain ('metro-isle'). From a deep reading of the language and terminology in the wills she demonstrates how '"reputed children" came to mean something more than merely "natural", whilst always less than "lawful"'. Sometimes present were the existence of a 'legitimate' family and the evidence Bottomley finds about the extent to which an 'illegitimate' family could 'destabilise a legal family unit' resonates painfully with contemporary narratives in adoption practice and for care experienced people more widely,[14] as Edwards and Collins explore in more detail later.

Bottomley's identification of paternal desires to create a 'legitimate' lineage, including by way of explicitly racist conditional clauses, forms part of the wider history of 'establishing a phenotypically white hierarchy on-island and the erasure of mixed-African heritage in Britain'. A later chapter by Wright recounts another context of legitimacy and white supremacy in her analysis of how DNA is mobilised in succession law by far-right white nationalist groups in the US. Bottomley demonstrates how the intimate stories within the wills she examines are a key archive for thinking about the legacies of empire and provide an essential tool for engaging conceptually and historically with 'the emergence of "race", "family" and "property"'. This framework resonates beyond the geography and timeframe of her study and is pertinent for thinking about the legacies of colonialism more widely. Exploring motivations behind the wills is, however, always a complex task – and Bottomley also brings into play the possibilities of familial affection, and guilt and shame, to contrast the contingencies of the timing of recognition: at birth through Christian baptism or at death. The possibility of spiritual factors and a will as a tool for redemption reemerges in the next chapter.

In chapter four, '"Charitable Inclinations": Women's Bequests to Ireland's Magdalene Laundries', feminist legal scholar Máiréad Enright demonstrates, in the same way as Bottomley, how rich a resource uncontested wills are for socio-legal history and how overlooked they are in throwing a light, in particular, on obscured and hidden aspects of women's lives.[15] Through painstaking searches of newspaper notices and official archives, Enright identifies twentieth-century charitable bequests from privileged women to Magdalene laundries: residential institutions which women and girls who had somehow 'transgressed Irish Catholic norms around female sexuality' were sent to, many for life, and which are now officially acknowledged as sites of abuse. The role of these bequests in enabling these carceral institutions has been overlooked[16] and indeed one donor, Mary Ryan

[14] Monk and McVarish (2018).

[15] See Whittle (2005); Ainsworth (2019); Hodges (2019); Bennett and Whitick (2007); Fellow (1991); Pölönen (2002); Owens (2001); Porter (2015); Hasson (2013).

[16] For comparative perspectives see Sigh (2017); Hansen (2017); Jürgensen (2017).

(1873–1961), the first woman university professor in Ireland, is celebrated by University College Cork as a feminist trailblazer. Enright makes a compelling case for viewing these bequests as 'vectors of "structural complicity" with the abuses'.

The argument is multi-layered as the motives for the bequests are shown to be varied and complex. This is not an attempt to establish direct responsibility for or indeed knowledge of the abuses. The challenges in reading motivations and intent from wills is a complex task that many scholars of inheritance face.[17] As Enright notes here: 'Wills offer some clues as to women's knowledge and motivations but cannot give us the whole messy picture of an individual's intentions'. In mapping the myriad of motives Enright takes us deep into the social and political cultures and milieu of the testators. Centre stage is the place of religion, here, the Catholic Church, in the women's lives, and indeed of the laundries: a recurring theme in much scholarship about wills.[18] The wills examined by Enright reveal the centuries old practice of bequests in wills for masses to be said. They provide evidence of a belief in purgatory but also that 'Guaranteeing that others would be prayed for was often a widow or spinster's last act of familial care, ensuring that the family could benefit from her spiritual attentions after she was gone'. But spiritual beliefs as a motive go hand in hand with familial connections with individual members of the church hierarchy or a particular nun; and genuine charitable desires to 'rescue' and 'benefit penitants' also reflects an opportunity for privileged women to establish political or communal influence, a prospect that Enright notes 'was especially attractive to women, whose economic and political agency was curtailed in ways that their male relatives' was not. In explicitly seeking to politicise charitable giving, Enright's research not only illuminates the past but resonates with contemporary inheritance practices of posthumous philanthropy. Individual desires to benefit causes and communicate values are incentivised and deeply entwined with taxation privileges which distinguish charitable from non-charitable. These are contemporary practices and laws which go to the heart of political debates about the contested delineation of state and private welfare.[19]

Part Two: Legal Fiction and Wills in Fiction

Bottomley's call to take seriously the revelations and the silences in wills goes beyond real wills and reminds us of the importance of fictional stories in literature, for example the allusions to reported paternity and slavery in Jane Austen's novels.[20] She also takes seriously visual representations,[21] in this case the painting

[17] On the challenges of using wills as a biographical tool, see Lafler (1997); Millgate (1992); Monk (2013).

[18] Bezzina (2019); Goose and Evans (2000); Craig and Litzenberger (1993); Coster (1999); Breathnach (2009).

[19] Cunliffe and Erreygers (2013); Braun and Röthel (2016).

[20] See for example Said (1989, 1993); Ferguson (1991); Park and Rajan (2000).

[21] See also Bottomley (1996).

of *The Reading of the Will* (1819) by David Wilkie, an engraving of which is reproduced on the front cover of this book. They serve to remind us how both popular understandings and debates about inheritance have often been based on fictional and non-legal texts. Wilkie's famous and mass-produced image, and not least the competition between rival rulers to own it,[22] attests to the extent to which inheritance narratives had, as they still do, the ability to fascinate a wide audience and to be the object of diverse projections. Indeed, it is not too disingenuous to see a direct link between Wilkie's painting and a contemporary television drama such as *Succession*, one of the most successful television dramas in recent years.[23] The question 'Who will inherit?' has long been the subject of fictional representations much loved by writers. Indeed, the fact that nineteenth-century novels almost always involve at least one 'reading of the will' has ensured that literary scholars have frequently been better informed about the formalities of will writing than many lawyers.[24] LS Lewis, writing in 1897, wondered: 'Goodness only knows what novelists and dramatists would do without wills.'[25] These narratives are too easily dismissed as 'melodramatic', a concept that has become a pejorative term. Brooks' towering challenge to this too-quick-dismissal is particularly pertinent here:

> Melodrama starts from and expresses the anxiety brought by a frightening new world in which traditional patterns of moral order no longer provide the necessary social glue. It plays out the force of that anxiety with the apparent triumph of villainy, and it dissipates it with the eventual victory of virtue. It demonstrates over and over that the signs of ethical forces can be discovered and can be made legible.[26]

Dramas about wills are moral and ethical tales. The conversations they initiate grapple with the legitimacy of feelings of being wronged and of entitlement. They traverse the dynastic and the intimate. Prior to the literary turn to modernism, wills and the testamentary freedom provided writers with the vehicle or narrative hook to reveal and indeed sometimes to initiate social, political and, at times, revolutionary debates.[27] Emphasising the importance of taking literary texts seriously for the study of inheritance, the next two chapters draw on two very distinct moments in inheritance fiction making.

In chapter five, 'Surnames and Inheritance: Will-Plotting and Female Economic Power in the Eighteenth-Century Novel', literary scholar Jolene Zigarovich opens

[22] For a detailed account of the history and literary inspirations of the painting, see Pintens and Declerk (2008).

[23] R Wikeley, 'Why Are We So Obsessed with *Succession*?' *Harpers Bazaar* (13 December 2021), available at www.harpersbazaar.com/uk/culture/entertainment/a38481460/why-are-we-so-obsessed-with-succession; R Samadder, 'Breath of Fresh Heir: How Succession became the Must Watch TV of the Year' *The Guardian* (10 October 2019), available at www.theguardian.com/tv-and-radio/2019/oct/10/breath-of-fresh-heir-how-succession-became-the-must-watch-tv-of-the-year.

[24] Frank (2010); Counter (2010); Monk (2013); Lankester-Carthy (2019).

[25] Lewis (1897).

[26] Brooks (1976) 20.

[27] Frank (2010); Counter (2010); Monk (2013).

with the plot from *Cecilia, or, Memoirs of an Heiress* (1782) by the pioneering satirical women novelist Frances Burney. At the heart of the novel is a conditional clause in the will of Cecilia's uncle, which stipulates that in order to receive her inheritance she must continue the family name by bestowing it upon her future husband. Confronted by her betrothed's refusal to accept this, Cecilia chooses love over fortune. Yet at the novel's close Cecilia is rewarded for her choice by a female-to-female bequest from her husband's aunt. Placing the disinheritance of a woman at the heart of the novel and resolving the injustice through inheritance was a model subsequently followed, centuries later, by both George Eliot in *Middlemarch* (1871–72) and by EM Forster in *Howards End* (1910). Burney's novel consequently is a key text for anyone interested in the role of literature in the emergence of feminist thinking and the significance of inheritance as the site for drawing attention to the legal and social status of women in society. While Zigarovich does not shy away from the overwhelming weight of patriarchy that dominated women's lives at that time, she seeks to 'update, trouble, and revise previous assumptions and interpretations of patrilineal succession'. The novels and the real-life cases that she examines demonstrate the spaces available to women to exercise autonomy and agency in their navigation of their relationships with fathers and (potential) husbands.

As an aside, it is important to note that while the fictional and real-life cases Zigarovich draws on relate to the rich, foregrounding the question of names showcases a form of inheritance that forms part of everyone's history, identity and genealogy. The history of surnames recounted in this chapter emphasises their impact on women, but they also contain within them the violence of slavery, as Bottomley demonstrates. The history of names contains national as well as familial and patriarchal stories; most notably, the Napoleonic introduction of compulsory surnames is a complex story about the conditionality of citizenship linked to questions of gender, taxation and the assimilation of non-Christian minorities.[28] There is no doubting the connection of names with power, but as with inheritance more widely, they also provide the space for resistance. As Zigarovich notes, 'in modern times surnames have witnessed perhaps their most dynamic transformation in terms of freedom of choice and socio-cultural diversity'.[29] At the same time she reminds us of an earlier history such as the wide use of matronyms in the medieval period. Like other historians, Zigarovich complicates and challenges assumptions about the past concluding that in the context of some privileged women their rights were 'stifled but not extinguished'.[30]

The conditional clauses that Zigarovich examines are referred to as 'Names and Arms Clauses' and she traces the history of them in real life, drawing attention to how widespread they were, alongside the emerging practice of private

[28] Eichner (2014); Amos (1928); Scott et al (2002).
[29] For legal disputes about names see Emens (2007); Herring (2009).
[30] Goose and Evans (2000); Whittle (2005).

Acts of Parliament to achieve the same end. Conditional clauses in wills, their legality and their usage, remains a complex doctrinal question in many legal systems. Zigarovich notes that such clauses could also refer to religious practices, citing the novel *Henrietta* (1758) by Charlotte Lennox in which a niece inherits her aunt's estate only upon her conversion to Catholicism. The legality of an inheritance being conditional on a recipient adopting a particular religion, or marrying within a particular religious community is a live question.[31] Grattan and Conway, for example, have argued powerfully for such clauses to be treated as a violation of human rights,[32] while Cooper and Herman have noted the racialised and discriminatory approach of the courts to minorities for whom such clauses can be a way of resisting assimilation and conversion.[33] This is a complex debate that reveals the contingency of political and moral judgments about the motives behind exercises of testamentary freedom. This challenge and how the courts have responded to it is examined in more detail in subsequent chapters by Cartier, and Conway and Grattan.

Motive is central to the next chapter by UK legal historian and family law scholar Rebecca Probert. In chapter six, 'Murder, Inheritance and Family Provision in the Golden Age of English Detective Fiction', we enter the twentieth century, more specifically the 1920s and 1930s. By this time wills had lost their earlier central place in 'great literature' as vehicles for explicitly political concerns and, instead, had become firmly located within popular or 'middlebrow'[34] detective fiction. In this context inheritance is 'simply' a possible motive for murder. Probert makes a compelling case for taking this extensive body of literature seriously, a suggestion that has resonance for thinking about contemporary fiction and popular culture within this genre. Probert presents a close reading of a selection of the novels of Dorothy L Sayers and Agatha Christie, the doyennes of English crime fiction, alongside the contemporaneous debates about two significant statutory reforms of inheritance law: the Administration of Estates Act 1925 and the Inheritance (Family Provision) Act 1938.[35] The former revised the rules of intestacy and the latter allowed a spouse, an unmarried daughter, or an infant or incapacitated son to challenge a will on the basis that it did not make reasonable provision for them. Probert demonstrates that Sayers and Christie were both clearly aware of these reforms. Sometimes this is explicit; as Probert notes, Sayers' *Unnatural Death* (1927) 'is probably unique in English literature in investing the line "isn't there a new Property Act?" with a sense of urgency and excitement'. That novel concerns the legal status of a great niece as the sole surviving relative, and ignorance of the law, or at best its lack of clarity, is critical to the plot. These popular novels were arguably educational as much as entertaining.

[31] Sherman (1999); Harding (2011); Du Toitt (2011); Chalmers (2007); Sennene and Barbaix (2014).
[32] Grattan and Conway (2005).
[33] Cooper and Herman (1999).
[34] Humble (2001).
[35] See Hedlund (2021) and Dainow (1940) for analysis of this period of legal reform.

The principle of testamentary freedom and law reform debates are at the heart of the novels Probert examines. This had particular resonance for women. As Probert reminds us, while married women's right to own property was a significant victory for women at the end of the nineteenth century – indeed its non-existence is key to some of the texts explored by Zigarovich – the vast majority of wives owned very little property and for them 'the ability to make a will in whatever terms she wished was of little value when set against the fact that her husband could decide to make a will leaving her nothing'. The 'capricious and vindictive wills' of husbands who failed to provide for their wives was a key motivation underlying the legal reforms and one campaigned for by many of the same women who had been instrumental in fighting for women to get the vote.

Sayers and Christie did not use their novels to campaign for legal reform, and Probert hints at their potentially ambivalent views; for example, in one novel the respective merits of an estate being kept within the family or being left to a testator's companion becomes the subject of a discussion. What is evident, however, in particular from the novels by Christie, is a wry view of familial relations: for the murderers are spouses or close relatives. It is possible to read this as a challenge to an idealised investment in the family. But none of her novels concern nuclear families, and Probert comments that it may be 'less threatening' to read about murders in which the family was 'clearly untypical and dysfunctional'. Yet this may also be motivated by the realities of law, for 'such families are also the ones that pose particularly difficult questions for the law of inheritance'. Law provides the framework for narrative possibilities. Indeed, this is evident in the most stark way if one compares the crime novels here with Zigarovich's texts from the eighteenth century; for prior to the Married Women's Property Acts a husband had no need to murder his wife to obtain her fortune, which is the plotline in two of Christie's novels. Consequently, these novels inadvertently provide a further window onto the violence of law.

An explicit example of this is the status of children deemed 'illegitimate' by law and in the UK denied inheritance rights of any form until 1969. In a novel from 1938, in which an unacknowledged illegitimate son murders his father, Christie has her detective Hercule Poirot observe wryly that, 'A son born the wrong side of the blanket may inherit many things', including his father's features and his 'revengeful spirit'. The centrality of marriage, and in particular the status of illegitimacy in inheritance law is, as noted above, a recurring theme in all the preceding chapters.

Part Three: Resistance, Rights and Agency

The next two chapters look more deeply into the experiences of two groups that have been, and in many respects remain, outside of dominant discourses of inheritance. Monk has noted elsewhere that for 'those whose lives have been lived outside of traditional familial norms inheritance takes on an added significance, partly because their lives are invisible in intestacy laws, which remain firmly rooted in blood and marital status'.[36] In taking seriously the efforts to redress law's silences, it is noteworthy that these two chapters foreground personal narratives. Both attest to the legacies and ongoing impact of law's violence and by giving a voice to the excluded, demonstrate how inheritance practices can provide creative spaces for resistance, agency and activism.

In chapter seven, 'The Story of the Pink Cat: An Exploration of the Ways Care-Experienced People Navigate Inheritance', UK sociologists Delyth Edwards and Rosie Canning trace the history of the legal framework and experiences of people who have been subject to the care of the state, that is, people who have 'spent some or all of their childhoods in the care of a Local Authority, whether that be foster care, children's homes, residential care or kinship care'. The ruptures and complexity of the practices and doing of 'family' is key here as is the long legacy of 'illegitimacy', which, they remind us, was criminalised in England in the 1660s. Loss is a recurring theme, taking many forms, and it informs their making a case for the importance of 'inheritance rights'.

How courts in civil and common law systems respond to claims by 'disappointed heirs'[37] – in particular adult children – are examined in subsequent chapters. But it is noteworthy that inheritance as a 'human right' is not one explicitly recognised by international human rights treaties. Edwards and Canning's recourse to the language and strategy of rights claiming is distinctive and in this context powerful and compelling. This is particularly pertinent, for the everyday and often oral family practices of inheritance are, for many, taken for granted, assumed, unremarked. This is viscerally evoked in findings from Edwards and Canning's empirical research with care-experienced people. They show how confronted by the absence of legal support and resistant professional practice, care-experienced people often become 'detectives of one's own story'; uncannily Agatha Christie emerges once again but here as an inspiration for unravelling the masking of the past to discover an inheritance. Key here is the emphasis upon the importance of thinking of inheritance beyond the financial, where names and objects come to the fore.

That names matter echoes the texts explored by Zigarovich and contrasting the productive role of law in the context of rich families in the eighteenth century with those examined here provides further evidence to support Tait's argument about the contingency of law's creativity and imagination. Aristocratic Names and Arms clauses and double-barrelled names present a stark contrast to the casual violence of renaming care-experienced children and the active participation in the denial of access to knowledge of identity; that the latter is often undertaken 'in the best interests of the child' – that ever malleable concept[38] – reasserts the vulnerability of care-experienced young people and, again, the importance of speaking of rights.

[36] Monk (2014) 24.
[37] Hacker (2014).
[38] Monk (2008). See also Finch and Mason (2000) and Finch et al (1996).

In foregrounding objects, and in making the argument that 'For too long, the importance of belongings for children in care has been largely underestimated and misunderstood', Canning shares her own story of the pink cat in the chapter's title. Embodying her care story, containing 'a history and a beginning', the story of the pink cat encapsulates the importance of and possibilities of producing heirlooms for future generations. Some of the legal issues relating to 'heirlooms' and the concept of 'sentimental attachment' are pertinent here and examined in a later chapter by Purewall and Gilmartin.

Personal narratives, heirlooms, intergenerationality, and inheritance-as-activism as performative, creative and as an affective and effective tool of resistance all come to the fore in chapter eight, 'Queer Property', by the UK-based American artist Russell Perkins. Inheritance has until relatively recently been overlooked by LGBT and queer scholars. Dismissed or reduced too quickly to an equal rights claim for couples in same-sex marriage or civil unions – the focus of campaigns in many jurisdictions – what has been overlooked are the experiences of gays and lesbians and queer people (the terminology inevitably changes) prior to same-sex relationship recognition and those whose lives are lived outside of a couple-norm. What these stories reveal are both marginalisation by the law but also creative strategies that draw on the possibilities of testamentary freedom and inscribe will-making as, potentially, a remarkably queer activity.[39]

Edwards and Collins argue in the previous chapter that 'storytelling is part of this way of "doing" and "making" family, but it is also a way that we do and make ourselves'.[40] Perkins demonstrates what this storytelling can feel and look like as his chapter weaves an intensely personal story embedded in broader queer experiences and history. At the heart of his work is his recounting of a friendship with an older gay man, Harry, a friend of his parents; a classic example of the type of relationship Eve Sedgwick emphasised the importance of in her essay, 'Tales of the Avunculate' in which she encourages us to 'forget the name of the father and think of your uncle and aunts'.[41] Intergenerationality is key here: Harry's gay life, one indelibly marked by social and legal homophobia, is 'passed on' and becomes part of Perkins' reading of a collective queer history, viewed from his own more liberal and accepting environment. This inheritance takes a tangible form as Perkins navigates the bequest in Harry's will of a collection of homoerotic photography – objects which are themselves redolent, for Perkins, of a distinctive generational queer male aesthetic. Going back further, adding an older branch and in so doing queering the imaginary possibilities of genealogical trees, is the presence of EM Forster (1879–1970), an ambivalent figure read as both closeted and 'haunted by Wilde' and at the same time as profoundly and proudly queer. Forster's own navigations of posthumous life[42] inform the legacy-making practice

[39] Sherman (1991); Berendt and Michaels (1991); Monk (2011, 2014); Sorainen (2014, 2018); Westwood (2015); Robinson (2022).

[40] Lenon (2017).

[41] Sedgwick (1994).

[42] Monk (2013).

of both Harry and Perkins. Language from Forster's will is weaved into the text of Harry's and his ambivalence about property, and in particular his ownership of a wood, results in Perkins taking the reader on a mystical queer journey and he transforms the legacy and bequest from Harry into a queer performative art form. Change and continuity go hand in hand here. The intertwining of the inheritance practices of three gay men from different generations makes visible the challenges and possibilities of non-conventional family 'display'[43] that transcends the liberal legal imagination of coupledom and reproduction. It was a theme Forster himself returned to frequently in his novels: 'the problem of continuity without direct physical begetting'.[44]

Whether a pink cat or a collection of homoerotic photography, Edwards, Canning and Perkins richly demonstrate the significance of objects in inheritance practices. This issue is centre stage in chapter nine by Sarah Gilmartin and Anita Purewal, 'Sentimental Value: Keeping Inheritance in the Family'. As they note, the law plays relatively little attention to objects or heirlooms.[45] Sharing the starting point of the previous authors – that inheritance can be about feelings and attachments and personal storytelling and memories and memory-making – the method they adopt draws on sociological texts and English case law in order to unpack the meanings and judicial application of the concept of 'sentimental attachment'. They identify four key elements: length of property ownership; subjective associations and involvements with the property; objection to the sale of the property; and emotional harm upon the property's loss. How these considerations impact on judicial decision-making, the weight attached to them in cases which are fundamentally about monetary disputes varies. It is important to note that the case law goes beyond inheritance conflicts, for trusts law and divorce proceedings also feature disputes about inherited property. Indeed, in divorce proceedings in England and Wales, where the distinction between matrimonial and non-matrimonial property is not always clear, questions can arise as to when inheritance property becomes so 'intermingled' with matrimonial assets that it effectively changes its status. Moreover, the desire to protect inherited property can be a motivation for making a prenuptial agreement. While Purewal and Gilmartin's focus is on sentimentality with respect to material heirlooms, we can also consider the role of emotions and affect in what Goodall Jr calls 'narrative inheritance', that is, the familial stories we inherit and/or are kept secret – what Barnwell terms 'hidden heirlooms'.[46] Underlying the case law that Purewal and Gilmartin examine are deeper questions about the challenge in determining 'fairness' and law's ability to adjudicate on questions requiring emotive evidence of

[43] 'Displaying' here refers to both the artistic practice but also the concept of 'family display' (introduced by Finch (2007)) a key framework in the chapter by Edwards and Canning.

[44] Martin (1997) 255.

[45] For an early analysis of the concept of an 'heirloom' see Garden (1926). See also Dawson (2000); Sidarov (2016); Roth (1992).

[46] Barnwell (2017); Bennett (2015); Goodall (2005).

degrees of attachment. Purewal and Gilmartin also remind us of Perkins' experience in the previous chapter that 'Testators may … hold a different sentimental attachment to property than their beneficiaries'. Moreover, law's aim here, as demonstrated in the cases discussed by Purewal and Gilmartin, to be sensitive to 'keeping it in the family' begs questions about law's role in sustaining norms and genealogies embedded in complex power relations. Such questions are all the more urgent when we consider the colonial looting and theft of sacred and cultural objects that are part and parcel of the legacies and inheritance of empire. These were assuredly *not* 'kept in the family', broadly defined, but were transferred to private collections and public museums who continue to actively curate the spoils of empire. As Purewal and Gilmartin remark, the loss of objects 'carries historic significance, and arguably with it a broader sentimentality, the loss of which could be of concern to more people than just the family involved, potentially being relevant to a country's historic or cultural heritage'. Indeed, contemporary debates about cultural restitution, repatriation, and the decolonisation of museums form a broader public discourse[47] about heirlooms and inheritance, one that connects to Enright's analysis of 'structural complicity'.

Part Four: Adjudicating Inheritance/Adjudicating 'Family'

The next three chapters collectively present a comparative perspective on the shifting boundaries and practices that determine the resolution of inheritance disputes. These contributions bridge the common and civil law divide, the key starting point for much research in this field.[48] Collectively, they identify underlying changes in expectations and understandings of familial life and the legal and social application of duties, obligations and responsibilities.[49] In all three contexts the role of legal professionals is also brought to the fore, an emerging issue in the wider literature.[50]

In chapter ten, 'How Social Norms and Values Influence the Balance between Wills Variation Claimants and Testators', Canadian legal scholar Allison A Cartier traces the movement across the common law world from an explicit commitment and privileging of the principle of testamentary freedom to the introduction of limitations imposed by statute. The first of these was New Zealand's Testator's Family Maintenance Act 1900, followed by British Columbia's Testator's Family Maintenance Act 1920. The focus here is on provisions that enable claimants to

[47] Douglas (2017); Hicks (2020); Coombes and Phillips (2015); B Gervais, 'Sacred items returned to Siksika Nation after 144 years in U.K. museum' *Calgary Herald* (20 May 2022), available at calgaryherald.com/news/local-news/sacred-items-returned-to-siksika-nation-after-144-years-in-uk-museum.

[48] Reid et al (2020).

[49] Douglas (2020).

[50] Gordon (2010), Horton (2012) and Hacker (2010) highlight how lawyers have a negative impact on the possibility of wills expressing emotion. See also Seddon (2011) on the language in wills.

raise an explicit objection to the terms of a will. It is important to note that there are and always have been alternative, less explicit ways for 'disappointed heirs' to raise legal challenges. These take the form of questioning the capacity of the testator, making an allegation of 'undue influence', disputing the meaning of a clause or the lack of certainty. The manifold ways in which these claims can be made and the fundamental evidential problem resulting from the fact that the testator is dead is such that a number of commentators have made compelling arguments questioning the reality of testamentary freedom.[51] Moreover, analysis of the extensive case law across jurisdictions reveal the extent to which judicial interpretations are informed by raced and gendered assumptions.[52]

The space for judicial valued judgement is central to Cartier's examination of statutory provisions. References to 'just', 'equitable', 'adequate provision' and 'reasonable dependency' across the statutes examined here inevitably and possibly intentionally enable and enhance judicial discretion – intentionally, because it is arguable that as social and cultural values evolve it is appropriate for this to be reflected by the courts. While the statutory goalposts differ significantly between Canadian provincial courts, Cartier identifies and contrasts the weight attached to claims by infant children and adult children with disabilities, which are deemed 'uncontroversial', with those by able-bodied and independent adult children – where judicial consensus collapses. The shifting ways in which claims by women are understood highlights both the impact of and tensions within feminist perspectives. As Probert's chapter makes clear, statutory interference with testamentary freedom was a key plank in early feminist campaigns. Alongside similar initiatives in divorce law, underlying the debates are changing understandings of marital duties and, for women in particular, tensions between aspiring for increased financial autonomy at the same time as addressing the lived realities of financial vulnerability and dependency. In western jurisdictions women's social and economic status has of course changed considerably since the introduction of the will variation statutes at the beginning of the twentieth century. But the family and economic social structures remain highly gendered. Moreover, moves to equality have gone hand in hand with individualisation. In tracing recent judicial navigations of inheritance disputes, Cartier tentatively suggests that they may be 'indicative of the pendulum swinging away from dependants' relief and towards testamentary freedom, but only time will tell'. Looking beneath the principal and continuingly asking 'who benefits from testamentary freedom?' remains essential.

In chapter eleven, 'Testamentary Freedom in Debate: The Prerequisite of the Notary to Pass Down and to Inherit', Corinne Delmas takes us to France and reveals similar trajectories, but from the perspective of a civil law system where testamentary freedom has been restricted by the countervailing imposition of a

[51] Blumenthal (2006); Leslie (1996, 2014); Sneddon (2015); Frolik (2001); Champine (2003); Watkins (2012).

[52] Maillard (2009); Monk (2011); Roberts (2015); Sneddon (2015).

'hereditary reserve' (*réserve héréditaire*). Like Cartier, Delmas takes a long view, reminding us of the revolutionary origins of the rejection of testamentary principle as the guiding principle and at the same time identifying how the pendulum, here too, is moving towards testamentary freedom.

Delmas' research adopts a mixed method, drawing on archival, statistical and a variety of empirical research with legal professionals, in particular Notaries. Legal professionals, as other inheritance scholars have found,[53] offer a rich sociological resource. Delmas notes: 'Every year, notaries meet with almost twenty million clients. This enables them to gauge the changing attitudes and lifestyles of our fellow citizens, their expectations and the limits of the rules that govern us.' The role of notaries, a profession similar to but in many respects very distinct from lawyers in common law systems, offers a particular perspective because of their explicit public role as reformers. Indeed, as Delmas shows, in their own national reports they perceive themselves not only as family and property law experts but 'even as sociologists'.[54] From their grassroots and broader public policy vantage point, their desire for increased testamentary freedom is premised on what Delmas describes as an enhanced focus on 'emotional choice' and 'the vagaries of relationships' over state-enforced obligations. Family here is an activity, a practice, and not just a status.[55] While this impacts on decision-making within traditional family structures, whether it extends to those explored by Edwards and Canning and Perkins is questionable.

In foregrounding shifting expectations and the importance of emotions, what both Cartier and Delmas attest to is the broader contemporary shift to what Reece described as 'post-liberalism', that is, a political culture in which 'psychological norms have replaced social norms, and therapeutic correctness has become the new standard of behaviour'.[56] The role of judgement in inheritance disputes – in popular and internal familial narratives, in individual familial discourse and by the courts – remains, but the language and moral frameworks have shifted. As Cartier and Delmas note, parental obligations to independent adult children is the terrain that brings these tensions to the fore. The marked lack of consensus reveals the extent to which private inheritance disputes reveal public debates about the meaning of contemporary citizenship.[57]

In chapter twelve, 'Children in Need and the Great Intergenerational Wealth Transfer: Squaring the Impossible Circle of Testamentary Freedom, Family Obligations and the Role of the State', UK legal academic and practitioner Heather Conway and Sheena Grattan return us to the common law system. Their focus is the 2017 UK Supreme Court judgment of *Illot v The Blue Cross*. Much debated

[53] Hasson (2013); Monk (2016).
[54] For a comparative view of the role of social sciences in policy reform see Cottier (2014).
[55] Morgan (2011).
[56] Reece (2003) 217.
[57] Douglas (2020); Hacker (2014).

in the UK and attracting wide public attention,[58] it encapsulates all the issues discussed so far and more.[59] The facts were simple. A mother wishing to disinherit a long-estranged physically able, but welfare-dependent, adult daughter left everything in her will to an animal charity. The rights of a testator were pitted against those of a child, 'estate provision' against 'state provision', and charities against 'the family'; and indeed humans against animals. Conway and Grattan illuminate the unpredictability of the 'family provision' legislation introduced in 1975 and suggest that while the case disappointed practitioners seeking a degree of certainty, that unpredictability is inherent in the legal framework.[60] This is made clear by the at times conflicting desires, some evidenced and others assumed by politicians, that inform popular opinions: a belief in testamentary freedom but also a less explicit but evident sense of entitlement to parental estates and in particular homes, the legacies of 'dynastic' thinking. Conway and Grattan are clear in their opposition to the latter. However, they complicate the picture by acknowledging the wider economic context in which the decision took place, a context mirrored to varying degrees in most western European jurisdictions: a growing elderly population with, proportionally, considerably more wealth than younger generations, but, at the same time, increasingly in need of care. This is the background to the rise in inheritance conflicts.[61] The question of elder care has informed arguments in favour of enhancing testamentary freedom as an incentive for people to look after elders,[62] as well as more collective arguments that challenge law's understanding of 'vulnerability'.[63] Concern about elder abuse in the context of inheritance also informs extensive literature about disputes premised on allegations of 'undue influence'.[64] Intergenerationality is key here – 'baby boomers', 'generation rent' – become markers for a broader but not always acknowledged conversation about wider structural inequalities.[65] Individual judgments, even from a Supreme Court, cannot resolve these tensions, but they are explicitly referenced and apparent in the stark disagreement between the judges about the extent to which, if at all, the daughter being a recipient of welfare support should impact on the question of her inheritance. That the answer to this question from the Supreme Court in *Illot* was 'not at all' suggests that judicial understandings of the familial do not – led unquestionably by statute – extend to 'the social' or wider community interests. Inheritance disputes remain, in this way, firmly and resiliently located in the 'private'.

[58] Sloan (2017); McDonnell (2017).
[59] For civil law responses to similar issues see Reid et al (2020); Dethloff (2013).
[60] See also Douglas (2014).
[61] Izuhara and Köppe (2019).
[62] Tate (2008).
[63] Herring (2016).
[64] Sloan (2011); Scalise (2008); Harding (2015).
[65] On the relationship between old age and inheritance see Hartog (2012) and Weigle (2008), and for a critique of the 'generational war' argument see Segal (2014).

Part Five: Looking Backwards into the Future

The final four chapters ask hard questions about inheritance. The authors write from four jurisdictions, and adopt distinct methods and frameworks, traversing theology, tax, empirical narratives and abolition. Collectively they serve to demonstrate the breadth of scholarly approaches to the subject. But more than that, they reveal the historical and political contingencies underlying and informing the past and the present and in doing so, point to both the very real possibility of alternatives, of doing things differently and, at the same time, the weight of history that limits the collective imagination.

In linking the past with the present, US legal scholar Danaya C Wright makes a compelling and provocative case in chapter thirteen for connecting the rise of far-right, white supremist Christian Nationalism in the US with the theories and long history of significance being attached to blood in early Christian theology; a violent legacy that, she argues, is sustained by and complicit with inheritance laws and practices. Her chapter, entitled 'The Power of Blood: How Succession Law's Reliance on DNA Reinvigorates White Supremacy and the Politics of Biological Privilege', identifies continuities and paradoxes. An example of the latter is the decentering of the significance of biological links in contemporary family forms, identity and primary parenting alongside the extraordinary growth of people seeking to discover their DNA or genetic origins as part of a desire to 'find their place in our complex globalised world'. What is 'passed on', transmitted, inherited in this context is deeply malleable.[66] Wright, referring to US legal initiatives, foregrounds here the resilience and recentering of inheritance law around ideas of blood. Drawing on the high-profile dispute arising on the death of the US 'celebrity' Anna Nicole Smith, Wright demonstrates how these ideas attests again to the place of melodrama as a trope in cultural representations of inheritance. It is no surprise that this true story inspired an opera.[67]

Tracing the antecedents of contemporary white supremacy back to the Peace Council of Narbonne in 1054, in which Pope Gregory VII declared that it was not the shedding of human blood that was a sin but rather the shedding of Christian blood, Wright reminds us that what is perceived so often as 'natural' in terms of lineage, identity and 'descent' has a political and social history. The tension in early English history between Saxon and Norman inheritance practices is just one example of the inventiveness and contingency of law, and the extent to which powerful interests determined the rules for particular ends. The creativeness in the wills explored by Bottomley and Zigarovich in earlier chapters similarly become more comprehensible when located within systems premised on the raced and gendered

[66] See Lenon and Peers (2017).

[67] *Ann Nicole* (Turnage, 2011). Earlier operas based on disputes over wills include *The Makropolous Case* (Janáček, 1925); *Katya Kabanova* (Janáček, 1921) and most famously *Gianni Schicchi* (Puccini, 1918).

longer histories canvassed here. As Wright remarks, 'succession law's reliance on blood helps explain the stickiness of biology in inheritance and reveals its foundations in race supremacy'. For Wright, looking backwards is a tool for politicising the unremarked 'familial' of inheritance and a tool to consider the extent to which the political legacies premised on race are deeply entwined with 'private' practices deemed 'natural'.

In chapter fourteen, 'Women, Property and Agency: Contours of Matrilineal Inheritance among the Nayars in Kerala, India', Lekha NB and Antony Palackal turn the focus to the changing position of women in a highly distinctive system: one traditionally premised on a matrilineal social structure. Gender distinctions in inheritance laws and practice are a recurring theme in much of the literature on inheritance across a number of jurisdictions.[68] In many legal systems and cultures patriarchal assumptions and practices remain deeply embedded. But even in those where the laws are formally gender neutral, these coexist with highly gendered and explicitly patriarchal practices. For example, primogeniture in the UK still dictates the ownership of vast estates. And testamentary freedom permits parents to discriminate between sons and daughters for religious or other reasons. In England the latter came to the fore when the Law Society, which represents solicitors, prepared guidance for its members about how to write a 'sharia-compliant will' for lawyers' Muslim clients. Under pressure from feminist and other organisations, the Law Society removed this guidance. But it was notable that while these discriminatory – albeit perfectly legal – wills, by a minority religious community, were widely criticised, the practice of primogeniture is legitimised as sustaining British heritage.[69] Moreover, beyond formal law the challenges of elder care, a recurring theme in both individual disputes and broader policy debates, remain deeply gendered.

NB and Palackal contend that gendered elder care is one of the explanations provided for moves away from the matrilineal traditional practices whereby all the matrilineal descendants of a female ancestress would hold property collectively. The rationale for this is the increasing assumption that it is sons who will and should look after the family and elder parents; associated with this is the increase in the role of a dowry for daughters. They identify many other reasons for the decreasing significance of the matrilineal practices, including 'social conditions brought about by British colonisation and its notions of modernity and progress in the late nineteenth and early twentieth centuries which cast these rights as "immoral" and "primitive"'. The decline of agricultural activities and the monetisation of land are also factors.

The picture painted by NB and Palackal, however, is a complex one and the nuance they bring to thinking about the matrilineal legacies is embedded in

[68] Xynas (2011); Roy (2015); Richardson (2004); Cooper and Bird (2012); Dancer (2017); Forbes-Chilibeck (2005); Jacobs (2014).

[69] Monk (2018). See also Wilson et al (2016).

empirical research with women over three generations; an intergenerational method offering much potential for future inheritance research. Here it reveals the ways in which for women the culture and practices of matriliny 'accorded them bargaining power in gender relations in a patriarchal social milieu' and how in this way 'property seemed to gather different semiotic meanings'. Focused as it is on the Nayars in Kerala, this research is highly specific. But it powerfully demonstrates two points that are key to thinking critically about inheritance. First, that there are alternatives to what is too easily perceived as 'natural' and 'traditional'. Secondly, that inheritance practices and indeed even the memories of them have a deep impact on the dignity, status and identity of people that goes beyond the transmission of property.

Alongside disputes between individual potential heirs, familial or otherwise, and policy debates about the limits of testamentary freedom a further issue is the question of taxation. In chapter fifteen, 'Egalitarianism or Just a Need for Revenues? Debates on Inheritance Taxation in Scandinavia', Swedish historian Martin Dackling reminds us that nation states throughout history have, in different ways, often claimed a share of an estate on death. Referred to sometimes as death duties, these forms of inheritance taxation are an explicit reminder of the public interest in inheritance. At the same time these forms of taxation are closely linked to debates about the meaning and function of 'the family'. Indeed, as Dackling identifies, certain transfers of wealth, typically to spouses, have been exempt from taxation. Some jurisdictions go further and link taxation rates to the degrees of familial connection – reinforcing concerns discussed by Tait and Wright above.

Dackling complicates many of the received wisdoms about inheritance tax, in particular that it is a twentieth-century initiative solely motivated by egalitarian politics premised on the redistribution of wealth. This is, of course, an important part of the story but it cannot be reduced to this; and Scandinavia is a rich site for exploring this, because, perhaps more than anywhere else, it is associated strongly with egalitarian values. Drawing on Beckert's key comparative work, Dackling identifies the competing principles and values at play, how, 'family property is pitted against meritocratic ideals, and freedom to dispose of property is pitted against a social responsibility for all citizens, as is diligence and frugality against economic inequality'.

Examining inheritance tax across Norway, Sweden and Denmark in the period from 1880 to the 1950s reveals that from being the western countries with the lowest inheritance tax they did indeed adopt high rates, although not the highest. But by looking beyond the rate of tax to the underlying political debates in the respective legislatures, Dackling's analysis reveals important distinctions and motives: mass mobilisation of forces after both world wars is identified as a motive alongside redistribution of wealth and Social Democracy as a political force does not map neatly if at all on to the introduction of high rates of inheritance tax. Moreover, in Norway the importance of an agricultural family-based economy provides a distinctive argument against taxation.

In complicating dominant narratives about inheritance tax – of the left and the right – Dackling does not shy away from the starkness of inequality and the increasing significance of inheritance on this. The recent moves from the 2000s onwards to decrease and indeed to abolish inheritance tax (Sweden in 2004 and Norway in 2014) mirrors themes identified elsewhere in this collection about the rise of individualism and neoliberal economics. But Dackling also helpfully reminds us that inheritance tax has never been a particularly effective tool in raising revenue for the state or indeed in combating inequality, a point relied on by those arguing for such a tax to be abolished,[70] and indeed amply demonstrated by the research that identifies the role of trusts and alternative means of wealth protection.[71] As he concludes, it has been 'a tax that has resulted in more debate than income' and is not simply an 'economic question' but rather a discursive one on to which political theories and ideals can project competing understandings of 'the nature of property, family relations, and the role of the state'. Like so many debates about inheritance, the question of inheritance taxation is also an emotional debate, which in part explains why people who are unlikely to be liable for inheritance tax can sometimes object strongly to it. Understanding inheritance tax as a matter of emotions lends support to the sociologist Durkheim's ideas about the role of emotions underlying the construction of the realities and experiences of the social and indeed the constructions and possibilities of social solidarity.[72] It provides a valuable framework for understanding the past and imagining different futures.

In chapter sixteen, 'Émile Durkheim's Proposal to Abolish Inheritance', the French philosopher Mélanie Plouviez challenges us to confront the current paucity of bold thinking about inheritance; and reminds us once again, as was noted above in the context of literary texts, that 'in the nineteenth century, the subject of inheritance was omnipresent. It was impossible to address the "social question": without first questioning the legitimacy of inheritance itself'. The need to redress this is all the more urgent as she also reminds us that in relation to the economic wealth of households, inheritance is as significant now as it was in the late nineteenth century. Bold thinking is required and Plouviez provides this by dusting off the ethnographic studies and policy proposals of the sociologist Émile Durkheim (1858–1917). Locating his thinking on inheritance alongside other 'abolitionist' writers demonstrates how core inheritance was considered to society as a whole, from the French Revolution onwards. The very word 'abolition' is a provocation to deep-seated commonsense assumptions and values. Indeed, in its ability to disturb and trouble mainstream thinking there are parallels with the use of the term in the context of contemporary debates about policing and incarceration[73]

[70] Lee (2007).
[71] Friedman (2009); Leslie (2014); Madoff (2010); Horton (2017); Harrington (2012).
[72] See Cotterrell (1999).
[73] See for example, Alexander (2010); Davis (2003, 2005); Pasternak, Walby and Stadnyk (2022); Stanley and Smith (2015); Jones (2022).

as well as queer and feminist provocations to abolish the family.[74] Chapters thus far that highlight the significance of race in inheritance (Tait, Bottomley, Wright) and the varied terrains of kinship made and un/done by inheritance (Edwards and Canning, Perkins, Conway and Grattan) bridge ideas of abolition and inheritance. While Durkheim's call for the abolition of inheritance is undoubtedly radical and premised on a demand for social justice what makes his arguments distinctive is, as Plouviez demonstrates, its basis in sociology as opposed to political theory, for he reaches his position not by looking at statistics about inequality but by undertaking ethnographic research about clans, kinship and the function of property. From this perspective locating inheritance within the modern family is simply an anachronism and ill-suited to addressing the necessary functions of property and work. Far removed from earlier forms of kinship networks, the family collective is, simply outdated, not fit for purpose. But crucially, and in contrast to other thinkers, both then and now, Durkheim rejects the idea of simply replacing the family with the state. In other words, taxation at a dramatically higher rate is not the answer.

Instead, Durkheim proposes that inheritances should be transferred to the deceased's occupational group. An initially startling proposal it is legitimised through an understanding of this collective corporation as a diverse, democratised body best placed to protect people through social insurance funds, health insurance funds and retirement funds. By consequently linking inheritance with work this form of 'occupational solidarity' not only provides a motivation, which simple taxation is perceived to lack, and far from simply replacing 'the family' brings inheritance back to its earlier functional core as identified in earlier kinship models. As Plouviez notes: 'The hypothesis of this work is that there is, in past discourses on inheritance and inequalities, a possible source of profound renewal of our contemporary ways of thinking about the problem of social justice'. Inheritance in this way is not per se the problem, rather, it can provide 'the ideal tool for extending democracy beyond the defence of political rights, through the acquisition of new social rights'.

In ending this collection of essays with a call for the abolition of inheritance is not to suggest that Durkheim's proposal offers the answer or the solution. His work has inevitably been subject to extensive critique, most effectively by his ardent apologists.[75] But in its boldness, its denaturalising of inheritance 'by historicising and de-essentialising its link to the family and to private property', it does not so much point us in a particular direction of travel but opens the space for questions about collective living and what inheritance might achieve. In other words, a proposal that provocatively calls for abolition reminds us why and how much inheritance matters.

[74] See for example, Kollontai (1902/1977); Firestone (1970); and more recently Care Collective (2020) and Lewis (2022).

[75] Cotterrell (1999).

References

Ainsworth S, 'Willing Women: Wills as Constructs of Female Self-Identity in the Seventeenth-Century South-West (1625–1660)' (University of Exeter, 2019).

Alexander, M, *The New Jim Crow: Mass Incarceration in the Age of Colorblindness* (New York, The New Press, 2010).

Allison, D (1997) 'The Importance of Estate Planning within the Gay and Lesbian Community' 23 *Thurgood Marshall Law Review* 445.

Amos M, 'The Code Napoleon and the Modern World' (1928) 1 *Journal of Comparative Legislation and International Law* 222.

Atkinson, AB, 'Wealth and Inheritance in Britain from 1896 to the Present' (2018) 16 *The Journal of Economic Inequality* 137.

Barnwell, A, 'Hidden Heirlooms: Keeping Family Secrets across Generations' (2017) 54 *Journal of Sociology* 446.

Beckert J, *Inherited Wealth* (Princeton, NJ, Princeton University Press, 2008).

Bennett, J, 'Narrating Family Histories: Negotiating Identity and Belonging through Tropes of Nostalgia and Authenticity' (2015) 66 *Current Sociology* 449.

Bennett, J and Whittick, C, 'Philippa Russell and the Wills of London's Late Medieval Single Women' (2007) 32 *The London Journal* 251.

Berendt, E and Michaels L, 'Your HIV Positive Client: Easing the Burden on the Family through Estate Planning' (1991) 24 *Journal of Marshall Law Review* 509.

Bezzina, D, 'The Two Wills of Manuele Zaccaria: Protecting One's Wealth and Saving One's Soul in Late Thirteenth-Century Genoa' (2019) 1 *Ianuensis non nascitur sed fit. Studi per Dino Puncuh, Società Ligure di Storia Patria* 205.

Bottomley, A, 'Figures in a Landscape: Feminist Perspectives on Law, Land and Landscape' in A Bottomley (ed), *Feminist Perspectives on Foundation Subjects of Law* (London, Cavendish, 1996).

Braun, S and Röthel A, *Passing Wealth on Death: Will-Substitutes in Comparative Perspective* (Oxford, Hart, 2016).

Breathnach, C, 'An Exploration of Testamentary Behaviour in Twentieth-Century Ireland' (2009) 14 *The History of the Family* 309.

Brophy, AL, 'What should Inheritance Law Be? Reparations and Intergenerational Wealth Transfers' (2008) 20 *Law & Literature* 197.

Blumenthal, S, 'The Deviance of the Will: Policing the Bounds of Testamentary Freedom in nineteenth-century America' (2006) 119 *Harvard Law Review* 959.

Care Collective, *The Care Manifesto: The Politics of Interdependence* (London and New York, Verso, 2020).

Chalmers, J, 'Testamentary Conditions and Public Policy' in KGC Reid, M de Waal and R Zimmerman (eds), *Exploring the law of succession* (Edinburgh, Edinburgh University Press, 2007).

Champine, P, 'A Sanist Will?' (2003) 22 *NYLS Journal of International and Comparative Law* 13.

Champlin, E, *Final Judgments: Duty and Emotion in Roman Wills 200BC – AD250* (Berkeley, University of California, 1991).

Clymer, J, *Family Money: Property, Race, and Literature in the Nineteenth Century* (Oxford, Oxford University Press, 2012).

Cooke, E, 'Wives, Widows and Wicked Step-Mothers: A Brief Examination of Spousal Entitlement on Intestacy' (2009) 21 *Child and Family Law Quarterly* 423.

Coombes AE and Phillips RB (eds), *Museum Transformations: Decolonization and Democratization* (Hoboken, Wiley Blackwell, 2015)
Cooper, D and Herman, D, 'Jews and Other Uncertainties: Race, Faith and English Law' (1999) 19 *Legal Studies* 339.
Cooper, E and Bird, K, 'Inheritance: A Gendered and Intergenerational Dimension of Poverty' (2012) 3 *Development Policy Review* 527.
Counter A, *Inheritance in Nineteenth-century French Culture: Wealth, Knowledge and the Family* (Oxford, Legenda, 2010).
Coster, W, 'Community, Piety, and Family in Yorkshire Wills Between the Reformation and the Restoration' (1999) 12 *Studies in Church History* 511.
Cottier, M, 'Adapting Inheritance Law to Changing Social Realities: Questions of Methodology from a Comparative Perspective' (2014) 4 *Oñati Socio-Legal Series* 196.
Cotterrell R, *Emile Durkheim: Law in a Moral Domain* (Edinburgh, Edinburgh University Press, 1999).
Cownie, F and Bradney, A, 'Divided Justice, Difference Voices: Inheritance and Family Provision (2003) 23 *Legal Studies* 566.
Craig J and C Litzenberger, 'Wills as Religious Propaganda: The Testament of William Tracy' (1993) 44 *Journal of Ecclesiastical History* 415.
Cunliffe, J and Erreygers, G, *Inherited Wealth, Justice and Equality* (London, Routledge, 2013).
Dainow, J, 'Limitations on Testamentary Freedom in England' (1940) 25 *Cornell Law Review* 337.
Dancer, H, 'An Equal Right to Inherit? Women's Land Rights, Customary Law and Constitutional Reform in Tanzania' (2017) 26 *Social and Legal Studies* 91.
Davis, A, *Are Prisons Obsolete?* (New York, Seven Stories Press, 2003).
—— *Abolition Democracy: Beyond Empire, Prisons, and Torture* (New York, Seven Stories Press, 2005).
Davis, AD, 'The Private Law of Race and Sex: An Antebellum Perspective' (1999) 51 *Stanford Law Review* 221.
Dawson, N, '"Heirlooms": The Evolution of a Legal Concept' (2000) 51 *Northern Ireland Legal Quarterly* 1.
Dethloff, N, 'The Protection of Children in German Inheritance Law' in T Frantzen (ed) *Inheritance Law – Challenges and Reform* (Berliner, BWV, 2013).
Douglas, G, 'Family Provision and Family Practices – The Discretionary Regime of the Inheritance Act of England and Wales' (2013) 4 *Oñati Socio-Legal Series* 222.
—— *Obligation and Commitment in Family Law* (London, Bloomsbury, 2020).
Douglas, G, Woodward H, Humphrey A, Mills L and Morrell G, 'Enduring Love? Attitudes to Family and Inheritance Law in England and Wales' (2011) 38 *Journal of Law and Society* 245.
Douglas, S, *Curating Community: Museums, Constitutionalism, and the Taming of the Political* (Ann Arbor, University of Michigan Press, 2017).
Du Toit, F, 'The Constitutionally Bound Dead Hand? The Impact of Constitutional Rights and Principles on Freedom of Testation in South African Law' (2001) 12 *Stellenbosch Law Review* 22.
Eichner, CJ, 'In the Name of the Mother: Feminist Opposition to the Patronym in Nineteenth-Century France' (2014) 39 *Signs: Journal of Women in Culture and Society* 659.
Emens, EF, 'Changing Name Changing: Framing Rules and the Future of Marital Names' (2007) 74 *University of Chicago Law Review* 761.

Fellows, ML, 'Wills and Trusts: "The Kingdom of the Fathers"' (1991) 10 *Law & Inequality Journal* 137.

Ferguson, M, 'Mansfield Park: Slavery, Colonialism, and Gender' (1991) 13 *Oxford Literary Review* 118.

Finch, J and Mason, J, *Passing On: Kinship and Inheritance in England* (London, Routledge, 2000).

Finch, J, Mason, J, Masson, J, Wallis L and Hayes, L, *Wills, Inheritance and Families* (Oxford, Oxford University Press, 1996).

Finch, J, 'Displaying Families' (2007) 41 *Sociology* 65.

Firestone, S, *The Dialectic of Sex: The Case for Feminist Revolution* (New York, Farrar, Straus and Giroux, 1970).

Forbes-Chilibeck, E, 'Have you Heard the one about the Farmer's Daughter? Gender-bias in the Intergenerational Transfer of Farm Land on the Canadian Prairies (2005) 24 *Canadian Woman Studies* 26.

Frank, CO, *Law, Literature and the Transmission of Culture in England, 1837–1925* (Farnham, Ashgate, 2010).

Friedman, L, *Dead Hands: A Social History of Wills, Trusts and Inheritance Law* (Stanford, CA, Stanford Law Books, 2009).

Frolik, L, 'The strange interplay of testamentary capacity and the doctrine of undue influence: Are we protecting older testators or overriding individual preferences?' (2001) 24 *Journal of Law and Psychiatry* 253.

Gardner JC, 'The Legal Antiquity of Heirlooms' (1926) 36 *Juridical Review* 299.

Goodall, HL Jr, 'Narrative Inheritance: A Nuclear Family with Toxic Secrets' (2005) 11 *Qualitative Inquiry* 492.

Goose, N and Evans, N, 'Wills as an Historical Source' in T Arkell, N Evans and N Goose (eds), *When Death Do Us Part: Understanding and Interpreting the Probate Records of Early Modern England* (Oxford, Leopard's Head Press, 2000).

Gordon, DS, 'Reflecting on the Language of Death' (2010) 34 *Seattle Law Review* 379.

Graetz, M and Shapiro, I, *Death by a Thousand Cuts: The Fight over Taxing Inherited Wealth* (Princeton/Oxford, Princeton University Press, 2005).

Grattan, S and Conway, H, 'Testamentary Constraints in Restraint of Religion in the Twenty-First Century: an Anglo-Canadian Perspective' (2005) 50 *McGill Law Journal* 511.

Hacker, D, 'Soulless Wills' (2010) 35 *Law & Social Inquiry* 957.

—— 'Disappointed 'Heirs' as a Socio-Legal Phenomenon' (2014) 4 *Onati Socio-Legal Series* 243.

Harding, M, 'Some Arguments against Discriminatory Gifts and Trusts' (2011) 31 *Oxford Journal of Legal Studies* 303.

Harding, R, 'The Rise of Statutory Wills' (2015) 78 *Modern Law Review* 945.

Harrington, B, 'Trust and Estate Planning: The Emergence of a Profession and its Contribution to Socioeconomic Inequality' (2012) 27 *Sociological Forum* 825.

Hartog, H, *Someday All This Will Be Yours: A History of Inheritance and Old Age*, (Harvard, Harvard University Press, 2012).

Hansen, PW, 'The Age of Miracles? Alms Culture and Charitable Donations in Copenhagen, c. 1770–1830' in OA Rønning, HM Sigh and H Vogt (eds), *Donations, Inheritance and Property in the Nordic and Western World from Late Antiquity until Today* (London, Routledge, 2017).

Hasson, E, 'Where There's a Will There's a Woman': Exploring the Gendered Nature of Will-Making (2013) 21 *Feminist Legal Studies* 21.

Hedlund, R, 'The End to Testamentary Freedom' (2021) 41 *Legal Studies* 55.
Herring J (2016) *Vulnerable Adults and the Law* (Oxford, Oxford University Press).
Hicks, D, *The Brutish Museums: The Benin Bronzes, Colonial Violence and Cultural Restitution* (London, Pluto Press, 2020).
Hodges, M, 'Widows of the "Middling Sort"' and their Assets in Two Seventeenth-Century Towns' in T Arkell, N Evans and N Goose (eds), *When Death Do Us Part: Understanding and Interpreting the Probate Records of Early Modern England* (Oxford, Leopard's Head Press Ltd, 2020).
Horton, D, *Tomorrow's Inheritance: The Frontiers of Estate Planning Formalism* (2017) 58 *Boston College Law Review* 539.
Humble, N, *The Feminine Middlebrow Novel, 1920s to 1950s: Class, Domesticity, and Bohemianism* (Oxford, OUP, 2001).
Izuhara, M and Köppe, S, 'Inheritance and Family Conflicts: Exploring Asset Transfers Shaping Intergenerational Relations' (2019) 8 *Families, Relationships and Societies* 53.
Jacobs, S, 'Gender, Land and Sexuality: Exploring Connections' (2014) 27 *International Journal of Politics, Culture, and Society* 173.
Jamoussi, Z, *Primogeniture and Entail in England: A Survey of their History and Representation in Literature* (Cambridge, Scholars Publishing, 2011).
Johanson, SM and Bay, KF, 'Estate Planning for the Client with AIDS' (1989) *Texas Bar Journal* 217.
Jones, E, *Abolitionist Intimacies* (Halifax & Winnipeg, Fernwood Publishing, 2022).
Jürgensen, MW, 'Pious Donations: The Act of Giving in the Lutheran Church and its Spatial Implications' in CA Rønning, HM Sigh and H Vogt (eds), *Donations, Inheritance and Property in the Nordic and Western World from Late Antiquity until Today* (London, Routledge, 2017).
Kollontai, A, 'Communism and the Family' in A Holt (ed), *Selected Writings of Alexandra Kollontai* (New York & London, W W Norton & Company, 1920/1977).
Lafler, J, 'The Will of Katherine Maynwaring: An Autobiographical Reading' (1997) 20 *Biography* 156.
Lankester-Carthy, N, *The Hereditary Curse: Inheritance and Legacy in Early Modern Revenge Tragedy 1550–1610* (Lancaster University, 2019).
Law Commission, *Intestacy and Family Provision Claims on Death* (2011) Law Com 331.
Lee, N, Inheritance Tax – An Equitable Tax No Longer: Time for Abolition? (2007) 27 *Legal Studies* 678.
Lenon, S, 'Inheritance's Intimacies and Social Change' (2017) 54 *Canadian Review of Sociology* 366.
Lenon, S and Peers, D, '"Wrongful" Inheritance: Race, Disability and Sexuality in Cramblett v Midwest Sperm Bank' (2017) 25 *Feminist Legal Studies* 141.
Leslie, M, 'The Myth of Testamentary Freedom' (1996) 38 *Arizona Law Review* 235.
—— 'Frustration of Intent in the Wealth Transmission Process' (2014) 4 *Oñati Socio-Legal Series* 283.
Levenbook, B, 'Harming Someone after His Death' (1984) 94 *Ethics* 407.
Lewis, LS, 'Some Peculiar Wills' (1897) 14 *Strand Magazine* 441.
Lewis, S, *Abolish the Family: A Manifesto for Care and Liberation* (London and New York, Verso, 2022).
Macdonald D, *Born to Win: Wealth Concentration in Canada since 1999* (Ottawa, Canadian Centre for Policy Alternatives, 2018).
Madoff, R, *Immortality and the Law: The Rising Power of the American Dead* (New Haven, Yale University Press, 2010).

Maillard, KN, 'The Color of Testamentary Freedom' (2009) 62 *Southern Methodist University Law Review* 1783.

Marquis, D, 'Harming the Dead' (1985) 96 *Ethics* 159.

Martin MK '"It must have been the umbrella": Forster's queer begetting' in RK Martin and G Piggford (eds), *Queer Forster* (Chicago, University of Chicago Press, 1997).

McDonnell C, 'Blurring the Focus? The Supreme Court's Decision in *Ilott v The Blue Cross*' (2017) 23 *Trusts & Trustees* 748.

Miller R and SJ McNamee (eds), *Inheritance and Wealth in America* (New York, Plenum Press, 1997).

Millgate, M, *Testamentary Acts: Browning, Tennyson, James, Hardy* (Oxford, Clarendon Press, 1992).

Monk, D, 'Childhood and the Law: In Whose "Best Interests?"' in MJ Kehily (ed), *An Introduction to Childhood Studies* (Berkshire, Open University Press, 2008).

—— 'Sexuality and Succession Law: Beyond Formal Equality' (2011) 19 *Feminist Legal Studies* 231.

—— 'E M Forster's Will: An Overlooked Posthumous Publication' (2013) 33 *Legal Studies* 572.

—— '"Inheritance Families of Choice"? Lawyers' Reflections on Gay and Lesbian Wills' (2016) 43 *Journal of Law and Society* 167.

Monk, D and McVarish, J, *Siblings, Contact and the Law: An Overlooked Relationship?* (London, Nuffield, 2018).

Morris, D, Charities and the Big Society: A Doomed Coalition? (2012) 32 *Legal Studies* 132.

Olsen FE, 'The Myth of State Intervention in the Family' (1985) 18 *University of Michigan Journal of Law Reform* 835.

Owens, A, 'Property, Gender, and the Life Course: Inheritance and Family Welfare Provision in Early Nineteenth Century England' (2001) 26 *Social History* 299.

Park, Y and Rajan, RS (eds), *The Postcolonial Jane Austen* (London and New York, Routledge, 2004).

Pasternak, S, Walby, K and Stadnyk, A, *Disarm, Defund, Dismantle: Police Abolition in Canada* (Toronto, Between the Lines, 2022).

Perry, A, *Colonial Relations: The Douglas-Connolly Family and the Nineteenth-Century Imperial World* (New York, Cambridge University Press, 2015).

Piketty, T, 'On the Long-Run Evolution of Inheritance: France 1820–2050' (2011) 126 *The Quarterly Journal of Economics* 1071.

—— *Capital in the Twenty-First Century* (Cambridge, MA and London, Harvard University Press, 2014).

Pintens, W and Declerck, C, 'Inheritance and Art, A Mirror of Society' in B Demarsin, E Schrage, B Tilleman and A Verbeke (eds), *Art and Law* (Bruges, die Kleure, 2008).

Pölönen, J, 'The Division of Wealth between Men and Women in Roman Succession' in R Berg et al (eds), *Women, Wealth and Power in the Roman Empire* (Rome, Acta Instituti Romani Finlandiae, 2002).

Porter, AM, *Their Lives, Their Wills: Women in the Borderlands, 1750–1846* (Texas, Texas Tech University Press, 2015).

Povinelli, EA, *The Inheritance* (Durham NC, Duke University Press, 2021).

Reece, H, *Divorcing Responsibly* (Oxford, Hart, 2003).

Reid, K, de Waal, M and Zimmerman R, *Comparative Succession Law (Vol III: Mandatory Family Protection* (Oxford, Oxford University Press, 2020).

Richardson, A, 'Women's Inheritance Rights in Africa: The Need to Integrate Cultural Understanding and Legal Reform' (2004) 11 *Human Rights Brief* 6.

Roberts, D, 'Race, Care Work, and Inheritance' (2015) 40 *Law & Social Inquiry* 511.

Robinson, P, 'Gay Inheritance Decisions: Family of Choice or Family of Origin?' in *Mapping LGBTQ Spaces and Places* (Cham, Springer International Publishing, 2022).

Rønning, OA, Sigh, HM and Vogt H (eds), *Donations, Inheritance and Property in the Nordic and Western World from Late Antiquity until Today* (London, Routledge, 2017).

Roth, A, 'He Thought He Was Right (But Wasn't): Property Law in Anthony Trollope's *The Eustace Diamonds*' (1992) 1 *Stanford Law Review* 879.

Roy, S, 'Empowering Women? Inheritance Rights, Female Education and Dowry Payments in India' (2015) 14 *Journal of Development Economics* 233.

Said, E, 'Jane Austen and Empire' in *Contemporary Marxist Literary Criticism*, Francis Mulhern (ed) (London, Routledge, 1989).

—— *Culture and Imperialism* (New York, Alfred A Knopf, 1993).

Scalise, R, 'Undue Influence and the Law of Wills: A Comparative Analysis' (2008) 19 *Duke Journal of Comparative & International Law* 41.

Scott, JC, Tehranian, J and Mathias, J, 'The Production of Legal Identities Proper to States: The Case of the Permanent Family Surname' (2002) 44 *Comparative Studies in Society and History* 4.

Sedgwick, EK, 'Tales of the Avunculate: The Importance of Being Earnest' in *Tendencies* (London, Routledge, 1994).

Segal, L, *Out of Time: The Perils and Pleasures of Ageing* (London, Verso, 2014).

Shammas, C, Salmon M and Dahlin, M, *Inheritance in America from Colonial Times to the Present* (New Brunswick, NJ, Rutgers University Press, 1987).

Sherman, JG, 'Undue influence and the homosexual testator' (1981) 42 *University of Pittsburgh Law Review* 225.

—— 'Posthumous meddling: An instrumentalist theory of testamentary restraints on conjugal and religious choice' (1999) 99 *University of Illinois Law Review* 1273.

Sigh, HM, '"Immortal Mother and Benefactor": Honorable Dwellings for Unmarried Gentlewomen and the Dynamics of Donations among the Danish Elite from 1699 to 1745' in OA Rønning, HM Sigh, HM and H Vogt H (eds), *Donations, Inheritance and Property in the Nordic and Western World from Late Antiquity until Today* (London, Routledge, 2017).

Sloan, B, 'Due Rewards or Undue Influence? – Property Transfers Benefitting Informal Carers' (2011) 19 *Restitution Law Review* 37.

—— '*Ilott v The Blue Cross* (2017): Testing the Limits of Testamentary Freedom' in B Sloan (ed), *Landmark Cases in Succession Law* (Oxford, Hart, 2019).

Sneddon, KJ, 'In the Name of God, Amen: Language in Last Wills and Testaments' (2011) 29 *Quinnipiac Law Review* 655.

—— 'Not Your Mother's Will: Gender, Language, and Wills' (2015) 98 *Marquette Law Review* 1535.

Sorainen, A, 'Queer Personal Lives, Inheritance Perspectives, and Small Places' (2014) 19 *Lambda Nordica* 31.

—— 'How the Inheritance System Thinks: Queering Kinship, Gender and Care in the Legal Sphere' in P Agha (ed), *Law, Politics and the Gender Binary* (London, Routledge, 2018).

Stanley, E and Smith, N, *Captive Genders: Trans Embodiment and the Prison Industrial Complex* (Chico, California, AK Press, 2015).

Strand, P, 'Inheriting Inequality: Wealth, Race, and the Laws of Succession' (2010) 89 *Oregon Law Review* 453.

Swennen, F and Barbaix, R, 'Ethical Wills – a Continental Law Perspective' (2014) 4 *Oñati Socio-Legal Series* 323.

Tate, J, 'Caregiving and the Case for Testamentary Freedom' (2008) 42 *UC Davis Law Review* 129.

Watkins, D, 'The (Literal) Death of the Author and the Silencing of the Testator's Voice (2012) 24 *Law & Literature* 59.

Weigle, S, 'Inheritance Law, Heritage, Heredity: European Perspectives' (2008) 20 *Law & Literature* 279.

Westwood, S, 'Complicating Kinship and Inheritance: Older Lesbians' and Gay Men's Will-Writing in England (2015) 23 *Feminist Legal Studies* 181.

Whittle, J, 'Housewives and Servants in Rural England, 1440–1650: Evidence of Women's Work from Probate Documents' (2005) 15 *Transactions of the Royal Historical Society* 51.

Wightman, A, *Who Owns Scotland* (Edinburgh, Canongate, 1997).

Wilson, J, Rosenman, L, White, B, Tilse, C and Feeney, R, 'Cultural Considerations in Will-Making in Australia: A case study of Islamic or Sharia-compliant wills' (2016) *41 Alternative Law Journal* 23.

Xynas, L, 'Succession and Indigenous Australians: Addressing Indigenous Customary Law Notions of "Property" and "Kinship" in a Succession Law Context' (2011) 19 *Australian Property Law Journal* 199.

PART 1

Foregrounding Inequalities – Past and Present

2

Defining Family Trees and Building Family Fortunes

A Look into Dispossession and Enrichment Through Inheritance Laws

ALLISON TAIT

I. Introduction

Family forms and kinship networks take on a creative and evolutionary range of aspects, characteristics and participants as they build, reshape, and sometimes undo themselves. What defines a family, however, is not just a source of cultural contestation but also a political question and the subject of legal intervention. The extremely malleable concept of family is contingent on many factors including historical practice and community custom, which can be both embracing and exclusionary, as well as the will of lawmakers and those with legal influence.[1] Family trees, therefore, appear in a profusion of shapes and sizes, some blossoming and some not. And since legal rules recognise and support only certain trees, therein exists the linkage, a strong root connection, between select arboreal genealogies and their economic fortunes.

Within the ecosystem of kinship, the forest of family trees, legal rules can prevent the accumulation of family money just as they can further it. The myriad definitions of the family written into both state and federal statute books are a crucible in which economic inequality is crafted and tempered. What a family looks like and the connective threads of law and biology that attach family members to one another are, consequently, paramount in determining what economic benefits a family can claim, what inheritance rights family members possess, and how a family will be treated in contexts as diverse as tax and housing law. Historically, in the US, the most obvious and salient example of dispossession based on legal definition of the family has been the refusal of legal family status to enslaved

[1] See generally Lenhardt (2017); see also generally Quince Hopkins (2004).

individuals, a refusal grounded in the colonial and plantation politics of power and a root cause of the racial wealth gaps that have evolved and persisted over time.[2]

To this end, in the US the legal family has long been coextensive with the marital family. Marriage, and belonging within a marital family, has traditionally been the key to accessing resources, a fulcrum for distribution of funds within a political economy of privatised dependency.[3] At the state level, there are certain staple financial rights that spouses have through marriage to one another's wealth at both death and divorce.[4] Marriage has also over time become the means for accessing an extraordinary subsidy package providing a multitude of rights and entitlements to married couples, from social security benefits to the right to pursue certain claims like wrongful death.[5] Writing for the majority in *Obergefell*, the US Supreme Court decision that legalised same-sex marriage across states thereby granting same-sex couples access to the panoply of marital rights, Justice Kennedy explained that state law has, 'throughout our history made marriage the basis for an expanding list of governmental rights, benefits, and responsibilities'.[6] That is to say, the Government has over time directed significant streams of money to nuclear, marital families in the form of a robust subsidy package.[7]

[2] Bradway and Freeman (2022, introduction). This profound dispossession was a political demonstration of how 'kincoherence and anti-Blackness are deeply entwined in the production of Black people as kinless.' See also Burnham (1987) and Dixon Weaver (work in progress, forthcoming) (stating '[m]arriage and slavery were in fact antithetical to one another'). See also generally Harris (1993).

[3] There is a large literature on neo-liberalism and the privatisation of dependency discussing how, in the neoliberal economy, the family constitutes its own micro-economy, complete with rules governing both the flow of resources among family members and distributions to dependants at key moments within the life cycle of a family. As Martha Minow has said: 'States try to assert family or family-like relationships in order to avoid or reduce public responsibility for a family's economic dependency.' Minow (1991) 280. See also Eichner (2021) (forthcoming).

[4] Although there is some variation among states, it is generally true in all states that, at divorce, spouses have a right to equitable distribution of the assets earned or acquired (except through inheritance) during the marriage. A divorcing spouse may also have a right to spousal support. At death, surviving spouses are often the primary inheritor, through wills and trusts. Additionally, in the absence of an estate plan, surviving spouses inherit through the default rules. Moreover, even if the spouse who dies would like to disinherit the surviving spouse, the law makes it impossible. A surviving spouse – based either in support or partnership theories – has a right to some portion of the marital wealth, just as that spouse would if the marriage ended in divorce.

[5] At a federal level, there are myriad benefits for married couples, including wealth transfer benefits such as the tax-free transfer of property from one spouse to another at death. See, eg, *United States v Windsor*, 570 US 744; see also, for example, Joslin (2013).

[6] *Obergefell v. Hodges*, 576 US 644, 670 (2016). Selecting just a few of these benefits, Kennedy named taxation, spousal privilege in the law of evidence, hospital access, medical decision-making authority, the rights and benefits of survivors, professional ethics rules; campaign finance restrictions, and workers' compensation benefits.

[7] A recent study investigating 58 federal statutes defining family confirmed this notion. Spouses were included in 91% of the cases, only however in cases of legal marriage and almost never in the case of non-marital partners. Children were the other family members most commonly included – included in 98% of the statutes – but based on the understanding that these were either legal or biological children. Grand-children were included only 62% of the time and step-children only 55% of the time. Least frequently included in family-based statutes were 'nieces and nephews (36%), aunts and uncles (33%), and first cousins (33%). Center for American Progress, 'Expanding Definitions of Family in Federal Law' (26 May 2020) available at www.americanprogress.org/article/expanding-definitions-family-federal-laws.

This tireless governmental mono-focus on marital families has privileged those families that tend more typically to cohere around and embody the notion of an idealised nuclear family – a family formed through marriage, blood and adoption. And as a result, the legal specificity of family belonging has transformed kinship into 'an idiom of state power, white supremacy, and Western modernity'.[8] On the one hand, white families with a modicum of resources –inclusive now of many higher-wealth, often white, same-sex families[9] – tend to align more closely with the state-sanctioned vision and definition of family, while on the other hand non-white heterocentric families, many queer families of all racial backgrounds and ethnicities, and families brought together by economic need are more likely to live their daily lives outside of the marital and nuclear family paradigm.[10]

Findings show, for example, that Black Americans 'display lower marriage rates than do other racial and ethnic groups'.[11] Similarly, non-white, non-marital families are more likely to be constituted by single-parent families, extended families with collateral relations, and 'families that include children unrelated to their caregivers by marriage, blood, or adoption'[12] Underscoring the point, 'Among couples raising children, same-sex couples are seven times more likely than their different-sex counterparts to be fostering [a child]'. Moreover, cultural patterns particularly in immigrant communities shape families in such a way that 'Approximately 17 per cent of children under age 18 – or 12 million overall – are currently living with an extended family member.'[13] Encapsulating ethnographic studies of family and kinship, Elizabeth Freeman writes: 'racial, ethnic, and working class communities have maintained expansive notions of kinship that supersede the genealogical grid.'[14]

Families that do not align with the legal definition of family – the state-powered sorting mechanism for resource distribution – are not only more likely to be non-white, queer, or both; these families are also more likely to be in lower-income brackets that also include heterocentric white families with limited resources.[15]

[8] Bradway and Freeman (2022).

[9] The choice to pursue the fight for marriage equality in the US has been critiqued by many queer commentators as a political strategy designed to benefit primarily same-sex couples with wealth and resources, a boon for those families considered to be 'homonormative'. See Duggan (2002); Franke (2015); Adler (2018).

[10] '[I]nsofar as queerness denotes an excess or perceived deficiency in relation to the normative family, the term always includes and indexes racialization.' Bradway and Freedman (2022, introduction).

[11] Kelly Raley et al (2015).

[12] Sugarman (2008).

[13] Family Equality Council, 'Snapshot: LGBTQ Adoption and Foster Care Parenting in Delaware' (9 November 2022), available at www.familyequality.org/wp-content/uploads/2019/03/8-Delaware-Snapshot.pdf#:~:text=Same%2Dsex%20couples%20raising%20children%20are%20seven%20times%20more%20likely,be%20raising%20an%20adopted%20child.

[14] Freeman (2007).

[15] The marriage gap, for example, is starkly present according to income and wealth: 'poor Americans are almost three times more likely to cohabit, and working-class Americans are twice as likely to cohabit, compared with their middle- and upper-class peers age 18–55.' The study authors add: 'This stands in marked contrast to the 1970s, when there were virtually no class divides in the share of adults married, and a majority of adults across the class spectrum were married.' Accordingly, where 'a majority of

Non-white families and some queer families find themselves existing within the statistics alongside poor, white families – who themselves are prone to being racialised in derogatory ways[16] – for numerous reasons that generally stem from the myriad forms of discrimination, from labour-market to housing discrimination, that have created wealth and income gaps. Families, kin groups and household collectives that exist outside of the white, marital, nuclear family paradigm are, then, also more likely to live outside or on the fringes of the American middle class as defined by income and wealth as well as opportunity.[17] These are also the families who are least well served by narrow family definitions, which serve as obstacles to obtaining governmental benefits, finding housing and receiving tax credits. Narrow legal definitions of family, consequently, do not serve the needs of those lower-income families that fail to model a particular yet broadly embraced vision of middle-class status.

On the other end of the wealth spectrum, high-wealth families tend to be constituted by marital couples, like their more middle-class counterparts. Nevertheless, high-wealth families resemble their low-income counterparts in that statutes that provision benefits based on the nuclear marital family structure no more meet the needs of ultra-rich families than they do those of low-income families. High-wealth families think of themselves, often, in broad-ranging, corporate terms that capture the scope of family connections and the investment of all the family branches in collective family success. Marital families may be units in the complex structure of the high-wealth family but it is not one marital family alone that will generate business success, impart substance to the family legacy, and bring permanence to the family's wealth and privilege.[18] More expansive and corporatist definitions map on to the forms and patterns of money management and wealth planning that the ultra-rich engage in, and are more responsive to this demographic's particular concerns with respect to family business planning, wealth management, and the twinned work of estate and tax planning. Consequently, ultra-rich families, like their low-income counterparts, align with more expansive family definitions and eschew conceptualising family in a middle-class way, as predominantly marital and nuclear.

Accordingly, families at either end of the wealth spectrum tend to find the marital family norm – and rules mandating the embodiment of such a family in order to match the requirements for various benefits and rights – confining and not necessarily conducive to the needs and flourishing of their families. The critical and predictable difference between low-income and high-wealth families seeking more inclusive and forgiving definitions of family rather than the narrow,

middle- and upper-class Americans are married, … only a minority of working-class Americans are married.' W Bradford Wilcox and W Wang, 'The Marriage Divide: How and Why Working-Class Families Are More Fragile Today' 3, Institute for Family Studies (25 September 2017), available at ifstudies.org/blog/the-marriage-divide-how-and-why-working-class-families-are-more-fragile-today.

[16] For a formative analysis of racialisation, see Omi and Winant (2015).

[17] Reeves, Guyot and Krause (2018).

[18] See generally Tait (2019).

marital ones found in the majority of legal rules is that low-income families rarely succeed in obtaining more capacious definitions. High-wealth families, conversely, have in many cases manipulated and influenced the lawmaking process to produce incredibly expansive definitions of the family in the areas that matter most to the ultra-rich.

The rest of this chapter explicates this difference in regulation between low-income and high-wealth populations with respect to how family definitions operate within law and specifically within legal rules that govern inheritance. And if, as Susan Gary reminds us, succession laws can be described as 'an attempt to express the family in terms of property',[19] this chapter demonstrates how family as property and family property are shaped according to two completely different designs based on a family's situatedness on the wealth spectrum. For low-income families default inheritance rules are disciplinary, penalising non-conforming families with economic loss and inheritance failure, while the trust and investment rules that facilitate inheritance for high-wealth families are facilitative and supportive of complex forms of family wealth transfer. After this investigation into the lattice-work of legal rules, the chapter concludes by exploring the wages of these wealth-destabilising or wealth-facilitating rules in the context of inheritance and how the rules replicate historical patterns of dispossession and enrichment by compounding wealth gaps, characterised by gendered and racialised patterns, that both endure and increase over generations.

II. Narrow Definitions: Who Inherits the Family Money

When an individual dies without a will or any other form of estate plan, such as a living trust or any other non-probate transfers, state rules dictate how their belongings and assets will be distributed. These intestacy rules set forth how much a surviving spouse gets, what percentage of the estate children get, and who inherits in the absence of either a spouse or descendants. Because a majority of people do not have wills[20] –'The reality is that most people do not make wills'[21] – these rules ultimately govern a wide swath of the family money that is passed down from one generation to the next.

The phenomenon of intestacy is, however, more acute and widespread with low-income families than with any other segment of the population.[22] Low-income

[19] Gary (2000) 12 (citing T Plucknett, *A Concise History Of The Common Law* 711 (5th edn, 1956)).

[20] In a recent study 67% of the respondents said that they had no estate plan in place. L Konish, '67% of Americans have no estate plan, survey finds. Here's how to get started on one' CNBC (11 April 2022), available at www.cnbc.com/2022/04/11/67percent-of-americans-have-no-estate-plan-heres-how-to-get-started-on-one.html.

[21] Cahn and Ziettlow (2015).

[22] ibid, 343.

families often state that they see themselves as apart from a planning process designed to serve those with greater wealth (whereas at the opposite end of the spectrum, estate planning is quite literally denominated as wealth planning).[23] Moreover, low-income families and individuals avoid conventional estate planning and the probate process because of economic expense and the financial anxiety of hidden costs throughout the process.[24] And, because of the intersection between low-income families and non-white families, statistics also reveal that 'African Americans have much higher intestacy rates than the population as a whole: seventy per cent die without a will, a much higher rate than whites'.[25] The phenomenon is present as well with Latinx families and Native American families. Conversely, 'Demographic analyses reveal that individuals are more likely to have a will if they are white, male, married or formerly married, educated, older, and wealthy; this demographic pattern has endured over time.'[26]

Low-income and non-white families, then, are particularly likely to be subject to intestacy rules as they transfer whatever wealth they have from one generation to the next, and the intestacy rules offer a narrow and particularised view of the family and what it looks like.[27] One scholar has commented that intestacy rules 'constitute the legal vision of the family for the purpose of inheritance' and that, 'Despite various reforms over the years, intestate rules continue to privilege a family based on formal relationships: biology, adoption, and marriage.'[28] The marital family has indeed been the primary focus of these rules, despite some minor variation among states, as evidenced by the fact that the primary inheritors in intestacy are strictly limited to the decedent's legal spouse and children. This configuration of inheritance may successfully map on to the desires of some individuals, but mostly if the individuals live in 'traditional, white, heterosexual families'.[29] Other family members get left out and other family formations go unrecognised – as well as unenriched.[30]

The surviving legal spouse is the main inheritor in intestacy, especially if there are no children or if the children are all from the marriage between the decedent

[23] 33% of the respondents replied that they did not think they had sufficient assets to make a will; Konish (n 20).

[24] Stating '13% said the estate-planning process is too costly and 12% said they do not know how to get a will'; Konish (n 20).

[25] Spivack (2019) 204.

[26] Weisbord (2012) 896.

[27] Intestacy rules vary by state, but all are quite similar in the basic outlines. For 50-state survey information, see law-richmond.libguides.com/c.php?g=129545&p=846341.

[28] Kreiczer-Levy (2019) 349, 354 (internal citation omitted); see also Cahn (2019) (the UPC has steadfastly focused on marital relationships, not broadening provisions concerning intestacy, for example, to include civil unions or domestic partners).

[29] Kreiczer-Levy (2019) 349. This may vary across not only wealth lines but also geographical boundaries. See Douglas et al (2011) (finding that, despite a proclaimed decline in the notion of the traditional family, 'A sense of responsibility to one's partner, one's descendants and, in some instances, to one's ancestors, remains strong' with most decedents).

[30] Strand (2010) 492; Tritt (2010) 275–77 (discussing reforms in the definition of parenthood); Wright (2019); Gary (2000).

and the surviving spouse. In either of these scenarios, the surviving spouse inherits the entire estate. This is the rule in most states and it is the rule in the Uniform Probate Code.[31] The surviving spouse's right to the full estate decrease only when the decedent had children from a previous marriage. Accordingly, if there are children from a previous marriage, the surviving spouse inherits a smaller portion of the estate – often one-third – and the decedent's children and other descendants inherit the rest.[32] In almost no circumstance, however, will non-marital partners inherit.[33] Spouses are defined as legal spouses only (which, after *Obergefell* includes same-sex spouses) and even in the very few states that have common-law marriage, the common-law spouse must be legally determined to be such as spouse before inheriting.[34] Accordingly, cohabiting couples who have not been legally determined to be 'spouses' – which is the vast majority of such couples – have no rights.

If there is no legal spouse, the legal rule across all states is that children – biological or adopted children – share any inheritance in equal parts. Foster children, step-children who have not been legally adopted, and other informally related children do not inherit.[35] Following the branches of the tree out from the centre, if there are no children or other descendants (grand-children, great-grand-children), then the decedent's estate goes to parents, then siblings[36] and any nieces or nephews. The inheritance keeps flowing through the branches of the family tree until the legal family has been exhausted and, finally, when there are no more family members on the legal family tree, the money escheats to the state and goes into the state treasury. In some jurisdictions, intestacy rules have been modified to include in-laws and (unadopted) step-children as a last resort before the money goes to the state.[37] Friends and other chosen family members will never enter into the inheritance equation.[38]

In some cases, if there is little other than personal property to distribute – clothing, mementos, the remains of a savings account – intestacy may not pose such a

[31] Unif Prob Code § 2-102 (amended 2019).

[32] Unif Prob Code§ 2-103; see also, eg, Va Code § 64.2-200(A)(1). In that case, assumptions about how a step-parent will treat step-children when it comes to inheritance emerge and the rules presume that a step-parent will treat step-children worse, financially speaking, than biological or legal children.

[33] See generally *Estate of Fincher*, 119 Cal App 3d 343 (Cal Ct App 1981); *Peffley-Warner v Bowen*, 778 P2d 1022 (Wash 1989).

[34] As of 2022, Colorado, Iowa, Kansas, Montana, New Hampshire, Oklahoma, Rhode Island, South Carolina, Texas, Utah, and the District of Columbia recognise common law marriage. Washington State has a category of 'meretricious' relationships which is similar to common-law marriage.

[35] See, eg, 'Intestate Inheritance Rights for Adopted Persons', US Dept of Health and Human Services, Children's Bureau, available at www.childwelfare.gov/pubpdfs/inheritance.pdf.

[36] Generally, across states, half siblings have the same inheritance rights as full siblings, but there are some exceptions. See generally Brashier (2005).

[37] There is a robust literature concerning law and friendship. See, for example, Goodrich (2013) ('Friendship, or at least the explicit recognition of friendship in public, is surrounded by injunctions, inhibitions, passions, and laws' 23); see also Lieb (2011).

[38] Kreiczer-Levy (2019) 357. 'Friends, neighbors, and caretakers who are not related to the decedent will never inherit from her estate.'

problem and the family can ignore any rules that do not suit by circumventing the probate process and distributing the decedent's belongings according to the family's own collective design.[39] If, however, there is any real property involved – family homes, farms or land – the default rules create particular problems for low-income families and those living in non-normative family arrangements. When there is no will or other form of ownership that provides for survivorship rights, real property is considered to be owned in a tenancy-in-common, which means that it descends according to the rules of intestacy.

This distribution of real property interests through intestacy increases the possibility of fractionation (the more legal heirs there are, the more the property interest is split up) such that where there was one owner initially, intestate succession may result in five owners of the property. Compounding the problem, if the surviving spouse is a non-marital one, that person will have no property rights and distant heirs may gain rights that they are then willing to sell. Fractionation, in this context, works against low-income families because heirs of 'heirs property' lack clear title to the land. Consequently, these heirs face obstacles when seeking to qualify for a variety of loans and government programmes (including disaster relief) and, ultimately, are at increased risk of forced sale and eviction.

Regarding this phenomenon of what is called 'heirs property', one scholar has commented: 'Intestacy disrupts intergenerational economic continuity by causing inherited wealth to fractionate, a result that disproportionately affects decedents of middle or lower economic status.' Making the problem that much worse, 'For those decedents, the largest asset owned at death is typically the primary residence. Failure to execute a will can therefore lead to devastating consequences.'[40] As Carla Spivack notes, on a broader scale, fractionation and heirs property 'has led to considerable land loss among rural African American families, as well as Mexican Americans, farmers, and the rural Appalachian poor.'[41]

Thomas Mitchell and others have demonstrated how intestacy rules have been 'a major cause of African American land loss' by enabling land speculators to buy out land interests from 'far-flung' heirs and subsequently demand a partition by sale. And, in the Southwest, commentators 'have estimated that Hispanics in New Mexico alone in the late nineteenth and early twentieth century lost more than 1.6 million acres of property … and that partition sales accounted for much of this loss.'[42] Intestacy rules, in this way, not only dispossess intestate families, those already facing or enduring circumstances of poverty, but they simultaneously

[39] Cahn and Zeitlow (2015).

[40] Weisbord (2012) 878; Wright (2020).

[41] Spivack (2019) 206.

[42] See ibid and American Bar Association, 'Restoring Hope for Heirs Property Owners: The Uniform Partition of Heirs Property Act' (1 October 2016), available at https://www.americanbar.org/groups/state_local_government/publications/state_local_law_news/2016-17/fall/restoring_hope_heirs_property_owners_uniform_partition_heirs_property_act. See also Mitchell (2014) and Mitchell and Powers (2022).

enrich land speculators and investors who stand to profit and who seek to add wealth to their already lucrative portfolios.

Ultimately, as Felix Chang has stated: 'For lower-income households, intestacy stands as the greatest threat within T&E [trusts & estates] to the intergenerational transmission of wealth.'[43] And, on account of the intersection of poverty with race and other factors of oppression, non-white families are most subject to this threat, suffering persistent and compound economic loss through the failure of the inheritance system.[44] As Carla Spivack observes: 'These broken links of our property inheritance system deserve attention because they contribute to inequality and vulnerability. They also compound, rather than ameliorate, historical injustice.'[45]

III. Relaxed Rules: Building Bigger Scaffolds for Wealth

Enlarging the scope of analysis to capture rules governing high-wealth families, the statutory set of family definitions that operate within a landscape of wealth and privilege is wholly different and the definitions are as broad as the intestacy ones are narrow. Instead of rules defined by cramped and biased definitions of family, rules created to reflect the presumed intent of only a certain slice of families and decedents, the regulation of elite wealth transfer is replete with exemptions, preferential treatment and political favouritism. At the highest reaches of family wealth, there is and has traditionally been a separate set of legal rules benefitting only those families with top earnings, substantial inheritances (and often a combination of the two).

One of the clearest examples of how ultra-rich families manage and transfer their wealth differently than most families, is through the use of family offices and private trust companies, entities whose regulation plays directly into and reinforces the notion of high-wealth privilege and exceptionalism.[46] A family office is the mechanism for family investment – the site of wealth production and increase – and it can work in tandem with the private trust company, a family-centered entity designed to transfer the family fortune outside of probate, through private channels that provide both financial secrecy and asset protection. Family offices and

[43] Chang (2022) 93.

[44] Spivack (2019) 'inheritance law often fails to pass wealth as effectively among the already disadvantaged as it does among others. This failure contributes to higher rates of poverty among these groups'; 192.

[45] Spivack (2019) 192.

[46] Tait (2019). That these entities are meant for the super-rich is clear from the fact that, to establish any of these entities, wealth advisors recommend having somewhere around $100 million in investable assets. See Scherer (2018) 29–32. You may only be a 'single-digit millionaire'; S McGee, 'Millionaires' new challenge: they're not rich enough for private banking' *The Guardian* (11 September 2016), available at www.theguardian.com/money/us-money-blog/2016/sep/11/millionaires-private-banking-chase-wealth-management.

private trust companies constitute legal spaces where elite families can create their own familial networks of profit and privilege, escaping the gaze of governance while reaping economic benefit in a number of ways and transferring wealth from generation to generation through private processes.

With roots in the Rockefeller tradition of family financial management,[47] the family office is a multi-purpose and flexible vehicle that can be located anywhere[48] and 'designed to do anything [the family] wants'.[49] Some family offices handle the logistical issues of life: travel arrangements, event planning, and other household organisation.[50] One of the most common uses for a family office, however, is as an investment arm for the family, focusing 'primarily on the management and enjoyment of family wealth, ensuring that it is wisely invested for growth'.[51] Family offices are widely used for investment purposes by high-wealth families because these offices receive specialised legal treatment in the form of an exemption from the definition of 'investment adviser' under the Dodd-Frank Act of 2010, a federal piece of legislation enacted after the 2008 mortgage crisis in an attempt to create more transparency and accountability with financial institutions.[52]

Family offices are exempt from significant swaths of regulation – especially disclosure rules – based on the proposition that investing for family members is different than doing so for members of the public. Proponents of the exemption argued, when the bill was being considered, that the families in question deserved financial privacy and latitude when investing for themselves and other 'family members'. Lobbying by a group called the Private Investor Coalition, composed of a number of high-wealth families,[53] was a strong determinant in the outcome and the group essentially argued that 'wealthy families … should be able to risk

[47] EJ Poza and RD Hisrich, 'Family Governance: How Leading Families Manage the Challenges of Wealth' Credit Suisse (2016), available at perma.cc/4TVF-GYPQ.

[48] Collins and Thomhave (2021). Three-fourths of family offices are based in North America and Europe. An estimated 1,000 family offices are based in London, managing over $1 trillion in private wealth. Most family offices are in the US, which houses over 3,100 offices, or 42% of the global total. The seven emerging market regions of South America, Africa and the Middle East are home to an estimated 600 family offices.

[49] Maslinski (2006).

[50] A Hayes, 'What Is a Family Office and Do You Need One?', available at www.investopedia.com/terms/f/family-offices.asp. This is the 'service' model of a family office, in which the family office 'employs staff to provide bookkeeping, administrative services, personal property management, project management, and concierge services.' S Martiros S and T Millay, T, 'A Framework for Understanding Family Office Trends' (10 February 2017), available at silo.tips/download/a-framework-for-understanding-family-office-trends.

[51] Maslinski (2016) 27.

[52] Dodd-Frank Wall Street Reform and Consumer Protection Act, Pub L No 111-203, 124 Stat 1376 (2010).

[53] Dodd-Frank Wall Street Reform and Consumer Protection Act, Pub L No 111-203, § 403(2), 124 Stat 1376, 1571 (2010) (amending the Investment Advisers Act of 1940 and eliminating the Private Adviser Exemption). The Private Investor Coalition won an exemption in the 2010 Dodd-Frank financial reform bill, then spent much of the next year persuading the SEC to largely adopt its preferred definition of 'family office. H Scheiber and P Cohen, 'For the Wealthiest, a Private Tax System That Saves Them Billions' *New York Times* (29 December 2015), available at www.nytimes.com/2015/12/30/business/economy/for-the-wealthiest-private-tax-system-saves-them-billions.html.

money as they please'.[54] The final rule, released in June 2011, provided that family offices were exempt if the family office advised only 'family clients' with respect to securities, was wholly owned by 'family clients' and exclusively controlled by 'family members', and did not hold itself out to the public as an investment adviser.

As a result, family offices need only mind whether they have properly followed the definition of 'family clients' and 'family members' set forth by the Securities and Exchange Commission (SEC) in order to benefit from the exemption. And the definition of family employed by the SEC is a capacious one. The SEC defines a 'family client' as any family member, key employee,[55] or charity funded exclusively by family members. 'Family members' are subsequently defined as any lineal descendants of a common ancestor – as well as current and former spouses – provided that the common ancestor is no more than 10 generations removed from the youngest generation of family members. The definition includes adopted children, foster children, and current and former stepchildren.[56] It is a strikingly expansive definition that reveals the way in which high-wealth families understand their families differently, outside of the marital family norm.

Once a person is a family member or family client, that person can put money into or otherwise have a share in the family investment pool, managed by the family office staff – who can be either family members or, increasingly, finance professionals. And because the family office is by definition not an investment advisor, the office avoids public disclosure about office staffing, the amount of assets under management, and the office's trading history.[57] That is to say, this information is kept within the 'family' and not shared with either financial or governmental institutions or intermediaries. Accordingly, a family member's stake in the family fortune is invested and managed both privately and professionally, with the family office taking advantage of select investment opportunities in order to increase the family wealth and protect it from erosion.

Managed by the family office, the family fortune can subsequently be transferred through a private trust company. Another high-wealth family entity often operating in conjunction with the family office, the private family trust company likewise serves the financial needs of one family and is a time-honoured mechanism for facilitating family wealth preservation.[58] And, like the family office, what has traditionally been appealing about these private trust companies is that they

[54] R Frank et al, 'Soros Fund All in the Family' *Wall Street Journal* (27 July 2011) 864, available at www.wsj.com/articles/SB10001424053111903999904576469761599552.

[55] The definition generally includes senior executives and employees active in the investment process, but excludes employees providing solely clerical or administrative services.

[56] US Security Exchange Commission (2011).

[57] Dynastic families like the Phipps and the Rockefellers have used private trust companies since the 19th century to preserve wealth. In fact, a number of today's leading trust companies, such as the Bessemer and Northern Trust Companies, began as private trust companies formed for the benefit of elite families. EY Global Family Business Center of Excellence, 'EY Family Office Guide' (2017), available at www.ey.com/Publication/vwLUAssets/ey-family-office-guide/$FILE/1006031-family-office-guide-hr.pdf.

[58] Hughes (2004). See also Weeg (2016).

are legally sanctioned entities exempt from most state regulation. In every state a high-wealth family can create a 'lightly regulated' private trust company – that is to say a company that is regulated less than any bank or trust company that serves the general public.[59] Alternatively, some states permit the formation of unregulated private trust companies.[60] There is one consistent requirement across states if a high-wealth family wants to charter a private trust company: that the company make a statement under oath that it is not offering services to the general public and provide organising documents limiting the entity's purpose to serving the family.

Here, again, the definition of family is stunningly expansive. The definitions vary somewhat by state, but they are all substantially similar, drawing on the same definition used by the SEC with respect to family offices. This correspondence between the state rules and the SEC rule is intentional and strategic, based on the understanding that if the private trust company engages in any securities-related investment management, it could be required to register with the SEC as an investment advisor.[61]

Most of the statutes begin with the explicit requirement that the trust company designate either a 'designated relative' or 'common ancestor' who will determine what other family relationships are either within or without the scope of the family trust company.[62] Wyoming defines the 'designated relative' as:

> [T]he common ancestor of the family, who may be either living or deceased. With regard to a chartered family trust company or a family trust company applying to be chartered pursuant to this act, the designated relative is the person who is designated in the application for a charter under this act.[63]

Once the family selects a 'designated relative', it is then possible to determine the class of individuals who constitutes that person's family members. The Nevada statute, relatively typical of its kind, allows a family trust company to serve the following 'family' clients:

- a family member with lineal kinship to the designated relative within 10 degrees;
- a family member with collateral kinship to the designated relative within nine degrees;
- adopted children;

[59] Goodwin (2010) 473–74; states with this so-called 'light regulation' include Alaska, Delaware, New Hampshire, and South Dakota. see Alaska Stat § 06.26.200; Del Code Ann tit 5, §§ 773, 774, 779; NH Rev Stat Ann §§ 392.40-a, 392.40-b; SD Codified Laws § 51A-6A-4. Goodwin (2010) 473.

[60] States that permit private trust companies without regulation include Nevada and Wyoming. Goodwin (2010) 475.

[61] T Ganos, 'Putting "Family" In Private Trust Companies – A Follow-Up Discussion On Regulation' Forbes (10 November 2015), available at www.forbes.com/sites/toddganos/2015/11/10/putting-family-in-private-family-trust-companies-a-follow-up-discussion-on-regulation/#10f69ac728cd.

[62] Tenn Code Ann § 45-2-2002 (requiring 'A statement under oath of the name of the individual who will be the designated ancestor of the private trust company'); ibid, § 45-2-2001.

[63] WY Stat § 13-5-204 (2015).

- step-children;
- spouses and former spouses, including spouses and former spouses within five degrees of lineal kinship;
- any non-family member who is an individual beneficiary under a will or trust created by a family member;
- family affiliates and the affiliates' directors, officers and immediate family members;
- family member trusts;
- a trust not owned by a family member if at least one family member is a beneficiary;
- a charitable foundation, as long as a family member is 'an organiser, incorporator, officer, member of the governing board, trustee, major donor or noncharitable beneficiary'; and 'the officers, directors, individual trustees and managers of that foundation, trust or entity and their immediate families'.[64]

Some states are slightly more restrictive. Louisiana, for example, mandates that 'All individuals who control a private trust company … must be related within the second degree of affinity or consanguinity.'[65] Florida limits family members to six degrees of lineal kinship, but Florida also allows a private trust company to serve up to 35 current and former employees.[66]

One of the biggest draws of private family trust companies – as with family offices – is the unparalleled financial privacy they offer, through exemptions from state reporting requirements about their holdings, transactions or investments. Exposure of sensitive financial information to outsiders is minimal, limited only to any expert advisors a family chooses to bring into the company. Private trust companies therefore 'allow[] the true owners, beneficiaries or controllers of trust assets to keep hidden, especially from public scrutiny'.[67] Moreover, private trust companies protect family assets as well as information. Keeping earnings, transactions and even ownership out of sight from both the public and regulatory authorities creates optimal conditions for tax avoidance and evasion.[68]

[64] NRS 669A.070.

[65] La Rev Stat § 6:591 ('All individuals who control a private trust company … must be related within the second degree of affinity or consanguinity.'); Okla Stat tit 6, § 1740 (same language as Louisiana).

[66] Ganos (n 61).

[67] A Knobel (2017) 'Trusts: Weapons of Injustice?' Tax Justice Network, 1, 2 (13 February 2017), available at www.taxjustice.net/wp-content/uploads/2017/02/Trusts-Weapons-of-Mass-Injustice-Final-12-FEB-2017.pdf. For these reasons, trusts including private trust companies are the most commonly used vehicle for providing tax advantage and avoidance. 'Trusts, they said, prove such a hurdle to investigation, prosecution (or civil judgment), and asset recovery that they are seldom prioritized in corruption investigations.' E van der Does de Willebois et al, 'The Puppet Masters: How the Corrupt Use Legal Structures to Hide Stolen Assets and What to Do About It' World Bank (2011), available at: openknowledge.worldbank.org/handle/10986/2363 License: CC BY 3.0 IGO.45.

[68] Wealth managers, for the most part, firmly state that their clients who use these entities for tax benefit remain on the tax avoidance side. However, one advisor admits a more likely situation – 'at least half of the world's wealthiest families are using structures that would struggle to stand up

The private family trust is, then, an essential site of building wealth and supporting the preservation of family wealth through successive generations and spread among numerous, broadly defined family members. Here, foster children, employees and former spouses, wealth transfer beneficiaries and board members are all statutorily authorised to share in the privilege and wealth that family-based institutions create and manage. That is to say, there are no narrow definitions to automatically exclude those family members without legal connection to the family – such as employees, financial advisors, or wealth transfer beneficiaries – or those who may be a part of the family through affective but non-legal bond – foster children, former spouses. And marital families, though they are present, are nothing more than one component part of the larger family, a part subject to assembly and disassembly as the collective family moves through time, accumulating and preserving the family fortune. Wealth rules, then, facilitate family choice and flexibility for elite families as they organise their family affairs and manage the family fortune.

IV. The Fate of Family Fortunes Over Time

Some wealth transfers are – as we have seen through even this brief overview of low-income and high-wealth family definitions in the inheritance context – more successful than others. Wealth transfers on the low-income end of the wealth spectrum may frequently fail to secure what little family wealth may exist on account of a variety of factors, foremost among them being the narrow range of family inheritors in intestate succession. Alternately, in elite and high-wealth circles, wealth rules pertaining to investment and trust legally facilitate the transfer and inheritance of family assets to a chosen family, broadly defined. These definitions and the difference in a family's ability according to positionality on the wealth spectrum to self-define and successfully pass wealth down through generation are the how and the why of kinship's capacity to endure. Kinship and family identity 'do not exist without extension over time'[69] and, conversely, kinship's 'grounding in duration is exposed precisely when it fails'.[70]

The failure here is that over time, as the patterns of inheritance success and failure play themselves out, legal rules that govern elite forms of wealth transfer enable elite families to consolidate their kinship connections and wealth holdings through inheritance. In the middle – a broad and amorphous middle[71] – families

to a full and comprehensive audit.' H Burggraf (2016) 'Panama Papers and the Average Investor: Family Offices Report from the Front Line', International Investment (9 September 2016), available at www.internationalinvestment.net/products/panama-papers-average-investor-family-offices-report-front-line. 'This secrecy enables all manner of financial crimes and abuses.' Knobel (n 67).

[69] Bradway and Freeman (2022).

[70] ibid.

[71] See, for example A Shenker-Osorio, 'Why Americans All Believe They Are 'Middle Class' *The Atlantic* (1 August 2013), available at: www.theatlantic.com/politics/archive/2013/08/why-americans-all-believe-they-are-middle-class/278240; Sherman (2018).

are unlikely to use the sophisticated tax and wealth planning mechanisms available to elite families, possessing neither the means nor the motivation to engage in such wealth transfer strategies. Many middle-class families, however, suffer no harm from the narrowness of intestacy rules, designed to map on to the marital family. Alternately, middle-class families with a modicum of resources are able use basic estate planning tools like wills and revocable trusts to mitigate the worst outcomes of intestacy, like same-sex couples did for many years before *Obergefell* granted marital access to these families.[72] On the low-income side of the spectrum, the default rules of intestacy that govern wealth transfer for many ordinary- and low-wealth families routinely fail to strengthen kinship connections through structured property transfers or, more generally, the family's financial position through inheritance.

In this way, inheritance and the laws regulating inheritance are and have always been, 'an integral component of family, economic, and legal institutions, and a basic mechanism of class stratification'.[73] Moreover, inheritance rules underscore Cheryl Harris's foundational proposition that whiteness is property and property is white.[74] That is to say, the persistent failure to solidify family fortunes through inheritance creates and recreates wealth gaps defined by race, ethnicity, gender, and other measures of identity and marginalisation. And, while wealth transfer embeds class stratification along with other forms of hierarchies and privilege, it also compounds family-based wealth inequality since 'One of the primary mechanisms by which this sedimentation [of wealth] occurs is through inheritance.'[75]

In the US, for example, almost 30 per cent of white families report having received an inheritance or gift, while only approximately 10 per cent of Black families and seven per cent of Hispanic families report having received a similar inheritance or gift.[76] Even among those families receiving inheritances, Black families received less than their white counterparts; a study from 2015 found that 'White families are twice as likely to receive an inheritance as black families, and that inheritance is nearly three times as much.'[77] The outcomes for a family's

[72] Wills have always been particularly important for those families organised outside of the marital norm. Even executing a will, however, has not been a guarantee that non-normative testamentary desires will be actualised. See Maillard (2009); see also K Schroader, 'A Brief History of Pre-Obergefell Same-Sex Estate Planning: Adult Partner Adoption' 107 *Kentucky Law Journal Online* (27 September 2018). available at: www.kentuckylawjournal.org/blog/index.php/2018/09/27/a-brief-history-of-pre-obergefell-same-sex-estate-planning-adult-partner-adoption.

[73] Clignet (1992).

[74] Harris (1993) ('rights in property are contingent on, intertwined with, and conflated with race') 1714.

[75] Chang M, 'Lifting as We Climb' Insight Center for Community Economic Development (Spring 2010), available at static1.squarespace.com/static/5c50b84131d4df5265e7392d/t/5c5c7801ec212d4fd499ba39/1549563907681/Lifting_As_We_Climb_InsightCCED_2010.pdf.

[76] N Bhutta et al, 'Disparities in Wealth by Race and Ethnicity in the 2019 Survey of Consumer Finances' (28 September 2020), available at www.federalreserve.gov/econres/notes/feds-notes/disparities-in-wealth-by-race-and-ethnicity-in-the-2019-survey-of-consumer-finances-20200928.html#:~:text=White%20families%20are%20both%20more,15%20percent%20of%20other%20families.

[77] J Jones, 'Receiving an inheritance helps white families more than black families', Economic Policy Institute (17 February 2017) available at www.epi.org/publication/receiving-an-inheritance-helps-white-families-more-than-black-families.

wealth of these inheritances is hard to understate: 'The importance of inheritances to the wealth position of white families is staggering. At the median, an inheritance increases wealth by more than $100,000 for white families and only $4,000 for black families.'[78] For this reason, another study claimed that 'Careful economic studies actually demonstrate that inheritances, bequests and intra-family transfers account for more of the racial wealth gap than any other demographic and socio-economic indicators including education, income and household structure.'[79]

Consequently, looking at statistics for median wealth-holding, families of colour – particularly Black families – fall far short, stymied by the failures of not only earning but inheritance. To this point, in 2019, 'the median wealth … of Black households in the United States was $24,100, compared with $189,100 for white households.'[80] Looking at averages instead, the gap is much larger in dollar amounts: 'The average Black household had $142,330 in 2019 compared with $980,549 for the average white household. This means that, on average, Black households had 14.5 per cent of the wealth of white households, with an absolute dollar gap of $838,220.'[81] As Alyosha Goldstein remarks: 'For Native peoples, the descendants of enslaved Africans, and other racialised peoples dispossessed by colonisation, inheritance endures as struggle and demand.'[82] And, in this way, the structure of family-money rules replicates historical frameworks of legal and economic oppression in which those individuals and families at the bottom of the wealth pyramid are subject to narrow and unforgiving rules that constrain their ability to acquire, preserve, and transfer wealth.

At the same time, those individuals in the top slice of the pyramid are uniquely enabled in their wealth accumulation by bespoke rules that map on to the devices and desires of an elite population, finding enrichment where other families find dispossession. On the high-wealth end of the spectrum, populated by a blindingly white group of families, successful wealth transfers enabled by tailor-made investment and inheritance rules have crystallised and compounded the extraordinary wealth of elite families. The Forbes billionaires list and 'Richest 400' lists provide a window into the wealth of ultra-rich families and the signal importance of inheritance. Strikingly, 'Seven of the 20 wealthiest members of the Forbes 400 inherited their wealth from previous generations',[83] including Charles and David Koch, the Walmart heirs, and Jacqueline and John Mars of the Mars candy empire. In all these cases, elite white families strategically transferred wealth from one generation to the next through a complicated system of trusts, charitable foundations and corporate entities.

[78] ibid.

[79] Hamilton and Darity (2010) 212.

[80] C Weller and L Roberts, 'Eliminating the Black-White Wealth Gap Is a Generational Challenge' Center for American Progress (March 2021) 1, 3, available at www.americanprogress.org/wp-content/uploads/2021/03/BlackWhiteWealthGap-report11.pdf.

[81] ibid.

[82] Goldstein (2022).

[83] Collins and Hoxie (2018).

These inheriting families that populate the top of the Forbes lists underscore that more than 20 per cent of those individuals named on the list received sufficient wealth to make the list from this inheritance alone. Another sizeable group on the list of roughly 40 per cent – the 'born on third base' group – 'received a "significant economic advantage in their lives by inheriting a sizeable asset from a spouse or family member"'.[84] In addition, highlighting the role of the family office and investment decision-making, a recent study also found that inheritance-based inequality is intensified by the fact that only the very top tier of inheritors avoid depleting their inheritance within a decade, 'due to different rates of return on inherited wealth'.[85]

High-wealth methods of wealth transfer, then, cement family identity and family fortunes by facilitating the endurance of these elite families and their legacies.[86] The use of family offices and private trust companies correlate, then, with a concentration of wealth in elite sectors of society, as even a cursory look at the Forbes list indicates, and these institutions also likely aggravate wealth inequality. The link between these private family wealth institutions, wealth preservation and wealth inequality is so strong that one commentator has stated: 'Trusts are one of the primary vehicles used to create and perpetuate wealth concentration … and they must lie at the centre of debates about inequality.'[87] Consequently, while low-income families have dipped into negative wealth over the last several decades, America's richest families have bolstered their net worth in significant ways.[88] In fact, these recent decades have been defined, in the US (as well as globally), by a rise in wealth inequality and almost all of this increase is due to the rise of the share of wealth owned by the 0.1 per cent richest families, from seven per cent in 1978 to 22 per cent in 2012.[89]

The increase has been such that 'in recent years, U.S. wealth concentration seems to have returned to levels last seen during the Roaring Twenties'[90] and between 1983 and 2016, 'the number of households with $10 million or more skyrocketed by 856 per cent'.[91] On the flip side, during the same time period, 'the median Black family saw their wealth drop [between] by more than half after

[84] See S Moriarty et al, 'Born on Third Base: What the Forbes 400 Really Says About Economic Equality & Opportunity in America, United for a Fair Economy' (2012), available at: assets.nationbuilder.com/ufe/legacy_url/410/BornOnThirdBase_2012.pdf?1448056427.

[85] Nekoei and Seim (2021).

[86] See, for example, Pearson, Carr and Shaw (2008) 957. See also Tait (2019).

[87] Knobel (n 67).

[88] 'Wealth Inequality in the United States' Inequality.org, available agt inequality.org/facts/wealth-inequality.

[89] Saez and Zucman (2016).

[90] Zucman (2019).

[91] Collins et al (2019). Even in the upper echelons of wealth, Black families hold less wealth than white families do: 'The 99th percentile black family is worth a mere $1,574,000 while the 99th percentile white family is worth over 12 million dollars.' W Darity Jr et al, 'What We Get Wrong About Closing the Racial Wealth Gap' (Duke, Samuel DuBois Cook, Center on Social Equity Insight Center for Community Economic Development (April 2018) 2, available at socialequity.duke.edu/sites/socialequity.duke.edu/files/site-images/FINAL%20COMPLETE%20REPORT_.pdf.

adjusting for inflation, compared to a 33 per cent increase for the median White household.'[92] This widening wealth inequality has been accompanied by the resurgence of what Thomas Piketty calls 'patrimonial capitalism',[93] a form of capitalism grounded in ownership of capital through inherited wealth and an economic regime in which 'unequal asset ownership proves hugely determinative (if not completely dispositive) of an individual's life chances'.[94]

The result of this capital-enabling framework of dense and sometimes arcane rules that govern wealth and poverty is a root system that, *sub rosa*, nourishes some family trees and starves others. This highly cultivated and legally curated tangle of roots supports the joint production of racialised dispossession and white entitlement and, when unearthed, makes clear the workings and the wages of a highly differentiated set of inheritance rules.

V. Conclusion

Inheritance rules and the legal mechanisms that facilitate wealth transfer between family generations are grounded in legal definitions of the 'family', and these definitions vary materially according to the transfer system in question. Families that live outside the marital norm on the low-income end of the wealth spectrum – disproportionately non-white and often queer – transfer family property using the default rules of intestacy because they do not engage in estate planning on account of cost or other obstacles that confront them. These default intestacy rules, which privilege the middle-class ideal of the marital, nuclear family – do not serve or reflect the needs of many low-income families and they can even work against the financial interests of these families by directing wealth away from individuals whose important family roles are not captured in the legal rules. Their family trees are not enriched by the legal framework of family definition. In another, wholly different ecosystem, however, high-wealth families and their family trees – disproportionately white and multi-generational in terms of wealth holding – are carefully fed and financially nurtured by idiosyncratic rules and legal definitions that embrace expansive family definitions in order to better reflect the corporatist nature of family wealth preservation. These definitional differences underscore the presence of a bimodal inheritance system that directs the flow of family money through channels shaped by historical patterns of privilege. And, although the two sets of legal rules governing wealth and poverty are generally studied in isolation from one another, this brief inquiry gestures toward the understanding that, in reality, the systems are extensively intertwined with one another, as the same legal lever – *family definition* – produces and reproduces extreme variance in the family arboretum.

[92] Collins et al (2019).
[93] Piketty (2014).
[94] Grewal (2014) 732.

References

Adler, L, *Gay Priori: A Queer Critical Legal Studies Approach to Law Reform* (Durham, Duke University Press, 2018).

Bradway, T and Freeman, E, *Queer Kinship: Race, Sex, Belonging, Form* (Durham, Duke University Press, 2022).

Brashier, RC, 'Consanguinity, Sibling Relationships, and the Default Rules of Inheritance Law: Reshaping Half-Blood Statutes to Reflect the Evolving Family' (2005) 58 *SMU Law Review* 137.

Burnham, MA, 'An Impossible Marriage: Slave Law and Family Law' (1987) 5 *Minnesota Journal of Law and Inequality* 187.

Cahn, N 'Dismantling the Trusts and Estates Cannon' (2019) 2019 *Wisconsin Law Review* 165.

Cahn, N and Ziettlow, A, 'Makings Things Fair: An Empirical Study of How People Approach the Wealth Transmission System' (2015) 22 *Elder Law Journal* 325.

Chang, FB, 'How Should Inheritance Law Remediate Inequality?' (2022) 97 *Washington Law Review* 61.

Collins, C and Thomhave, K, *Family Offices: A Vestige of the Shadow Financial System* (Washington, Institute for Policy Studies, 2021).

Collins, C and Hoxie, J, *Billionaire Bonanza 2018: Inherited Wealth Dynasties of the United States* (Washington, Institute for Policy Studies, 2018).

Collins, C, Asante-Muhammad, D, Hoxie, J and Terry S, *Dreams Deferred: How Enriching the 1% Widens the Racial Wealth Divide* (Washington, Institute for Policy Studies, 2019).

Clignet, R, *Death, Deeds, And Descendants: Inheritance in Modern America* (Aldine de Gruyter, New Brunswick, 1992).

Dinner, D, *The Sex Equality Dilema: Work, Family, and Legal Change in Neoliberal America* (Cambridge, Cambridge University Press, forthcoming).

Dixon Weaver, J, 'Uncovering Race in Family Law' (forthcoming; draft on file with author).

Douglas, G, Woodward, H, Humphrey, A, Mills, L and Morrell, G, 'Enduring Love? Attitudes to Family and Inheritance Law in England and Wales' (2011) 38 *Journal of Law and Society* 245.

Duggan L, 'The New Homonormativity: The Sexual Politics of Neoliberalism' in R Castronovo and D Nelson (eds), *Materializing Democracy: Toward a Revitalized Cultural Politics* (Durham, Duke University Press, 2002).

Eichner, M, 'The Free-Market Family: Liberalism, Families, and Government's Responsibility to Regulate the Market' in A Bhandary and A Baehr (eds), *Caring for liberalism: dependency and liberal political theory* (London, Routledge, 2021).

Franke, K, Wedlocked: The Perils of Marriage Equality (NY, New York University Press, 2015).

Freeman, E, 'Queer Belongings, Kinship Theory and Queer Theory', in GE Haggerty, M McGarry and MA Malden (eds), *A Companion to Lesbian, Gay, Bisexual, Transgender and Queer Studies* (Oxford, Blackwell, 2007).

Gary, S, 'Adapting Intestacy Laws to Changing Families' (2000) 18 *Minnesota Journal of Law and Inequality* 1.

Goldstein, A, '"In the Constant Flux of Its Incessant Renewal": The Social Reproduction of Racial Capitalism and Settler Colonial Entitlement' in S Koshy, JA Byrd, LM Cacho and B Jeffersonn (eds), *Colonial Racial Capitalism* (Durham, Duke University Press, 2022).

Goodrich, P, 'Laws of Friendship' (2013) 15 *Law & Literature* 23.
Goodwin, IJ, 'How the Rich Stay Rich: Using a Family Trust Company to Secure a Family Fortune' (2010) 40 *Seton Hall Law Review* 467.
Grewal, DS, 'The Laws of Capitalism' (2014) 128 *Harvard Law Review* 626.
Hamilton, D and Darity, W Jr, 'Can "Baby Bonds" Eliminate the Racial Wealth Gap in Putative Post-Racial America?' (2010) 37 *Review of Black Political Economy* 207.
Harris, C, Whiteness as Property' (1993) 106 *Harvard Law Review* 1707.
Hughes JE Jnr, *Family Wealth: Keeping it in the Family* (Princeton, Bloomberg Press, 2004).
Joslin, NG, 'Marriage, Biology, and Federal Benefits' (2013) 98 *Iowa Law Review* 1467.
Kelly Raley, R, Sweeney M and Wandra D, 'The Growing Racial and Ethnic Divide in U.S. Marriage Patterns' (2015) 25 *Future Child* 91.
Kreiczer-Levy, S, 'Big Data and the Modern Family' (2019) 2 *Wisconsin Law Review* 349.
Lenhardt, RA, 'The Color of Kinship' (2017) 102 *Iowa Law Review* 2071.
Lieb, EJ, *Friend v. Friend: The Transformation of Friendship – and What the Law Has to Do with It* (Oxford, OUP, 2011).
Maillard, KN, 'Color of Testamentary Freedom' (2009) 62 *SMU Law Review* 1783.
Maslinski, M, 'The Family Office: adapting modern needs in a changing world' (2006) 12 *Trust and Trustees* 27.
Minow, M, 'Redefining Families: Who's In and Who's Out?' (1991) 62 University of Colorado Law Review 269.
Mitchell, T, 'Reforming Property Law to Address Devastating Land Loss' (2014) 66 *Alabama Law Review* 1.
Mitchell, T and Powers E, *Heirs' Property and the Uniform Partition of Heirs Property Act: Challenges, Solutions and Historic Reform* (Chicago, ABA Publishing, 2022).
Nekoei A and Seim, D, 'How do Inheritances Shape Wealth Inequality? Theory and Evidence from Sweden' (CESifo, Working Paper No 9017, 2021).
Omi, M and Winant, H, *Racial Formation in the United States: From the 1960s to the 1990s* (New York: Routledge, 2015).
Pearson, AW, Carr, JC and Shaw, JC, 'Toward a Theory of Familiness: A Social Capital Perspective' (2008) 32 *Entrepreneurship Theory and Practice* 949.
Piketty, T, *Capital in the Twenty-First Century* (Cambridge, Harvard University Press, 2014).
Quince Hopkins, C, 'The Supreme Court's Family Law Doctrine Revisited: Insights from Social Science on Family Structures and Kinship Change in the United States' (2004) 13 *Cornell Journal of Law and Public Policy* 431.
Reeves, RV, Guyot, K and Krause, E, 'Defining the Middle Class: Cash, Credentials, or Culture?' (Brookings Institute Report, 2018).
Saez, E and Zucman, G, 'Wealth Inequality in the United States Since 1913: Evidence from Capitalized Income Tax Data' (2016) 131 *Quarterly Journal of Economics* 520.
Scherer, B, 'Are You Rich Enough for a (Single) Family Office?' (2018) 20 *Journal of Wealth Management* 29.
Sherman, R (2018) 'A very expensive ordinary life': consumption, symbolic boundaries and moral legitimacy among New York elites' 16 *Socio-Economic Review* 411.
Spivack, C, 'Broken Links: A Critique of Formal Equality in Inheritance Law' (2019) 2019 *Wisconsin Law Review* 191.
Strand, PJ, 'Inheriting Inequality: Wealth, Race, and the Laws of Succession' (2010) 89 *Oregon Law Review* 453.
Sugarman, S, 'What Is a "Family"? Conflicting Messages from Our Public Programs' (2008) 42 *Family Law Quarterly* 232.

Tait, AA, 'The Law of High-Wealth Exceptionalism' (2019) 71 *Alabama Law Review* 981.
Tritt, L, 'Technical Correction or Tectonic Shift: Competing Default Rule Theories Under the New Uniform Probate Code' (2010) 61 *Alabama Law Review* 273.
US Security Exchange Commission, 'A Small Entity Compliance Guide' (2011).
Weeg, C, 'The Private Trust Company: a DIY for the Über Wealthy' (2016) 52 *Real Property, Trust and Estate Law Journal* 122.
Weisbord, RK, 'Wills for Everyone: Helping Individuals Opt Out of Intestacy' (2012) 53 *Boston College Law Review* 877.
Wright, D, 'Disrupting the Wealth Gap Cycles: An Empirical Study of Testacy and Wealth' (2019) 2019 *Wisconsin Law Review* 295.
—— 'What Happened to Grandma's House: The Real Property Implications of Dying Intestate' (2020) 53 *UC Davis Law Review* 2603.
Zucman, G, 'Global Wealth Inequality' (National Bureau of Economic Research, Working Paper No 25462, 2019).

3

'My Reputed Children'

Legacies of Enslavement in Atlantic-Island Wills

ANNE BOTTOMLEY*

'I am the bastard child of Empire and I shall have my say'[1]

I. Introduction: Atlantic-Island Children

English–Jamaican author Andrea Levy's novels explore her Caribbean heritage and a history which she described as having been 'forgotten, just left on the margins':

> In Jamaica, I realised what happened there is about the world, empire, a story about humanity – this was not a small place, this was not a small story that affected only a few. It is so much a part of British history and global history. And most of these stories are untold.[2]

Levy's literary legacy gives voice(s) to 'the bastard child of Empire'. This claim of recognition, made by a character whose experience resonates with Levy's own sense of recovery, is defiant and proud. It should be read (heard) as a thick compendium of literal and figurative references (people, islands, legacies), and as shaped by a process which Martinican author and theorist Edouard Glissant called 'creolisation': a process which enables an island-centred understanding of the

* With thanks to the editors of this volume, and to Nick Piska, Bea Bottomley and Kuba Ochocinski, and the late George Gordon. The image at the end of this chapter is composed of details taken from David Wilkie's 'The Reading of the Will' and David Martin's double portrait of Lady Elizabeth Murray and Dido Belle.

[1] Levy (1999) 385.

[2] A Levy 'This was not a small story' (November/December 2004) 70 *Caribbean Beat*, available at www.caribbean-beat.com/issue-70/was-not-small-story#axzz7p8E7l5CY.

potential (of a heritage) of hybridity. Recovering and asserting the history of the 'forgotten, just left on the margins' is a means through which to reimagine (all) our futures.[3] Opening this potential requires 'us' to take time to pay attention to what has previously been rendered marginal in order to recognise the significance of this remapping for (re)thinking (scholastically, politically) a new geography which challenges centrifugal metropolitan presumptions and privileges.

This chapter explores a literal aspect of Levy's 'bastard child of empire': children born on 'British' Caribbean islands to colonial (white) fathers and island (of colour, often enslaved) mothers. Within processes of colonisation, one factor which differentiates colonial sites is the extent to which they were 'settled' by colonisers who intended, personally, to permanently remain rather than return 'home'. In Jamaica the plantation economy was owned and managed by a significant proportion of 'self-improving' transient men. Lacking fortune and social position at home, they were focused on securing sufficient wealth to return and establish themselves, respectably, on metro-isle. Although they might spend most of their adult lives on-island, they did not bring wives with them: wives (and heirs) would be sought 'on return', when their acquired wealth would assure a socially advantageous marriage. Importing a transient, non-familial colonial class resulted in a very high number of sexual 'encounters' (across the full spectrum of sexual relations from non-consensual acts to long-term cohabitation) between colonial (white) men and island (of colour) women, with many children born as a consequence.

These 'Atlantic-island' children shared the characteristic of being born illegitimate. Even those born to cohabitating parents, however affectionate and committed, did not benefit (legally or socially) from their fathers marrying their mothers. It was not illegal; it was simply not done.[4] A consequence of prejudice derived from the early colonial heritage of white male sexual aggression targeting enslaved women with impunity; it was also a consequence of the presumption that many men made that they would be returning 'home' to marry. Marriage on-island was not, to these men and the social milieu they moved in, an option. In 1808, an anonymous author published (in London) a novel in which a daughter (Olivia) describes her father's refusal to marry her once enslaved mother: 'the pride of the man, the quick feeling of the European, the prejudices which he had imbibed in common with his countrymen, forbade his making this affectionate and heroic

[3] Glissant (1992).

[4] Marriage between colonial (white) men and local (of colour) women was not illegal on the British colonial islands (unlike legislative codes introduced in some mainland North American colonies). Marriage for enslaved women was deemed legally impossible on the basis that they lacked legal capacity to consent (to this or any other contract), and, if not baptised, would not have had capacity to enter into Christian marriage anyway, Free(d) women did have legal capacity, but the prejudices of the established church (the administrators of marriage law) as well as colonial society operated 'as if' a legal ban was in place. See Collins (2022).

girl his wife'.[5] Her father dies, unmarried, in Jamaica, leaving his fortune to Olivia on the condition that she goes to England and marries her English cousin (his closest male relative). Through this device, her father contrives the transfer of his fortune to his (legitimate) English family, ensuring the legacy of combining wealth with name, as well as making provision for his daughter through inheritance and marriage.

The narrative illustrates a number of issues which will be addressed in this chapter. Most Atlantic-island children would not, of course, have been as economically fortunate as Olivia (an heiress). For the majority, the question was simply the extent to which (and how) their fathers might make some economic provision for them and, if enslaved, ensure their freedom.[6] Underpinning these issues was the extent to which, and how, putative fathers recognised children as 'theirs'. Put simply: the greater the extent of paternal recognition, the more likely children would be given the benefits of economic support (and freedom, if still enslaved). Recognition was carried initially in being given the paternal/family name, and thereby a lineage. The first formal potential for this was in being given the paternal family name on a baptismal certificate, and, even better, with the father's paternity also registered. However, as we shall see, being named in a father's 'final testament', especially along with the use of the phrase 'my reputed child', provide the strongest form of recognition a father could bestow on putative children. Paternal recognition carried a social benefit on-island, and, for a small proportion of children, but a not inconsiderable number, being recognised was a first step towards becoming 'received' (however marginally) within the British paternal family 'back home' on metro-isle. Whether on-island or in metro-isle, recognition was a move away from maternal heritage (of colour) towards a paternal (white) lineage.

The factors which informed decisions to extend recognition through this process of public documentation will be considered, as well as the legacies of testamentary recognition within a wider social framing. Investigating these questions requires recognition of the (then and ongoing) 'entanglement'[7] between the

[5] Dominique (2008). Resonant with an English anti-slavery sentiment which, whilst recognising a common humanity increasingly advocated separation between distinctive 'races', Olivia sacrifices (for the good of the English family) her marriage and fortune and returns (alone) to Jamaica. See eg Hall (2002).

[6] Livesay (2018) 3 references estimates that only c20% of 'island children' were provided for, freed (if enslaved) or recognised by putative fathers. However, the numbers involved were such that the small minority sent by fathers to Britain (for education or permanent residency) was numbered in thousands. In a sample taken of Jamaican wills 25% included bequests to island children (at 101).

[7] 'Entangled' is used by Stuart Hall, see eg Hall (with Bill Schwarz) (2017); and Catherine Hall 'Entangled histories: Britain and Jamaica in slavery days and beyond', lecture delivered to Society of Antiquarians, Burlington House, London, 7 July 2021, available at www.sal.org.uk. 'Entanglement' is signalled through my use of 'Atlantic-island'. 'Atlantic' is commonly used to recognise the complex interrelations between 'old' and 'new' worlds: bracketing it with 'island' is a recognition of the specificity of colonial relations between the Caribbean archipelago and 'metro-isle'.

Caribbean archipelago and metro-isle, and in order to understand the processes determining a paternal inheritance on-island, the chapter begins in metro-isle. This was the frame of reference which colonists carried with them into the islands; and to begin this way affirms the significance of recovering 'forgotten' histories 'left on the margins' as critical to an understanding of the metropolitan inheritance.

II. Nobody's Child

> The rights of an illegitimate child are only such as he can acquire; he can inherit nothing, being in law looked upon as nobody's son, but he may acquire property by devise or bequest. He may acquire a surname by reputation, but does not inherit one.[8]

When women's rights campaigner Barbara Leigh Smith included a chapter on 'Illegitimate Children and Their Mothers' in her 1854 book the *Most Important Laws concerning Women*, she emphasised that it was within the gift of fathers to make economic provision for putative children, by 'devise or bequest', as well as to allow them to carry a (paternal) surname 'by reputation'. Leigh Smith knew this well: her father, the reformist Whig MP Ben Smith, had chosen not to marry the mother of his five Leigh Smith children. Named on their baptismal certificates, and living with them as 'his' family in a single household, he had withheld the status of legitimacy from them, denying them legal benefits as well as social respectability. Barbara and her siblings lived on a margin, loved and well provided for by a wealthy upper-class father but without the security of legitimate status to embed them in the supportive inclusiveness of a wider paternal family and social class.

'Nobody's child' carried a doubled meaning. Born outside of marriage, children lacked the paternal linkage which delivered legitimate status and, because women lacked legal capacity, it was presumed that mothers themselves could not convey legal status to children born to them.[9] Children with no legally recognised parent were therefore 'nobody's child': 'illegitimate' in the sense of being without outside-of-law.[10]

[8] See Hirsch (1998) 88. Unlike civil law, common law made no provision for formal recognition or adoption by putative fathers. Adoption only became available in English law in the early 20th century, and then only for children (to provide for a home, rather than an heir). See eg Graveson and Crane (1957).

[9] The only exception (introduced by colonial statutes) was that an enslaved mother passed on her enslaved 'status' to her children. In 1802, a Jamaican document referred to 'the reputed children of Mary Hay a free woman of colour', reflecting the presumption that (free) women lacked the ability to convey status. CO/139/51, 'Details of Private Acts of the Jamaican Assembly relating to people of African or part African descent from 1774 to 1784' extracted by Edward Crawford from the list of Jamaican Assembly Acts at the Public Record Office, Kew, London (rootsweb.com).

[10] Statutory reforms in the early 20th century finally allowed for the recognition of a legal relationship between mother and child. See eg Graveson and Crane (1957).

Without destabilising this fundamental distinction, paternal links could be recognised by imposition or election. Putative fathers of children whose mother's sought parish relief, could, under legislation introduced in the sixteenth century, be made responsible for their 'bastards'' upkeep. Fathers of higher socio-economic status could avoid the legal processes of public judgment and condemnation by voluntarily providing for their 'natural' children. In *Emma*, Jane Austen introduces Harriet Smith, 'the natural daughter of somebody' who has placed her 'out of the way' in a boarding school, 'no-one knowing', including Harriet, who 'somebody' was.[11] 'Somebody' is a putative father (her maternal heritage is never referenced), who has chosen not to recognise Harriet and is unlikely to carry the name Smith.

Leigh Smith's account of the law introduces a spectrum to illegitimacy: through to the best-case scenario of a child not merely provided for, but openly recognised by the putative father through the gift of the paternal (sire-)name.[12] Investigations carried out by parish authorities concerned to fix fathers of 'bastards' with their maintenance began with seeking 'reputed fathers'; men named as 'reputed' to be responsible. In a neat reversal, from accusation to claim, fathers began to use the same referent to identify children they chose to acknowledge as: 'my reputed children'. In documents such as wills, 'reputed children' came to mean something more than merely 'natural', whilst always less than 'lawful'.

If men like Smith were free to marry, why not marry the mothers of their children? The answer was simple: the women were not (sufficiently) socially respectable to be 'received' within the paternal family or social milieu. For Smith, the issue was class: he withheld marriage from his lower-class partner, and consequently legitimacy from his children. A great deal of hard (and often imaginative) labour was then invested in crafting and presenting such socially marginal families in a form which allowed fathers to remain, as far as possible, respectably

[11] J Austen, *Emma* (London, Penguin, 2012) 20. First published 1815. At the end of the novel we are told that Harriet 'proved to be the daughter of a tradesman, rich enough to afford her the comfortable maintenance which had been hers, and decent enough to have wished for concealment' (at 473). Not rich enough, however, for social respectability: 'The stain of illegitimacy unbleached by nobility or wealth would have been a stain indeed' (at 474). Would the very large fortune of the British-Antiguan 'half-mulatto' Miss Lambe, in Austen's unfinished novel *Sanditon* (1817), be enough to overcome her disadvantages of heritage and birth to attract the attention of the scheming Lady Denham seeking an heiress for marriage to the impoverished heir of her late husband's title? J Austen, *Sanditon and Other Stories*, P Washington (ed) (New York, Alfred A. Knopf, 1996). There are too few chapters to be able to anticipate Austen's plot design, but she is likely to have echoed contemporary concerns, evident in the British evangelical anti-slavery movement, with the threat of West Indian 'corruption' (wealth, manners, health and purity) and avoided marriage (or brought it to a quick end). Miss Lambe is described as 'sickly' which does not bode well for her. See n 5, and Reed (2019) 501.

[12] Or one closely aligned to it. Smith gave the mother of his children an assumed name, Mrs Leigh; creating the surname Leigh Smith for their children. After her death he fathered a second family, named Bentley Smith. His first family had no knowledge of this until reference was found to them (with modest economic bequests) in his will. No effort was made to incorporate them into the Leigh Smith family: they remained strictly extra-familial (Hirsch, 1998).

embedded in their own class and natal family. It was a balancing act often requiring considerable levels of collusion from all involved. Somewhat paradoxically, a not infrequent paternal concern was to do everything possible to ensure that 'his' children would eventually share the advantages of his birth: not merely economic security, but social respectability. Others negotiated a more marginalised position for their children: no natal family recognition, a lower social class or weaker economic position.[13]

Underlying all these scenarios was the problematic existence of mothers: now doubly unrespectable, having become unmarried mothers as well as mistresses. Some fathers simply 'hid' them in clear sight, often in the role of 'housekeeper'; others placed them more discreetly in separate establishments. For some mothers, the lack (or end, or denial) of a relationship with fathers, and/or paternal concerns with securing the best advantages for their children, could result in marginalisation to the point of erasure. Separation from children (placed as borders like Harriet or Miss Lambe,[14] or taken to live with fathers, or within the extended paternal family) would (was intended to) make continued contact with mothers difficult, if not impossible.[15]

Maternal separation was a particular feature for one group of 'reputed children': those who, like Miss Lambe, were born to island mothers of colour and then sent (or brought) to Britain by colonial fathers. However distasteful we now find the choices made by someone like Smith in holding class at a distance, it is so much more difficult to encounter the attitudes held, and decisions made, by putative fathers based on a woman's heritage and the legacy of enslavement. For these children, and even more so their mothers, all the prejudices and discriminatory practices carried in colonisation and enslavement impacted starkly and directly: particularly given that marriage and legitimacy was always out of the question.[16]

For Atlantic-island children, the use of 'by repute' to distinguish between children a father chose to acknowledge and those he did not, became extensively used and with much greater consequence than on metro-isle. It would, however, be a mistake to engage with the colonial evidence as if it is simply a question of/for colonial sites and their respective histories. To refuse the distancing strategy of an off-island, overseas, account of remote 'colonial' stories (to actively listen for/to the silence which pervades, haunts, Jane Austen's *Mansfield Park*), is to confront and accept that Atlantic-island families are a metro-isle legacy as much as an on-island

[13] See, eg, n 12.

[14] n 11.

[15] Most mothers would not have been able to undertake single parenthood, for social and/or financial reasons. To have their children provided for, rather than being left as a single parent, would have been a benefit they may well have advocated and negotiated. My point here is simply that provision made for children was often at the cost of separation from mothers.

[16] n 4.

heritage: we remain entangled islands.[17] Within this framing, the issue, from the limited perspective of metro-isle, is one of 'recovery'. The recovery of a forgotten, marginalised or supressed, legacy, which we can begin to diagram in an image of a significant moment when an uncomfortable secret might be exposed.

III. Reading the Will

When, in 1818, the King of Bavaria commissioned David Wilkie to make a painting 'as purely English as possible', Wilkie chose as his theme a family and household gathered after the death of a husband/father/relative/master to hear 'the reading' of the deceased's will.[18] The past, carried in a written text, reaches forward to shape the future of those gathered to hear, conventionally for the first time, the decisions (which have been) made by the deceased. One life is over, and those who remain anticipate futures revealed in a sealed document extracted from a locked box.

As common law allows 'freedom of testation', it is in the gift of the testator to decide who will benefit 'by bequest'.[19] And as conventionally the will is a private document, the contents of which are known only to the testator (and lawyer), it is not made public – that is, known to the family – until after death.[20] When technologies for communication were limited, it was convenient to 'read the will' after the family had gathered for the funeral of the deceased.[21] The event of 'reading' is therefore framed, temporally and spatially, as a revelation. Wilkie peoples his picture with a range of characters posed to intrigue us in terms of possible narratives of past, present and future relations between them: moulded and negotiated through the decisions of the absent central figure (a ghostly presence manifested in his wall-hung portrait).

Wilkie's consummate dramatic twist is that the scene he portrays is sufficiently opaque to be open to numerous interpretations. Pulling his audience into the image, he provokes questioning and speculation drawing on the persistently

[17] J Austen *Mansfield Park* (London, Penguin, 2003). First published 1814. See further Bottomley (2022). On 'haunting', see Gordon (2008).

[18] Cunningham (1843) The painting now hangs in the Neue Pinakothek, Munich. In the 1990s, the picture was used as a cover illustration for editions of Jill Martin's *Modern Equity* (published by Sweet and Maxwell). The image used on the cover of this collection is a sketch made by Wilkie of one section of the painting.

[19] There were some restrictions, most obviously property held in trust, and widows had limited rights at law. In the 20th century, legislation introduced rights to provision for some family members whilst maintaining the foundation of testamentary freedom.

[20] The wider public can access the contents of a will after it has been probated and entered into the public record. Before the state administered probate system, introduced in 1858, this fell under the jurisdiction of the established church.

[21] After the event of 'reading' ceased to have a pragmatic purpose it slipped into disuse, but the drama of revelation before a gathered family continues to engage the public imagination.

popularist thematic of death and testamentary disposition as a potent time for the revelation of (life) secrets. Not only does expectation (or hope) of benefit fuel this dramatic moment, so does the thrill of anticipation of the unknown and unexpected.[22] This is not just about bequests as gifts: it is a 'last testament', a time for coming to terms with truth (especially for those who live and die in the expectation of divine judgment), and for the imposition of obligations as 'last wishes' (not only by law, but also by appeals to sentiment and honour). The will is a threshold: between life and death; past and future; public and private. In this sense, we need to think of the will as a potent document designed to carry (sometimes difficult) messages. The questions are always: what is the message designed to achieve, and who is this message intended for? (And, as a supplementary: what did they already know?)[23]

Wilkie Collins,[24] a godson of David Wilkie, died in 1889. A bachelor, his will revealed paternity of three children: 'I hereby acknowledge the said three children as my children by the said Martha Rudd.'[25] Under the assumed name of 'Mr Dawson', he had installed Martha Rudd (Mrs Dawson) and their Dawson children in a discrete establishment without his family, his housekeeper-mistress, or most of his friends, knowing about them.[26]

Collins used simple and direct language, 'children', 'mine', 'acknowledge', for the posthumous admission that he had fathered children and (until then) hidden the truth. The tension is obvious: through open acknowledgment he accepts responsibility and in so doing makes visible the design which had kept hidden his secret. For whom was this revelation intended? It is tempting to think that Collins enjoyed being the author of his own drama of revelation, but it does not read that way. There is a kind of brutality in the way he casts his admission: no words of affection are employed. It could have been the result of a promise made to Martha Rudd that he would admit to paternity and make provision for the children at some point in the future, but that he did not want to face the (personal) consequences of revelation during his lifetime. It could be that he was concerned that, without some explanation, the bequests made to Martha and the children might not be respected (taken seriously enough and in good time), or even challenged.

[22] George Eliot's *Middlemarch* (serialised in the 1870s) describes, to great comic effect, one such scenario of expectations shattered and secrets (alluded to rather than) revealed. In Ch XXXIV, expectant relatives of a deceased bachelor are astounded when an unexpected and unexplained heir is revealed at 'the reading'. Under the terms of the will, he will take the deceased's family name: linking the bequest of wealth (land) with the direction/gift of name (lineage) makes clear that the inheritance is designed as much as for the future of family and estate as for the benefit of the nominated heir.

[23] On colonial wills and island children, see eg n 32.

[24] Collins authored numerous novels and short stories using the dramatic plot device of family secrets (illegitimacy, problematic marital status, socially inappropriate liaisons etc), see eg *No Name* published in 1862.

[25] P Lewis, 'Wilkie Collins – The text of his Will', posted March 1997 on clarahost.co.uk.

[26] In 1874, the year that (state) birth certificates became compulsory, he was registered as the father on his youngest child's birth certificate (under the name of Dawson).

Whatever the key factors which influenced him, his will operated to carry and record his revelation as part of a granting of bequests and imposition of obligations (on his executors) in a design intended to protect his Dawson children after his death.

Extending the potential introduced in Wilkie's narrative-image allows us to mould and recreate that image in order to explore other narrational settings: thinking about why and how something has been revealed, to whom, and with what (potential) consequences.

When Moses Benson, a 'Liverpool merchant', died in 1806 he left a lengthy 36-page will creating a strict settlement reaching forward across future generations of 'lawful heirs'.[27] Any break in succession through the direct male line was covered by allowing for a collateral heir, on the condition that the family name (and recently purchased crest) be adopted by private act of parliament within one year of coming into the inheritance. Benson used property, will and settlement to secure for his family (and himself) a legacy of establishment in the respectable security of the landed gentry. Having made his money in trade, he had then become focused on acquiring the key indices for becoming a 'gentleman': a landed estate with manorial rights carrying the title of 'esquire'. Benson died before the transition into land was accomplished, but his executors fulfilled his game plan by purchasing a country estate and thereby securing the material and socio-cultural assets needed to ground the family within the landed gentry.

The narrative arc of moving from trade to land is familiar, but Benson's plan for transition contained an odd feature: he lacked 'lawful heirs'. A bachelor, he had, and made bequests to, four children and created a settlement 'to the use of his son or reputed son Ralph Benson for life, remainder to trustees on trust to preserve, remainder to use of the testator's grandson Moses Benson, eldest son of Ralph … (etc)'.

'Reputed' slips in as if Benson would have preferred not to have had to use it. It is likely that this admission of illegitimacy was advised by lawyers in order to deflect a possible legal challenge based on the (then) presumption that 'child' only covered 'lawful issue' (his namesake, Moses, having been born legitimate, is described as 'grandson' and 'son'). Benson's children carried his name and, until they married, lived with him as his family. It is quite possible that a certain amount of ambiguity, even subterfuge, had allowed their legitimacy to be presumed within local society; if so, the will carried an unwelcome admission.

Benson exemplifies a father working hard to build his (family) legacy whilst (and because of) not having provided the most basic of foundational blocks: the

[27] PROB 11/1451/254. The complications of the settlement were such that, in 1839, a private act of parliament was required to assist the trustees. 'Moses Benson', Legacies of British Slavery database, available at wwwdepts-live.ucl.ac.uk/lbs/person/view/2146652071.

legitimacy of his children. The key to making 'sense' of this paradox is found in his description as a 'Liverpool merchant'. Austen's very deliberate pause in *Emma*, 'a Bristol – merchant, of course, he must be called.',[28] is apposite. Benson, like the Bristol merchant, made his fortune trading in enslaved persons. He lived between Jamaica and Liverpool before finally returning 'home' with four Jamaican-born children who carried his family name. His paternity is recorded in their baptismal records, which record their mother, Judith Powell, as a 'mustee' (a person of seven-eighths white ancestry, that is with one Black ancestor three generations back).[29]

In contrast to Collins, Benson had done everything he could to present the children as his, but colonial prejudices would not allow any formal recognition of a relationship with Judith Powell; only his children would be acknowledged.[30] However, like Collins, his will became a record of paternity: a future-orientated concern made necessary by a past decision which had deprived his children of legitimate status.

Benson's narrative is one of the problematic origins of wealth and family, simultaneously covered and revealed within a document designed to distance and protect (the inheritance of) the future family from (the legacy of) the past. Transposed into a version of Wilkie's painting, the significance of 'a reading' reimagined as a colonial narrative would be to signal the (denied and obscured) absent-presence in the room (of an English estate) of (island plantation) colonisation and enslavement (as Austen achieved in *Mansfield Park*).[31]

[28] n 11, 179. The source of the 'profits of his mercantile life' are underscored by Austen naming him 'Hawkins' (an Elizabethan 'slave trader').

[29] Jamaican baptismal records were 'white blind'. Persons of solely European heritage were not recorded by ancestry. European-white was so embedded as the normative standard that it was (necessarily) rendered invisible. Naming a specific degree of European/African ancestry was inherited from the Spanish practice of treating the fourth generation as if white. This was adopted in Jamaica (once Spanish) in practice, and then in law in 1733. Reference was made to 'how far … corruption of the blood should extend' in debates concerning the legislation, but as Livesay (2018) points out: the adoption of the Spanish precedent meant that Jamaica did not follow the 'one drop rule' used in continental American colonies (at 38). This, and the large number of 'people of colour' in the islands created a very different environment for the development of constructions (and policing) of racial identity between island and American continental colonies. (See also n 4.) However, towards the end of the 18th century, and increasingly in the next, divisions into and between 'races', and a determined effort to protect (the privileges of) white identity took root on-island (especially following significant uprisings by enslaved people supported by some free people of colour), as well as in metro-isle (carried in concerns of what might follow after the ending of enslavement and drawing from the rise of biological essentialism), see eg Livesay (2018) and Hall (2002). A full-blown fear of 'contamination' entering metro-isle is, notoriously, evident in Charlotte Bronte's *Jane Eyre*, published in 1847. Sarah Collins, in *The Confessions of Frannie Langton* (London, Penguin, 2019), depicts as part of her narrative colonial attempts to find scientific evidence to ground racial categories.

[30] I have found only one record of marriage between Atlantic-island parents. Thomas Legall Yates brought Dorothy Smellie, mother of his nine reputed children, to England and married her in 1834. She is variously recorded on baptismal certificates as 'free quadroon' or 'free mustee'. 'Thomas Legall Yates of Brockhurst', Legacies of British Slavery database, available at wwwdepts-live.ucl.ac.uk/lbs/person/view/1318320185.

[31] n 11.

In Benson's will it was social approval which was jeopardised by the revelation of illegitimacy raising questions of heritage, but in some cases a testamentary acknowledgment of 'reputed children' came as an unwelcome surprise to the paternal family, especially if the testator had married and had lawful heirs:

> Many colonists hid illegitimate children of colour from British family members and did not disclose their existence until death freed them from the burden of maintaining the secret. Wills frequently served as official messengers, bearing witness to their authors' colonial indulgences.[32]

A conflict over bequests might well arise as a consequence. In 1741, Richard Codrington's will was proved in England.[33] From his extensive colonial and metropolitan estates, he made ample provision for his wife and legitimate children, and then included modest bequests for a number of island women ('my negro woman') and more generous bequests for their children ('my mulatto boy'), along with giving them all their freedom. He did not openly acknowledge parentage, and the children had not been given his family name. The use of 'my' can be read as simply indicative of the fact that he 'owned' enslaved persons, or can (also) be read to imply a more personal connection. His wife blocked the bequests by simply ignoring them. Was she angry that he had had island children (and not told her?), or that he had made it (almost) public knowledge, or that he had taken some wealth away from his legitimate family?

When the terms of the will and her failure to act became known on-island, litigation was begun in London to enforce the bequests. In a judgment which instructed payment to be made, Lord Hardwicke recognised that the wife 'must have some resentment against this kind of conduct by her husband', but that 'when he had these children, in whatever way, or with whatever colour, it was a natural duty incumbent upon him to provide for them'.[34]

The Codrington litigation evidences the tensions which could arise between the interests of a legitimate family ('at home'), and a paternal wish to undertake some responsibility for island children. Evidence presented during and after the trial suggests that Codrington had, during his lifetime, taken an interest in his island children and financially supported them (some had been sent to school in England). If Codrington had chosen to be discrete (at least in metro-isle) during his lifetime, and continued a level of discretion in his will, he nevertheless was concerned enough about their futures to allow a level of posthumous visibility as a consequence of testamentary inclusion. In this sense, Codrington, like Benson, was forced to make a(n implied) public admission, but Codrington had to negotiate this within the context of a wife and lawful heirs. Conversely, for Benson his island children were his only family and heirs and he wanted to treat them as-if legitimate.

[32] Livesay (2018) 221.
[33] PROB 11/713, NAE.
[34] *Williamson v Codrington*, 1750, see Livesay (2018) 60.

Hardwicke's argument that fathers had a natural obligation to support all their children, resonates with a contemporary concern that illegitimate children could destabilise a legal family unit, emotionally and economically. A perceived need to increase the regulation of families in order to stabilise financial wealth led to (the same) Lord Hardwicke's Marriage Act of 1753. However, the tone of Hardwicke's judgment can also be read as supporting the basic value of freedom of testation (allowing for responsible choice and future legacy), and as a reminder that it is the obligation of those who remain to uphold the wishes of the deceased. In this sense, it is supportive of male (husband, father) choice, and requires female (wife, mother) compliance, whilst encoding a message of the need to be paternally responsible towards the legitimate family and lineage.

IV. Thresholds: Decisions and Documents

The threshold passages of life and death were opportunities for recording paternity: at the birth of a child, and on the death of a father. Until 1874, baptismal records kept by the established church were the only record of birth. But this depended on baptism taking place, and baptism was a crucial divider between Christian and non-Christian, free and enslaved. A father deciding that children born of an enslaved woman should be baptised was a significant step away from enslavement and towards the potential of becoming free(d). Even for children born to free(d) mothers, baptism was still important in marking a continued move away from enslaved origins towards a safer, more respectable, future; in part through providing a(nother) record of freed status. The gift of baptism, especially with the entry of a paternal name, was therefore an important act of recognition and support. However, for some children freedom and baptism were only gained after the father's death under testamentary provisions. Both threshold-moments therefore framed major paternal decisions: if he had not done so already, should he make provision for the freedom, baptism and naming of his children in his will (his last testament)? How might he design the terms of his will to try and secure the future of his children (or their mothers)? How should he balance the interests of his various family members, on-island and in metro-isle?

It is in the final document of record, the will, that we gain some insight into how putative fathers led their lives and structured their decision-making. Wills as a last testament were a father's final chance to create (and attempt to protect) a legacy for himself and his children: they could be used to admit to what had been hidden (or not dealt with) *inter vivos*, or record and confirm previously made decisions.

Wills are unique in combining temporal/spiritual authority and purpose. On the one hand, the role of executors and enforced publicity are designed to protect and enforce the wishes of the testator, and on the other hand, the seriousness of the intentions of the settlor's last wishes is underscored by a kind of sanctity attached to the processes of (and preparation for) dying.[35] We might almost say that recognition in baptismal certificates is a potential, whereas to be evidenced as a 'reputed child' in a will is a final confirmation.

Between these thresholds, lives were lived out in mundane struggles of messy and muddled complexities, underpinned by the harsh realities of colonial enslavement and prejudice. Life factors such as how relationships developed; whether the deceased had had other children; whether he married and had legitimate children; and where he was resident, were then critical factors determining his final, testamentary, decisions.

Edward Earl, a Jamaican lawyer and planter, died on-island in 1821. His will recognised several 'reputed' children, all born to enslaved women.[36] He had purchased the freedom of some, but not others:

> To a negro woman named Hardtime, … the property of Hebert Jarrett, £100 currency.
>
> I am the reputed father of the two following (groups of) mulatto people whose freedom I purchased 05/04/1808 viz John (and named others), the sons and daughter of a negro woman named Lucretia that did belong to Orange Valley Estate[37] and Betty (and named others), the sons and daughters of Hardtime.
>
> Since I manumised the above 10 people of colour I am the reputed father of another mulatto child named Rosee, a daughter of Hardtime. I beg that my executors will use every means in their power to have my said reputed daughter and also her mother Hardtime purchased and manumised at the expense of my estate. If Rosee's freedom cannot be obtained then my executors to pay into the hands of the Orange Valley estate £300 currency, the interest to be paid to Rosee each year for life and the capital to then go to her children.

His testamentary design carries two temporalities: providing for a future and protecting a past.[38] It is a reminder of how fragile recognition of legal status could be, and that therefore every repetition of record(ing) was significant, especially

[35] Wills written on-island often have a particular sense of awareness of the closeness of death. See Brown (2010).

[36] 'Edward Earl', Legacies of British Slavery database, available at wwwdepts-live.ucl.ac.uk/lbs/person/view/2146634282.

[37] He had been the estate manager of Orange Valley.

[38] He made small bequests for four other (we can surmise) daughters born to enslaved women, without acknowledging paternity or making provision for manumission. Economic provision without open acknowledgment was common; see eg nn 33 and 39, and 'Thomas Hercey Barritt', Legacies of British Slavery database, available at wwwdepts-live.ucl.ac.uk/lbs/person/view/2146632224. Barritt's three legatees, all female, carried his family name but were not recognised as 'reputed'. His legitimate children in England were also female. Lacking sons, he was concerned about the continuation of the family name and requested in his will that any future sons-in-law should allow 'their children (to) take and use the name of Barritt in addition to their own name and that they will apply for and obtain proper authority for that purpose'. The significance of family name across a range of circumstance is very visible in Barritt's testament.

when endorsed in a last will and testament.[39] In Earl's text, the use of the term 'reputed' combines evidence of past treatment (informal, 'lived', recognition), with a statement of record (formal 'documentation', in law, of recognition). Recognition 'by repute' in the paternal final testament became a kind of imprimatur. George Besson, a Trinidadian author, characterised this, and the legacies which still flow from it, as 'the cult of the will'.[40]

Dr John Drummond died in Jamaica in 1804. His will evidences processes of being (re)moved from enslavement within a complex of sexual/paternal relations, alongside the use of enslaved persons as inheritable property 'settled' between generations to provide capital and income:[41]

> I give devise and bequeath unto a free Negro woman named Mary Drummond alias Juno the following slaves … to hold … with their issue … for and during the term of her natural life … and immediately give devise and bequeath said several slaves with their issue … unto Thomas Drummond the younger my reputed son … to hold to him for and during the term of his natural life and from and immediately after his decease I give and devise the said slaves … unto such child or children of the said Thomas Drummond as shall be alive at the time of his decease and acknowledged by him …
>
> … at the end of 2 years after my decease if not sooner … I hereby direct my executors … to purchase a mulatto boy child reputed to be mine named William the son of a Negro woman named Eleanor the property of the said Mary Drummond and a mulatto girl child named Maria also reputed to be mine by a Negro woman named Kitty belonging to the said Mary Drummond and to make both the said children free at the expense of my estate. And I hereby give and bequeath unto the said 2 mulatto children an annuity or yearly sum of £25.

The once enslaved Mary Drummond had lived with the doctor as his housekeeper; whilst he extended his sexual activities to include enslaved women within her household. Whilst he made provision for the purchase and freedom of the children born to Eleanor and Kitty, along with a modest annuity, their mothers

[39] Thomas Burton used his will to provide further documented evidence of having freed his children and their mother, without acknowledging them as 'reputed': 'Whereas I did by two several instruments of writing or record in the secretary's office of this Island manumise enfranchise and set free one negro woman Hannah (alias Hannah Mendez) and two mulatto boys named Nicholas & Francis (alias Nicholas Burton & Francis Burton). It is my will and desire that they & each of them and each of their offspring & increase be and are hereby declared free to all intents and purposes whatsoever hereby corroborating ratifying and confirming the said instruments of writing in the fullest and amplest manner possible.' www.antonymaitland.com/wright01f.htm. Using wills to provide documentary evidence of freedom could also be useful in England: when Lord Mansfield died in 1793, he included a provision designed to protect Dido Belle (unacknowledged daughter of his wife's nephew and an enslaved African woman), who had been living in his London household: 'I confirm to Dido Belle her freedom.' Ian Trackman 'The Will and 19 Codicils of the 1st Earl of Mansfield, with particular reference to Dido Elizabeth Belle', available at www.academia.edu/44557559.

[40] Besson (2009).

[41] 'Will and Descendants of Dr John Drummond', available at www.jamaicanfamilysearch.com/Members/wdrummon.htm.

remained enslaved. Their children were treated very differently from Mary's son, not only in provision (the use of enslaved person as inheritable property to provide an 'estate') but also in how they are named (no surname), and the subtle distinction between 'reputed to be mine' and 'by repute'. Drummond designed very different outcomes for the children, reflecting differences in the relations/hips he had with their mothers, as well as their, and therefore their children's, status as enslaved or free(d).[42]

Differences in treatment between children (and mothers) undoubtably arose in part as a result of the nature (affection, duration, dynamic etc) of the parental relationship. But there is also evidence of a generalised prejudice against children born of enslaved mothers rather than free(d) women, one that becomes more pronounced with generational distancing from enslavement. Baptismal records of ancestral heritage for people of colour evidence a very explicit correlation between the measure of African (black) heritage and the treatment of mothers and children by colonial (white) fathers. Reputed children brought 'back' to Britain are far more likely to have been phenotypically white, having mothers recorded as 'mustee' rather than 'mulatto'.[43] Clearly many fathers hoped that children brought to Britain would be presumed to be or capable of 'passing' as 'white' and thereby take the benefits of a 'status' which might not be achievable on-island (too much memory, gossip, prejudice and judgment).

For children who remained resident on-island a route to (some of) the benefits of white privilege became available in 1733 when, under local legislation, persons of colour could apply through a private act of the Jamaica Assembly to be treated as having 'white' status with associated legal privileges (most importantly holding land over a certain value, as well as civic rights). This built on the locally widely accepted social understanding (a legacy of Spanish colonisation) that a distance of four generations from one black ancestor was sufficient to move a person of colour into being (treated as-if) white.[44] Designing a legal framing for 'becoming white' allowed this to be achieved and protected 'by law' (and, in practice, petitions could be made before four generations had passed). The majority of applications were made on behalf of 'reputed children', underlining the extent to which colonial men (and society) went in finding strategies to afford privileging their (nearly white) children (if they chose to), without recourse to the route of marriage and legitimacy. In 1793, a privilege act was passed for some reputed children of Dr Drummond, 'by which Thomas Drummond (and three others) .... free mulattos, reputed children of John Drummond of Westmoreland, practitioner of physic and surgery, were given all rights and privileges, subject

[42] Drummond's executors purchased, freed and baptised William and Maria. Their father's name was recorded, and they were given the family name.

[43] See eg Benson (n 27).

[44] See n 29.

to certain legal limitations'.[45] Petitions referenced heritage, a family name and baptism, as well as wealth, educational and social skills (especially when acquired through residence in Britain) to argue that the applicants should 'be raised above the level of people of colour in general'.[46]

Petitions were particularly significant for those who remained on-island, but they also evidence becoming 'white by law' as part of a process of 'becoming British'. Francis Hall, who died 1848, left bequests for four reputed children: 'To my four reputed children by Elizabeth Evans, my former housekeeper, named Charles Hall (and three others) … £10,000 sterling each payable in England at the age of 23, the interest to pay for their maintenance and education'.[47] Jamaican baptismal records describe the children as 'white by law', and the bequests evidence a presumption that the children will be resident in England.

Linking testamentary bequests with baptismal records, privileges petitions and references to residence in Britain provides evidence which underscores the extent to which becoming phenotypically white was a significant factor in paternal decision making and differential treatment between children.[48]

V. Return(ed) to Metro-Isle

When reputed children were sent to Britain it was usually, initially, for education.[49] The question of whether they then returned to the islands was a matter of individual prospects, and paternal family circumstances. John Graham

[45] CO/139/48/873. This 'Thomas' is the older of the Drummond children given that name. Restrictions on privileges was standard practice: operating to open an 'as-if-white' category, rather than full assimilation.

[46] eg From a 1784 Privileges Act: 'Jane Charlotte Beckford hath been Baptised Educated and Instructed in the principles of the Christian Religion and in the Communion of the Church of England as by Law Established and hath caused her said children to be Baptised the elder of whom hath been sent to England and where it is intended that the younger of them shall also be sent at a proper age to be brought up in the like principles and Educated in such manner as to make them useful to the Community which with the assistance that will be afforded them will raise them above the level of people of Colour in general.' 'Ann Eliza French', Legacies of British Slavery database, available at wwwdepts-live.ucl.ac.uk/lbs/person/view/19966. This petition is evidence of the ability of some island mothers to use their children to enhance their own social position, see also n 56.

[47] 'Francis Hall', Legacies of British Slavery database, available at http://wwwdepts-live.ucl.ac.uk/lbs/person/view/13871.

[48] An English father writing from India was open about the factor influencing whether to send children 'home': 'The two eldest – [who] are almost as fair as European children – should be sent to Europe. I could have made no distinction between the children if the youngest was of a complexion that could possibly escape detection; but as I daily see the injurious consequences resulting from bringing up certain [darker-skinned] native children at home, it has become a question in my own mind how far I should confer a service in recommending the third child (to proceed to England)'. See Dalrymple (2012) 51.

[49] See eg legacies of 'Joseph Green', Legacies of British Slavery database, available at http://wwwdepts-live.ucl.ac.uk/lbs/person/view/2146645815.

died in 1801, having returned to Scotland where he married and had children. His will provided for two reputed children:[50]

> To my reputed son John Graham, a free quadroon, £600 sterling to enable him to rent a farm in Scotland and to stock the same or to be applied for his … benefit in any manner my executrix (his wife …) may think best for his advantage.
>
> To my reputed daughter, Mary Graham, a free quadroon, as much money as will purchase three new negroes if she remain in Jamaica, but if she go to Britain then £200 sterling to her.[51]

Other fathers, particularly those without legitimate issue, were focused on ensuring that their reputed children made the transition into becoming white and British, and thereby able to contribute to the building of family wealth and lineage. For these fathers, a design for assimilation into metropolitan respectability often required emphasising a need to keep reputed children away from their Jamaican maternal origins. Andrew Wright died in England in 1806, leaving a will which made provision for two 'reputed daughters', also resident in England. His will made his concerns clear:[52]

> [T]o pay … for the education and benefit of my reputed daughters Ann Wright and Rebecca Wright born of Ruth Sinclair, until aged 21 or married …
>
> I also direct that if Ann Wright or Rebecca Wright shall at any time after my decease without the consent in writing of the trustees … return to Jamaica unmarried then any share … shall be in trust for … such persons as would … be entitled to such shares of my estate if … (either of them) were … virtually dead without issue …
>
> Two copies of my will be delivered to (them) after my decease that they may be fully acquainted with the contents and particularly the clause prohibiting their return to Jamaica.

Jamaican baptismal records record Ruth Sinclair as a 'free mustee', and the children as 'reputed white'. Both daughters married in England, but into Atlantic-island families, and Ann returned with her husband to live in Jamaica. In the baptismal records of Ann's children, he is described as a 'free man of colour'.[53] Not the profile her father had intended for her and the (his) future family: in fact exactly what he had been trying to avoid. Clearly he had intended his daughters to (have) become metropolitan, absentee beneficiaries of the Jamaican estates whilst continuing their journey into a social order of white respectability.

[50] PROB 11/1361/159. 'Charles Graham of Jamaica', Legacies of British Slavery database, available at wwwdepts-live.ucl.ac.uk/lbs/person/view/2146647887.

[51] It was not unusual for a once-colonial married man to appoint a widow as executrix: a neat symmetry in a widow inheriting responsibility for colonial children may also have been a placatory gesture as it placed her in control of their destinies. However, the presence of legitimate children seems to have usually resulted in holding reputed children at a (discrete) distance from both the legitimate family and their home. See n 32.

[52] www.antonymaitland.com/maitwils.htm#__RefHeading___Toc34930244 at 5.8.1.

[53] 'Wrights of St Elizabeth Family', www.stclairresearch.com/alex/jamaica.html.

Two aspects of Wright's will resonate with that of Moses Benson.[54] The first is that both returned with significant fortunes, but did not acquire legitimate heirs. Their 'reputed children' became the only ones who could carry forward a legacy of family respectability and lineage. The second is that their baptismal records evidence a generational 'distance' from Africa (black) heritage, and in Britain they may well have been able to be presented as if of 'European' heritage, even if of Jamaican birth. It is also quite possible that they were presumed to be legitimate within the British social milieu they moved in. But as their father's wills had to ensure their inheritance by admitting to their 'reputed' status,[55] wills as public testimonies carried an inevitable tension of revelation.

Transitioning into the paternal legacy of becoming white required a distancing from maternal origins, and from any chance that children might be drawn back into a Jamaican social order which would recognise and treat them as people of colour. In Wright's case, Ann subverted his intentions, and his design of/for 'white' aspiration, whilst managing to still secure her fortune. Ann and her husband, Francis Maitland, became wealthy, respectable Jamaican citizens. Paradoxically, their wealth was built in part on Francis' inheritance through his maternal line. His mother (and grandmother) had been enslaved, but both were freed and gifted property (of land and enslaved persons) after becoming mothers to children of (white) colonial fathers. They became successful business women, and in 1782 the grandmother made a successful application for privileges, on behalf of herself, her daughter and Francis on the basis of holding 'real and personal Estate in this Island to a very Considerable Value … in such manner as to raise them above the level of people of colour in General but for the Unfortunate Circumstances of their Birth.'[56]

Francis and Ann were in fact half-cousins, and their marriage combined a family inheritance derived from the Jamaican maternal line as much as the British paternal legacy. From an island perspective, their marriage continued a transition towards assimilation into white respectability.[57] The British family member who documented the history of the Maitland/Wright families had not, before undertaking his task, any knowledge of family links back into maternal enslavement. He describes the family legacy as 'an example of how a mixed-race family evolved

[54] n 27. (Benson's will contained a provision forbidding his reputed daughter from marrying an Irishman on penalty of loss of her inheritance: she didn't.).

[55] To avoid opening a potential for legal challenges by others (relatives) who might then benefit. Acrimonious and expensive litigation between legitimate and illegitimate families could arise when legal loop-holes were 'found' in testamentary dispositions, see eg the drawn-out Morse litigation, Livesay (2018).

[56] See n 53.

[57] The majority of reputed children on-island joined the growing numbers of children 'of colour' networked between resident colonial fathers. Daniel Nairne died in 1816 leaving bequests for his six 'reputed children' (including a daughter 'now resident in Scotland'), and four 'reputed sons' of male friends, two of whom were his godchildren. 'Daniel Nairne senior', Legacies of British Slavery database, available at wwwdepts-live.ucl.ac.uk/lbs/person/view/2146633398.

in Jamaica (and then) took steps to lose their African background and integrate into 19th Century England'.[58]

VI. Legacies

Livesay suggests that two motives persuaded fathers to support Atlantic-island children, even to the extent of sending them 'home'.[59] The first, and one he is keen to emphasise, is paternal 'affection'. He argues that whilst evidence of close and committed family units, cohabiting as-if married, are the clearest example of bonds of familial affection, even in less committed relationships paternal affection was the significant explanation for extending support to island children. The importance of this, for Livesay, is that it recovers evidence of familial affection which had been forgotten, suppressed or denied in later decades when island children, let alone island families, were less, to the point of 'no longer', tolerated on either side of the Atlantic.[60] He finds a second motive in fathers expressing guilt and shame for having sired children outside of marriage (and with island women), who then sought to make some atonement for their sins through making provision for the children. Seeking redemption, particularly through the device of a final testament, could certainly be bracketed with a concern for salvation. In his Jamaican will of 1775, Nathaniel Milward, who had sent his 'swarthy illegitimates' to Britain, apologised (indirectly) to his British executor for imposing the responsibilities of guardianship upon him:

> I am at a loss what apology to make in their behalf (who are blameless) I must rely on his humanity … I hope his good nature will excuse the follies of youth, and … consider the provision here made as the most eligible atonement to render them useful to society.[61]

[58] 'Introduction' at www.antonymaitland.com/maitland.htm. The author excuses 'concubinage amongst his ancestors' by asserting that inter-racial marriage was not legal, and that men had no choice but to have 'reputed children' with partners (but see n 4). Loss of knowledge of island heritage is also evidenced in the successful assimilation into Scottish society by the Atlantic-island descendants of Sir John Lindsay, arguably facilitated by differential treatment between his reputed (more acceptable) and non-acknowledged children: one of whom was Dido Belle, the daughter of an enslaved African woman (n 39). See further 'Dido Elizabeth Belle – New information about her siblings' All Things Georgian, available at georgianera.wordpress.com/2018/06/26/dido-elizabeth-belle-new-information-about-her-siblings; and Bottomley (2022). My interpretation runs counter to the popularist account of Dido's benevolent reception into British society, promulgated in Amma Asante's 2002 film, *Belle*, and see also Byrne (2014), Gerzina (2022) and 'Dido Belle', available at: www.scone-palace.co.uk/dido-belle. Asante's film was inspired by the recovery of a double portrait of (half-cousins) Lady Elizabeth Murray and Dido Belle, attributed to David Martin, and painted c 1779. It was commissioned by Lord Mansfield and now hangs in Scone Palace. See further Suntherland (2021) and Bottomley (2022).

[59] n 6. His scholarship is focused on the decision to send island children 'home', rather than on processes of recognition.

[60] See n 29. Dalrymple (2012) traces a similar trajectory in India.

[61] Livesay (2018) 102.

A plea for forgiveness and an appeal to/for personal honour underpins the legal obligation, and the testator's (last) wishes ('to render them useful to society'), combined with a public admission of guilt, does suggest a redemptive imperative.

However, I want to press the evidence rather further. The consequences of both affection and guilt/atonement are, noticeably, focused on the children: there is little (if any) equivalent concern for mothers. This omission could be a result of a general discrimination against women, particularly mothers of illegitimate children and even more so when carrying the legacy of enslavement. But an extra clue to paternal imperatives (if not conscious 'motives') might be found in the advice given by an elder brother, in 1777, to a man about to take up residence in Jamaica: not become one of those men, 'who have mulattoes as their offspring, yet can neither patronise, educate, not enrich them; and must see their own blood and substance grovelling in low insensibility or shame'.[62]

'Low sensibility and shame' is linked with 'own blood and substance', suggesting very strongly that it is a concern with children who share 'blood and substance' with fathers, and will carry it forward, which is at issue here. Within the context of having mothers of colour, this creates a paternal (patriarchal) imperative to assert the priority of 'their' lineage against (overcoming) the maternal inheritance.

At a minimum, it would be a question of pride and honour (a counter to shame) that a man's progeny should be as well provided for as he could afford (and circumstances allowed). At a maximum, even illegitimate children could carry his family name (making visible his lineage of 'blood and substance') forward. In the absence of legitimate children, they could become resources for acquiring and extending family respectability and wealth: although on metro-isle this would require good marriages and subsequent 'lawful' descendants, as well as establishing sufficient distance from (maternal) origins.

In 1773, George Hall, having sent two 'mulatto children' to Britain, died in Jamaica. His will specified that his son's inheritance would only be secured by marrying a white woman (thereby, by implication, remaining in Britain), whereas if 'he live in a lewd way with any woman' he would only inherit a small number of enslaved persons (and, by implication, return to Jamaica). His sister had a similar restriction placed on her.[63] The lodestones of moving descendants into metropolitan respectability were simple: marriage and becoming 'white(r)'.[64] Livesay recognises that 'moving to Britain increased the prospect of a biological whitening of the family line',[65] but I think he underestimates the paternal imperative to achieve this.

Establishing a phenotypically white hierarchy on-island and the erasure of mixed-African heritage in Britain, are consequences of the practices of paternal recognition. It is now well recognised that modern (Western) constructions of 'family' (drawn out from kinship) and 'race' (consolidated around an essentialist

[62] Livesay (2018) 188.
[63] ibid 103.
[64] See also n 59.
[65] Livesay (2018) 104.

biologism) were mutually constitutive, mediated through and around 'property' (not merely as assets, but also as the ability to access and consolidate wealth), but what needs to be more recognised are the differences in specific familial (race, and property) patterns between island and metropole. And whilst Atlantic-island history is clearly relatable to established historical accounts based on American-continental material and scholarship,[66] it is a specific history carrying a different legacy of inter-relations between race/family/property. Recognising these distinctions offers comparative material and (re)opens questions concerning the emergence of 'race', 'family' and 'property'. How might we engage (scholastically, politically) with the island legacy?

The challenge for metropolitan scholars is to give space for the recognition and recovery of the 'forgotten, just left on the margins'.[67] In Britain, this requires listening for/to the 'haunting'[68] of the absence/presence which we have been so distanced from, geographically and historically. Rereading canonical authors such as Austen, to listen for/to the marginalised and repressed, and reimaging iconic paintings such as Wilkie's, to reframe history and legacy, provides a means through which to re-engage with 'our' heritage. We are 'entangled islands', and the extent of, and responsibility for, the legacies of colonisation and enslavement are, necessarily, a focus for most contemporary post/colonial work. But the question of a post/colonial potential is also significant, and it may be that one way to think (image, diagram) this potential is to embrace a common heritage as hybrid 'bastard children of empire' and pursue an aspirational horizon of becoming-creole: 'It is the composite reality of the bastard that obsesses Glissant, not the longing for a remote paternity.'[69]

[66] eg Clymer (2013).
[67] Levy (1999).
[68] See Gordon (2008).
[69] See Glissant (1992) introduction by J Michael Dash xii, see further Bongie (1998). Hall (2015) emphasises that we cannot ignore the legacies of power and privilege carried in the existent island-creole, and hence the need to distinguish the aspirational horizon of 'becoming-creole'.

References

Besson, G, *The Cult of the Will* (Port of Spain, Paria Publishing, 2009).
Bongie, C, *Islands and Exiles: The Creole Identities of Post/Colonial Literature* (Bloomington, Stanford University Press, 1998).
Bottomley, A, 'Legacies' in P Goodrich et al (eds), *Research Handbook on Law and Literature* (Cheltenham, Elgar, 2009).
Brown, V, *The Reaper's Garden: Death and Power in the World of Atlantic Slavery* (Boston, Harvard University Press, 2010).
Byrne, P, *Belle: The True Story of Dido Belle* (London, William Collins, 2014).
Clymer, J, *Family Money: Property, Race, and Literature in the Nineteenth Century* (Oxford, Oxford University Press, 2013).
Collins, J, *Tracing British West Indian Slavery Laws: A Comparative Analysis of Legal Transplantations* (London, Routledge, 2022).
Cunningham, A, *The Life of Sir David Wilkie* (London, J.Murray, 1843) vol 2.
Dalrymple, W, *White Moguls* (London, Harper Press, 2012).
Dominique, LJ (ed), *The Woman of Colour: A Tale* (Peterborough, Broadview Press, 2008).
Gerzina, G, *Black England* (London, John Murray, 2022).
Glissant, E, *Caribbean Discourse* (trans J Michael Dash) (Charlottesville, University Press of Virginia, 1992).
Gordon, A (2008) *Ghostly Matters: Haunting and the Sociological Imagination* (Minneapolis, University of Minnesota Press, 2008).
Graveson, RH and Crane, FR (eds), *A Century of Family Law*, (London, Sweet and Maxwell, 1957).
Hall, C, *Civilising Subjects: Colony and Metropole in the English Imagination, 1830–1867* (Chicago, University of Chicago Press, 2002).
Hall, S, 'Creolite and Processes of Creolisation' in EG Rodriguez and SA Tate (eds), *Creolising Europe: Legacies and Transformations* (Liverpool, Liverpool University Press, 2015).
Hall, S (with B Schwarz), *Familiar Stranger: A Life Between Two Islands* (London, Allen Lane, 2017).
Hirsch, P, *Barbara Leigh Smith Bodichon* (London, Chatto and Windus, 1998).
Levy, A, *Fruit of the Lemon* (London, Tinder Press, 1999).
Livesay, D, *Children of Uncertain Fortune: Mixed-Race Jamaicans in Britain and Atlantic Families* (Williamsburg, University of North Carolina Press, 2018).
Reed, J, 'Moving Fortunes: Caribbean Women's Marriage, Mobility, and Money in the Novel of Sentiment' (2019) 3 *Eighteenth Century Fiction* 509.
Suntherland, K, 'Giving Voice to a Portrait: The Intersection of Gender, Race, and Law in Belle' (2021) 10 *European Journal of Life Writing* 106.

4

'Charitable Inclinations': Women's Bequests to Ireland's Magdalene Laundries[1]

MÁIRÉAD ENRIGHT

I. Introduction

Mary Ryan (1873–1961) was the first woman university professor in Ireland.[2] University College Cork,[3] where she taught Romance Languages, celebrates her as feminist trailblazer.[4] She was a director of the family firm; a soap and candle manufacturer. Her brother Finbar was Provincial of the Dominican Order in Ireland, and later Archbishop of Port of Spain, Trinidad. In her youth, the Catholic church disapproved of women attending university, and so she studied for her BA at St Angela's School, run by the Ursuline nuns. An obituary noted her 'great personal charm and gentle enthusiasm' for scholarship. '[H]er conversation was always so lively that she became almost breathless when she warmed to any subject that excited her.'[5] Happy in academia, she believed that 'there was no exhilaration like that of good work'.[6] Professor Ryan was a member of the Third Order of St Dominic.[7] The Third Order were lay people, affiliated to the Dominicans, who did not join a convent or monastery but committed themselves to religious study. She died in 1961, aged 88. Like many of Cork city's wealthy Catholic women,[8]

[1] Part of the research for this piece was funded by a Leverhulme Research Fellowship 2020–21.

[2] 'Mary Ryan' *Cork Examiner* (13 October 1961) 15.

[3] She was hired by Professor (later Monsignor) Alfred O'Rahilly, a conservative and one-time member of the far-right Blueshirts, who sought to run the nominally plural University according to a strict Catholic ethos.

[4] 'Professor Mary Ryan' University College Cork, available at www.ucc.ie/en/heritage/historicpeople/ucc-staff/prof-mary-ryan.

[5] D Gwynn, 'Now and Then' *Cork Examiner* (20 June 1961) 6.

[6] 'Laments for Loss of Status' *Cork Examiner* (16 December 1935) 13. She was speaking as guest of honour at a dinner where other feminist speakers made rather more critical remarks.

[7] Bryan (2009).

[8] See especially 'Isabella Honan' *Cork Examiner* (12 September 1913) 4.

Prof Ryan remembered several charities in the will she wrote in 1957. The Third Order encouraged its members to give to charitable causes.[9] She gave £100 each to convent institutions on the north side of the city, run by the Religious Sisters of Charity at Peacock Lane and the Good Shepherds, just a mile from the University, at Sunday's Well.[10]

Today, these convents are remembered as two of Ireland's Catholic Magdalene laundries.[11] These were residential institutions, committed, as Ingrid Holme observes, to 'spiritual eugenics';[12] women and girls who had somehow transgressed Irish Catholic norms around female sexuality were removed from the world on the pretext that they would be reformed and made fit once more to participate in society, perhaps as wives and mothers. In practice, many remained in Magdalene institutions for life. 'Magdalene', from 'Mary Magdalene', refers to the regime of penitence imposed within the institutions. 'Laundry' describes their labour regime; many women worked unpaid in industrial laundries to generate income for the institutions, while enduring the physical discipline of 'respectable' hard work.[13] Magdalene laundries were carceral institutions. Most women were sent to the laundries by family members, priests or social workers rather than by the courts or state authorities; this demonstrates that the laundries were part of a wider system of social control.[14] For most of the twentieth century, Irish Magdalene laundries were widely treated, not as sites of abuse, but as respectable charities; appropriate recipients of wealthy women's bounty. In recent years, survivors have spoken publicly about their experiences, demanding a state response.[15] The state eventually commissioned a limited investigation into the history of the Magdalene laundries[16] and established a redress scheme for surviving women.[17] Magdalene laundries are now associated in the public mind with human rights abuses including forced unpaid labour,[18] physical and emotional neglect, complete denial of privacy,[19] cruel punishment,[20] forced separation of family members and denial of identity in life and in death. As a teenager in the 1960s, Elizabeth Coppin was detained in both laundries which benefitted from Prof Ryan's will.[21] She was

[9] Stephens (1934) xxv.

[10] She also left money to the 'mother and baby home' at Bessborough, outside the city.

[11] See generally O'Donnell (2022); McGettrick et al (2021); Hamill (2021).

[12] Holme (2018). Holme contrasts spiritual eugenics with medical eugenics. The tools of eugenics used elsewhere – contraception and sterilisation – were not readily available in Ireland for much of the 20th century.

[13] Gott (2021).

[14] Fischer (2016).

[15] O'Mahoney (2018).

[16] McAleese (2013).

[17] The Department of Justice and Equality, 'The Magdalen Restorative Justice Ex-Gratia Scheme', available at justice.ie/en/JELR/Pages/WP15000111.

[18] Gallen and Gleeson (2018).

[19] O'Mahoney, Grieve and Torn (2019).

[20] Benítez-Castro and Hidalgo-Tenorio (2018).

[21] See *Elizabeth Coppin v Ireland* CAT/C/68/D/879/2018.

put to work six days a week without pay. In Peacock Lane, she slept in a locked cell with no running water and was held in solitary confinement for an alleged minor theft. In Sunday's Well, her hair was shorn, she was made to answer to a male name and given a degrading uniform to wear. Hundreds of women have testified to similar treatment.[22]

In this chapter, I suggest that we can think of bequests like the ones Prof Mary Ryan made to Cork's Magdalene laundries as vectors of 'structural complicity' with the abuses perpetrated there, against women (once girls) like Elizabeth Coppin. I begin by explaining some of the background to charitable giving to the laundries; the kinds of women who gave and the religious context of their bequests. Next, I introduce the concept of 'structural complicity', using it to show how bequests reinforced the social and gendered orders of power that legitimated the Magdalene laundries in the first place. The point is not to say that all or any of the women who gave money to the Magdalene laundries were themselves directly responsible for abuses that took place in the institutions they funded,[23] but to better understand the range of potential relationships between abuse, will-making and charity. Finally, I suggest how attention to structural complicity might help to clarify the stakes and possibilities of new legal histories of the Magdalene laundries.

II. Leaving Money to the Magdalene Laundries

Prof Mary Ryan was not the only Irish Catholic woman who 'devised, gave and bequeathed' some of her estate to a Magdalene laundry. I identified others by searching newspaper notices of charitable bequests published in Irish national and regional newspapers[24] between the foundation of the Irish Free State in December 1922 and the commencement of the Charities Act July 1973.[25] I also reviewed archived copies of wills where available, but newspapers often provided equivalent detail of bequests. Ordinarily, details of bequests were published in a 'Legal Notices' or equivalent section of the newspaper. Sometimes they were printed as small news items with their own headlines; for instance,

[22] Williams (2022).

[23] Complicity is not guilt. Guilt generally describes individuals who participated, voluntarily and directly, in discrete episodes of violence. I cannot draw direct links between individual bequests and specific human rights abuses, in part because religious congregations' financial archives are not publicly accessible and so it is not possible to trace, except in very general terms, how any one bequest was spent.

[24] Based on a search of the online *Irish Times* archive and Irish Newspaper Archives database (1920–70) using search terms (Magdalen*, refuge, or 'Good Shepherd' or geographical descriptors) combined with 'bequest', names of a relevant congregation and gendered terms (eg widow or spinster, Miss or Mrs, lady or woman).

[25] The requirement to publish notices of charitable devises and bequests was amended by s 16 of the Charities Act 1973, which exempted most wills from this requirement. The high point of published notices of bequests to Magdalene laundries in the 20th century seems to have been 1935–45.

'Many Charitable Bequests of Dublin Lady',[26] but a 'Notice of Charitable Bequests in the Goods of' a named individual was more usual.

Bequests were not the laundries' main external source of income. The state funded some Magdalene institutions, including through lucrative laundry contracts.[27] For the greater part of the twentieth century, lay women played a limited role in the state's relationship with the laundries, because they were less likely to occupy public office. However, they made important contributions to the laundries' wider economies. Women of all classes made small donations to convent laundries during their lifetimes or paid to have their personal laundry done in the convents. Some women held in the Limerick laundry manufactured fine lace, for sale to wealthy families, and well-off families hired domestic servants who had spent time in a convent laundry or in an associated institution. Written records of these kinds of private contributions to Magdalene laundries in the twentieth century are relatively scarce. Wills, by contrast, are readily accessible as public records.[28]

Newspaper notices show that laundries inherited money, stocks and shares, proceeds of sale of property, or a portion of the residue of the estate after other legacies and debts had been paid. The testatrix was typically from the same prosperous social class as the senior members of the religious congregations who ran the laundries. Several were wealthy enough to employ servants, at least in old age. In the wills I have found, a servant was sometimes a witness. Some were described as a 'gentlewoman' or 'of independent means' on their death certificates. Others had inherited from wealthy men;[29] they were the daughters, sisters or widows of merchants[30] and strong farmers.[31] More had been landladies[32] or shopkeepers;[33] their wills distributed money derived, in some measure, by their own commercial skill. A rare few, like Mary Ryan, were retired professionals.[34] Some were public figures in their own right. Laura Anne Rorke, for example, had been a governor of the Royal Hospital, Donnybrook and had sought election as a Poor Law guardian in 1902.[35] The very wealthiest women who gave to laundries left wider marks on

[26] *Cork Examiner* (6 April 1936) 8.

[27] See further Enright (2021).

[28] Jaconelli (2012).

[29] Until the Succession Act 1965, married women did not have a statutory right to a share in their husbands' estates.

[30] 'Mary McDonnell' *Limerick Leader* (3 May 1930).

[31] 'Margaret Nash' *Limerick Leader* (10 August 1940) 6; 'Kitty Holme's, *Evening Echo* (22 February 1966) 3; 'Aloysia M O'Donnell', *The Nationalist* (11 January 1930) 6.

[32] 'Maria Egan' *Irish Independent* (15 June 1925) 5.

[33] Mary O'Sullivan had kept a draper's shop with her brother; *Southern Star* (11 December 1937) 9. Frances O'Grady's death certificate describes her as a tobacconist; her shop was on Patrick Street in Cork City.

[34] Catherine Mary Dwyer was a retired primary school teacher, *Irish Independent* (24 March 1938) 14. Eileen Sutton's death certificate shows that she was a retired hospital matron; *Irish Examiner* (20 April 1968) 6. She had worked at St Vincent's Hospital, Dublin. Her father's family were coal merchants.

[35] 'Laura Rorke' *Irish Independent* (10 December 1929) 13.

their cities and towns. Fannie Andrews died in Dublin in 1931 with an estate of £100,000; equivalent to millions today. Alongside bequests to a Magdalene laundry, her will made several provisions in memory of her younger sister, Jeannie de Verdon Corcoran[36] including a hospital bed[37] a lifeboat at Howth,[38] and a seventeenth-century cabinet donated to the National Gallery.[39]

Women's wills were, in large part, religious documents. Women funded parish projects, church-building and renovation projects and scholarships for student priests. Where a will funded physical memorials to the testatrix or to her deceased family these almost always did double duty in adorning a church; stained glass, religious statues, or stations of the Cross. They rarely left money to secular organisations. One exception was Mary Imelda Forde, a breeder of show-dogs,[40] who gave money to the RSPCA.[41] In writing their wills, many women's minds seemed set firmly on Purgatory, where their souls or those of their loved ones would await the purification of any sins for which they had not already atoned in life. Bridget Murray provided for the 'Holy Souls in Purgatory'[42] while Martha Blake left money for Masses for 'the poor souls in Purgatory who have no-one to pray for them'.[43] The Catholic church taught that time spent in Purgatory and admission to Heaven could be shortened through the prayers of the living on behalf of the dead. Women used their wills to ensure that Masses would be said after their deaths for the repose of their own souls, and for the souls of those they had prayed for in life. Guaranteeing that others would be prayed for was often a widow or spinster's last act of familial care; ensuring that the family could benefit from her spiritual attentions after she was gone. Mary Murphy provided for 150 Masses.[44] Rathgar's Nanny Andrews wanted Masses to be said in 22 different churches.[45] Kate Nevins, whose husband had made his money in New York, paid for an anniversary High Mass each year in Castlebar.[46] Some women nominated specific priests to say Masses for them.[47] They paid for religious devices to ensure others'

[36] The two women had lived together following the death of Jeannie's husband, and Fannie inherited from Jeannie on her death.

[37] 'Fannie Andrews' *Irish Times* (31 October 1931) 3.

[38] This part of the bequest was the subject of litigation involving the Archbishop of Dublin; 'Woman who left £90,000' *Irish Times* (20 December 1932) 2.

[39] The cabinet was reputed to have been a gift from Oliver Cromwell to his daughter on her wedding day; 'A Cromwell Relic' *Cork Examiner* (16 May 1931) 12; Andrews also contributed to the cost of a Harry Clarke stained glass window at St Joseph's Church in Terenure in memory of her sister and brother-in-law. An inscription invites those visiting the window to pray for their souls. She also paid for the high altar at the Church of the Holy Name in Ranelagh to be dedicated to them.

[40] 'Irish Kennel Club Sued' *Belfast Newsletter* (5 December 1928) 15.

[41] 'Mary Imelda Forde' *Irish Press* (31 July 1942) 3.

[42] 'Bridget Murray' *Dundalk Democrat* (10 August 1929) 1.

[43] 'Martha Blake' *Irish Press* (17 May 1938) 14.

[44] 'Mary Murphy' *Irish Independent* (2 February 1938) 6.

[45] 'Nannie Andrews' *Irish Independent* (5 May 1927) 6.

[46] 'Catherine Mary, 'Kate' Nevins' *Connaught Telegraph* (22 November 1930) 1.

[47] 'Bridget Fahey' *Cork Examiner* (9 June 1934) 4.

prayers; entries on a church's altar list of the dead, to be remembered at Mass every November;[48] a gift towards a convent's 'perpetual lamp' which would be constantly burning in memory of those sharing in the community's prayers and sacrifices;[49] a cycle of 30 'Gregorian Masses' said over 30 days to release the deceased's soul from Purgatory.[50]

Will-writing enabled women to make very deliberate choices about the afterlife of their wealth.[51] A bequest carries an element of generativity; 'a desire to invest one's substance in forms that outlive the self'.[52] Bequests can ensure the continuity of important institutions and communicate moral lessons to those remaining behind.[53] Perhaps because of their connection to faith and sin, it is tempting to doubt women's agency in will-making. In 1902, the barrister Michael McCarthy had written bitterly of charitable bequests:

> [Testators] back every horse in the field, male and female, Passionist and Poor Clare in the hope that one of them is bound to win. Such seems, without irreverence, to be the frame of mind in which these terrified testators and testatrices approach death.[54]

Precise instructions as to division of a woman's assets between institutions, however, may indicate that the decision to benefit a Magdalene laundry was made with some care and deliberation. Martha Blake split the residue of her estate into eighths, with one eighth to the laundry at Gloucester Street.[55] Laura Rorke divided her estate of £4,000 into sixteenths.[56] Annie Blake, daughter and granddaughter of mayors of Galway, and a descendant of one of the city's 14 'tribes', shared cash, clothing and jewellery between 32 separate beneficiaries, almost all of them Catholic charities.[57] Bridget O'Neill's estate in 1928 was comparatively small, with the largest individual bequest at £5, but she managed to divide it between 15 different institutions, including a Magdalene laundry.[58]

[48] 'Anna Mary Fitzsimons' *Drogheda Independent* (11 January 1941) 3.

[49] 'Mary Josephine Giblin' *Irish Independent* (7 July 1939) 1.

[50] 'Mary Fitzgibbon' *Irish Independent* (30 July 1937) 15.

[51] An exception may be made for women who only enjoyed a life interest in property inherited from someone else, and whose deaths triggered a bequest provided for in that earlier will. See for example, Letter (7 January 1931) from WR Meredith Solicitors to the Superioress of High Park Convent, concerning the will of John Joseph Burke, who had died in 1906. On his wife's death, part of his property passed to the convent. The letter is in the Mary Raftery Archive, which is privately held by Sheila Ahern. My thanks to Claire McGettrick for supplying a copy.

[52] Kotre (1996) 10. On testamentary intention in socio-legal studies see Monk (2013).

[53] Routley and Sargeant (2014) 881–82.

[54] McCarthy (1902) 143.

[55] 'Martha Blake' *Irish Press* (17 May 1938) 14. Gloucester Street was renamed Sean McDermott Street in 1933. I have referred to it as 'Gloucester Street' throughout this chapter for consistency.

[56] 'Laura Rorke' *Irish Independent* (10 December 1929) 13.

[57] 'Annie Mary Josephine Blake' *Irish Independent* (27 March 1945) 4. Her father, Edmond Blake, received Galway's ancient mace and sword in lieu of salary and Miss Blake sold them after his death; 'Galway's insignia' *Irish Press* (31 May 1935) 1. The items were subsequently purchased by William Randolph Hearst, whose wife returned them to Ireland in 1960.

[58] 'Bridget O'Neill' *Irish Independent* (23 June 1928) 12.

Mary Ellen Lavelle from Newport in County Mayo[59] left a detailed will with specific instructions for the distribution of her best possessions; her money, 'wearing apparel', silver plate and cutlery and her shares in some of the most successful companies of her time; Guinness brewers, Lever Brothers and Imperial Tobacco. Her shares in the Hibernian Bank (later part of the Bank of Ireland) she left to the Gloucester Street laundry.

III. Structural Complicity: The Wrongs of Leaving Money to a Laundry

There is nothing in these women's wills, or in newspaper reports of their bequests to suggest that the act of leaving money to a Magdalene laundry was considered tainted by wrongdoing. The law showed little concern for these wills. In cases involving bequests to Magdalene laundries, the courts focused on giving effect to the testator's intentions,[60] rather than on evaluating the uses to which their money would be put.[61] Magdalene laundries enjoyed significant social support, and the women who funded them were celebrated for their generosity. For example, Kate Greene[62] left legacies to 26 separate Catholic causes, including the Gloucester Street laundry. Her obituary in the *Drogheda Independent* remarked on the large crowd attending her funeral and on her friendships with influential churchmen.

> Noted for her charitable inclinations and her readiness to support every laudable local movement, it was through her generosity that a great many parochial works were made possible of achievement, and she never had to be asked twice to subscribe to any deserving object.[63]

Now that the Magdalene laundries are associated with human rights abuses and the question of inheritance, in that respect, carries a different moral weight. In constructing a critical legal history of laundry bequests, it is imperative that we

[59] *Irish Independent* (24 February 1948) 1. Miss Lavelle had inherited some wealth from Martin Carey, her aunt's widower for whom she had cared in old age. One of Carey's nieces challenged his will but was unsuccessful. 'Newport's "Model Merchant's" will challenged in High Court – 90 year saga' *Mayo News* (24 November 1999) 22; 'Mayo Will Suit' *Irish Independent* (26 June 1910) 7.

[60] For a broader discussion of the law on charities and taxation see Enright (2022). It is likely, of course, that some judges were sympathetic to the laundries. On succession and judicial sympathies see Monk (2011).

[61] For instance, in a 1928 case Mr Justice Meredith had to decide what should be done with money left to the 'Good Shepherd' convents in Galway and Dublin. The Good Shepherds had no convent in either city, but the order claimed both amounts. The judge determined that the testator's aim was to fund 'good works' in particular areas. The money went to the Sisters of Mercy laundry in Galway, and the Our Lady of Charity of Refuge laundry at Gloucester Street in Dublin; 'Thomas Hayes' *Irish Times* (15 February 1928) 3. See similarly, 'Cavan Solicitor's Will' *Irish Times* (26 March 1942) 3.

[62] 'Kate Greene' *Drogheda Independent* (18 June 1938) 1.

[63] *Drogheda Independent* (19 March 1938) 7.

pay attention to the relationships between inheritance and institutional abuses and scrutinise their role in the networks of benefit and legitimation that enabled the laundries to operate. Borrowing from Aragon and Jaggar,[64] I argue that it may be helpful to think of women who left money to Magdalene laundries – the Kate Greenes, the Mary Ellen Lavelles and the Prof Mary Ryans – as 'structurally complicit' with abuses perpetrated there. 'Structural complicity' describes how specific individual actions may reinforce wider, unjust societal structures. As a concept, it allows us to account for the specific quality of bequests as contributions to those structures, without allowing them to be absorbed into a larger homogenous whole. It may be that all lay Irish Catholics were, in some way, 'institutionally' complicit in the abuses perpetrated in Magdalene laundries during their lifetimes. In making bequests, some women became more than mere bystanders to the laundries' activities, actively reproducing the violent social conditions against which they acted. Wealthy and accomplished women were not immune from punishment when they transgressed Catholic social norms. Their position was a complex one.[65] However, their position allowed them to invest in Magdalene institutions and perform belonging on the right side of moral and economic boundaries. Their bequests reflected, and reinforced, hierarchies that were rooted in deeply gendered conceptions of sin and poverty, morality and desert; hierarchies that normalised and legitimised the Magdalene institutions and their activities.

We have already seen how women's wills performed piety and religious belonging. Bequests to Magdalene laundries depended on additional religious commitments which positioned women held in the laundries as sinners, and as the subordinates of good affluent Catholics. As we have discussed, a bequest to a Magdalene laundry fit neatly within what Olivia Frehill terms the 'divine economy', by securing valuable prayers for the testatrix after her death. As Frehill writes, faithful Catholics understood that giving to poor and institutionalised women in exchange for prayer was an investment in their own salvation. Penitents' prayers were especially valuable since they were considered closer to God.[66] A bequest to a Magdalene laundry produced symbolic capital for the benefactor; capital rooted in concepts of other women's sinfulness and redemption.[67]

'Structural complicity' does not depend on an individual's intentions or state of knowledge. It describes women who did not themselves directly participate in any wrongful activity but who indirectly facilitated it, whether purposely or recklessly. Wills offer some clues as to women's knowledge and motivations but cannot give us the whole messy picture of an individual's intentions.[68] At the same

[64] Aragon and Jaggar (2018).

[65] For historical studies of feminist women's positions in oppressive societies see eg Ware (2015); Midgley (2007).

[66] Frehill (2020) 78.

[67] McGonegal (2007) 294–97, 304–05.

[68] There is a contrast here with, for example, the letters documented in Earner-Byrne (2017).

time, it is important to acknowledge that some women who left money to the laundries cannot have been entirely ignorant of life within them; they must have known or ought to have known something of the activities they were choosing to fund. Mary Howe[69] of Buxton Hill in Cork left money to the Sunday's Well laundry, whose grounds were separated from her own garden by a high stone wall. Isabella Mary Corcoran's 'picturesquely situated' house, Rita Ville in Sunday's Well was sold at auction to benefit the nearby laundry.[70] Others who gave to Magdalene laundries lived for a time in associated homes, such as St Michael's guesthouse in Drumcondra, Dublin City, which was linked to the nearby High Park laundry. Wealthy elderly women could live there as paying guests.[71] Several St Michael's women remembered the laundry in their wills.[72] It is likely that they had some understanding of the High Park regime. Maria Hamill[73] and Helen Sheil[74] both died in St Michael's, and both left money to High Park. The same 'inmate', a Margaret B,[75] is marked on their death certificates as witnessing each woman's death, a decade apart. Even without saying precisely what these women knew of one another, their proximity, in life and in death is quite clear.

Leaving money to a laundry was as much a political as a personal decision. Bequests to the laundries reinforced quasi-secular orders of political and economic power which placed the fate of poorer women and girls in the hands of private religious institutions at a time when there were few other sources of support. Women who gave money to the laundries also gave to 'the poor', more generally though usually through Catholic charitable intermediaries such as the Society of St Vincent de Paul. They gave to voluntary hospitals, money to orphanages and industrial schools, hostels and institutions for disabled people; all typically run by Catholic religious sisters. Charitable giving was always politically charged. In the early decades of the state, papal encyclicals and the Irish Catholic hierarchy encouraged subsidiarity in welfare and social policy.[76] This religious teaching suited affluent Catholics. As Maria Brenton writes, charities enabled the 'control and patronage of the poor by the wealthy classes, for whom any more radical changes in the distribution of wealth would have been unthinkable'.[77] At the same time, those who

[69] *Cork Examiner* (1 December 1938) 1.

[70] *Irish Examiner* (1 April 1948) 4; *Irish Press* (24 April 1948) 5. She appears to have inherited the house from a priest.

[71] Margaret Geoghegan was the sister of a priest; *Freeman's Journal* (17 December 1923) 4. Rosanna Murphy had been a teacher and was the mother of two priests; 'Mother of Two Priests, Cousin of Cardinal' *Northern Standard* (2 February 1945) 1.

[72] See eg see 'Margaret Mary Walshe' *Irish Independent* (23 March 1964) 18; 'Margaret O'Neill' *Irish Independent* (2 August 1967) 18; 'Ellen Ross' *Irish Independent* (12 October 1954) 10; 'Maria Hamill' *Irish Independent* (9 May 1930) 1; 'Frances Curran' *Irish Independent* (7 March 1953) 8; 'Mary Jane Brady' *Irish Independent* (10 November 1930) 10.

[73] Maria Hamill's cousin was a priest, and left her his home on his death. She is buried in his vault in the O'Connell Tower Circle in Glasnevin Cemetery.

[74] 'Helen Sheil' *Irish Independent* (30 November 1940) 5.

[75] Her full name is given on the certificate.

[76] See more broadly Powell (2017).

[77] Brenton (1985) 16.

might give enough to direct the flow of charity might 'multiply their influence, guide the destiny of others, and co-opt redistribution'.[78] This prospect was especially attractive to women, whose economic and political agency was curtailed in ways that their male relatives' was not. As Sarah Roddy[79] shows, participation in charitable or philanthropic activity was an important route to the public sphere for wealthier women at a time when many jobs and political positions were closed to them. Some wills indicate that testatrices framed their commitment to Magdalene institutions in the language of charity, rather than in terms of recognising a need to discipline or reform other women who had transgressed the social order. I have only found one bequest which referred to a Magdalen institution overtly as a 'laundry'.[80] The wills are not more specific because the nun receiving the bequest on behalf of her community or order[81] usually enjoyed significant discretion as to how the money should be spent.[82] Although wills do not precisely stipulate how the testatrix's money should be used, they clearly indicate that the women making them thought of laundries as charities.[83] Wills referred to 'the charitable purpose of the [Magdalene] asylum',[84] 'for their respective charities',[85] for 'the use and benefits of the *inmates*'[86] or for 'the assistance and maintenance'[87] of the institution. Some wills directly associated the institutions with poverty; and sought to make provision 'for the poor and neglected under [the superioress'] care'[88] or 'the upkeep of the poor girls in the Home'.[89] Mary Lonergan left money to the Sisters of Charity in Cork's Peacock Lane 'to be applied in training poor pupils in any work which might enable them to earn a livelihood'.[90]

Some wills were more direct in associating the laundries with their role in controlling gendered disobedience. Here the hierarchy between the testatrix and

[78] Hanson (2015) 516.

[79] Roddy (n 23) 49.

[80] *Irish Times* (2 July 1960) 16. This was the will of Edith Couturier de Versan, daughter of a former Registrar of the Court of Appeal, and descendant of Lord Chief Justice Whiteside.

[81] Catholic lay women's direct participation in the work of institutions was limited because this work was done by Catholic nuns; Roddy (2022) 50.

[82] Fannie Andrews' will included one of the more ambitious recorded legacies; providing £1,000 for the Sisters of Our Lady of Charity of Refuge at High Park to establish a 'penitents' retreat' on the south side of Dublin city, to accompany the two they already ran to the north of the Liffey. 'In default of [this] being possible' the money was to remain at High Park. In the end, no new foundation was built, suggesting that the decision on how the money should be used remained with senior members of the congregation and their supervising Bishop; 'Fannie Andrews' *Irish Times* (31 October 1931) 3.

[83] In some cases, the use of the word 'charitable' may have as much to do with a solicitor's efforts to give effect to a client's practical intentions as with an individual's own characterisation of a convent's work as 'charitable'.

[84] 'Kathleen Barker' *Irish Times* (27 August 1949) 7; 'Kathleen Free' *Irish Independent* (11 November 1963) 15.

[85] 'Anna Maria O'Leary' *Cork Examiner* (15 November 1947) 6; See similarly 'Fanny O'Connor' *Cork Examiner* (7 April 1925) 1; 'Alice Elliott' *Irish Independent* (13 June 1927) 5.

[86] 'Margaret Donnelly' *Irish Press* (15 November 1957) 6.

[87] 'Catherine Mary 'Kate' Nevins' *Connaught Telegraph* (22 November 1930) 1.

[88] 'Mary Elizabeth O'Sullivan' *Irish Press* (19 March 1938) 6.

[89] *Irish Independent* (14 February 1949) 3.

[90] *Cork Examiner* (24 June 1938) 1.

the imagined recipients of her generosity is more plainly expressed. These wills referred to 'the *rescue* of poor girls',[91] 'the benefit of the *Penitents*',[92] the 'support and maintenance of the poor *penitents* sheltered in the Magdalen Asylum'[93] and 'the benefit of the *Magdalens* under [the convent's] care'.[94] This language indicates that the decision to leave money to a Magdalene laundry could reflect a commitment to a specific kind of religious charitable work; the 'rescue' of women who had transgressed prevailing social norms around reproduction and sexuality.[95] This commitment might also be reflected in legacies to more than one Magdalene laundry; an especially common practice among Dubliners. For example, Rose Smyth's money went to laundries at Gloucester Street, High Park and Donnybrook, and to the Sisters of Mercy laundry at Dun Laoghaire.[96] Annie J O'Donoghue gave to both High Park and its associated Sacred Heart Home for children.[97] Women who left money to a Magdalene laundry commonly gave to other charities associated with 'rescue'. St Joseph's Night Refuge for homeless working women and their children, run by the Sisters of Mercy near Cook Street in Dublin, often received legacies from women who also gave to laundries. The laundries' supporters also funded organisations seeking to 'reclaim' the children of unmarried Catholic mothers, such as the Catholic Protection and Rescue Society and Fr Craven's Crusade of Rescue. The moral fate of Irish emigrants was a particular concern for some women. As well as Irish laundries, they might support Catholic institutions in English cities with large Irish populations like Birmingham and Liverpool. Their wills often reflect networks between Irish institutions and equivalents abroad. Annie Gallagher, once landlady of Dublin's Buswell's Hotel,[98] left bequests to both Magdalene laundries run by the sisters of Our Lady of Charity of Refuge in Dublin, and to their equivalent convent at Waterlooville near Portsmouth, which had many Irish nuns.

How were women encouraged to view 'rescue' within the laundries as a positive charitable object? Three possibilities are reflected in their bequests: family, fundraising and faith groups. A bequest to a Magdalene laundry sometimes reflected a wider family's interest in 'rescue' work. Some women went further than simply identifying a Magdalene institution to benefit from their wealth and

[91] *Freeman's Journal* (1924) 9.
[92] 'Ellen Reeves' *Irish Independent* (2 June 1949) 4.
[93] *Irish Press* (21 December 1938) 16.
[94] *Cork Examiner* (30 March 1948) 4.
[95] Well into the 20th century, religious orders were often understood to be rescuing women and girls, not so much from themselves, but from the society around them. See, on this point Dr Jerome McMahon, who left money to two Magdalene laundries and Bessborough mother and baby home; 'Validity of Cork Doctor's Will Disputed' *Cork Examiner* (5 March 1952) 7.
[96] 'Rose Smyth' *Irish Independent* (21 October 1954) 11.
[97] 'Annie J O'Donoghue' *Irish Press* (15 January 1934) 9. See also 'Annie Josephine Murph' *Irish Independent* (18 October 1954) 5.
[98] 'Annie F Gallagher' *Irish Times* (29 July 1933) 1.

specified an individual religious sister by name.[99] Ordinarily,[100] a will might refer to the superioress or Reverend Mother 'for the time being'[101] or 'at the time of the testatrix's death',[102] and so a specific name may suggest a personal relationship or at least admiration for the work the sister was involved in. Sometimes the nun named was a close relative or family friend. For example, Annie Fitzgerald of Limerick directed that her nine Guinness shares should be sold, and half the proceeds given to the Magdalene laundry in Cork's Sunday's Well 'in remembrance of her dear sister the late Sister Mary Stanislaus [Bridget Mangan]'[103] who had been a nun in that convent. Agnes Mary Sims of Donnybrook left £100 to the Gloucester Street laundry and £400 to High Park when she died in 1924.[104] Her husband Frederick, a silk merchant, was a generous subscriber to public appeals for the High Park and Gloucester Street laundries during his lifetime.[105] He himself left £100 to High Park on his death. Iza Farrelly[106] left £100 to the Gloucester Street laundry when she died in 1945. The Superioress of the Donnybrook laundry received £1,000 on the death of Iza's bank manager brother John, just a few years later.[107]

Some women were likely influenced by the fundraising tactics employed by the congregations who ran the institutions, and by the men who appealed for money on their behalf.[108] Fannie Andrews named several priests in her will, among them the Jesuit Fr John Verdon. Verdon had been a minister first at the

[99] 'Bridget Houlihan' *Cork Examiner* (3 August 1968) 7; 'Margaret Martin' *Irish Press* (6 November 1936) 8.

[100] The words quoted are designed to avoid the rule against perpetuities. Religious congregations were treated as voluntary associations and could have both charitable and non-charitable purposes. A non-charitable gift to a voluntary association tends to a perpetuity. One way to avoid this issue was by specifying that the gift was to go to an identifiable class within the association; to the sisters of a specific convent community (as joint tenants), or to a particular member of the community, such as the superioress; *Morrow v McConville* (1883) LR Ir 11 Ch 236; *Re Delany's Estate* (1881) 9 L IR 236; *Bradshaw v Jackman*, [1887] 21 LR Ir 12; *Re Keogh's Estate*[1945] IR 13.

[101] 'Bridget Fahey' *Cork Examiner* (9 June 1934) 4; 'Kate Dowling' *Freeman's Journal* (9 February 1923) 1.

[102] 'Margaret Hallinan' *Irish Independent* (26 September 1944) 4.

[103] *Cork Examiner* (19 February 1926) 1. The Mangans were aunts of the revolutionary leader The O'Rahilly.

[104] 'Agnes Mary Sims' *Freeman's Journal* (18 December 1924) 1.

[105] 'The Magdalen Asylum High Park', *Freeman's Journal* (27 January 1883) 2; 'Gloucester Street Magdalen Asylum' *Irish Times* (14 May 1892) 8; 'Catholic Notices', *Freeman's Journal* (25 February 1893) 3; 'The Magdalen Asylum, High Park Drumcondra, *Freeman's Journal* (30 January 1900) 9.

[106] *Irish Independent* (1 August 1945) 4.

[107] *Irish Independent* (4 November 1949) 2.

[108] It is difficult to say what role solicitors had in shaping the expression of women's intentions. Firms of all kinds are mentioned in the published advertisements. Not all will have had exceptional expertise in religious matters. Several of the wills discussed here were handled by Arthur O'Hagan Solicitors, which represented the Archbishops of Dublin for decades. The firm's former principals included Richard Ryan (uncle of the Fine Gael Minister for Finance), who was made a Knight of St Gregory by the Pope at the request of Archbishop John Charles McQuaid. Ryan was also chairman of Irish Catholic Church Property Insurance Ltd, which insured church buildings and schools.

influential Clongowes Wood College,[109] and later at Gardiner Street in Dublin. As a younger man, he was a popular preacher, who gave many sermons on behalf of Catholic women's institutions. These were sometimes published in national newspapers. In 1897, he implored his congregation to give money to enlarge the Gloucester Street laundry and make the women inmates, 'the poor creatures, respectable members of society'. Their 'own people would not take them back. No respectable family would receive them'. Fr Verdon described women 'hedged in by circumstances', sinking 'deeper and deeper' into vice, forever at risk of 'rotting' in a prison, or dying 'degraded' in a hospital. '[A]ngel tongues alone,' he said, could describe the wonders done for 'poor strayed souls' in Gloucester Street laundry.[110] Fundraisers like Fr Verdon used language reinforcing moral and class divisions between benefactors and their imagined women beneficiaries.[111] They encouraged their listeners to imagine themselves as heroic agents of rescue.[112] Through their bequests, Catholic women took their place in that imaginary.

Finally, some women will have been motivated by their commitments to lay religious organisations.[113] Genevieve McDermott was a member of the Third Order of St Francis,[114] as was her brother Valentine. On her death in 1967,[115] she left over 50 legacies to Catholic organisations, including the Magdalene laundries at Drumcondra, Gloucester Street and Donnybrook in Dublin. Miss McDermott was bound for life to observe the Order's rules. Her will itself was made in obedience to the rules; members (called Tertiaries) were required to leave a clear will as soon as possible after they joined the Order.[116] Miss McDermott may also have had a strong sense of the boundaries of women's transgression under Catholicism. The Order's rule instructed her to resist purportedly obscene behaviours in wider society[117] including 'dangerous dancing', 'corrupt literature' and 'suggestive plays'.[118] An observant member would have worn a scapular around her neck and a cord around her waist,[119] under her clothing, at all times; the cord

[109] A Jesuit boys' boarding school, strongly associated with the education of leading lawyers.

[110] 'The Magdalen Asylum Gloucester Street' *Irish Independent* (25 October 1897) 4. The sermon was preached at Gardiner Street, less than a kilometre from the laundry. See a similar sermon on behalf of Prisoners Aid in 1898; 'Discharged Prisoners' Aid Society' *Irish Daily Independent* (17 January 1898) 2.

[111] Siegel (2012) 32.

[112] Brouillette (2011) 169.

[113] See De Cléir (2014) 44–47.

[114] Well-known Irish members included Venerable Matt Talbot and the revolutionaries Tomás MacCurtain and Terence McSwiney.

[115] 'Genevieve McDermott' *Irish Independent* (27 February 1968) 16.

[116] Misericors Dei Filius, Constitution on the Law of the Franciscan Third Order Secular (1883), Chs II, VII. The rule was created by St Francis and may have been intended to encourage members to avoid intestacy, and to deal with their affairs before they became old or infirm.

[117] See, for example, 'St Francis: A Plea for the Third Order' *Cork Examiner* (26 October 1926) 8.

[118] Fr Augustine O'Neill, *The Third Order and You* (John English & Co, Wexford, 1928) 2.

[119] Fr Canice, *The Perfect Christian* (Dublin, Gill, 1933) 21. Although members of the Third Order of St Dominic, to which Prof Mary Ryan belonged, were encouraged to dress modestly, to avoid dances and similar entertainments, and to wear a scapular, there was not the same apparent emphasis on dress as controlling lust.

signifying her obligation to control the 'passion of lust' within her.[120] It may be that this emphasis on control of individual passions steered Miss McDermott towards support for 'rescue' work. Charitable giving, too, was consistent with the Order's rules, which discouraged members from spending their money on needless luxuries. Tertiaries were encouraged to share any material fortune with God and with those around them. In some senses, the property and money Miss McDermott left behind may be read as the result of a life of self-denial; conserving her wealth for redistribution to religious congregations.

IV. Bequests in Histories of the Magdalene Laundries

What is the purpose, for legal history, of telling the stories of women and the money they left to Magdalene laundries decades ago? One purpose is to trouble gaps or omissions in the official record. The McAleese Report, containing the conclusions of a government-commissioned inquiry into the facts of state involvement with the Magdalen laundries was published in 2013.[121] It does not deal with bequests at any length except, in a few paragraphs of strikingly legalistic language, to acknowledge that the Irish Commissioners of Charitable Donations and Bequests facilitated religious congregations in deriving benefit from bequests made to Magdalene laundries under their control; for instance, by authorising the sale of certain properties. Jim Smith of the campaigning group Justice for Magdalenes had written to the Committee charged with preparation of the Report identifying the administration of bequests as a key point of connection between the state and the laundries. He provided supporting research; details of individual bequests.[122] His intervention is not reflected in the Report. The bequests themselves are never examined in any detail, although the Report later asserts, in just one sentence, that they were crucial to the laundries' financial sustainability.[123] So, even in the context of a state inquiry into institutions associated with historical injustice, bequests are made uncontroversial. The Report twice reminds readers that the Commissioners' role was 'facilitative' or 'enabling' rather than 'regulatory'.[124] 'Facilitation' is never problematised, but the word 'facilitative' itself may denote a certain division of moral labour. McAleese describes itself as a report into 'state involvement' with the Magdalen laundries; by declining to

[120] Ferdinand Gruen and Eugène Oisy, *Catechism of the Third Order of St Francis* (Franciscan Herald, 1914) Ch IV.

[121] McAleese (2013) 851–53.

[122] See J Smith (2012) 'Email of 2nd April 2012 (No 4: Charitable Donations & Bequests) from Prof James Smith to Nuala Ní Mhuircheartaigh'. Bundle 8, Tab 242 and 243, 2542–545, Justice for Magdalenes Archive, University College Dublin Archives.

[123] McAleese (2013) 994.

[124] ibid 848, 851.

analyse bequests, the report may signal that responsibility for a bequest lies with the testator. She forms an intention, which organs of state merely 'facilitate'.

This chapter's emphasis on 'structural complicity' tells a more complex story, resisting the silence and abstraction of this 'official' history. Charitable bequests enabled many women to fulfil a personal desire for religious salvation and, to some extent, to possess and direct the flow of wealth and property within their towns, cities and country. Simultaneously, their bequests reinforced unequal distributions of wealth and power that were in no small part animated by class hierarchy and gendered ideologies of 'rescue'. In this way, bequests participated in a complex web of interlocking forces that held up the wider system of admission, containment, exploitation and abuse of women in laundries and allied institutions. They contributed to a charitable and political imaginary that persisted long after the money bequeathed had been spent and the properties sold on. This chapter, then, actively politicises bequests, offering one route to unsettling too-easy divisions of labour between the testator and the state.

References

Aragon, C and Jaggar, AM (2018) 'Agency, Complicity, and the Responsibility to Resist Structural Injustice' 49 *Journal of Social Philosophy* 439.

Benítez-Castro, MA and Hidalgo-Tenorio, E (2018) '"We Were Treated Very Badly, Treated Like Slaves": A Critical Metaphor Analysis of the Accounts of the Magdalene Laundries Victims' in P Villar-Argáiz (ed), *Irishness on the Margins: Minority and Dissident Identities* (London, Springer International Publishing, 2018), available at doi.org/10.1007/978-3-319-74567-1_6.

Brenton, M, *The Voluntary Sector in British Social Services* (Harlow, Essex, Longman Publishing, 1985).

Brouillette, S, 'Human Rights Markets and Born into Brothels' (2011) 25 *Third Text* 169.

Bryan, D, 'Ryan, Mary' in J Quinn (ed), *Dictionary of Irish Biography* (Royal Irish Academy, 2009), available at www.dib.ie/biography/ryan-mary-a7874.

De Cléir, S, *Popular Catholicism in 20th-Century Ireland: Locality, Identity and Culture* (London, Bloomsbury Publishing, 2014).

Earner-Byrne, L, *Letters of the Catholic Poor* (Cambridge, Cambridge University Press, 2017).

Enright, M, 'Contract, the State, and the Magdalene Laundries' in *Legacies of the Magdalene Laundries: Commemoration, Gender, and the Postcolonial Carceral State* (Manchester, Manchester University Press, 2021).

—— '"Benefactors and Friends": Charitable Bequests, Reparation and the Donnybrook Laundry' in M Coen, K O'Donnell and M O'Rourke (eds), *A Dublin Magdalene* (London, Bloomsbury 2022).

Fischer, C, 'Gender, Nation, and the Politics of Shame: Magdalen Laundries and the Institutionalization of Feminine Transgression in Modern Ireland' (2016) 41 *Signs: Journal of Women in Culture and Society* 821.

Frehill, O, 'Serving the "Divine Economy2: St Joseph's Asylum for Aged and Virtuous Females, Dublin, 1836–1922' (2020) 48 *Irish Economic and Social History* 70.

Gallen, J and Gleeson, K, 'Unpaid Wages: The Experiences of Irish Magdalene Laundries and Indigenous Australians' (2018)14 *International Journal of Law in Context* 43.

Gott, CK, 'Productive Bodies, Docile Women and Violence: Exploring "Respectable Work" as Physical Abuse within Ireland's Magdalene Laundries' (2021) 11 *Religion and Gender* 167.

Hamill, C, 'The Atlas of Lost Rooms' in M Shehade and T Stylianou-Lambert (eds), *Emerging Technologies and the Digital Transformation of Museums and Heritage Sites* (Springer International Publishing, 2021).

Hanson, JH, 'The Anthropology of Giving: Toward a Cultural Logic of Charity' (2015) 8 *Journal of Cultural Economy* 501.

Holme, J, 'Spiritual Eugenics as Part of the Irish Carceral Archipelago' (2018) 31 *Journal of Historical Sociology* 154.

Jaconelli, J, 'Wills as Public Documents – Privacy and Property Rights' (2012) 71 *Cambridge Law Journal* 147.

Kotre, JN, *Outliving the Self: How to Live on in Future Generations* (New York, WW Norton, 1996).

McAleese, M 'Report of the Inter-Departmental Committee to Establish the Facts of State Involvement with the Magdalen Laundries' (2013), available at www.justice.ie/en/JELR/Pages/MagdalenRpt2013.

McCarthy, M, *Priests and People in Ireland* (Dublin, Hodges Figgis, 1902).

McGettrick, C et al, *Ireland and the Magdalene Laundries: A Campaign for Justice* (London, Bloomsbury Publishing, 2021).

McGonegal, J, 'The Tyranny of Gift Giving: The Politics of Generosity in Sarah Scott's Millenium Hall and Sir George Ellison' (2007) 19 *Eighteenth Century Fiction* 294.

Midgley, C, *Women Activists in Imperial Britain, 1790–1865* (New York and London, Routledge, 2007).

Monk, D, 'Sexuality and Succession Law: Beyond Formal Equality' (2011) 19 *Feminist Legal Studies* 231.

—— 'EM Forster's Will: An Overlooked Posthumous Publication' (2013) 33 *Legal Studies* 572.

O'Donnell, K, 'A Certain Class of Justice: Ireland's Magdalenes' in L Black, L Brangan and D Healy (eds), *Histories of Punishment and Social Control in Ireland: Perspectives from a Periphery* (Bingley, Emerald Publishing Limited, 2022).

O'Mahoney, J, 'Advocacy and the Magdalene Laundries: Towards a Psychology of Social Change' (2018) 15 *Qualitative Research in Psychology* 456.

O'Mahoney, J, Bowman Grieve, L and Torn, A (2019) 'Ireland's Magdalene Laundries and the Psychological Architecture of Surveillance' in S Flynn and A Mackay (eds), *Surveillance, Architecture and Control: Discourses on Spatial Culture* (New York, Springer International Publishing, 2019), available at doi.org/10.1007/978-3-030-00371-5_10.

Powell, P, *The Political Economy of the Irish Welfare State: Church, State and Capital* (Bristol, Policy Press, 2017).

Roddy, S, 'Doing Good? Irish Women, Catholicism and Charity, 1852–1922' in *Gender and History* (Routledge, India, 2022).

Routley, C and Sargeant, A, 'Leaving a Bequest' (2014) 44 *Nonprofit and Voluntary Sector Quarterly* 869.

Williams, AM, '"The Whole Thing Was Numbingly Bland and It Was Deliberately So": Food and Power in Ireland's Magdalene Laundries, 1922–1996' (2022) 34 *Gender & History* 648, available at onlinelibrary.wiley.com/doi/abs/10.1111/1468–0424.12667.

Seal, L and O'Neill, M, *Historical Spaces of Confinement 2: Magdalene Laundries* (Bristol, Bristol University Press, 2019), available at bristoluniversitypressdigital.com/view/book/9781529202656/ch003.xml.
Siegel, D, *Charity and Condescension: Victorian Literature and the Dilemmas of Philanthropy* (Ohio, Ohio University Press, 2012).
Stephens, JW, *Manual of the Third Order of Saint Dominic* (St Saviour's Dublin, 1934).
Ware, V (2015) *Beyond the Pale: White Women, Racism, and History* (London, Verso Books, 2015).

PART 2

Legal Fiction and Wills in Fiction

5

Surnames and Inheritance: Will-Plotting and Female Economic Power in the Eighteenth-Century Novel

JOLENE ZIGAROVICH

I. Introduction

Frances Burney's *Cecilia, or, Memoirs of an Heiress* (1782) charts Cecilia Beverley's financial dispossession and has been considered by literary critics to be a 'dismal commentary on women's potential for retaining individual property rights'.[1] By robbing Cecilia of her uncle's inheritance, Burney effectively shifts the emphasis to the acquiring of autonomy not through proprietorship and economy but through individual development and awareness. An heiress only because she is an orphan, Cecilia inherits £10,000 upon her father's death (which she rapidly borrows against under unfortunate circumstances). Though the inheritance will provide her future independence, she is also trapped by the patriarchal economy. When her paternal uncle, Dean Beverley, dies, Cecilia learns that his will dictates that in order to receive her inheritance she must continue the family name by bestowing the surname Beverley upon her future husband. His will makes her 'heiress to an estate of 3000*l*. per annum; with no other restriction than that of annexing her name, if she marrie[s], to the disposal of her hand and her riches'.[2] I wish to suggest that this name clause ostensibly gives her the modern right to independent thought and action: upon marriage she will keep her surname and identity, have a certain amount of power in her marriage negotiation, and will be a female recipient of family wealth.[3]

[1] Cope (2009) 57.

[2] Burney (1999) 5–6.

[3] Straub (1987) recognises that the stipulation 'frustrates her marriage and re-entry into domestic security', but it doesn't impact her final achievement of 'emotional and social equilibrium through marriage' (113). Terry Castle (1986) remarks that the name clause essentially gives Cecilia the ability to unman her future husband, that she 'will make him into a wife' (275). I agree with König (2014) who finds that the name clause 'undermines patriarchal institutions of marriage and patrimonial succession' (80). Other readers of the clause disagree, finding that women are merely conduits for patrilineage. For instance, Ganz (2013) believes that 'it constricts rather than enhances Cecilia's liberty' (34).

Yet these forms of empowerment aren't without painful personal and financial sacrifice. In fact, she eventually experiences disinheritance. Recoiling from the thought of changing his surname in order to marry Cecilia, Mortimer Delvile pronounces that the 'barbarous and repulsive clause' would 'degrade me forever.'[4] Reeling from this insult, Cecilia sarcastically responds: 'Well, let him keep his name! since so wondrous its properties.'[5] The middling-class readers of the novel 'thought no man would turn down a solid fortune of £3000 per annum for such a trifle.'[6] Giving up her uncle's estate and dowry when Mortimer Delvile and his family refuse to accede to the name clause, and having spent most of her sizeable paternal inheritance, Cecilia limits her agency. She explains to Mortimer:

> I have ever thought myself secure of more wealth than I could require, and regarded the want of money as an evil from which I was unavoidably exempted. My own fortune, therefore, appeared to me of small consequence, while the revenue of my uncle ensured me perpetual prosperity.–Oh had I but foreseen this moment! –.[7]

Choosing love over fortune and interest, she marries Mortimer and relinquishes her name and estate in what is seen as an 'extraordinary sacrifice.'[8] The narrator describes Cecilia's indifference to wealth as such:

> At the proposal of parting with her uncle's fortune, which, desirable as it was, had as yet been only productive to her misery, her heart, *disinterested*, and wholly careless of money, was prompt to accede to the condition (added emphasis).[9]

As Linda Zionkowski details, reviewers and admirers of the novel such as Hester Chapone and Mary Delany expressed frustration with Cecilia's choice to give up her fortune.[10] In 1782, the writer in *The Critical Review* remarks, 'Cecilia's conduct, in sacrificing so large a fortune to gratify the pride of the Delvile family, is an example which we would by no means wish to propose as an object of imitation for the fair sex.'[11] We can certainly agree with contemporary and current readers of the novel that the heroine's indifference to fortune is a form of defeat; a diminishing of her agency. But with some form of financial independence, she still retains the *choice* to marry for love. And ultimately, Cecilia's disinheritance for not upholding the name clause points to failed attempts for will stipulations to guarantee male lineage.

[4] Burney (n 2) 512.
[5] ibid.
[6] Doody, Introduction, *Cecilia* (n 2) xxix.
[7] Burney (n 2) 808.
[8] ibid, 939.
[9] ibid, 804.
[10] Quoted in Zionkowski (2016) 114. Burney relates this conversation in a letter to her sister Susan Burney Phillips (4 January 1783). Attending the opera, Burney overhears Delany and Chapone's conversation with a 'Dutchess' discussing the name clause in *Cecilia*. See Crump (2002) 223–27. Doody (1989) notes that even Burney's father and close family friend Samuel Crisp 'tried hard to think of expedients that would preserve Cecilia's estate for her and Mortimer–they were quite tender hearted at seeing the fictional girl robbed of her treasure' (145).
[11] *Critical Review* 54 (December 1782) 414. Doody (1989) speculates that 'the approving review in this periodical may have been written by Charles Burney's old friend Thomas Twining' (405 fn 66).

This patriline failure is symbolised by an optimistic female-to-female bequest. At the novel's close, Burney reinstates Cecilia's economic power through a modest female inheritance: her husband Mortimer's maternal aunt who admired the extraordinary sacrifice Cecilia made, 'left to her, and to her sole disposal, the fortune, which almost from his infancy she had destined for her nephew'.[12] This *deus ex machina* is extraordinary: Cecilia receives the fortune of the late aunt – someone previously unknown to her – which enables the couple to live comfortably. Mortimer generously remarks that he was 'delighted to restore to her through his own family any part of that power and independence of which her generous and pure regard for himself had deprived her'.[13] While Zionkowski interprets her charity as confined to the domestic, and 'limited gestures of good will that would not impinge upon the resources of the patriarchal household', I wish to emphasise not the failure of Cecilia's dream of charitable paternalism remaining unrealised, but the power of females investing in each other.[14] With this unconditional female-to-female legacy, Cecilia benefits from a clearly discernible chain of female charity, perhaps fashioning a new model of economy that critiques patriarchal capitalism. Mortimer's future inheritance, though perhaps not significantly altered or threatened, has suddenly been reduced. Essentially, Cecilia is rewarded for not upholding legal attempts to maintain male property and name.[15]

The powerful name clause in *Cecilia* has received much critical attention and interest in terms of its uniqueness to the eighteenth-century novel. But how frequent were these clauses in actual practice? Were the clauses included solely in male-authored wills? Were they typically followed or rejected, as *Cecilia* depicts? Could they be challenged in court? This essay will first address these legal questions in order to better assess how the name clause is interpreted in fiction. While Deborah Anthony states that 'increasingly strict surname rules for women served as a mechanism by which patriarchy was both reflected and reinforced', which is certainly true, I hope by examining both real and fictional surname situations we can also locate opportunities for women's social and perhaps financial empowerment and choice.[16] My essay will interrogate both actual and fictional cases of female inheritance under the name clause in order to update, trouble and revise previous assumptions and interpretations of patrilineal succession. The larger aim is to collate examples that reimagine an eighteenth-century culture that experienced female inheritance and its powerful potentials.

In *Law, Land, and Family, Aristocratic Inheritance in England, 1300 to 1800*, Eileen Spring observes that the trend in the 'invention of the name and arms

[12] Burney (n 2) 939. In her earlier novel *Evelina*, surnames also play an important role. Supposedly a natural daughter, and legally unable to use her father's surname, Evelina is given the anagram-ish surname 'Anville' by Mr. Villars, the kindly reverend who looks after her.

[13] ibid.

[14] Zionkowksi (2016) 117; Zigarovich (2023) 231–32.

[15] Burney never reveals which relative receives the uncle's bequest rejected by Cecilia, perhaps suggesting that this information is irrelevant. We can assume that the Beverley line is extinct, and that the inheritor is not blood related.

[16] Anthony, 'Analyzing the Disappearance' (2018) 17.

clause' found its apotheosis in the eighteenth century.[17] This was a clause by which the beneficiary of a will or settlement was required to change his name to that of the testator or settlor as a condition of receiving his estate. She writes, 'The name and arms clause has sometimes been held to be a benefit to women', as seen in Lawrence Stone and Jeanne C Fawtier Stone's *An Open Elite? England 1540–1880*. It opened the possibility that a settlor could choose his daughter as heir, requiring her husband to take her name and thus preserving the family's name despite the succession of the female. Spring disagrees with this interpretation, arguing that the name and arms clause is evidence of the 'growth of the patrilineal ethos'.[18] Since 'women so seldom inherited', she sees this as a last resort, such as when a female heir has not married or bore children. 'Thus such clauses have had no notable effect in favoring female inheritance in gentry and aristocratic families', she claims.[19] 'Why surnames should have had a power akin to titles, a power to overcome the natural flow of family sentiment, remains puzzling', she further states.[20]

As *Cecilia* points to, often names and arms clauses were used to disguise the fact that a patriline was about to end or that it had actually ended, 'striking evidence of the growth of patrilineage', Spring claims. This surname condition arises in notable eighteenth-century novels, especially those written by women, and many depict women benefiting from the inheritance despite and even because of the troubling name clause. Studies such as Eva König's *The Orphan in Eighteenth-Century Fiction: The Vicissitudes of the Eighteenth-Century Subject* and Cheryl L Nixon's *The Orphan in Eighteenth-Century Law and Literature: Estate, Blood, and the Body* discuss foundlings and birthright restitution in law and literature, yet they primarily avoid the specific issues that arise in terms of gender and female entitlement.[21] Further interrogating Spring's sweeping statements about the clause acting as evidence of the growth of patrilineage, through the discussion of the roles gender and names play in courtship and inheritance, I assert that both actual and fictional cases of men being forced to take their wives' surnames in order for these women to keep their fortunes demonstrates the growing significance of female inheritors in the period. This gender reversal – where men give up a portion of their identity and power by taking on another man's surname – thereby reflects a broader cultural shift. Though not common, and a feudal remnant from wills of the wealthy, the practice of making an inheritance contingent on the beneficiary taking on a particular surname, or keeping a family name, saw increased use in the eighteenth century (eg Lord Byron taking the name 'Noel').[22] And importantly,

[17] Spring (1993) 95.

[18] ibid.

[19] ibid.

[20] ibid.

[21] See König (2014) and Nixon (2011).

[22] Though the persistent practice of surname substitution emerged during the Restoration, hereditary acquisition of surnames had become the norm by the fourteenth and fifteenth centuries. OM Stone (1963) remarks that name and arms clauses are 'relics of feudalism' (652). Squibb (1953) notes that the Tudors 'sought to prove that they were not really new at all, and that their families had their roots firmly embedded in the past'. He states, 'The heralds of the day had no lack of patrons anxious to be

female beneficiaries could find themselves navigating more powerful choices in terms of distribution of funds and even in spouses.

II. Eighteenth-Century Name and Arms Clauses in Wills and Courts

Historians have demonstrated that 'the relationship of English women to their surnames was historically quite dynamic and individualised'.[23] In modern times surnames have witnessed perhaps their most dynamic transformation in terms of freedom of choice and socio-cultural diversity. Yet the early history of surnames demonstrates a diversity of attitudes over time, including the wide use of matronyms, and the regularity of husbands taking their wives' surnames during the medieval period. Much work has been done on the history of surname usage and traditions, research that has necessarily informed this chapter, but my aim is to magnify the role of women's surnames in the eighteenth century as related to wills and inheritance practices, in order to suggest that despite the limitations women faced, name and arms clauses could extend to them independence and choice.[24]

In English law a will can be drafted to include a 'name and arms' clause, which typically transfers the land or any other property to another person on the condition that he (or more rarely, she) takes the name of the testator. Legal scholar Audrey Guinchard recognises that 'This possibility to dispose of one's own name seems to contradict completely the English Law's affirmation that a person has no property right to his/her name'.[25] The clause requires the beneficiary to apply for and obtain a licence from the Crown authorising the taking and use of the specified name and arms. By the middle of the eighteenth century about a quarter of all private Acts of Parliament were for name changes.[26] For example, in the *Journals of the House of Lords*, which lists divorces, the naturalising of illegitimate children, and other Acts, we see a typical application for a surname change: 'An Act to enable

provided with long illuminate pedigrees tracing their names and arms back to remote periods' (219). He cites *Wyleby v Maundeville* (1340) where the plaintiff propounded a pedigree of nine generations in the male line, and *Bon v Smith* (1596), which included a remainder 'to the next of the devisor's kin of his name' (220).

[23] Anthony (2018) 'Analyzing the Disappearance' 4.

[24] In 'Inheritance Strategies Among the English Landed Elite, 1540–1880', Lawrence Stone argues that major demographic changes arose in the second half of the eighteenth century that created the need for landed families to artificially continue the family name. After 1750, 'No fewer than 10 per cent of them changed their names, even if in some cases the change only took the form of hyphenation. it is significance of the values prevalent in this social class that it was thought preferable to alter the personal identity tag of the individual–his surname–than to separate the seat from the family name' (288). By 1900 old family surnames had been artificially inherited, and many heads of families hardly carried 'a drop of the blood of the family they purported to represent'.

[25] Guinchard (2008) 24.

[26] See Gibson (1992) 18. Gibson notes that 'between 1732 and 1762 this may reflect as many as 310 separate acts' (30, fn 9). See also Lambert (1971) 11. Surname changes were secured 'by royal license, an Act of Parliament, or more rarely a letter patent'. See Guinchard (2008) 29.

Thomas Purnell James Esquire, and his Issue, to take and use the Surname and Arms of Purnell'.[27] Many of the applications specify 'Issue Male', but there are also several like Purnell's which include both sexes ('his Issue'). Typically, the clause is followed by a shifting clause directing that in the event of non-compliance with the directive, the settled estates shall go to the next beneficiary named in the will. The list of period Acts reflects some of the problems that arose from the change of surnames, including the request to amend a previous name clause Act: 'An Act to amend an Act, made and passed in the Fourteenth Year of His present Majesty's Reign' instituted

> An Act to enable John Medows the Elder, Gentleman, and his Issue Male, to take the Surname and Arms of Theobald, pursuant to the Will of Elizabeth Theobald Widow, deceased; and also to enable John Medows, eldest Son of the said John Medows (now John Theobald), and the Heirs of his Body, to take the said Surname, and bear the said Arms of Theobald.[28]

Here it is important to note the important fact that women's wills – such as that of Elizabeth Theobald – also designated the name and arms clause, reminding us that women's will-making not only played an integral role in maintaining the transference of *male* property and name, but that with this they also gained a certain amount of financial and familial power.

Historians have established that it is not until the eighteenth century that wills consistently included a name clause.[29] JD Squibb observes that

> The fashion seems to have gained considerable popularity in the early years of the eighteenth century, and it was not long before the requirement to take the settlor's or testator's name had added to it a requirement to bear his arms. From then onwards the name and arms clause came to be used with increasing frequency.[30]

Stone and Stone have estimated that between 1760 and 1879 4,000 families changed their names. In a survey of three counties they estimated that in Northumberland surname substitution among the landed classes rose from about five per cent in 1700 to 20 per cent from 1850–79.[31] And subsequent historians have suggested that this may have been an underestimate.[32] Facing the possibility that their name

[27] 14 GEO III *Journals of the House of Lords* (1774) 39. Such a Private Act was costly and time-consuming. Gibson notes that 'it became more common to apply to the monarch for permission to change name' (18).

[28] 16 GEO III *Journals of the House of Lords* (1774) 717.

[29] Squibb (1953) remarks, 'Who first sought to perpetuate his name in this way we do not know. It was a comparatively late introduction into settlements and wills. The earliest instance known to the writer is in the will of Ralph, last Lord Grey of Warke, who died in 1706' (220).

[30] Squibb (1953) 220. Squibb goes on to note that 'By the time of the passing of the Stamp Act of 1815 it had become sufficiently common to warrant the imposition of a heavier rate of duty (£50) upon changes of name and arms 'in compliance with the Injunctions of any Will or Settlement' than upon a voluntary application (£10)–a distinction that persisted until both charges were abolished by the Finance Act, 1949' (220).

[31] Stone and Stone (1984) 89.

[32] See Gibson (1992); Erickson (1993); and others.

might become extinct and the property pass through the female line thus resulting in a change of name, men of property especially took up the clause as some sort of patriarchal assurance that their name wouldn't die with them.[33] This condition of entail was considered ultra vires ('beyond the powers'), meaning an act which requires authority (eg conditions in a will subject to apportionment) but is done without it. In other words, stating in a will, for instance, that the heirs of entail assume, bear and constantly retain a particular surname and arms is an *obligation*; it restrains heirs from altering the course of succession (but then also opens up the possibility to fight the obligation in a court of law).[34] The contested will of Scottish Sir Thomas Dundas is a typical example of these legal statements, and also demonstrates the critical role women played in entailed estates and name clauses. The entail states:

> That the whole heirs of tailzie above mentioned, both male and female, who shall succeed to my said lands and estate above written, shall be holden and obliged to assume, bear, use, and carry, and constantly to retain, the surname of Dundas, and arms of Dundas of Kerse, as their proper surname and arms, and no other surname or arms, in all time after their succession.[35]

Reflecting the frequency of these clauses in the period, the Dundas will acknowledges the problem that could arise with an heir who receives multiple settlements, and directs the heirs accordingly:

> Yet if any of the heirs of tailzie, male or female, above mentioned, shall happen to marry an heiress or heir of another estate, or shall succeed to another estate settled under the like condition of carrying a particular surname and arms, and under the like irritancy, it shall be lawful to the person so marrying or succeeding to such an estate to make such addition to their surname and arms as shall be necessary, they always retaining the surname of Dundas, and arms of Dundas of Kerse, and using the same in the first place, and carrying the arms first and fourth, where that may be consistent with the settlement of the said other estate.[36]

The Dundas proviso underscores the significant role of women's surname usage in the period. Passing on the patronym through the female line, women could experience more social visibility and status, as well as some independence and autonomy.

[33] Gibson notes that there is evidence that the name clause was also popular among the untitled landed classes. Robert Harper, the lawyer and drafter of private parliamentary bills, drafted 23 bills for name changes from 1732 to 1762. Of these only three were for members of the peerage. See Gibson (1992) and Lambert (1971) app 1.

[34] In this period, typically ultra vires cases involved entail. For example, if the granter of an entail prohibited any alteration of the order of succession, the entail could be reduced as ultra vires upon the ground that no power was reserved in the marriage contract to impose this prohibition. In the court of equity, deeds designated by the maker should be considered rational, therefore a deed *ultra vires* is considered null and void (eg a property owner who only has the power to grant a lease for ten years grants it to a renter for 20). See cases such as *Marjory Row v Charles Row* (1706); *Gordon v Gordons* (1731); *Ker v Kers* (1747); *Strang v Strang* (1751).

[35] Dundas (1783) 4.

[36] ibid.

The name change of Admiral Everitt to his wife's name, Calmady, in 1783, reflects this important female role. The Admiral's wife, Pollexfen Calmady, was in a bitter legal battle over her brother's will, which had bequeathed large Calmady estates in Devon and Somerset to her. It was perhaps helpful that her husband adopted his wife's surname, but it was her own retention of the surname that 'gave her an important psychological advantage in the legal cases'.[37] In another example, Sir Arthur Langford of Summerhill, County Meath, who died unmarried in 1716, left his Antrim estates to his brother Henry Langford, but also added in the will that in default of issue male to Henry Langford then it was to go to Henry's daughter, 'provided always that such daughter or daughters and the heiresses of their bodys to whom the said estate shall come take on them the sirname of Lanford'.[38] In this case, the estate would not be entailed to solely male issue or relatives, thus underscoring the increased value placed on female heirs in the period. So as surnames were aligned with rules of coverture and the formal legal restrictions of common law, as Spring, Anthony and Gibson have identified, their role in name and arms clauses as beneficiaries of property also signal a type of social and financial empowerment for women.

While men's wills were the primary source for entailed estates with the name and arms clause, numerous women's wills either continued or instigated the clause.[39] In March 1788 Martha Turner, sister of Philippa á Beckett and widow of George Turner of Penleigh, included the fashionable clause. Carefully crafted, the will designated that it was not permissible to assume the surname as part of 'a double-barrelled name', hence Thomas could become Thomas á Beckett Turner but not á Beckett-Turner.[40] Not only does the clause enforce the surname change for male heirs, it has the effect of entailing an estate. While women were obviously the primary victims of entail, Martha Turner's will also demonstrates the authority given to her as a will-writing widow. Later in the next century, we still see several examples of will-making widows who use the name and arms clause for female beneficiaries. Anne Cranmer, a descendant of Archbishop Cranmer, inherited the estate from her cousin Martha Cranmer, subject to a name and arms clause. Anne Cranmer, widow, by a holograph will, dated in October 1854, after other devises and bequests, gave

> in trust to my executors for my niece, Mary Anne Byng, and her children, all my Quendon Hall estate in Essex, provided she takes the name of Cranmer and arms, and

[37] Gibson (1992) 23. See the court case Somerset RO DD/X/BKE 2.

[38] Will of Arthur Langford, 1715 (PRONI, T168/1). Quoted in Whan (2013) 70. The spelling and use of 'sirname' instead of 'surname' reflects 'sir' (a man of rank) as well as the appropriation of 'sire' to mean quite literally, owned by the male alone and conferred upon others by the father exclusively. For helpful discussions of the history of women and surname usage, see the work of Deborah Anthony such as 'Analyzing the Disappearance of Women's Surnames' and 'Eradicating Women's Surnames'.

[39] Women made approximately 20% of the two million wills that survive from the 1550s to the 1750s. See Erickson (1993) 204, and Davis (2004) 219–36.

[40] Martha Turner's will is included in John Michael Bennett's *Sir William a'Beckett: First Chief Justice of Victoria 1852–1857* (Annandale, New South Wales, Federation Press, 2001) 2–3.

> her children, with my mansion house, furniture, plate, books, linen, etc., Archbishop Cranmer's portrait by Holbein, the India cabinet in drawing-room, and striking watch, and my diamond earrings and pins, as heirlooms with my estate.[41]

Born Anne Webb, Anne Cranmer changed her surname when she inherited the estate from her cousin, as did her husband at their marriage.[42] In my view, these female-authored wills indicate a keen awareness of the legal and social implications of transmitting property. The will becomes a type of narrative framework for identity, property, and gender.

While wills from both men and women included name and arms clauses, and also imposed the continuation of the surname through the male issue of an heiress, rarer is the condition of imposing a name change upon the man who marries an heiress (seen in the previously discussed Calmady will). Perhaps this is one of the reasons why novelists take up this dramatic plot line. Robert Whan remarks that 'full surname and arms change was always much more likely to be accepted when a man of inferior status and income, rather than one of a more illustrious name, was concerned'.[43] Stone and Stone also endorse this view (*Open Elite* 130). The will of Archibald Edmonstone of Duntreath and Redhall reflects this possibility. In the disposition of his estates, he stipulated that 'in case of any such heirs-female shall … happen to be married to a peer' then the Edmonstone estates were to go to the second son of such marriage and 'shall only be capable to succeed who, and everyone of them, shall from that time forward assume the sirname of Edmonstone, and bear the arms of the family of Duntreath'.[44] Edmonstone's will foresees the complications a name and arms clause could bear on the male peerage. But for non-peers marrying an heiress of the peerage, there could be potential benefits of the name clause, such as being the beneficiary of a title and arms.[45] Therefore, women of the peerage who were beneficiaries of an estate with this proviso could play important roles in their marriage choice, potentially offering a suitor the ability to apply for a Royal Licence to assume an esteemed name, noble title, and ancient arms.

While there were some legal detractors and critics (Lord Mansfield famously described the surname condition in the Irish case *Gulliver v Ashby* as 'silly'), the

[41] vlex.co.uk/vid/byng-and-others-v-803046381.

[42] The distribution of items listed in Anne's will were contested by beneficiaries and led to the case *Byng v Byng* in the later 1860s. The name and arms clause was not contested, but it did play a part in the court determining that the will intended to create an entail through the female line. Missing the typical wording 'and the heirs of her body', the will was challenged by relatives who questioned its distribution of gifts and 'heirlooms'. For more on this fascinating and important case, see Norma Dawson, '"Heirlooms": The Evolution of a Legal Concept' (2000) 51 *Northern Ireland Legal Quarterly* 1.

[43] Whan (2013) 70.

[44] Edmonstone (1769) 3.

[45] Yet the clause also had advantages for non-peers in that they could marry an heiress and potentially inherit a title themselves In a well-known example, Winston (Spencer) Churchill was a descendant of this name clause. His paternal ancestor George Spencer married one of the daughters of John Churchill, first Duke of Marlborough, and thereby took the name of Churchill by Royal Licence dated 26 May 1817 and became fifth Duke of Marlborough.

practice of imposing a surname on beneficiaries remained popular.[46] For the wealthy, the changing of a surname or adding a double surname (whether legally imposed or not) was almost an aristocratic rite of passage, or stamp of class approval. Problematic situations did arise, of course (such as a benefactor of two separate wills with two separate name clauses, or a testator requiring his beneficiary to 'lawfully assume' arms to which he had no colour of right),[47] and several required legal intervention, but there were relatively few court cases compared to the large amount of name provisions.[48] But I wish to highlight a few of these cases to demonstrate first, how wills with a name and arms clause could be challenged in court and, secondly, to highlight the role of heirs female and name clauses. These cases reflect the anxieties felt by male benefactors when they did not have any male issue to carry on an ancient name and estate, as well as reinforce the significance of female heirs in the transmission of wealth and patronym.

To return to the 'silly' surname proviso in *Gulliver v Ashby*, Lord Mansfield was referring to the case from 1766 which involved an heir of William Wykes who refused to change his surname. According to Wykes's will (1736),

> That whenever it shall happen that the said mansion-house and said estates, after my wife's decease, shall defend or come unto *any* of the persons herein before named, [that] the person or persons to whom the same from time to time shall descend or come, [that he or they] do or shall *then change their sirname*, and *take upon them and theirs the sirname of Wykes only*, and *not otherwise*.[49]

In 1759 Ambrose Saunders, the testator's nephew and sole heir at law, came into the inheritance. When he did not take the name of Wykes, other potential heirs at law filed a suit against him 'for *breach of the proviso*' and sought the estate's remainder. Saunders' position was that the proviso 'operated as a *limitation* to the devise'. Ultimately, Mansfield agrees, noting that the will did not include an additional proviso that the estate be forfeited if the name condition was not met. Citing several principles set out in previous cases, Mansfield states that 'These cases show that the court leans strongly against defeasance clauses of this nature'. Despite the fact that the continuation of the surname was the highest expression of the concept of the inseparability of name and land, even King George II expressed 'great uneasiness about it'.[50]

[46] *Gulliver v Ashby* (1766) 4 Burr 1941.

[47] *Re Berens; Re Dowdeswell* involved a beneficiary required to take different names and arms under the wills of two benefactors. Squibb notes that 'Fortunately for the plaintiff the name and arms clause in one of the wills was held to be not binding, since it was impossible for the plaintiff to obtain a grant of that testator's arms'. *Re Croxon* involved the legal bearing of arms to which the testator had no legal right. (1904) 1 Ch 252. See Squibb, 221, fn 13, 16.

[48] Using *An Index to Changes of Name* (1905), in 1953 Squibb claims that 'By the beginning of the present century several thousands of families, principally in the upper and well-to-do classes of society, had changed their names' (221).

[49] *Reports of Cases Argued* (1794) 1930, available at deedpolloffice.com/change-name/law/case-law/Gulliver-v-Ashby-1766-Burr.

[50] Cannon (1988) 116.

Perhaps for this reason men did not reject the name clause, as Mortimer Delvile does in Burney's *Cecilia*. The Scottish court of appeals case *Steel v Steel* (1817) involved the will of George Steel (1790); this included a name and arms clause which was not the source of appeal:

> That every person and heir, whether male or female, who shall succeed to the foresaid lands, etc. and their heirs and successors whatsoever, shall immediately upon their succession, assume and take, and afterwards bear and carry, the surname and arms of Steel of Baldastard.[51]

There is no directive in the Steel will as to female heirs and surname changes due to marriage. In *Healey v Copley* (1777), Thomas Copley's will (1765) doesn't designate if heirs female can change their surname upon marriage, but it does state that heirs who refuse to take the surname Copley, or

> should at any time during his life, take upon himself any other surname than that of Copley only, then and in such case the testator did by virtue of the powers reserved to him by the said recited indentures declare, that such grant and conveyance, so far as related to the respondent Thomas Copley, and his children, should be immediately void; … and that his said freehold, copyhold, and personal estates, should go and descend to the next in remainder … who should take upon himself, and write and stile himself by the surname of Copley only.[52]

The Steel and Copley examples demonstrate *assumptions* about female heiresses and surnames, foremost that if a married woman is to become a beneficiary, or if she is single and then plans to marry, the name obligation is not upon her alone, but upon her husband as well. Therefore, provisos that an heiress's husband or future husband must also change his name are relatively rare, and when they emerge in fictional wills, such as we saw earlier in Burney's *Cecilia*, they can be inflammatory, and considered a 'disgrace'.[53] In one notorious case, the first Duke of Montagu bequeathed his estate to his heirs with the name clause condition. In the 1740s, John, third Duke of Montagu, introduced a Bill to Parliament requiring the husband of any female Montagu to change his surname to Montagu if he wished to hold any of the Montagu estates or income. The Act even stated that 'Montagu' was to be used directly after a Christian name

> which … name [Montagu] is hereby given and settled upon the husband or husbands of every such woman or women … to be subscribed immediately following after his name of baptism and shall take, use and bear the ensigns and arms of Montagu.

According to Gibson, all his sons-in-law obliged: 'The Duke of Manchester, the Earl of Cardigan, and Sir Edward Hussey meekly changed their names to Montagu on marriage to Montagu heiresses'.[54] By using the adverb 'meekly', Gibson

[51] *Steel v Steel* (1817) 5 Dow 73.

[52] *The English Reports* (1901) 323.

[53] Squibb (1953) traces the fascinating history of 20th-century cases in order to demonstrate that 'the possible scope of a name and arms clauses was much reduced' by this time (223).

[54] Gibson (1992) 24. He cites J Wake, *The Bridenells of Deene* (London, 1953) 260–61. Gibson remarks that 'Ironically, the Montagu line died within two generations in spite of this' (32, fn 58).

underscores the lack of male agency in this transaction which requires a level of humility and submissiveness. Next, turning to the novel, we can now better assess the import of these stipulations for female characters, and understand them as a potential source of their agency.

III. Surnames and Name Clauses in Female-Authored Novels

As depicted in Burney's *Cecilia*, period novels often reflect anxieties about birthright and rightful inheritance by incorporating wills with very specific directives and stipulations, such as: a daughter inherits only upon marriage to a particular male relative (Anon, *The Woman of Colour* (1808)); a niece inherits her aunt's estate only upon her conversion to Catholicism (Charlotte Lennox's, *Henrietta* (1758)). Many of these plots in fact emerge from news headlines and court cases in the period, where provisos and stipulations in wills were challenged in the court system.[55] Legal scholar OM Stone remarks that:

> With a name and arms clause, the object is to attempt to ensure, by a conditional gift, that members of other families assume names which, in the natural course of events, would otherwise cease to be connected with particular land and armorial bearings. The underlying motive of perpetuating *by a fiction* the name of a particular family in a particular part of the country is a curious one' (emphasis added).[56]

In a similar literary fashion, Gibson describes that:

> [S]urname substitution, by creating a *myth* of dynastic continuity, provided an *allegory* of stability – establishing in the mind of the rural community a sense of legitimacy. The landed families were like the rivers and hills, an immovable part of the landscape (emphasis added).[57]

It is no coincidence that OM Stone and Gibson see the name and arms clause as a type of myth or fiction, a false legal narrative, and it is no coincidence that as fiction, the name clause perfectly adapts to novel plots.

Since legal debates and practices often inform literature, it is not surprising to see name and arms clauses creatively plotted in period fiction. For example, in Jane

[55] Eleanor Shevlin's excellent work on this interplay between courts and novel plots does not discuss name and arms clauses, but it does argue that female protagonists who change their own surnames (to be incognita, to not be associated with a former husband, and so on), challenge the legal and social notion of the 'value of fixed identity derived from real property' ('The Titular Claims of Female Surnames', 273). One example that involves a name and arms clause Shevlin does provide is from Hugh Kelly's novel *Memoirs of a Magdalen* (1767) where a male character inherits 'no less that eighty thousand pounds to take the name of Melmoth' (273).

[56] Stone (1963) 652.

[57] Gibson (1992) 25.

Austen's *Emma* (1815), the son of Mr Weston, Francis ('Frank') Weston drops his surname when he comes of age and assumes 'Churchill' in order to inherit from his maternal uncle, Mr Churchill, whose will stipulates Frank adopt the surname: 'It had become so avowed an adoption as to have him assume the name of Churchill on coming of age'.[58] His mother having died, Frank is adopted by his childless aunt and uncle, and is estranged from his father. Frank Churchill's aunt directs every aspect of his life and uses his dependency upon her and her husband to control his movements and choices. Though not a major plot line, the name clause does demonstrate how important patronyms were to male legacies.[59] Essentially, Mr Churchill 'bribes' his legatee, making Frank's inheritance contingent upon the name change. This would be of course socially embarrassing for his father, the kind and generous Mr Weston. Emma's sister, Mrs John Knightley, remarks that the adoption and name clause is 'shocking'.[60]

Charlotte Smith's novels are often plotted around intricately detailed lines of inheritance, including surname clauses. For instance, Orlando Somerive, in *The Old Manor House* (1793), must take his widowed aunt's surname, Rayland, in order to inherit Rayland Hall. While his older brother is placed to carry on the Somerive name, Orlando is deliberately placed in the female Rayland line of descent. Mrs Rayland is granted sole control over her property and has freedom of choice that money and power typically bring a man in the period. Both Frank Churchill and Orlando pander to their aunt's demands, and both aunts in Austen's and Smith's novels are endowed with significant control over future beneficiaries. When Mrs Rayland dies, Orlando marries the orphan Monimia (niece of the housekeeper), recovers his property, becomes a Rayland only through a legal act, and buys a baronetcy, a money-based return to a title that we are told was originally 'granted' by James I. Jacqueline Labbe observes, that 'in this way, the re-invigoration of the male line is achieved artificially, while the bloodline is mixed with Monimia's unknown genetic heritage'.[61] She adds, 'The happy ending is contained in the passing of property from the sterile female line to the fertile male line'. This is underscored by the novel's ending where the narrator tells us that Orlando has a son 'to whom he gave his own name'.[62]

While these name and arms clause plots can dramatically affect male characters' trajectories and choices, surnames and inheritances involving female heiresses see much more attention in period fiction. Charlotte Smith, who notoriously fought

[58] Austen (1993) 9.

[59] Jane Austen was no stranger to surname clauses. The father of Harris Bigg-Wither, who was to propose to Jane, had been 'Lovelace Bigg' before receiving his inheritance. James Leigh, Jane's maternal uncle, had changed his name to 'Leigh Perrot' in order to inherit property of his great-uncle Thomas Perrot. Jane Austen's older brother, Edward, adopted by the wealthy, childless Knights to continue their line, took their name when he came into their fortune. See Doody (2015) 164.

[60] Austen (n 58) 62.

[61] Labbe (2002) 26.

[62] Smith (2002) 522.

in court for her own rightful inheritance and that of her children for years, places heiresses at the centre of her plots to dramatise the financial strength of matriarchal economies.[63] A demonstrative example is that of *Emmeline, The Orphan of the Castle* (1788), which opens with a complex legacy of female inheritance, symbolised by Mowbray Castle and its inhabitant Emmeline, the supposed 'natural' (illegitimate) daughter of the deceased Mr Mowbray. How Emmeline eventually secures her birthright and inherits the castle at the end of the novel is intricately detailed by Smith, as is the female role in the castle's ownership history which is dependent upon a name and arms clause. With the extinction of her family's male line, Lady Eleonore Delamere became 'sole heiress, her husband took the name of Delamere; and obtaining one of the titles of the lady's father, was, at his death, created Viscount Montreville'.[64] In her will Lady Delamere leaves her eldest son, Mr Mowbray, 'the large estate', and he then marries, having a son and two daughters. When Mr Mowbray and his wife are deceased, the castle passes to his younger brother Frederick Mowbray who must also change his surname in order to inherit the estate and the title of Lord Montreville. Now owner of Mowbray Castle, he finds the orphaned infant Emmeline as its inhabitant. Her parents having eloped and thought not to have been married when she was born, Emmeline is allowed to remain in the castle with its servants and is given the surname 'Mowbray' by her uncle. Later, when there are suspicions that she may be the true heir of the castle, Emmeline is threatened by her uncle with the loss of her father's name: 'you must drop the name of Mowbray, to which in fact you have no right, and take that of your mother, whatever it be'.[65] Refusing to contract an engagement with his son, her cousin Delamere, and the uncle opposing the match since she has no fortune, Emmeline is forced to leave her childhood home. While Lord Montreville and his son Delamere are confident the castle's ownership is not at risk, Smith consistently gestures to the Cinderella myth through Emmeline's sympathetic and disenfranchised position. At the close of the novel, Emmeline locates documents that not only prove her parents were indeed married (Mr Mowbray marries Miss Stavordale in France after Lady Delamere dies), but that Emmeline had been left the Mowbray estate by her father. After some legal intervention, Emmeline is declared owner of the estate. In fact, a set of lawyers helps Emmeline avoid a public lawsuit and instead reach a private agreement.[66]

[63] Charlotte Smith found herself locked in a lengthy legal battle over her father-in-law's will. In fact, the inheritance ends up being tied in Chancery for almost 40 years. Bypassing his profligate son and leaving a large portion of his estate instead to Charlotte's children, the father-in-law creates a legal quagmire that is supposedly the basis for Charles Dickens's seemingly infinite legal proceedings in *Bleak House*. By the time Charlotte's legal case succeeds, most of her father-in-law's £36,000 is spent. See Fletcher (1998).

[64] Smith (2002) 45.

[65] ibid, 117.

[66] For an explanation of Private Acts see Spring (1993) 55–62 as well as König's discussion of Smith's novels and Parliament's Private Acts which allow the law to navigate private agreements, most typically to resolve concerns of the propertied person.

Effectually, this legal intervention results in Emmeline disinheriting her uncle Lord Montreville and his son (her cousin) Delamere. Smith recognises this financial triumph by stating that:

> [Emmeline] saw an infinite deal for which to be grateful, and failed not to offer her humble acknowledgements to that Providence, which, from dependance and indigence, had raised her to the highest affluence; given her, in the tenderest of husbands, the best and, the most generous and most amiable of men; and had bestowed on her the means and the inclination to deserve, by virtue and beneficence, that heaven where only she can enjoy more perfect and lasting felicity.[67]

Mowbray Castle has become a symbol of matrilineal bonds; as a site of contestation, it eventually becomes the site of Emmeline's mastery and advantage, no surname change required.[68] Loraine Fletcher writes, 'Emmeline's intelligence and humanity make her, rather than the Montrevilles, the right person to inherit and renovate Mowbray Castle, and to use the power that goes with it'.[69] I agree, yet Fletcher doesn't address the female legacy that has enabled Emmeline's proper inheritance. Indeed, Emmeline transforms into a heroine of economic *interest* and success; she is allowed economic considerations to play a part in her marriage choice and her virtue is rewarded in the end. Smith politicises her heroine's position, creating a powerful fantasy of disinheriting the male domain of property ownership. Emmeline benefits from the fact that her cousin Delamere, the last owner of the castle, dies in a duel and that legal documents surface proving her parents' marriage and Emmeline's inheritance of the castle and estate. In certain ways, the Mowbray surname in fact empowers Emmeline. Casually bestowed upon the orphan, it becomes the moniker of the estate: she symbolises Mowbray Castle and is its proper owner. What happens to the Delamere name that was so critical to previous owners of the castle? It dissolves off the page with the death of her cousin. In the end Emmeline marries William Godolphin, and both retain their inherited homes. In fact, Godolphin retains his surname and lives with Emmeline at Mowbray Castle, which we may assume is now his property. And despite the efforts of Emmeline's father and uncle, in the end no one bears the name Mowbray and the line dies out. The castle stands alone as the symbolic reminder of the Mowbray lineage.

Novels such as Charlotte Smith's *The Old Manor House* and *Emmeline*, and Frances Burney's *Cecilia* trouble the practice of female inheritance through wills that stipulate particular beneficiaries (as well as their future spouses) maintain their surnames. Obviously, these stipulations and clauses in wills reinforce patriarchal power and economic control, as Spring attests, but I hope I have shown how they can also provide females forms of independence (a possibility Spring never engages with). In their novels Smith and Burney explore the positive ways

[67] Smith (2002) 476.
[68] For more on the role of women bequesting to other women, see Zigarovich (2023).
[69] Fletcher (2003) 22.

in which female beneficiaries under the name clause are allotted paths of choice and agency. In this light, Cecilia is empowered from the inheritance and the name clause; she needn't rely on marriage for financial support and she continues to independently support charities of her choosing.

IV. Conclusion

Clearly, Cecilia is financially harmed by the name and arms clause in her uncle's will, but in my reading these fictional instances of female marriage choice also signal forms of independence and autonomy. Do the novel's readers wish that Mortimer Delvile's ego not interfere in his future wife's disinheritance? That he value her living conditions and financial protection enough to not see the clause as 'repulsive', but instead as an opportunity for his wife to prosper and grow? Yes, of course. It is apparent that these troubling fictional moments represent the growing concerns over women's financial independence and power in the period. The late eighteenth century will witness a decline of the heiress for this same reason. But during this period, the relationships between surnames and women also witnessed flexibility. Women sometimes retained their birth names after marriage. Men could adopt the surnames of their wives if they were beneficiaries. Inheriting women could pass their surnames instead of their husbands' on to their children. Anthony remarks that 'surname usage is a reflection of women's rights more generally, especially with property and inheritance rights, and as those rights disappeared, so did their names'.[70] I agree, but I also believe that in the eighteenth century those rights were, yes, stifled but not extinguished. The curious instance of name clauses in the novel reflects how the law interacts with society, culture, and tradition, and in my view, this fascinating history also reflects the potential for women to be stewards of wealth and property, even of titles and peerages. Surnameless women abound as titles for novels in the period (*Clarissa*, *Pamela*, *Evelina*, *Amelia*, *Henrietta*, *Emma* to name just a few). Maybe we can see this not as representing their lack of identity, or their single-status as they look to marry and acquire their husbands' surnames, but as symbols of their own potential for identity-making. And with this, I hope perhaps a brighter view of Emmeline Mowbray's and Cecilia Beverley's fates can be envisioned.

References

Anon, *Critical Review* 54 (December 1782) 414.

Anthony, D, 'In the Name of the Father': Compulsion, Tradition, and Law in the Lost History of Women's Surnames' (2014) 25 *The Journal Jurisprudence* 59.

[70] Anthony (2014) 92.

—— 'Analyzing the Disappearance of Women's Surnames and the Retrenchment of Their Political-Legal Status in Early Modern England' (2018) 29 *Hastings Women's Law Journal* 7.
—— 'Eradicating Women's Surnames' (2018) 37 *Columbia Journal of Gender and Law* 1.
Austen, J, *Emma* (New York, WW Norton, 1993).
Burney, F, *Cecilia, or Memoirs of an Heiress* (P Sabor and MA Doody, eds) (Oxford, Oxford University Press, 1999).
Cannon, J, *Aristocratic Century* (Cambridge, Cambridge University Press, 1988).
Cope, V, *Property, Education, and Identity in Late Eighteenth-Century Fiction: The Heroine of Disinterest* (New York, Palgrave Macmillan, 2009).
Critical Review (December 1782) 54, 414.
Crump, J (ed), *A Known Scribbler: Frances Burney on Literary Life* (Peterborough, Broadview, 2002).
Edmonstone, A, *Disposition and tailzie, by Archibald Edmonstone of Duntreath, to Archibald Edmonstone, his eldest son* (Edinburgh, 1769).
Doody, MA, *Frances Burney: The Life in the Works* (Cambridge, Cambridge University Press, 1989).
—— *Cecilia, or Memoirs of an Heiress* (P Sabor and MA Doody, eds) (Oxford, Oxford University Press, 1999). Introduction, xi–xxxix.
—— *Jane Austen's Names: Riddles, Persons, Places* (Chicago, University of Chicago Press, 2015).
Dundas, Ch et al, *Information for William, Charles, Margaret, [and other] Dundases, children procreate of the marriage betwixt Sir Thomas Dundas ... and Lady Charlotte Fitzwilliam ... and the trustees of the said children, and Robert Bruce, Esq, of Kennet [and others] ... defenders; against Sir Thomas Dundas of Kerse, Baronet, pursuer* (1783).
The English Reports (United Kingdom, W Green, 1901).
Erickson, AL, *Women and Property in Early Modern England* (New York, Routledge, 1993).
Fletcher, L, *Charlotte Smith: A Critical Biography* (London, Macmillan, 1998).
—— Charlotte Smith, *Emmeline, The Orphan of the Castle* (Peterborough, Broadview Press, 2003) Introduction.
Ganz, M (2013) 'Clandestine Schemes: Burney's *Cecilia* and the Marriage Act' (2013) 54 *The Eighteenth Century: Theory and Interpretation* 25.
Gibson, WT, '"Withered Branches and Weighty Symbols": Surname Substitution in England, 1660–1880' (1992) 15 *British Journal of Eighteenth-Century Studies* 17.
Guinchard, A, 'Is the Name Property? Comparing the English and the French Evolution' (2008) 1 *Journal of Civil Law Studies* 21.
Journals of the House of Lords 14 GEO III (HM Stationery Office, 1774).
—— 16 GEO III (HM Stationery Office, 1774).
König, E (2014) *The Orphan in Eighteenth-Century Fiction: The Vicissitudes of the Eighteenth-Century Subject* (Houndmills, Basingstoke, Palgrave Macmillan).
Labbe, JM, Charlotte Smith, *The Old Manor House* (Peterborough, Broadview, 2002) Introduction, 9–29.
Lambert, S, *Bills and Acts* (Cambridge, University of Cambridge Press, 1971).
Nixon, CL, *The Orphan in Eighteenth-Century Law and Literature: Estate, Blood, and the Body* (New York, Routledge, 2011).
Reports of Cases Argued and Adjudged in the Court of the King's Bench, During the Time of Lord Mansfield's Presiding in that Court (1794) Vol 4, 1929–44.
Smith, C, *The Old Manor House* (Peterborough, Broadview Press, 2002).
—— *Emmeline, The Orphan of the Castle* (Peterborough, Broadview Press, 2003).

Spring, E, *Law, Land, and Family: Aristocratic Inheritance in England, 1300 to 1800* (Chapel Hill, The University of North Carolina Press, 1993).
Squibb JD, 'The End of the Name and Arms Clause?' (1953) 69 *The Law Quarterly Review* 219–25.
Stone, L and Stone JF, *An Open Elite? England 1540–1880* (Oxford, Oxford University Press, 1984).
Stone, OM, 'Name Worship and Statutory Interpretation in the Law of Wills' (1963) 26 *The Modern Law Review* 652.
Straub, K, *Divided Fictions: Fanny Burney and Feminine Strategy* (Lexington, University Press of Kentucky, 1987).
Whan, R, *Presbyterians of Ulster, 1680–1730* (Suffolk, Boydell Press, 2013).
Zigarovich, J, 'Matriarchal Economies: Women Inheriting from Women in Eighteenth-Century Wills, Courts, and Fiction' (2023) 52 *Studies in Eighteenth-Century Culture* 227.
Zionkowski, L, *Women and Gift Exchange in Eighteenth-Century Fiction: Richardson, Burney, Austen* (New York, Routledge, 2016).

6

Murder, Inheritance and Family Provision in the Golden Age of English Detective Fiction

REBECCA PROBERT

I. Introduction

Within the 'Golden Age' of English detective fiction in the 1920s and 1930s,[1] it is common to find murders being committed for the purpose of securing an inheritance.[2] Moreover, the inevitable suspicion that falls on any persons who might benefit financially from the murder, particularly where the victim was wealthy, means that discussions of inheritance loom large even where the inheritance motive was a red herring. Those investigating the murder will almost inevitably be involved in scrutinising wills and codicils, or, in the rare cases where the victim did not leave a will, seeking to ascertain who stands to benefit under the intestacy rules. As a result, the detective fiction of this period provides an ideal lens through which to examine ideas about inheritance and the law.

This period also merits particular attention because of the two key changes to the law that occurred during this time. The Administration of Estates Act 1925 revised and simplified the rules that operated when an individual died intestate. Thirteen years later, the Inheritance (Family Provision) Act 1938 addressed the rules governing testate succession, allowing certain key family members the option of claiming financial provision from the estate of the deceased.

This chapter will focus on how these changes (and the accompanying debates) were reflected in the detective novels published by two of the leading writers of detective fiction from this period, Dorothy L Sayers and Agatha Christie. Quite

[1] For discussion of the 1920s and 1930s as the 'Golden Age' of this genre see Symonds (1972) and Worsley (2013).

[2] See eg Edwards (2015) 7. The term 'inheritance' is here used in its everyday meaning of succession to any assets on the death of another rather than to refer to the rules that governed succession to land before 1926 (on which see Baker (2019) 288.

apart from their reputation in this field, three considerations determined the choice of these two women. Both were writing detective fiction across the 1920s and 1930s.[3] Both constructed a number of plots in which inheritance and issues of provision for family and dependants played a key role. And both, as this chapter will show, were clearly aware of the changes to the law in this area. Sayers made the 1925 reforms the lynchpin of her 1927 novel *Unnatural Death*, while Christie included more veiled allusions to the debates over what became the 1938 Act in *Dumb Witness* and *Appointment with Death*, published in 1937 and 1938 respectively.

Section II of the chapter examines the salience of inheritance as a motive for murder in the detective novels that Sayers and Christie wrote in this period, and how Christie in particular puts family relationships under the spotlight.[4] Section III turns to the passage of the Administration of Estates Act 1925 and how Sayers and Christie both in different ways raise questions about the changes it effected. As section IV will show, the 1925 changes to the default rules also raised questions about whether those who stood to inherit automatically in the absence of a will should be protected against disinheritance in the event of a will being made and, if so, how such protection should be afforded. The novels that Christie published in this period amply illustrate the difficulty of devising a solution, with a particularly high proportion of novels featuring a spouse as a murderer. Section V considers the limitations of the Inheritance (Family Provision) Act 1938, and how these are reflected in Christie's final novel from the period, *Hercule Poirot's Christmas*.

II. The Salience of Inheritance as a Motive for Murder

Both Sayers and Christie regularly feature murders being committed to secure an inheritance, whether directly or indirectly. Some are straightforward in that the murder is committed by someone who believes that they stand to benefit under the victim's will[5] or who will inherit from them under the intestacy rules.[6] In other cases the exact mechanism by which the murderer stands to benefit is left

[3] Christie's first novel was published in 1921 and Sayers' in 1923. The two women often grouped with them as the 'Queens of Crime', Margery Allingham and Ngaio Marsh, did not begin writing detective fiction until a little later, with Allingham's *The Crime at Black Dudley* being published in 1929 and Marsh's *A Man Lay Dead* in 1934.

[4] Collections of short stories have been excluded from analysis for present purposes. While a number do feature inheritance plots (see eg 'The House of Lurking Death' in Christie's *Partners in Crime* and 'Absolutely Elsewhere' in Sayers' *In the Teeth of the Evidence*), the short-story format means that the family dynamics underpinning the murder are less well developed.

[5] See Christie's *The Mysterious Affair At Styles* (1921), *Murder at the Vicarage* (1930) and *Dumb Witness* (1937). *Why Didn't They Ask Evans?* (1933) also features a complex inheritance plot in which a will is forged and the supposed testator murdered.

[6] See Sayers' *Unnatural Death* (1927) and Christie's *Death on the Nile* (1937).

unspecified, but the closeness of the relationship between them and the victim makes it plausible that it could be either under a will or the intestacy rules, or possibly even as a result of an earlier settlement.[7] Other murders are committed to remove the person who stands in the way of the murderer benefiting from a third party,[8] or by someone who is planning to marry the person who they believe will inherit from the victim.[9]

There are, however, significant differences between Sayers and Christie in terms of how they depict the relationship between the victim and the murderer. Sayers' murderers are rarely drawn from the immediate family circle of the victim. The murderers in *The Unpleasantness at the Bellona Club* (1928) and *Busman's Honeymoon* (1937) are not related to their victims: they do not stand to inherit directly but were planning to marry the main beneficiary under the will. In *Have His Carcase* (1932) the situation is reversed, with the victim being a young man who was planning to marry the murderer's wealthy mother.[10] Only in *Strong Poison* (1930) and *Unnatural Death* (1927) are the murderer and their victim related, and even then the relationship is relatively remote: in the former they are cousins, while the latter features a great-niece who is caring for her great-aunt. Within Christie's novels, by contrast, the person who commits a murder for the sake of an inheritance[11] is more likely to be a spouse or close relative. While she also uses the plot device of the murderer who is planning to marry the beneficiary in both *The Murder on the Links* (1923) and *Death in the Clouds* (1935), in the latter the murderer goes on to murder the beneficiary once he has married her. Murders by spouses also feature in *The Mysterious Affair at Styles* (1921), *Murder at the Vicarage* (1930), and *Death on the Nile* (1937). *Why Didn't They Ask Evans?* (1934) and *The A.B.C. Murders* (1936) both feature the murder of a brother, while in *Dumb Witness* (1937) a niece kills her aunt. Even more horrifyingly in *Why Didn't They Ask Evans* the murderer also brings about the death of a young child, his own nephew.

In addition, Sayers rarely shows us the victim alive, preferring to adopt the convention of the dramatic discovery of the body in the opening chapters or beginning the narrative at a later stage in the proceedings. The perspective she

[7] See Christie's *The A.B.C. Murders* (1936). There is also a sub-plot in *Why Didn't They Ask Evans?* in which a man murders his brother and nephew in order to inherit the family estate.

[8] See Sayers' *Strong Poison* (1930) and *Have His Carcase* (1932).

[9] See Christie's *The Murder on the Links* (1923) and *Death in the Clouds* (1935), and Sayers' *The Unpleasantness at the Bellona Club* (1928) and *Busman's Honeymoon* (1937). Christie's *Peril at End House* (1932) provides yet another variation: the murderer is planning to pass as the fiancée of a wealthy man who has recently died in an accident and so kills the true fiancée, who shares her name.

[10] The inheritance motive is made clear when the mother explains how she had planned to make a will in favour of her new husband once they were married, which would have resulted in him receiving around £100,000 – the equivalent of £7.5 million today – while her son would receive only a life interest in £30,000: Sayers (1930) 222.

[11] Or indeed for any other reason: the victim in *Murder in Mesopotamia* is also murdered by her husband, while in *Lord Edgware Dies* the murder is committed by Lord Edgware's wife.

offers is that of those investigating the murder rather than those under investigation. In *The Unpleasantness at the Bellona Club* (1928), for example, the two brothers who are potential suspects are never seen together, only through their meetings with Lord Peter Wimsey, Sayers' amateur sleuth who is investigating the murder. Christie, by contrast, tends to introduce a cast of characters and allow the reader an insight into the relationships between them before the murder is committed. In many cases the perspective she offers switches between characters, showing how the family and dependants of the deceased come under suspicion as potential murderers from each other as well as from those investigating the case.

Alison Light sees Christie as disrupting idealised images of the family, noting that 'In the process of a murder inquiry every member of the family can be found guilty of having it in for someone else, of being at heart a potential murderer'.[12] Yet although Christie depicts murders by spouses and close relations, and takes the reader into the heart of the family during the process, it is striking that none of her novels revolve around a nuclear family consisting solely of two parents and their biological children. Even where it is a spouse who commits the murder, the marriage is invariably childless. Christie's households often contain stepchildren and in-laws: that of Roger Ackroyd, for example, includes his sister-in-law and niece as well as his stepson, while, in *The Mysterious Affair at Styles* (1921), Styles Court contains Emily Inglethorp and her new (and much younger) husband, her two stepsons from her first marriage (one of whom is himself married), her orphaned protegée who was the daughter of an old schoolfriend, and her companion-secretary (who turns out to be the lover of Emily's husband). While Light comments that 'we are asked to take it for granted that members of a family will be at each other's throats, squabbling and often petty',[13] the reader need not have an unduly jaundiced view of family life to be unsurprised by the tensions within *this* family.

It is of course unsurprising that Christie is not presenting an idealised version of the family: she is, after all, setting the scene for a murder. Even if – or perhaps especially if – many murders were, in real life, committed within the family circle, it was more less threatening to read about ones in which the family was clearly untypical and dysfunctional. But such families are also the ones that pose particularly difficult questions for the law of inheritance, as the following sections will show. This was particularly true in the context of the default rules that applied upon intestacy.

III. Intestacy and Assumed Intentions

Throughout the 1920s and 1930s, it was the rules that applied on intestacy that determined the division of the estate in the vast majority of cases. Just 15 per cent

[12] Light (1991) 92.
[13] ibid, 67.

of adults who died in 1910 left a will.[14] By 1922 this had risen only slightly, to around 18.6 per cent, and even by 1938 it was still only 22.7 per cent.[15] Admittedly, many of those who died intestate would have had little to leave: grants of probate outnumbered letters of administration by roughly two to one. And many of the wealthiest members of society would have made lifetime transfers in an attempt to reduce future death duties,[16] or would only have had a lifetime interest under a settlement.[17] Even so, the default rules were still of considerable importance to the majority of the population.

Prior to 1926, there were different rules for real and personal property in the event of an individual dying intestate. Real property would pass to the person identified as the heir under the common-law rules of descent. Gender and birth order determined who inherited: a son (or his issue) would be favoured over a daughter, and the eldest son over any younger ones.[18] Personal property would be divided between the spouse and children, or, in the absence of issue, to the next of kin.

These default rules could of course be displaced by the making of a will. Nonetheless, they still shaped expectations about how assets would – and should – be divided. The tensions within the family depicted in Christie's first novel, *The Mysterious Affairs At Styles* (1921), are generated at least in part by a sense of resentment about the will made by Mr Cavendish. His decision to leave Styles Court – and the larger part of his income – to his second wife, Emily, for her lifetime is described by the narrator, Captain Hastings, as 'distinctly unfair' to his two sons from his first marriage.[19] As the elder of the two sons later tells him, Styles Court 'should be mine now by rights, if my father had only made a decent will'.[20] The younger son, too, will only inherit the money that his father has left to him upon Emily's death. While it is going too far to suggest that these arrangements lead to Emily's eventual murder,[21] they create an atmosphere in which the reader can believe that almost any member of the household would have taken the life that stands between them and their 'rights'.

[14] Cornish et al (2010) 10.

[15] The figures were calculated by comparing the number of deaths recorded each year with the number of grants of probate: see respectively ONS, 'The 20th Century Mortality Files' (1921–1930 ICD3 and 1931–1940 ICD4) and 'Judicial Statistics, Civil (England & Wales)' for 1922 and 1938.

[16] Death duties were raised to 40% in 1919: see Cornish et al (2019) 173.

[17] Although the Settled Land Act 1882 had given the tenant for life increased powers to lease, mortgage or sell the land: Cornish et al (2019) 171.

[18] Baker (2019) 286–88.

[19] Christie (1921) 2. Whether the reader is meant to share this view is another matter: given that the house in question was purchased by Mr Cavendish during his second marriage, it does not seem unreasonable to give his wife the right to live there rather than leaving her dependent on the goodwill of her stepson. Even in the 21st century, though, there remains little support for leaving the entirety of the estate to a second wife if there are children from an earlier marriage: Law Commission (2011) 44.

[20] Christie (1921) 16.

[21] *cf* Bright (2022) 237, who suggests that 'if the family were aristocrats, John Cavendish would be his father's heir, and his stepmother a dependent, so the fortune-hunter Inglethorpe would not have conspired to marry, and murder, her'. Since Emily has only a life interest in Styles Court, it cannot pass to her new husband upon her death. She is, however, independently wealthy, as well as having inherited some money from her first husband that she is free to leave to whomsoever she chooses.

But with the passage of the Administration of Estates Act 1925, the default rules changed dramatically.[22] Real and personal property were brought under a common set of rules that recognised the surviving spouse and treated other classes of relatives equally regardless of birth order or sex. In all cases the surviving spouse was to receive the personal chattels of the deceased together with the first £1,000 of the residuary estate.[23] In most cases, of course, this sum would far exceed the value of the estate and so no one other than the spouse would be entitled to anything. Where the estate exceeded this sum, what else a spouse might receive depended on which other relatives had survived the deceased: if the deceased had left issue, the spouse was entitled to a life interest in half of the remaining residuary estate, with the issue sharing the remainder equally. In the absence of issue, the spouse was entitled to a life interest in the entirety of the residuary estate if the deceased had left any other relatives within the classes set out in the statute,[24] and to the entirety of the residuary estate in the absence of any such relatives. In the absence of a spouse then the estate was held on trust for the issue of the intestate, or, in the absence of issue, for the relatives within the classes set out in the statute. In the absence of a spouse, issue or any relatives within the class listed, the residuary estate was classified as *bona vacantia*.[25]

The new rules were generally seen as much fairer than the old ones. As one barrister noted, intestate estates would henceforth be 'distributed in a manner far more in accordance with modern ideas of justice than under the rules hitherto prevailing'.[26] The gender neutrality of the new rules – which reflected other post-war developments in women's rights – was particularly welcomed.[27] Another commentator expressed the view that the new rules provided 'a very reasonable distribution of property for those who do not make wills', and would in most cases operate fairly as between the surviving spouse and other members of the family.[28] But both Sayers' *Unnatural Death*, published in 1927, and Christie's *The Mystery of the Blue Train*, published in 1928, raise questions about the application of the new default rules, the former directly and the latter more obliquely.

Unnatural Death is probably unique in English literature in investing the line 'isn't there a new Property Act?' with a sense of urgency and excitement.[29] Indeed, the Administration of Estates Act 1925, and its impact on the claims of remoter relatives, is the lynchpin of the plot. The scenario is that Mary Whittaker has been caring for her elderly great-aunt Agatha for a number of years. Agatha, who is predicted to have only a few months to live, has not made a will, partly because she

[22] Mortimer and Coates (1927) 284.
[23] Administration of Estates Act 1925, s 46(1)(i).
[24] In order: parents, siblings of the full blood, siblings of the half blood, grandparents, uncles and aunts of the full blood, and uncles and aunts of the half blood.
[25] Administration of Estates Act 1925, s 46(1)(vi).
[26] 'The New Law About Wills: By A King's Counsel' *Daily Mail* (13 August 1925).
[27] For an insight into the range of equality measures in this period see Rackley and Auchmuty (2018).
[28] 'Will-making in 1926: By A Solicitor' *Daily Mail* (29 December 1925).
[29] Sayers (1927) 162.

is unwilling to contemplate her impending death and partly because she assumes that Mary will inherit automatically under the intestacy rules as her next of kin. However, Mary, having learnt of the provisions of the 1925 Act, believes that there is a possibility that she will no longer be entitled to inherit once it comes into force and so takes steps to ensure that Agatha dies before its commencement date of 1 January 1926. Since the murder method is sufficiently subtle to escape detection, and Agatha's death was not unexpected, it initially seems as if Mary will get away with it. Even when the doctor voices his suspicions to Wimsey, there seems no obvious motive for Mary to have murdered a dying woman to inherit her estate a few months earlier than she would otherwise have done. Only when Wimsey recalls reading a newspaper account of the 1925 Act explaining how it would curtail the claims of remoter relatives does a motive for murder present itself.

Of course, a great-niece in Mary's position, as the only surviving relative, *would* still have been entitled to the estate under the reformed intestacy laws.[30] But the Act could have been more clearly drafted; some contemporary accounts reflected a degree of confusion about the effect of the new law,[31] and it is thus entirely plausible that an individual in the position of Mary Whittaker might not want to run the risk of the estate going to the Crown. The property lawyer Robert Megarry was perhaps unduly unkind in his assessment of the novel in griping that 'Modern novels into which the law intrudes usually make lawyers wish that the law had kept out',[32] since Sayers' characters do acknowledge the possibility that the term 'issue' in the new Act will encompass a great-niece.

What Sayers does show very clearly is the impact of changing long-settled expectations about how the law would and should operate. As Agatha's lawyer explains to Wimsey, one of the reasons why she had been so resolute in her refusal to make a will was because she would not believe that the law could be changed in the way proposed, or that any court would be so 'wicked' as to interpret the new legislation in such a way as to give the money to anybody other than her great-niece, 'when she was clearly the proper person to have it'.[33] While there is humour in Agatha demanding why the Duchy of Lancaster should have any right to it – as she tells her lawyer, 'I don't even know the Duke of Lancaster' – there is also a serious point here. As John Orth points out, the intestacy rules are intended

[30] By virtue of s 47 of the Administration of Estates Act 1925, which provides that the issue of the relatives listed in s 46 will take the share that their parent would have taken if living. See also Mortimer and Coates (1927) 890, which clarifies that a great-niece (or nephew) is included as the issue of a brother or sister.

[31] See eg 'Lawyers Return to School to Learn Intricate New Act' *Daily Mail* (17 November 1925), which claimed that in default of any relatives closer than first cousins the property would go to the Crown. A few years later there was an exchange in the letters page of *The Times* in which one correspondent claimed that a first cousin would be barred from inheriting under the new law, only to be corrected a few days later by a practitioner 'New Law of Intestacy' *The Times* (8 February 1930; 22 February 1930).

[32] Megarry (1944) 102.

[33] Sayers (1927) 196.

at least in part to reflect the assumed intentions of the ordinary individual, and 'Few testators ... choose the state government as their ultimate devisee'.[34]

Christie's *The Mystery of the Blue Train* (1928) by contrast, obliquely questions the newly privileged position of the spouse under the reformed intestacy rules. In the opening chapters we learn that the wealthy Ruth Kettering is contemplating a divorce from her unfaithful husband Derek. She has, however, taken no formal steps to this end. Nor has she made a will. Upon her subsequent murder, Derek accordingly benefits 'to the tune of a couple of millions', as Ruth's father grimly informs Poirot.[35] While there is a strong suspicion that Derek is guilty of Ruth's murder, this is a typical red herring and his innocence is eventually established.

As a result, however, the novel opens up questions about the automatic entitlement of a spouse under the intestacy rules that would not have arisen if he *had* been the murderer: found to be guilty, he would forfeit the estate (and his life); innocent, he gets to enjoy it despite the unlikelihood of his estranged wife having wanted him to benefit. And there are a number of factors, quite apart from his infidelity, that raise questions as to the justice of him inheriting her money. First, that money was not generated during the marriage but was given to Ruth by her father Rufus at the time of her marriage. Given that Rufus is still alive, justice might suggest that the money should return to him.[36] Second, Derek is upfront about the fact that he only married Ruth for her money. And, third, by the end of the novel he has fallen in love with, and is planning to marry, another woman. Any one of these factors by itself might call into question the fairness of a spouse being privileged over other family members; combined, they make a powerful case against it.

In other words, even if the intestacy rules operated well in most cases, there would inevitably be ones where they caused a perception of injustice.[37] But as the next section will discuss, there was also concern that the intestacy rules could be displaced – and close family disinherited – by the making of a will.

IV. Freedom of Testation, and the Campaign for Reform

Although the 1925 Act assumed that an individual would want their spouse and children to inherit in the event of their death, it imposed no obligation to make any provision for them at all.[38] It remained open to any adult of sound mind to displace

[34] Orth (2013) 324.

[35] Christie (1928) 134.

[36] Christie does not allude to the fact that the intestacy rules only give Derek a life interest in Ruth's estate, with the remainder passing to Rufus (Administration of Estates Act 1925, s 46(1)(i)(a) and (iv)) but that would be of scant comfort to the latter, given the age difference and the unlikelihood of him outliving Derek.

[37] See also 'Will-making in 1926: By A Solicitor' *Daily Mail* (29 December 1925), noting that privileging the surviving spouse might not produce a fair outcome where the estate was small and the deceased had children from a previous marriage, since the new spouse 'takes everything and may send her step-children to the workhouse'.

[38] *cf* Frank (2010) 218–19, who wrongly claims that the 1925 Act brought 'freedom from the testator's potential caprices or mercurial moods'.

these default rules by making a will in whatever terms they chose, however unfair or unjust to their family and those who were dependent on them.

In the late 1920s a campaign to curtail the freedom of an individual to disinherit their family was instigated by the National Union of Societies for Equal Citizenship (NUSEC). This organisation had previously been known as the National Union of Women's Suffrage Societies but after (some) women had been granted the vote in 1918 it 'renamed itself in order to expand its remit to cover a wide range of political, social and economic rights for women'.[39] As it recognised, the question of whether an individual should have any responsibility to make provision for their spouse in the event of their death was linked to the issue of how assets were owned during the marriage. The campaigns of the late nineteenth century had succeeded in establishing the principle of separate ownership of property during marriage and the right of wives to deal with their property as they wished, but such changes had made very little difference to the many wives who had no assets of their own and did not work outside the home.[40] For such a wife, the ability to make a will in whatever terms she wished was of little value when set against the fact that her husband could decide to make a will leaving her nothing.

At the behest of NUSEC,[41] Viscount Astor put forward a motion in the House of Lords asking for a Select Committee to be appointed 'to see whether a change is necessary in the laws governing testamentary provision for wives, husbands and children'.[42] As well as giving a number of examples of wives and children who had been disinherited, he drew attention to the changes in the law that applied upon intestacy, noting how in this context Parliament 'had decided that it was right to make more generous provision for the spouse and children of those owners of property who might die intestate'.[43] In the debate that followed, however, expressions of sympathy for cases of hardship were tempered by a strong sense that the issues were complex and that individuals, rather than courts, might be best placed to determine what provision should be made for their family.[44]

While the motion was withdrawn, the reformers persisted. Private members' bills were brought forward in 1928, 1929 and 1930,[45] and were welcomed in the press as restraining individuals' power to make capricious and unjust wills.[46]

[39] Hamilton (2022) 215.

[40] For discussion of this point see further Thompson (2022) ch 2.

[41] Cretney (2003) 486.

[42] *Hansard*, HL Deb, Vol 71, cols 37–38 (16 May 1928).

[43] ibid, col 41. The *Daily Mail* similarly drew attention to the provision made for the widow under the intestacy rules and the possibility of a husband making a will that disinherited her entirely: 'The Widow's Inheritance' *Daily Mail* (17 May 1928).

[44] For analysis of the debates see Hedlund (2021).

[45] Each bore the same title: the Wills and Intestacies (Family Maintenance) Bill.

[46] 'Capricious Wills: Lord Astor's Measure to Protect Dependents' *Daily Mail* (10 August 1928); 'Testators' Families: Lord Astor's Bill to Defeat Unreasonable Wills' *The Times* (10 August 1928); 'Unjust Wills: What Lord Astor's Bill Would Do' *Daily Mail* (18 August 1928); 'Cut Off By The Dead: Lord Astor's Move Against Unjust Wills' *Daily Mail* (8 November 1928); 'Capricious Wills: Lord Astor's Proposed Reforms' *The Times* (16 March 1929).

Although the first two bills failed to progress beyond a first reading,[47] the third, introduced by Eleanor Rathbone MP,[48] had sufficient support to be referred to a Joint Select Committee.[49] Despite the Committee rejecting the solution put forward in Rathbone's bill – which had been modelled on the intestacy provisions – it did express the view that it was 'wrong' that a surviving spouse or child should be left without adequate means of support, and advocated that some mechanism should be devised whereby a dependent spouse or child could apply for provision from the court.[50] The Powers of Disinheritance Bill 1934 subsequently proposed that the court should have an absolute discretion to make provision for a surviving spouse or (legitimate) child left without 'adequate provision for his or her property maintenance, education or advancement in life'.[51] Again, this was widely discussed in the press. In a letter to the *Manchester Guardian* at the time that the Bill was due to be debated, Marjorie Green, the Secretary of what was now the National Council for Equal Citizenship, commented that while most men and women were 'only too anxious that their dependents should be properly provided for after their death', the 'number of widows (more rarely widowers) and children who suffer under capricious and vindictive wills, although small in proportion to the whole, is actually considerable'.[52]

In her earlier novels, Christie had depicted a number of capricious and controlling individuals and the constant risk of being disinherited. In *The Mysterious Affair At Styles* (1921), for example, it is reported that the wealthy Emily Inglethorp had generally made a new will at least once a year. As her lawyer tells Poirot, she 'was given to changing her mind as to her testamentary dispositions, now benefiting one, now another member of her family'.[53] The murdered Roger Ackroyd is even more blatant in using his wealth to control his family, arranging a marriage between his stepson and niece. As Poirot later notes, 'Roger Ackroyd dictated his wishes – they agreed to them'.[54] And *Murder on the Links* depicts a son being disinherited by his (multi-millionaire) father, an action that various characters agree is unfair.[55]

[47] Wills and Intestacies (Family Maintenance) Bill 1928, *Hansard*, HL Deb, Vol 71, col 1540 (1 August 1928); Wills and Intestacies (Family Maintenance) Bill 1929, *Hansard*, HL Deb, Vol 73, col 85 (6 March 1929).

[48] Rathbone had served as President of NUSEC and was one of the prime movers behind the campaign to reform the law. The Bill also had the support of a number of other female MPs: 'Bill To Prevent Disinheritance: Woman MPs Unite' *Daily Mail* (16 February 1931).

[49] Wills and Intestacies (Family Maintenance) Bill 1930–31.

[50] 'Report by the Joint Select Committee of the House of Lords and the House of Commons appointed to consider the Wills and Intestacies (Family Maintenance) Bill and to Report to the House' (HC 127, 17 June 1931) para 7.

[51] Powers of Disinheritance Bill 1934, cl 1(1).

[52] 'Inheritance Bill: Capricious and Vindictive Wills' *The Observer* (23 April 1934). See also 'MPs Discuss Unjust Wills' *Daily Mail* (30 April 1934).

[53] Christie (1921) 73.

[54] Christie (1926) 257.

[55] Given that the novel is set in France, this would not in fact have been possible given the law there.

However, the novels that Christie published in the 1930s, against the backdrop of the debates about curtailing testamentary freedom, are distinctly ambiguous about the merits of mandatory provision for a spouse. In *Lord Edgware Dies*, Christie presents us with a wealthy man who has disinherited his wife, an act that Poirot describes as 'vindictive'.[56] But the novel is hardly a plea for a vulnerable and deserving spouse to have a right to provision: the wife has left her husband and resumed her career as a highly successful actress. She asks Poirot to persuade her husband to divorce her so that she can marry an even wealthier man. Moreover, although inheritance is not her motive, she nevertheless goes on to murder her husband. Indeed, it is striking just how many of Christie's novels from this period do feature a spouse as the murderer. *The Murder at the Vicarage* depicts a wife who plots with her lover to murder her husband. The fact that she stands to inherit a substantial sum under his will is a key factor here: as Miss Marple dryly notes, her lover 'is not the kind of young man who would dream of running away with a penniless woman'.[57] Murders by a husband who has deliberately entered into the marriage with the intention of killing his wife and inheriting her fortune feature in both *Death in the Clouds* and *Death on the Nile*.

An autobiographical reading of Christie might link this particular concentration of murderous spouses to her own divorce and remarriage.[58] But an alternative reading is that this was her oblique take on the debates taking place in Parliament and the press. Certainly in both *Dumb Witness* and *Appointment with Death* there are exchanges that closely echo the debates between those who championed the idea of protecting family members and those who favoured retaining freedom of testation. In *Dumb Witness*, the wealthy Emily Arundell has made a will in favour of her companion Minnie Lawson, disinheriting her nephew and two nieces. Upon her death a few weeks later, the terms of her will attract some comment locally, as the waiter at the local pub reports to Poirot, with some people taking the view that assets should not be left away from the family and others holding that the owner of property can dispose of it as they wish. While the scenario is at one remove from the debates in Parliament – no one was suggesting that nephews or nieces should have any claims to provision from the estate of an individual who had failed to make provision for them by will – these comments concisely distill the rival arguments that were being made. Similar points are made in *Appointment with Death*. Here the ability of the monstrous Mrs. Boynton to exercise absolute control over her daughter and step-children is enhanced by the fact that they are all financially dependent upon her, the deceased Mr Boynton having left his entire fortune to her for her lifetime. One character, the French Dr Gerard, is critical of the Mr Boynton's actions, commenting that in his country 'it is impossible by law to do such a thing'.[59] The American Mr Cope, however, defends Mr Boynton's decision

[56] Christie (1933) 158.
[57] Christie (1930) 280.
[58] Christie divorced her first husband in 1928 and married her second in 1930: Worsley (2022).
[59] Christie (1938a), 37.

on the basis that 'In America ... we're great believers in absolute freedom'.[60] Dr Gerard is unimpressed by this claim, musing to himself that 'no race, no country and no individual could be described as free', but that there are 'different degrees of bondage'.[61]

Dumb Witness is also deeply ambiguous as to the rival merits of freedom of testation and fixed expectations. The irony is that Emily, while exercising her freedom to change her will as she sees fit, has not achieved the result she intended. Her original will had left the bulk of her considerable estate to her nieces and nephew. Her decision to change it is not an act of malice or caprice but an attempt at self-preservation, as she suspects her nephew Charles of trying to murder her. The suspicion is not an unreasonable one: upon a weekend visit, he responded to Emily's refusal to give him more money by telling her that she was giving him a motive to 'bump her off', and that very same evening she tripped over something at top of the stairs and sustained a nasty fall. Having informed Charles of the fact that she has changed her will, she assumes that she will be safe from further attempts on her life. The new will is intended as a stop-gap rather than reflecting her real intentions: she has no particular affection for her companion Minnie, the new beneficiary, who has been with her only a short time. Unfortunately, the person who laid the booby-trap at the top of the stairs was in fact Emily's niece Bella, who is unaware that Emily has changed her will and who makes a second attempt on her life by poisoning her. Aware that she may be dying, Emily asks Minnie for her will. But Minnie – who knows that she is now the main beneficiary and is worried that Emily is going to destroy it – pretends that the will has been sent to the solicitor for safe-keeping. The upshot is that when Emily dies, the will in favour of Minnie takes effect. And the law, as the characters discover, offers no redress.[62]

Appointment with Death is also more ambiguous than it might at first appear in terms of the relationship between freedom of testation and the ability of individuals to exercise tyranny over their family and dependants. The reader is left in no doubt as to Mrs Boynton's love of power. She is a former prison wardress who 'loved tyranny',[63] unflatteringly described by Dr Gerard as 'a gross spider in the centre of the web'.[64] But her power is ultimately time-limited: after all, her husband has not left his fortune to her absolutely, only for her lifetime: his freedom constrained hers.

Both *Dumb Witness* and *Appointment with Death* would have been read against the backdrop of debates about reform. *Dumb Witness* appeared in July 1937, as a new bill was awaiting consideration in Parliament.[65] The publication of *Appointment*

[60] ibid. For discussion of the position in the US see Dainow (1940).

[61] ibid.

[62] With the discovery of the true facts (and the suicide of Bella) an extra-legal solution is found, with Minnie agreeing to share the estate with Emily's other niece, Bella's two children, and Charles.

[63] Christie (1938a) 41.

[64] ibid, 14.

[65] The Inheritance (Family Provision) Bill was introduced as a Private Member's Bill late in 1936: *Hansard*, HC Deb, Vol 317, col 39 (16 November 1936). By July 1937 it had had its second reading and been considered in Committee.

with Death, on 2 May 1938, coincided with its first reading in the House of Lords.[66] With government assistance,[67] this bill finally became law. But, as the final section will show, it was a more limited measure than had originally been envisaged.

V. The Limitations of the Inheritance (Family Provision) Act 1938

The Inheritance (Family Provision) Act 1938 eventually allowed a spouse, an unmarried daughter, or an infant or incapacitated son to challenge a will on the basis that it did not make reasonable provision for them. While limited in its terms,[68] it nonetheless marked an important change of principle, signalling that individuals (primarily husbands and fathers) had an obligation to provide for such dependants and that if they chose not to do so their wishes could be disregarded.

In the course of the earlier debates, Eleanor Rathbone had spoken passionately about the power that freedom of testation gave to bad or 'tyrannical' husbands and fathers.[69] As she pointed out, such 'thoroughly bad husbands', while a tiny minority, could 'hold the power of inheritance like a sword over the unfortunate wife's head'.[70] Yet while the 1938 Act reduced the power of individuals to use their wealth to dictate and control by means of threats of disinheritance, it did not eliminate it. And in *Hercule Poirot's Christmas*, published later in 1938, Christie gives us a picture of an individual who is fully aware of the power that his wealth gives him.

Simeon Lee, a self-made multi-millionaire, exercises a high degree of control over those within his household, with his daughter-in-law Lydia commenting that 'he expects us to behave like slaves'.[71] He also takes a malicious pleasure in tormenting his family through hints that he is going to change his will. Having invited all of his (known) family to Christmas under his roof, he deliberately arranges for them to overhear him telephoning his solicitor late on Christmas Eve, asking him to come over to make a new will for him to reflect the fact that circumstances have changed. He reassures the solicitor that it is not urgent and that he does not need to come over immediately, telling him that he doesn't want to spoil his Christmas. Of course, as several of the family recognise, his intention was very much to spoil *their* Christmas by creating uncertainty, doubt and mutual suspicion between the different members of his family about the terms of any new will.

Moreover, there is no one within his family who can take any comfort from the possibility of bringing a claim under the 1938 Act in the event of being

[66] *Hansard*, HL Deb, Vol 108, col 709 (2 May 1938).
[67] Cretney (2003) 493.
[68] For discussion of its limits see Probert (2014) and Douglas (2014).
[69] *Hansard*, HC Deb, Vol 319 col 528 (22 January 1937).
[70] *Hansard*, HC Deb Vol 288 col 2076 (27 April 1934).
[71] Christie (1938b) 17.

disinherited: his wife is dead, his daughter married before her own untimely death, and his sons are all adults. In the event, Simeon is murdered before he has the opportunity to change his will. The final twist is that the murder is committed by one of Simeon's illegitimate sons, who does not stand to benefit under the will and who was never acknowledged by him during his lifetime. As Poirot notes, 'A son born the wrong side of the blanket may inherit many things', including his father's features and his 'revengeful spirit'.[72] But that only served to underline how such children remained out in the cold legally, with limited rights upon intestacy or no right to claim provision from the estate.[73]

All this illustrates the limits of the new Act. And, as in *Dumb Witness*, Christie also questions the ability of the law to provide a fair solution. When faced with the question of whether provision should be made for their niece, the daughter of their dead sister, the family are divided between those who insist that 'the law is the law' and that they should abide by the terms of the will, and those who take the view that they have a moral responsibility beyond the law. In the event their willingness to share is not put to the test as the supposed niece admits that she is an imposter. But the message remains that generosity is more to be admired than adhering to one's legal entitlement.

VI. Conclusion

The question posed at the start of the chapter was how far the changes to inheritance law in the 1920s and 1930s were reflected in Sayers' and Christie's detective fiction. In the case of Sayers, the answer is a simple one: Sayers engaged directly with one of the key changes made by the 1925 Act and raised some difficult questions about the change in legal policy. In the case of Christie, the answer is more complex. In novel after novel there are oblique references to contemporary legal debates. Often they are so subtle that it is only when they are read against the context of the contemporary debates that their significance becomes clear.[74] She does not hold up a mirror to the debates but rather a prism that refracts them through multiple disturbing possibilities.

Wade has suggested that the detective fiction of the Golden Age 'promised order restored from chaos, justice delivered by a detective of apparent omniscience, and transgression punished'.[75] Almost all of the murderers depicted by Sayers

[72] Christie (1938b) 211.

[73] The Legitimacy Act 1926 had given illegitimate children the right to inherit from their mother if she died intestate and left no legitimate issue. Their right to inherit from their father, or to claim provision under the 1938 Act, was not established until the Family Law Reform Act 1969: Cretney (2003) 561–62.

[74] As Evans (2022) 255 notes in her chapter on law and justice in Christie's novels, 'Christie engaged so thoroughly and so frequently with her country's legal system and with the concept of justice that an entire volume approaching her work from a law and literature standpoint would be worthwhile'.

[75] Wade (2020) 116.

and Christie either die or are brought to justice, and none are able to enjoy their ill-gotten gains.[76] Nonetheless, the salience of inheritance within the detective fiction of the 1920s and 1930s provides a disturbing and distorting lens on family dynamics and the transmission of property. Ultimately, however the law was reformed, it could always provide someone with a motive for murder.

References

Baker, JH, *An Introduction to English Legal History*, 5th edn (Oxford: Oxford University Press, 2019).

Bright, B, 'House and Home: The Country House' in MA Evans and JC Bernthal (eds), *The Bloomsbury Handbook to Agatha Christie* (London, Bloomsbury Academic, 2022) 226–46.

Christie, A, *The Mysterious Affair At Styles* (London, HarperCollins Publishers, 1921, 2013).

—— *The Murder of Roger Ackroyd* London, HarperCollins Publishers, 1926, 2013).

—— *The Mystery of the Blue Train* (London, HarperCollins Publishers, 1928, 2015).

—— *The Murder at the Vicarage* (London, HarperCollins Publishers, 1930, 2016).

—— *Lord Edgware Dies* (London, HarperCollins Publishers, 1933, 2016).

—— *Appointment with Death* (London, Fontana Paperbacks, 1938a, 1988).

—— *Hercule Poirot's Christmas* (London, HarperCollins Publishers, 1938b).

Cornish, W, Anderson, S, Cocks, R, Lobban, M, Polden, P and Smith, K, *The Oxford History of the Laws of England: Vol XII* (Oxford, Oxford University Press, 2010).

Cornish, W, Banks, S, Mitchell, C, Mitchell, P and Probert, R, *Law and Society in England, 1750–1950* (Oxford, Hart, 2019).

Cretney, S, *Family Law in the Twentieth Century: A History* (Oxford, Oxford University Press, 2002).

Dainow, J, 'Limitations on Testamentary Freedom in England' (1940) 25 *Cornell Law Quarterly* 337.

Douglas, G, 'Family Provision and Family Practices – The Discretionary Regime of the Inheritance Act of England and Wales' (2014) 4 *Oñati Socio-Legal Series* 222.

Edwards, M, 'Introduction' to Charles Kingston, *Murder in Piccadilly* (London, The British Library, 2015).

Evans, MA, 'Agatha Christie, the Law, and Justice' in MA Evans and JC Bernthal (eds), *The Bloomsbury Handbook to Agatha Christie* (London, Bloomsbury Academic, 2022) 247–68.

Frank, CO, *Law, Literature and the Transmission of Culture in England, 1837–1925* (Farnham, Ashgate, 2010).

Guest, AG, 'Family Provision and the *Legitima Portio*' (1957) 73 *Law Quarterly Review* 74.

Hamilton, F, 'Equality Arguments, Contemporary Feminist Voices and the Matrimonial Causes Act 1923' (2022) 43 *Journal of Legal History* 210.

Hedlund, R, 'The end to testamentary freedom' (2021) 41 *Legal Studies* 55.

[76] A rare example of a murderer who escapes occurs in *Why Didn't They Ask Evans?* but his flight to South America means that he is unable to enjoy the family estate for which he brought about the deaths of his brother and nephew.

Law Commission, 'Intestacy and Family Provision Claims on Death', Law Com No 331 (TSO, 2011).
Light, A, *Forever England: femininity, literature and conservatism between the wars* (London, Routledge, 1991).
Megarry, RE, 'Review: The Just and the Unjust' (1944) 60 *Law Quarterly Review* 102.
Mortimer, C and Coates, HHH, *The Law and Practice of the Probate Division of the High Court of Justice*, 2nd edn (London, Sweet & Maxwell Ltd, 1927).
Orth, J, '"The Laughing Heir" – What's So Funny?' (2013) 48 *Real Property, Trust and Estate Law Journal* 321–26.
Probert, R, 'Freedom of testation in Victorian England' in A-J Zwierlein, K Boehm and A Farkas (eds), *Interdisciplinary Perspectives on Ageing in Nineteenth-Century Culture* (Abingdon, Routledge, 2014) 115–31.
—— 'Disquieting thoughts: who will benefit when we are gone?' in B Häcker and C Mitchell (eds), *Current Issues in Succession Law* (Oxford, Hart Publishing, 2016) 31–49.
Rackley, E and Auchmuty, R (eds), *Women's Legal Landmarks* (Oxford, Hart, 2018).
Sayers, DL, *Unnatural Death* (London, Hodder and Stoughton, 1927, 2003).
Symonds, J, *Bloody Murder: From the Detective Story to the Crime Novel* (London, Faber and Faber, 1972).
Thompson, S, *Quiet Revolutionaries: The Married Women's Association and Family Law* (Oxford, Hart, 2022).
Wade, F, *Square Haunting: Five Women, Freedom and London Between the Wars* (London, Faber & Faber, 2020).
Worsley, L, *A Very British Murder: The Story of a National Obsession* (London, BBC Books, 2013).
—— *Agatha Christie: A Very Elusive Woman* (London, Hodder & Stoughton, 2022).

PART 3

Resistance, Rights and Agency

7

The Story of the Pink Cat

An Exploration of the Ways Care-Experienced People Navigate Inheritance

DELYTH EDWARDS AND ROSIE CANNING

I. Introduction

Most people would be fairly confident in answering the question: *what does inheritance mean?* They would likely say that it involves 'passing something on' between family members. This would be understood as the distribution of assets: money, property, titles, important heirlooms or objects. In many respects, this is correct. Along with such tangible inheritance, people might also acknowledge more intangible forms of inheritance, such as genetic and cultural inheritances. But when asked: *what does inheritance mean to you?* some may struggle with relating this directly to their own experiences. This could be because they have not inherited anything in the shared understanding of passing on or receiving something. Inheritance is bound up with our heritage, our identities, our families and kinship. Whilst inheritance may be both tangible and intangible, *family* seems to be at the centre of current understandings of it. But, what if you are estranged from family? How does inheritance play out then?

'Care-experience' is the preferred term used to describe people who spent some or all of their childhoods in the care of a Local Authority, whether that be foster care, children's homes, residential care or kinship care. As Monk suggests, for 'those whose lives have been lived outside of traditional familial norms' – such as those with care-experience, as we argue in this chapter – 'inheritance takes on an added significance, partly because their lives are invisible in intestacy laws, which remain firmly rooted in blood and marital status'.[1] Families with care-experience are largely missing from inheritance research and narratives, yet care-experienced families have been engaging in inheritance practices for centuries. We know from the Foundling Token exhibition that between 'the 1740s and 1760s, mothers leaving

[1] Monk (2014) 24.

their babies at the Foundling Hospital would also leave a small object as a means of identification. The hope was that they would one day be able to reclaim their child'.[2] This ritual was a way of 'doing' and 'displaying' family, of sharing love and creating connection between mother and child. Inheritance for care-experienced people is firmly rooted to the journey of finding out who they are.

This chapter sets out to interrogate the practice(s) of inheritance from the viewpoint of families with care-experience, with the aim of instigating further research and for inheritance to be acknowledged in policy. Drawing on sociological theories of 'family practices',[3] it will first discuss what is known about inheritance and care-experience. It will then discuss the novel ways inheritance is practiced within care-experienced families, to show the ways that such families are (un)made and remade. Using our own examples as a care-experienced person (Rosie) and the daughter of a care-experienced mother (Delyth), we consider what is inherited, such as stories and identities through storytelling and the possession and creation of material objects of significance. In fact, the title of this chapter comes from Rosie's 'The Pink Cat', a story that Rosie shares later in this chapter which exemplifies the creativity of inheritance for care-experienced families. We wanted to explore the ways that other care-experienced people negotiate inheritance, so we reached out to ask others about their inheritance practices. Using Twitter and Facebook, we asked[4] the care-experienced community and our friends to share with us what inheritance means to them. We found that care-experienced people have actively had to fight unjust systems to get access to parts of their inheritance that have been hidden from them, lost or are simply the unknowns and absences that remain. Access to one's care file is a well-known example of care-experienced people trying to unearth their inheritance. A care file is a record that is kept by the Local Authority or agency in charge of the care of a child. Although the contents of a person's file vary, it usually contains information about the child's time in care (a record of the past) and also any information about the young person's family and their reasons for going into care. As adults, many care-experienced people request access to their care files in order to find out information about their lives. Edwards has noted that the Care Leavers Association (CLA)[5] in the UK 'has found that adults who try to retrieve their files experience a number of problems, including: their files being lost or damaged, files with numerous redactions (suggesting

[2] See the Foundling Museums Token exhibition: foundlingmuseum.org.uk/our-art-and-objects/foundling-collections/tokens.

[3] Morgan (2004) and (2011).

[4] In order to collate the views of other care-experienced people and families, we put out a question through our individual Twitter and Facebook accounts. We asked, for those followers who were happy to share, 'what does inheritance look like to you?'. We had several responses to our posts and we gained consent to share these stories and experiences in this chapter.

[5] The CLA is a UK-wide organisation run by care-experienced people aimed at improving the lives of care leavers of all ages. It fights continuously for the right for all care leavers to be able to access their memories.

that memories are still being managed by the institution); failures to respond to requests; people being told 'you can't have your file because it will damage you' and others being asked 'why you would even want the information' as though to suggest 'one should get over it'.[6] Therefore, we argue that inheritance has also become a site of activism for care-experienced people, who campaign for fairer and socially just access to the care files that contain information about their life. Ultimately, we conclude by arguing that inheritance, in all its forms, needs to be a right for care-experienced people.

II. Inheritance as a 'Family Practice'

Monk argues that 'inheritance, broadly understood, has long been the crux and almost the raison d'être of conventional, albeit subtly shifting, familial practices'[7] and has largely been examined through a legal lens of the processes surrounding death and the constructing and enacting of wills.[8] Sociologist David Morgan contends that a 'family practice' is a way of understanding families as what people *do* rather than as a static structure.[9] Seeing family as a practice allows us to foreground the mundane routines and habits through which we make sense of and produce and reproduce family as a set of relationships (bathing our children, making and eating dinner, celebrating Christmas are examples of such practices). To be an effective family practice, 'the actions which constitute family practices need to be linked in a sufficiently clear way with the "wider systems of meaning" … to enable them to be fully understood as such'.[10] Furthermore, 'an important part of the nurturing and development of relationships so that their "family-like" qualities are positively established' is through 'displaying' as well as 'doing' family.[11] This means individuals conveying to each other and for others that their practices and 'actions do constitute "doing family things" thereby' confirming 'that these relationships are "family" relationships'.[12]

Inheritance is part of this way of 'doing', 'making' and 'displaying' family. However, we have to be careful in our discussion of 'family' given the shifting meaning of what 'family' means.[13] If we accept inheritance as a 'family practice' we need to understand what family means for care-experienced people and

[6] Edwards (2017) 186.
[7] Monk (2014) 240.
[8] Monk (2016) 168.
[9] Morgan (2004) and (2011).
[10] Finch (2007) 67.
[11] ibid, 80.
[12] ibid, 67.
[13] Smart (2007).

how family practice is displayed. When researching this chapter, we found clear and plentiful information about the rights of children who were adopted, but inheritance rights for people not adopted is less straightforward.[14] For example, we found no information for adults whose care-experience was in foster care or children's homes. Adoption is an inheritance topic because it is an experience embedded in what is widely understood and accepted as the 'family', whereas other experiences of care are found to be peripheral in scholarly literature on inheritance. As Boddy[15] notes, the concept of family is troubling for care-experienced people. First, because it is a lived experience that traverses non-normative practices (such as having a birth and foster family that you spend time with) and normative practices (such as attending weddings or celebrating important holidays), family is something that is 'negotiated and practiced across time and in multiple (and changing) care contexts'.[16] Second, despite recognition of the shift from family to personal life, 'family' is also something that is constructed through the language used within children's social services and therefore 'remains an important concept for policy'.[17] For example, children have 'contact'[18] with or are 'reunified' with their families. This discourse around what and who constitutes 'family' in social policy fails to account for 'the complex temporality of "family" for young people who have been in care'.[19]

In what follows, we recognise that 'family practices' are experienced very differently for children, young people, and their birth and care families. We also recognise that there needs to be further work on understanding this topic and we hope that this chapter, with its focus on inheritance as family practice, can help advance this area of research. As a 'family practice', inheritance can be a way of showing or displaying care, but it can also be a way to cut off, punish or abandon family members. It can bring families together or destroy families.[20] But what is missing from these socio-legal and academic discussions of inheritance and family is care-experience. In the following section, we begin to explore what is known about inheritance and care-experience.

[14] For example the Inheritance (Provision for Family and Dependants) Act 1975 was updated in 2014 to identify what 'child of the family' means and this implies that people who have been treated as a child of the family, without formally being adopted could (emphasis on could) be eligible to claim inheritance. But we were unable to find further information on this.

[15] Boddy (2019).

[16] ibid, 2239.

[17] ibid, 2241.

[18] H Yoeli, D Edwards, C Diaz, L Ridley, D Williams, M Robson and J Young (2021) 'Family Time experiences of care experienced children and young people during the Covid-19 pandemic: A rapid scoping review', available at static1.squarespace.com/static/571e40539f72665367f6d2bc/t/60a3d02464e66350b0038775/1621348406263/BC-TT-LitReview-Outlined-May21.pdf.

[19] Boddy (2019) 2239.

[20] In our small research project, we found examples of adoptive parents threatening disinheritance when their adopted children expressed the wish to legally change their surname.

III. What is Known about Inheritance and Care-Experience?

> When children enter the care system, many children lose their kin identity, receive a collective identity (children in care) and are identified by different labels given by professionals (reflecting the legal jargon) or by society (often reflecting stereotypes about them).[21]

In 2022 there were over 100,000 children living in care in the UK.[22] This is an all-time high.[23] Children are separated from their families for a variety of reasons including parental ill health, loss of parent/s, neglect, or seeking asylum. Children may live with foster carers, in children's homes, in secure units, or in kinship care; and a minority of care-experienced children will go on to be adopted and will obtain a new legal identity. When a child enters the care system they immediately experience the loss of family, identity, inheritance and each time they are moved, there is more loss and then a fundamental and final loss after adoption. For some, the law is used to violently (un)make families. *Mohamed Hasan v Norway* [2018] ECHR 27496/15 is an example where a mother, whose children were taken into foster care because of domestic violence perpetrated by her ex-husband, had her parental rights forcibly removed when both of her children were adopted by their foster carers without her consent. This way of (un)making families happens in family courts all over the UK[24] and globally where mothers are victim-blamed and children are compulsorily adopted or the abused mother loses custody.[25]

Laws which assist in the victim-blaming, punishment and (un)making of certain families who do not adhere to the normative ideology of the family set out by society have existed for centuries. The contentious relationship between care-experience and inheritance in England can be traced to laws created to criminalise illegitimacy in the 1660s. Those deemed 'illegitimates' were used alongside orphan and foundling characters in novels, plays and poetry to explore social mobility, property inheritance and familial bonds of blood and affection.[26] From the eighteenth century onwards, many children in the UK and Ireland became

[21] Neagu and Sebba (2019) 2.

[22] Gov.uk (2022); Department for Health (2022); Scottish Government (2022); and Welsh Government (2022).

[23] Thomas (2018).

[24] See Katz (2022); and H Yoeli and D Edwards, 'Contactless Time: No-touch rules hit vulnerable children and birth families where it hurt' *The Sociological Review Magazine* (8 February 2022), available at doi.org/10.51428/tsr.qcam932.

[25] Khaw et al (2021).

[26] Gibson (2018) 24.

care-experienced because of their illegitimate status.[27] Discussing her historical research Gibson states that:

> Before the English civil war, most unmarried parents were prosecuted for sex outside marriage by the church courts, but when the courts resumed in 1660, prosecutions declined considerably. Throughout this period illegitimacy was primarily regulated by the Old Poor Law; parish officials identified poor unmarried parents, forced mothers to name the father of their child and forced fathers to pay maintenance. All this changed under the 1834 New Poor Law, which shifted responsibility solely onto mothers and made it much more difficult to claim paternal maintenance.[28]

For illegitimate children, the rights to inheritance were severely limited,[29] yet throughout the nineteenth century stigmatising illegitimacy was a way to control behaviour, particularly women's behaviour,[30] and creating secrecy 'on this scale can cause considerable trauma, which can be inherited down the generations'.[31] It wasn't until the Family Law Reform Act 1987 that legal distinctions between legitimate and illegitimate children were removed.

The position of care-experienced people in relation to inheritance law has not improved with the passage of time. Foster children are still considered 'strangers in law' in relation to foster parents, but not birth parents. Under the rules of intestacy, adopted children are recognised, foster children are not, suggesting that the law can only comprehend one family for all purposes, failing to recognise the complexity of circumstances in which families are 'done' and 'displayed'. As we move through time, we can see that the 'system' of 'care', aided by the law in some cases, acts as a gatekeeper to inheritance for care-experienced people and manages all forms of their tangible and intangible inheritance (from knowing their heritage, their name, story and even monetary rights and objects). As an institution it alters their inheritance, lies about it and, as we show in the following section, can be accused of holding things back.

IV. Hidden Inheritance: What's been held Back?

When a child is taken into the 'care system', they are immediately displaced from everything they have known and who they ought to be. For instance, many children in care have had their birth names changed, part of their family history stolen.

[27] Edwards (2017).

[28] K Gibson, 'Illegitimacy, Family and Stigma in England, 1660–1834' (2022), available at notches-blog.com/2022/09/22/illegitimacy-family-and-stigma-in-england-1660–1834.

[29] ibid; and also see Edwards (2012).

[30] Women were sent away to give birth in secret in Mother and Baby Homes; many were coerced into giving up their babies for adoption. However, the babies of mothers with a mental health diagnosis often weren't put up for adoption due to 'bad blood'; similarly, babies of colour couldn't be put up for adoption due to racism. This was why some children, such as the author Paolo Hewitt, author Phil Frampton, Rosie and many others found themselves hidden away in the care system.

[31] ibid.

This is generally the case for those who are adopted, but also sometimes for those in foster care. For example, in his memoir, *My Name Is Why*, Lemn Sissay tells the story of what happened to him as a baby in the 1960s and how he was renamed by a social worker who used his own name: 'Mr Goldthorpe was adamant that my name would be Norman'.[32] 'The foster parents wanted to call me Mark from the Gospel of Mark, and their last name was Greenwood. My name is Norman Mark Greenwood … I am Norman Sissay in the files'.[33] Further, when Lemn was 17 he was given information from his care files, including a birth certificate which showed his real name as well as letters from his mother that had been withheld.[34] There are many instances of items withheld from children in care such as birthday cards from birth parents and yet it is likely that a child in care would, on their birthday of all days, think of their family regardless of the circumstances and wonder if they were remembered.

In writing about *The Last Foundling*,[35] an autobiography by Tom H Mackenzie, who grew up in the Foundling Hospital in the late 1930s and 40s, Dee Michell explains that at around the age of 20, Tom set out to find his mother, Jean. Upon meeting Jean (who consequently had to adopt Tom as she had given up her parental rights when she had handed over 'Derek' (the name she had given him) as a baby to the Foundling Hospital), Tom discovered that his maternal grandmother had sent him gifts for every birthday and Christmas, gifts he never received while in the Foundling Hospital as well as £2,000 for his 21st birthday.[36]

Like Lemn and Tom, as an adult, Rosie accessed her care files and found several letters and photographs that had been held back. One particularly poignant one was from a foster mother who, on hearing Rosie was back in care, wanted to refoster her – the photographs were Rosie as aged three and four. Prior to the ubiquity of mobile phones, it is well known that many children in care often did not have pictures of themselves as babies. Some years later, an aunt also wrote and offered to foster her. But Rosie never received these letters or photographs and we have to ask *why*? Why did social services make those decisions to keep the letters and precious photos, not share the information, and leave Rosie where she was, removing the chance for her to experience family life? The hidden inheritances of money, letters and information impacts *lived* childhood. Why didn't Lemn, Tom and Rosie receive what was rightfully theirs?

We have both heard it said in practice that holding back information is usually founded on the argument that it is done so in 'the best interests of the child', which is one of the pillars of the United Nations Convention on the Rights of the Child (UNCRC). Withholding information about their family or life story, presents

[32] Sissay (2019).
[33] ibid, 11.
[34] ibid.
[35] Mackenzie (2014).
[36] D Michell, 'Tom Mackenzie – the Foundling Who Exceeded Expectations' (2022), available at drdee-drdeethinkingoutloud.blogspot.com/2022/02/tom-mackenzie-foundling-who-exceeded.html.

no risk of harming or retraumatising children. Yet Articles 7 and 8 enshrine the 'importance of children's identity,[37] in which every child has the right to a name, nationality, the right to know his or her parents and to preserve these inherent elements of identity'.[38] This practice is both adhering to and contradictory to the UNCRC. Although the UNCRC was ratified after Lemn, Tom and Rosie's experience, children, young people and adults wanting to access their files in the UK are still being denied access to information about who they are.[39]

Withholding of information means care-experienced people often have significant gaps in their stories and unanswered questions about their lives.[40] It is not just that the system of care is guilty of stealing or hiding inheritance; withholding life history in this way is also withholding part of their heritage and their identity. Whether it is institutions, absent parents or social services doing the withholding, it affects the child's sense of self. Care-experienced artist Yusuf McCormack[41] explores the visible and invisible elements of his heritage to help him to come to terms with his childhood experiences and to forge pathways for those silenced by the inheritance of care. *In Marks of an Unwanted Rainbow*, he says:

> Identity is something we all cling onto and hold dear to ourselves. It starts with your name, your ethnicity, your culture and evolves and grows with you becoming part of you [but] children coming into care usually have only their name that belongs to them so to remove that too is to strip away every aspect of who they are. The child is no longer whole.[42]

As far as we know, there has been no other research or publication that explores inheritance from the perspective of care-experienced people. There is extensive literature about the right to know about your identity.[43] But understanding these rights and this experience within the broader concept of inheritance and also *asking* care-experienced people themselves what inheritance means to them is important. This is something we now explore in the remainder of this chapter.

V. Asking Care-Experienced People about Inheritance

When we initially asked our care-experienced friends what inheritance looked like some of those that responded wondered whether what we were asking was a

[37] Unicef, 'Summary of the UNCRC', available at www.unicef.org.uk/rights-respecting-schools/wp-content/uploads/sites/4/2017/01/Summary-of-the-UNCRC.pdf.

[38] Neagu and Sebba (2019) 1.

[39] See the Care Leavers Association website for further information: www.careleavers.com/what-we-do/access-to-records.

[40] Access has been made more difficult especially in today's 'suing' climate where local authorities who were responsible for children could remove reports/letters which deem them liable.

[41] Yusuf McCormack (25/1/1963–16/1/2021).

[42] McCormack (2022) 173.

[43] Willis (2009) and Shotton (2010).

'joke' because it is a known fact that care-experienced people do not inherit. This demonstrates our earlier point that inheritance can be understood as a familial practice. This response made us curious and so we put out a call on social media (Twitter and Facebook) to ask the wider community of care-experienced people to share their views, experiences and meanings of inheritance:

> Rosie Canning and I are working on a presentation about Care Experience and Inheritance. If you are #cep and happy to share, what does inheritance look like to you? Is it about stories or objects? As the daughter of #cep I got narrative inheritance.
>
> Call for responses Tweet from Delyth

We received several responses to our call-out and we made three significant findings. First, in terms of intangible forms of inheritance, it was common for people to have absences in their stories. Secondly, we discovered that tangible forms of inheritance can be a way for care-experienced people to start their own traditions of 'passing things on'. Finally, we found that inheritance is accepted as an intergenerational practice, albeit an ambiguous one.

A. Missing Histories: Being the Detectives of One's Own Life Story

> When you grow up in a family your parents keep mementos of your childhood. When you meet as a family, with parents and brothers and sisters, you tell and retell what happened, where you went, what you did, and what you felt. Each one has their own perspective, and memory is not always consistent or faithful, but this is part of how you understand where you came from and who you are.[44]

Stories and storytelling are vital to our sense of identity, of knowing who we are, of belonging, and are passed down through the generations. But what if you don't know your family story? As discussed in the previous section, when inheritance is held back, it can create gaps and absences for care-experienced people. Above is an excerpt from Anne Harrison's memoir. She was told that her care files had been destroyed in a fire, which meant she had no record of her time in care or family history. In January 2016, she received a telephone call from Warwickshire Police. They were making inquiries into allegations of misconduct made by people who were once children in a residential care home. A police officer visited and asked Anne about her time in the children's home. After the policeman left, Anne said: 'What surprised me was how much he knew about my own childhood.'[45] Like many care-experienced people wanting to know their story, Anne made a subject access request to Warwickshire County Council to ask what information they had about her. After a few weeks she received a reply and a file consisting

[44] Harrison (2020) xi.
[45] ibid, 15.

of 600 pages documenting her life from the moment she came to the notice of authorities as a baby in 1957 to the day she left the system as a young adult. Many of the 600 pages were illegible, redacted or blank pages. Redactions are usually made because of references to 'third parties'. The social care files constitute an important piece of Anne's heritage, her life story as well as her narrative inheritance. As she says 'I have a right to know my heritage on both sides, my father's as well as my mother's'.[46] She remembered that towards the end of her time in care she attended a case conference, which is where they discuss the child in care. It was at this meeting that she was shown a file and her father's name was pointed out. At that time there was no legislation on data protection and her files would not have been subject to redactions. Being misinformed that her files had been destroyed meant she had lost her entitlement to know his name. Anne appealed to Warwick County Council for a fuller version of her files and particularly the name of her father. She also appealed to the Information Commissioner. She received one more document which stated, 'her father is a Nigerian male nurse'.[47] Anne's experience reflects the extent to which the 'care system' holds back inheritance for care-experienced people. But her story also shows the way that care-experienced people have to search for clues of their inheritance.

Like Anne, participants who responded to our social media requests also shared that their narrative inheritance consists of gaps:

> Would have been nice to have stories of family and history.
>
> Response from Twitter
>
> I don't have much of a narrative because there's no one left to tell stories.
>
> Response from Twitter

These gaps, like Anne's, lead care-experienced adults to become the *detectives* of their own inheritance searching for clues amongst the documents in their files to piece together the stories of their lives. Rosie also explains this really well:

> I have been a lover of Agatha Christie novels since I was a teenager. This could partly be because I could and loved to work out who had dunnit! Back then I didn't even know it was the most unlikely person – there were clues if you knew how to spot them. I was a child of extremes, at times insular and withdrawn lost in my books and own world and at other times, fully engaged, vocal – very vocal at times. I spent much of my childhood mining information from those around me. This could be from social workers or members of staff talking about me behind closed doors, or my family whenever I saw them. I would listen to stories about Ireland, family and heritage. The insular child becoming hypervigilant, that budding detective listening out for clues. I would go so far as to say I grew an outer ear! Whenever I visited 'family' out popped the ear whilst

[46] ibid, 132.

[47] A Harrison, 'A conversation with Australian writer, Susan Francis, and UK writer, Anne Harrison, about their memoirs' Care Experience & Culture Book Club Event (9 April 2022), available at youtu.be/Q4lBKlp7PHg.

> in my mind I'd be scribbling conversations and clues. Whenever I learnt something new about my mum or family, I was so excited. I would carry the secret home adding to an imaginary family tree that I was part of. The more I knew about myself, the more I belonged, the more I had an inherited culture.
>
> What do you do when you don't know who you are, where you come from, your heritage, your family stories? Figuring out who I am and where I come from has become a lifelong project.[48]

Like Rosie and others in our research, inheritance is a lifelong project. One participant in our research noted how finding out parts of their family story from official documents enabled them to identify a connection and an inheritance from parents that they never knew:

> No property or money that makes a difference. But a sentence about my father working in the circus on the adoption papers, my mother dancing on ice. So many things fell into place when I discovered a creative inheritance. Using it well is ongoing.
>
> Response from Twitter

In the 1960s and early 1970s, when Rosie was in care, it was rare that anybody spoke to a child and explained what was happening in their lives or even why they were suddenly having to live with strangers. Today, some children engage in life-story work and have a life-story book,[49] which in itself is an object of both inheritance and narrative inheritance that can be kept and one day possibly passed on to family. This supports Rosie's understanding that finding out who you are 'is a lifelong project'. And as another respondent stated,

> growing up we did build a life story box filled with objects, photos, letters – memories. In the absence of a narrative this box is so valuable to me and is something I want to continue with my kids
>
> Response from Twitter

Although life-story work is well established for adoption, it is not standard practice for those in foster care or children's homes. Under the Children and Adoption Act 2002, all local authorities have a statutory obligation to support the life-story work of children in their care 'because it is regarded as a means for helping children feel a sense of well-being'.[50] Significantly, as our participant above notes, the tangible as well as the intangible benefits of life story work are important, a subject to which we now turn to.

[48] Canning (2023).

[49] 'Life story work is the process of helping children separated from their birth families to remember and make sense of their early lives. Children who have been through the care system often experience changes in social workers, carers and homes. Therefore this work, which usually includes making a Life Story Book and Memory Box, allows care experienced children and young people access to their heritage and past that may otherwise be missing, lost or forgotten' (Watson, Latter and Bellew (2015); Gibson and Edwards (2015) 17).

[50] Edwards (2017) 201.

B. Objects and their Stories: Entangled Inheritance

> It has been long established that objects can have a special role in infant attachment processes [...] These items are thought to represent a symbolic connection with the caregiver which provides the child with a sense of comfort and security.[51]

But what if one does not have a caregiver? For many children, it is not the object per se that is important, but the memories, emotions and meanings attached to that object, such that children will reject an identical object, such as a toy, because it is not 'their' toy.[52] The object's value lies in the meaning attributed to it by the child, which makes it irreplaceable. 'Inheritance' generally conjures up images of items passed from one generation to the next, and it is precisely these objects, invested with attachment and emotion, that are passed on to children and grandchildren. We saw this attachment to objects from childhood in the responses we received:

> I have two 50 yr old books from my childhood: a Superman annual and The Guinness Book of Answers by @GWR Both battered by all the moves and much treasured. One had a fun safe alternate fantasy world, the other showed me there was an interesting real world out there. I'll pass them on.
>
> Response from Twitter

Additionally, Rosie writes about an important object from her childhood, the star of our chapter, The Pink Cat, in *Hiraeth*, her PhD creative project:

> I was only eight when I first saw the pink cat. She was sitting on a table with her tail wrapped round her flank. Her little head was tilted to the right. One ear pointed straight up as though listening to the sound of the wind sighing through the trees or the beat of a butterfly's wings. The left ear is chipped now, dropped by a friend. The pink cat was never quite the same after that.
>
> Pink stripes shape the contours of her face, a tiny brown blob defines her nose, and her pink tongue has been captured licking her neck contentedly. This action endeared her to me when I first saw her sitting on a table in the garden at Mrs L's house. Mrs L liked to invite the kids from the children's home to help her with small stationery jobs like stamping her address, using an old metal stamp on the back of a pile of envelopes. I loved to run my finger over the embossed letters on the thick, cream-coloured paper. And when the jobs were finished, there was lunch in her beautiful garden followed by races in the afternoon. The pink cat was one of many prizes to be given out at the end of the day. I watched as each of the winners went up to the table to claim their prize. I held my breath and closed my eyes sure that when I opened them the pink cat would be gone. Eventually it was my turn, she was still there and I claimed her. I couldn't wait to take her home and place her on my shelf. The pink cat was mine.[53]

[51] Stevens et al (2019) 215.
[52] Hood and Bloom, (2008).
[53] Canning (2023).

Rosie knew albeit instinctively about the importance of objects from childhood that had emotional significance and memories. She writes:

> I placed the pink cat on the mantlepiece near my bed. As soon as I entered the bedroom, there she would be, all shiny and pink, as if to say hello like a real cat. As I grew older, she became the memory of the children's home cat, Marmalade. Cats made a home and I was sure, the pink china cat had come from a beautiful home. Maybe even Mrs L's house who reminded me of Miss Marple. Miss Marple who took girls from St Faith's Orphanage and trained them in housekeeping skills like Mrs L trained me in small stationery jobs.[54]

Rosie still has the pink cat! She has become an important heirloom that Rosie will one day pass her on to her children. She's beautiful even with her chipped ear and missing bits of paw. Entangled in the pink cat is a history and a beginning. The cat embodies Rosie's care story and is a journey they have travelled together. It also symbolises a new familial tradition of having and belonging with the aim of 'passing it on'. The Pink Cat allows Rosie to do and display family. In our mini social media research project, we found that other care-experienced people engaged in new beginnings when it comes to tangible inheritance practices:

> I learnt to knit. So I could knit my children's children (if they have any) a baby blanket. So they knew they were loved before they were even here.
>
> Response from Twitter

> Me and my sister began a Xmas tradition of each buying 2 of the same decoration and gifting each other one so we have some matching decs on each of our trees.
>
> Response from Twitter

As the first quote above suggests, objects can contain intangible meaning, for example they can signify love, which is a way of doing and displaying family. This resonates with the earlier mentioned 'tokens' that mothers left with their babies when leaving them at the Foundling Hospital in the 1770s. Objects can also represent longevity and a journey.[55] For children in care, objects 'are important for the development of a sense of identity for looked-after children (LAC)[56] to provide them with feelings of security, continuity and belonging'.[57] This is further supported by Coram's 'objects in social work' whereby feedback analysed from social workers and practitioners found that the use of objects in conversations enabled social workers, children and young people to better understand their life stories and therefore their needs. As a result, social workers were better able to

[54] ibid.

[55] Stevens et al (2019) 214–26.

[56] In the UK, LAC is the acronym used within children's social care. However, the term is outdated, and disliked by looked-after-children and adults with care-experience. See these project websites for a detailed discussion of the importance of language: Conversations for Care (conversationsforcare.wordpress.com) and The Care Experience Conference (info822785.wixsite.com/careexpconf).

[57] Watson et al (2020).

support children and young people, which in turn gave them more stability in their lives.[58]

We hope that the key message from the Coram research is shared and widely implemented in children's social services. For too long, the importance of belongings for children in care has been largely underestimated and misunderstood. As the below excerpt from Rosie's PhD novel recounts:

> She must double-check that nothing was left behind. Opening the wardrobe door, she thought of Narnia as she always did. Or else the memory of black bags filled with her belongings: a handmade silky orange tutu worn for a West-End theatre show, a jewellery box made from shells, and her treasure – a geode cut in two revealing its beautiful crystal inside that had come from Broadstairs and which she'd bought with pocket money saved throughout the winter. Last but by no means least (as Aunty D used to say), the painted moth postcards – a Barberry Carpet and beautiful Elephant Hawk – hours they'd taken as she painstakingly copied every tiny detail from the old Butterflies and Moths book. There were other things too some of which she couldn't remember. Worst of all though had been the black and white photograph of Aunty Mabel, her favourite foster mum. She'd moved the black bags from the wardrobe to under the bed, meaning to sort through and forgetting, forgetting.
>
> Uncle Rob, 'but-you-can-call-me-Rob', told her to tidy the rubbish under her bed otherwise it would be thrown away. Some weeks later, he'd asked with a nasty glint in his eye, if she'd checked the black bags under her bed. Up the stairs she ran and into the bedroom; they were gone. She flew back down and outside to the dustbins, all the while feeling sick because she knew today was the day they were emptied. Perhaps, just perhaps, the bags filled with her memories would still be there.
>
> Sorry, said Rob. How was he to know the bag contained photographs. I did warn you though.[59]

This excerpt is based on a true-life event when Rosie was living in a children's home in Muswell Hill:

> The manager decided to chuck out the black bags under my bed … Now I only have vague memories of what was in those bags, some of which have been forgotten in the mists of time. I remember the irreplaceable black and white photographs of my mother; and I so wish I still had the orange tutu to pass on to my granddaughter. Of course, nobody knows whether I would still have some or all of those belongings after so many more moves, but the chance to sort or throw or pass on objects, and the stories that went with them is lost.[60]

Sadly, this is often the case for children in care who are constantly moved about, and, in many instances, it is down to an individual social worker to decide what a child will and won't take with them (let's hope they are not still using black bags!). Even in 2021, one social worker recalled how 'they now pack service users'

[58] Patel et al (2021) 5.
[59] Canning (2023).
[60] ibid.

items that are of significance to them [the children] personally e.g. teddy bears, photos etc., rather than purely practical items considered important by the social worker'.[61] There must be instances where a child is involved in this process and of course, sometimes, reasons for leaving a home might involve safeguarding issues – eg people falling out; emergency factors – and it is not always possible to take their personal objects of significance. More work needs to be done around this subject. It should not be the responsibility of one person to decide what a child takes when they move: a mandatory policy that takes the child's view into consideration could improve things. Notes about what a child in care arrives with could be another way; a practical use of records rather than negative notes about behaviour. Precious objects should be kept safe, as these could be objects that the child or young person carries through with them on their transition to adulthood. As this section and the following section shows, inheritance in all forms is intergenerational.

C. Narrative and Oral Inheritance: Care-Experience as Intergenerational

Care is a very public story but also a very personal experience. By this we mean that care is part of the UK's national heritage. It is an experience that has always existed, an identity that is publicly known and widely discussed (in the media for example), and 'looking after' children is a practice that has existed for generations. But it is also a subjective experience for individuals that is shared with and passed down through families. The experience of care is often inherited through stories,[62] along with the gaps and the absences.

In our mini research, we found that this type of inheritance was discussed in two different ways. First, one participant described how, when thinking about their inheritance practices with their own children, their own missing childhood stories are amplified:

> I know with my kids, they love listening to me telling them funny stories of things they did when they were little, I've never had that and even those little things make me feel like I've missed out on knowing the child version of me that was nice or funny. (Our care records don't have these positive or funny stories about our characters).
>
> Response from Facebook

This quote demonstrates the loss of inheritance for care-experienced people, but also how oral and narrative inheritance can be a beginning for families and a way that they can make their own family inheritance practice. This participant is able to pass on stories to her children about their childhood that they in turn will pass

[61] Patel (2021) 5–6.
[62] Edwards (2017) and (2012).

on. Second, there was awareness that inheritance within care-experienced families is complex and not straightforward:

> Again, none of the family stories feel like mine to inherit either. My mum would tell loads which would have been passed down but they aren't mine genetically so I wont be passing them to my kids.
>
> Response from Twitter

This participant demonstrates the complexity, especially for adoptees, in inheriting stories that they do not see as their own. In the above response, stories are aligned with 'genetics' and this participant has made the choice not to pass on this inheritance, feeling that it doesn't belong to them or is part of their story. In this respect, family is being 'done', but not 'displayed' through storytelling.[63] We saw this discussion of the ambiguity of 'passing on' or *not* passing on, experiences of care and belonging in other examples from our research:

> Without being gloomy I think the inheritance from a care experienced parent to their child will be bitter sweet. Loss, family history (not for everyone but in my case it's written in files but they won't feel and experience it), not really understanding their parents experience but on the other hand resilience and a new beginning and maybe some stability through positive relationships, a childhood and hopefully some material stability.
>
> Response from Facebook

This participant identifies that for many children of care-experienced parents, inheritance can consist of loss and in some respects a distance between parent and child. This distance can lead to families being (un)made through silences.[64] However, in the above quote, this idea of 'a new beginning' comes through, which can be creating something from the start; stability, as mentioned here, that can be passed on and carried down generational lines. This is something that Delyth understands as the daughter of a care-experienced mother. Her mother does not have any objects of meaning from her childhood that she can pass down, but she has shared her story. Delyth has widely written about and discussed how her mother's care-experience is the story she has inherited, which has greatly shaped her identity and who she is as an academic.[65] Delyth continues to research, write and teach students about care-experience. Her mother's story and her personal/autobiographical inheritance have shifted from something that was very peripheral to something that is now very publicly shared. And we are now seeing more care-experience stories becoming public, such as Lemn Sissay's story mentioned above, as well as the work at the Foundling Museum. Some may argue that this is a way of 'flaunting' an identity and a family that was once stigmatised.[66] The stories

[63] Finch (2007).
[64] McNay (2009) and also see: D Edwards, 'Understanding Life Story Work as Family Practice' (2022), available at creativelifestorywork.com/latest/understanding-life-story-work-as-family-practice.
[65] Edwards (2017) and also see ibid.
[66] Michell (2021).

that get told, retold and inherited within care-experienced families support the view that inheritance is a 'family practice' and displaying our family publically in this way 'confirms the qualitative character of a given relationship, at a particular point in time, as "family"' for ourselves and others.[67] Storytelling is part of this way of 'doing' and 'making' family, but it is also a way that we do and make ourselves. This is an area of inheritance that needs further exploration within the broader field of inheritance studies.

VI. Conclusion: Inheritance as a Right

In this chapter, we set out to share some initial findings we made from our modest social media request asking care-experienced people what inheritance means to them. First, we explored how inheritance is an established field of research, in socio-legal fields and family studies. We argue that seen as a 'family practice', inheritance can be a way in which family is 'done' and 'displayed' but it can also be a way in which families are violently (un)made. Then we briefly traced the history of the hostile relationship between care-experience and inheritance. Given the strong correlation between illegitimacy and care, exploring laws around illegitimacy and inheritance (specifically monetary and land inheritance) can help us trace why care-experienced people are still highly marginalised in inheritance laws today. The chapter then considered how tangible and intangible inheritance is held back by the 'corporate parent'.[68] Inheritance is to a large extent always shaped by others, for example, intangible inheritances deemed uncomfortable or embarrassing can be kept as secrets within all types of families.[69] But for care-experienced people secrecy is a decision made by an unfair system *outside* of the family which for many, when formally requested, refuses to give up the secrets.

A key aim of this chapter, however, was to elevate the voice of care-experienced people. In the final section, we shared findings from our mini research. To really understand how care-experienced people feel about and practice inheritance, we need to ask them and their families. Drawing on this research and our own experience as a care-experienced person and the daughter of a care-experienced mother we made three key findings. First, because of the inheritance that is held back by the care system, care-experienced people must embark on a life journey of finding out who they are. Second, objects, as symbols of self, other and history, can

[67] Finch (2007) 80.

[68] In the UK 'The Children and Social Work Act 2017 says that when a child or young person comes into the care of the local authority, or is under 25 and was looked-after by the authority for at least 13 weeks after their 14th birthday, the authority becomes their corporate parent'. This means taking on parental responsibility and acting in the best interests of the child. Local Government Association, Corporate Parenting resource pack (2017), available at www.local.gov.uk/sites/default/files/documents/15.11%20Corporate%20parenting_v05.pdf.

[69] Smart (2011).

be a site of inheritance creation and negotiation in the face of absence. Finally, we found that care-experience itself is something that is passed on intangibly. Some parents try to protect their children from such inheritance, whilst others share their story of care, which can in turn shape the identities of the next generation.[70]

We want to end the chapter with two messages. First, further research should be focused on inheritance and care-experience, and in particular care-experienced people should be asked about their inheritance practices. Our own stories and those of our participants contain stories of loss, trauma and absence. But we also found inheritance being used as a way to create new beginnings, and this warrants further attention in research, law and policy. Finally, the creativity that care-experienced people have shown in negotiating unjust systems of inheritance should not overshadow the *rights* that care-experienced people should have to their inheritance, whether that is access to their care file and the information it contains, or letters or money that were bequeathed them by birth family members. When inheritance is held back, it creates absences in people's narratives and this results in many care-experienced people trying to piece together information about their lives 'in unsupported ways that put them at risk of experiencing trauma', and this should *never* be the case for any care-experienced person.[71]

References

Boddy, J, 'Troubling Meanings of "Family" for Young People Who Have Been in Care: From Policy to Lived Experience' (2019) *40 Journal of Family Issues* 2239.

Bowlby, J, *The making and breaking of affectional bonds* (Hove, East Sussex, Brunner-Routledge, 1979).

Canning, R, 'Hiraeth – finding a fictional home: the representation of care experience in contemporary literature' unpublished doctoral thesis, University of Southampton (2023).

de Beauvoir, S, *The coming of age* (New York, Warner, 1973).

Department of Health, Publication of 'Children's Social Care Statistics for Northern Ireland 2021/22' (2022).

Edwards, D, 'Remembering the Home: The intricate effects of narrative inheritance and absent memory on the biographical construction of orphanhood' in E Boesen, F Lentz, M Margue, D Scuto, and R Wagener (eds), *Peripheral Memories: Public and Private Forms of Experiencing and Narrating the Past* (Transcript, Bielefeld, 2012).

—— *Cultural, Autobiographical and Absent Memories of Orphanhood: The Girls of Nazareth House Remember* (Palgrave Macmillan, Basingstoke, 2017).

Finch, J, 'Displaying Families' (2007) 41 *Sociology* 65.

Gibson, L and Edwards, D, 'Valuing participation: The cultural and everyday activities of young people in care' School of Museum Studies, University of Leicester (2015).

[70] Edwards (2012) and (2017).

[71] Edwards (2022).

Gibson, K, 'Experiences of Illegitimacy in England, 1660–1834' unpublished PhD thesis, University of Sheffield (2018).

Gov.uk, 'Children looked after in England including adoptions' (2022).

Harrison, A, *Call Me Auntie: My Childhood in Care and My Search for My Mother*. Illustrated edition (Hampshire, Waterside Press, 2020).

Hood, BM and Bloom, P (2008) 'Children Prefer Certain Individuals over Perfect Duplicates' (2022)106 *Cognition* 455.

Katz, E, *Coercive Control in Children's and Mothers' Lives* (New York, Oxford University Press, 2022).

Khaw, L, Bermea, AM, Hardesty, JL, Saunders, D and Whittaker, AM '"The system had choked me too": Abused mothers' perceptions of the custody determination process that resulted in negative custody outcomes' (2021) 36 *Journal of interpersonal violence* 4310.

Mackenzie, T, *The Last Foundling: A Little Boy Left behind, The Mother Who Wanted Him Back* (On Demand edition, London, Pan Macmillan, 2014).

McCormack, PY, *Marks of an Unwanted Rainbow* (Kirwin Maclean Associates, 2022).

McNay, M, 'Absent Memory, Family Secrets, Narrative Inheritance' (2009) 15 *Qualitative Inquiry 15* 1178.

Michell, D, 'Australian Care Leavers' "Misery Memoirs" as Anti-Stigma Activism' International Australian Studies Association (InASA) Biennial Conference (8–10 February 2021).

Monk, D, 'The pleasures and perils of inheritance' (2014) 15 *Studies in Gender and Sexuality* 239.

—— 'Inheritance Families of Choice? Lawyers' reflections on gay and lesbian wills' (2016) 43 *Journal of Law and Society* 167.

Morgan, D, 'Everyday life and family practices' in EB Silva and T Bennett (eds), *Contemporary Culture and Everyday Life* (Durham, Sociology Press, 2004) 37–51.

—— *Rethinking Family Practices* (Basingstoke, Palgrave Macmillan, 2011).

Neagu, M and Sebba, J, 'Who Do They Think They Are: Making Sense of Self in Residential Care, Foster Care, and Adoption' (2019) 105 *Children and Youth Services Review*.

Patel, V, Taylor, S and Gilbert, L (2021) 'Evaluation of Objects in Social Work Project' (2021).

Rochberg-Halton, E, 'Object relations, role models and cultivation of the self' (1984) 16 *Environment and Behaviour* 335.

Scottish Government, 'Children's Social Work Statistics, Scotland 2020–21' (2022).

Shotton, G, 'Telling Different Stories: The Experience of Foster/Adoptive Carers in Carrying Out Collaborative Memory Work with Children' (2010) 34 *Adoption & Fostering* 61.

Sissay, L, *My Name Is Why* (Edinburgh, Canongate Books Ltd, 2019).

Smart, C, *Personal Life: New Directions in Sociological Thinking* (Bristol, Polity, 2007).

—— 'Families, Secrets and Memories' (2011) 45 *Sociology* 539.

Stevens, D, Camic, PM, and Solway, R, 'Maintaining the Self: Meanings of Material Objects after a Residential Transition Later in Life' (2019) 45 *Educational Gerontology* 214.

Thomas, C, 'The Care Crisis Review: Factors contributing to national increases in numbers of looked after children and applications for care orders' (London, Family Rights Group, 2018).

Tobin, S, 'Cherished possessions: The meaning of things' (1996) 20 *Generations: Journal of the American Society on Aging* 46.

Watson, D, Latter, S and Bellew, R, 'Adopters' views on their children's life story books' (2015) 39 *Adoption and Fostering* 119.

Watson, D, Hahn, R and Staines, J, 'Storying special objects: Material culture, narrative identity and life story work for children in care' (2020) 19 *Qualitative Social Work* 701.
Willis, R and Holland, S, 'Life Story Work: Reflections on the Experience by Looked after Young People' (2009) 33 *Adoption & Fostering* 44.
Welsh Government, 'Wales Children Receiving Care and Support Census: as at 31 March 2021' (2022).

8

Queer Property

RUSSELL PERKINS

A little over a year ago my friend Harry learned that the illness he had long been fighting was terminal. With a level-headedness I struggle to imagine, he turned his attention to the work of preparing for death.

While writing his will he asked if I would take care of a collection of homoerotic photography he had amassed from the mid-1980s through the '90s. He had tried to give the collection to a local art museum but they weren't interested. I gladly accepted with the understanding that we develop a care plan, as an artwork, in collaboration with one another.

Harry was a resident in my dad's pathology department, and the first openly gay person I knew as a child. Growing up he was among the adults with whom my brothers and I were entirely comfortable; he helped us with our homework, took us trick-or-treating, put us to bed. Once, he showed up at our house late at night with caviar, an alabaster spoon, and a book of Natalya Gorbanevskaya's poems to read aloud together. I never felt that he spoke to me like a kid and so our friendship extended easily into my adulthood, mainly over text messages and long, meandering phone calls. He was chronically depressive, but so warm and easygoing that it was a pleasure to keep him company at the bottom of a well. A polymath who wrote electronic music and taught himself Russian, he savored cruel ironies, offered his emotions plainly, and was readily overcome by beauty.

Harry pursued writing his will as an expressive exercise in tracing his chosen family – not just a private transfer of property but also a public statement of identity, values, and his ties to others.[1] He seemed to enjoy working on it, as though pairing objects and people in his life were an elaborate puzzle. I think one of the pleasures of this puzzle was that the pieces would only come together after his death. As a speech act with a delay built into it, the circuit from intention to receipt wouldn't need to be completed by the time he died, unlike every other communication with the people he cared about.

He was, I think, also eager to avoid being seen to be caught unready for death. Once he related the cautionary tale of a friend, another single gay man, who hadn't made any preparations to die. As a result this friends' heterosexual siblings ended up rifling through all his belongings trying to figure out what to do with them, to Harry an impossible and ghastly hermeneutic endeavor.

Because Harry's involvement in his will already exceeded its legal function, I wanted our project to infiltrate the document itself. Harry wanted his photographs to give other people pleasure as they had for him, and we agreed that any text we might insert into his will shouldn't circumscribe the possible future uses of the collection too tightly. Harry also didn't want to scandalise 'the money men' executing the will with anything too explicitly gay.

We decided to inscribe a stealth quotation from the writer EM Forster's will into Harry's will. Forster's will is notable because he famously withheld his queer classic *Maurice* from publication until after his death in 1970.[2] But more relevant here was the prospect, by connecting them, of reading these two wills as self-reflexive, literary documents on their own terms. Daniel Monk has invited just this kind of reading, arguing for Forster's will as a 'posthumous publication', an expression of 'ideas and feelings,' 'written with the same degree of care and consideration as his novels, short stories and other non-fiction'.[3]

Forster owned a small forest – a few acres of land in the countryside south of London – which he granted on his death to the UK National Trust. His will specifies that he gives this land 'for preservation as an open space'.[4] We lifted this statement of purpose into Harry's will, shifting the reference to the photography collection. As an imperative, it leaves the mechanics of the collection's preservation unresolved.

As I write this, Harry has been dead just over a month. I've received an initial letter from the lawyers managing his estate asking for my contact details and shipping address. It's almost time to start dealing with Harry's photographs themselves, setting our project into motion. The purpose of this chapter is to pause before this process begins in earnest.

What does it mean to hold someone else's desire? What resonances are there between the legal institution of inheritance at death and the social institution of the homosexual closet?

Harry's collection provokes these questions. In it, I see the ambivalences of the closet at a particular historical moment. To me his pictures of naked bodies are as much about secrecy as they are about disclosure, disavowal as much as wish-fulfillment, illness as much as health, shame as much as pride. Apprehending the legacy of these contradicting energies – practically, trying to figure out what to do with the photographs – seems to call for something other than either private ownership or conventional public display. An attempt to queer inheritance, I will suggest, requires us to find alternatives to private property that do not necessarily play out in public space. If the logic of the closet has traditionally made the public–private divide into a trap for queer people, maybe inheritance can offer an opportunity to play with this divide and begin to unravel its compromises.

My first encounter with Harry's collection was accidental. One afternoon – I must have been 12 or 13 – Harry was tasked with driving me to my piano lesson. As we approached his car he popped open the trunk, and lying inside face up were two black and white photographs showing a pair of naked men grappling one another against a neutral background. The men were muscular, hairless, and the high-key studio lighting accentuated the softness of their skin. Their heads and feet were cropped out of the frame so that the focus was on the posed composition of their interlocking limbs.

I remember a rush of feelings. One was recognition: I had recently discovered that my local Barnes & Noble had several books of similar photographs, with titles like *Men Together* or *In Defense of Beauty*, which I would secretively visit whenever I could contrive to pass by the bookstore alone. Another was a near immediate realisation of Harry's distress. He hadn't meant for me to see these pictures, and their accidental revelation evidently put him in some kind of danger. Awkwardly, he explained that they were artworks, that he had just picked them up from the framer, and that he didn't want my parents to think he was showing me porn.

I feel I can see the tension in his posture, elbows against his sides, but this is probably more projection than memory.

I wanted to comfort him, to reestablish the appropriateness of our interaction or assure him that it hadn't been interrupted. But the photographs' mutually interpellating force was too disorienting for me to unscramble. Since I already knew Harry was gay – a fact about him that was tacitly acknowledged in my family but which I don't remember actually having been told – it was hard to make sense of why the revelation of these photographs had the impact of an involuntary 'coming out'. If I hadn't actually learned anything new about Harry, how was it that our relationship to that knowledge had suddenly been rearranged?

More derailing was the fact that his being gay was somehow still not available for us to talk about. Although the photographs had outed him, he nonetheless hadn't come out to me verbally. The moment had taken away his narrative control of our interaction, and any effort by me to restore its normal terms seemed likely to just make things worse.

Moreover, I certainly wasn't prepared to come out to him, to tell him that I was already enthusiastically familiar with photos like this. (Much later on, I would learn that he and my dad had often spoken about my sexuality; I was a flamboyant kid.) I think even at the time I also felt sure he knew I was queer – simply because I felt more seen by him than by other adults – but I didn't quite appreciate that this information wasn't available for him to refer to unless I first volunteered it.

In short, neither of us knew what to say. Though wordless, our awkward impasse was a crash course in the closet as an arrangement of traps: how a secret can be mutually known but not shared, how the performance of coming out makes sexuality newly speakable but how, when this performance misfires, it reveals that it was involved in making 'inside' the closet unspeakable in the first place. My dawning knowledge of and immediate implication in this social bind was, if not a gift, an intergenerational transfer of property – an indelible inheritance.

I'm particularly grateful for this inheritance now in part because my adult life has been far more gently governed by the institution of the closet than Harry's was. With the historically recent, geographically specific, and wholly unearned luxury of being careless about who knows I'm queer, I certainly recognise the temptation to assign this baggage to a generational past tense.[5] So I'm glad to be prompted, by Harry's collection and against my own impulses, to reconstruct some understanding of the closet as an indispensable presence shaping what gay meant and means.[6]

Harry didn't have this same luxury. He endured years of bruising workplace discrimination, before and still after the Iowa Civil Rights Act was amended to include sexual orientation as a protected class in

2007.[7] His life was marked by disdain, fear and non-recognition in his midwestern American community. I learned from Harry that living in or out of the closet, when freighted with risk, is rarely a simple binary. Although he was unusually open about his sexuality given his surroundings, his openness was calibrated, different in Chicago than in Iowa City, with old or younger, conservative or liberal friends, and especially along the axis of work and home. Each new relationship conjuring another threshold to negotiate: this must have been exhausting.

Eve Kosofsky Sedgwick calls the closet a 'compromised metaphor'.[8] While the gay liberation movement 'vitally reinvigorated many people's sense of the potency, magnetism, and promise of gay self-disclosure,' she writes, 'nonetheless the reign of the telling secret was scarcely overturned with Stonewall.'[9] Needing to say the same thing over and over, or not being able to say the thing that everyone already knows – the closet imposes 'contradictory constraints on discourse' that multiply these compromising predicaments.[10] As a metaphor, the closet maps 'in' and 'out' onto a proliferating list of pairings: silence and speech, shame and pride, illness and health, private and public. One problem,

though, is that these mappings are often misleading or incoherent for those who find themselves needing to navigate them.

These binarisms break down, for example, whenever I imagine Harry with his photography collection. I picture the naked men lining his walls electrifying the threshold of his home. He described buying them – researching different photographers and photographic movements, seeking out and claiming images that spoke to him – as a practice flushed with pleasures of self-affirmation. Especially after he moved from Chicago to Iowa City and no longer had the same access to queer community, the collection allowed him to claim an erotic life that didn't otherwise feel available.

As a pathologist diagnosing disease, he would have also spent his working life with pictures of the human body, immersed in photographic technologies for describing the body's interior and the many ways it breaks down. I wonder what emotional resources were needed to analyse and discuss these bodies in a professional context where one's own body is an object of alarm and stigma. I imagine him being welcomed back from a hostile workplace by a chorus of gleaming men.

I imagine Harry's engagement with his collection, in other words, as a vital form of avowal and world-making, but not one that coherently maps onto the metaphorical fulcrum of in versus out of the closet. The same is true of the photographs themselves. While the collection is too diverse to sum up easily, an ambivalence around gay identity cuts through many of the photographs. Especially in some older images, queerness is a vibrant availability to double reading that can just as easily be shut down. Some others seem to bait a gay viewer while still preserving the deniability of their address. The viewer is implicated as gay just by looking, while the model might be a straight boy who is letting himself be looked at but isn't reciprocating the camera's desiring gaze. Several photographs feature adult twins, whose pretext of familial closeness licenses homosocial behavior that would otherwise read as explicitly homosexual.

The most common deflection, though, is just the shining surface of the models' skin. They are overwhelmingly youthful, able-bodied, pristine. I can't help reading them against the backdrop of the AIDS crisis – which wasn't just killing Harry's friends but also would have been an ever present reality in his working life as a physician – as reflecting a desire to reconstitute an unmarked and sanitised male body. Whenever I try to make sense of the collection I find myself asking – are these prideful images or mechanisms for gay disavowal? I think the answer is both, or neither.

The disconnect between these multiple energies and the binary logic of the closet turns this queer inheritance into a problematic endeavour. Writing a will is a bit like coming out, and not just because coming out still figures in the homophobic imaginary as a social death. Both require an explicit performative utterance, the will's 'I give' and coming out's status-transforming 'I am'. Both are revelations on the axis of private and public. And both, of course, are a giving away – of valued property or coveted information.

Maybe this is why wills so often feature in literature as inflammatory sites of speculation, unveiling, and surprise. EM Forster's will – because of *Maurice's* presence among his unpublished papers – just was a coming out. Harry's will, by contrast, gives me the role of coming out on his behalf every time the collection is exhibited. It is first and foremost a portrait of him. But what does it mean to come out for someone who is already dead? How is this different from outing them?

The prospect of displaying Harry's collection in a conventional exhibition format makes me uncomfortable. Although he gave me permission to do whatever I wanted with it, and although he did want it to be enjoyed by others, simply showing the collection in public transgresses the private context of the home that so crucially animated it. This personal and equivocal register of his desires and attachments isn't asking to be disclosed for our contemporary scrutiny, and isn't legible under the spotlight of public display. Keeping it for myself is also out of the question; these aren't my desires and attachments, and I don't want to hold them indefinitely. What to do with the sense of shame that seems to creep in on both sides?

For Forster, ownership is itself a mortification. In his delightfully titled essay 'My Wood', Forster offers an extended reflection on the shame, weight, and ultimate impossibility of private property ownership. Interestingly, this reflection is triggered in the text by the fact that his wood actually isn't fully private. 'It is intersected, blast it, by a public footpath.'[11] Forster imagines the weekend hikers passing through his property who, speculating about its owner, 'should participate in my shame'. Indeed, it is in the inquiring voices of these passersby – 'in accents that will vary in horror' – that he places the text's motivating question: 'What is the effect of property upon the character? … What's the effect on me of my wood?'[12]

Forster's wood is a space of intense introspection because he *isn't* alone there. This framing captures the incongruous, dual aspect of shame that Sedgwick found so fascinating, its simultaneous

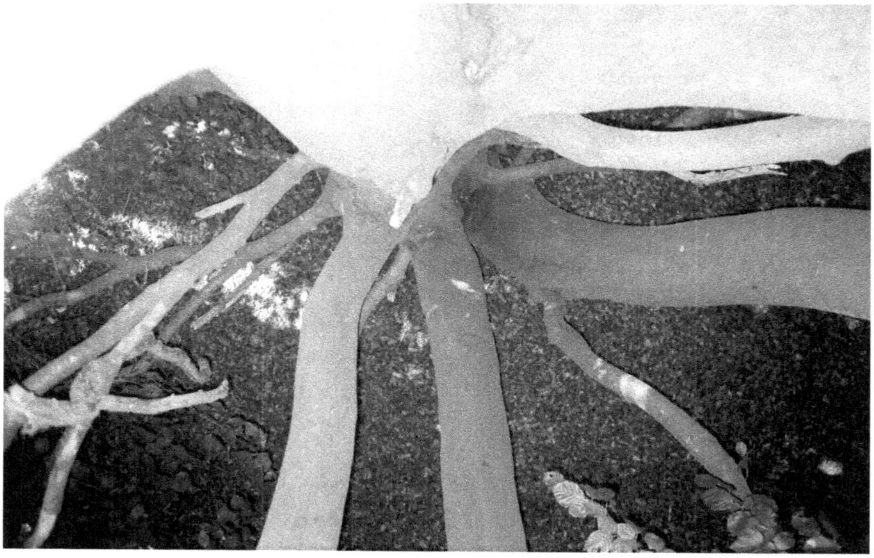

movement 'toward painful individuation' and 'toward uncontrollable relationality.'[13] Shame makes us feel both isolated and exposed. Just as much as it represents a break in communication – something I've done fails to produce the positive response I expected, or makes my interlocutor suddenly foreign – it is also itself an acute form of communication, the surface of the skin flooding with the 'desire to reconstitute the interpersonal bridge.'[14] By becoming an owner of property Forster has cut himself off from others, in space and in status. And yet the footpath literalises the infiltrating movement of these same others into his paranoid self-regard, which in turn instigates the remedial outflow of the text. The outside is inside: as Sedgwick writes, paraphrasing Silvan Tomkins, 'shame turns itself skin side out.'[15]

Maybe we can think of inheritance, along the axis of time, as akin to the public footpath's function in space. Like the footpath, inheritance brings inquiring eyes to the spectacle of property. Even aside from the public performances of will reading imagined in literature, wills are public documents, readily available in public records registries on request.[16] Property that passes through a will is catalogued for anyone to see and potentially exposed to contestation in court or scrutiny in the media. Like the self-consciousness Forster feels on account of the people walking through his property, wills inspire a concern with representing one's public image for posterity.

A will also literally marks an inevitable interruption in private property. Choosing your inheritors is very simply a reminder that your stuff won't always be yours. Yet both inheritance and the right of way interrupt private property without truly contesting it. Inheritance is of course among the core privileges linking private property and

heteroreproductivity to enable the consolidation of wealth across generations, while the footpath accommodates public access into the framework of private ownership, thereby insulating that framework from dispute.

Collapsing this analogy, the public footpath is itself an inheritance of English class struggle over the nature and extent of private property. The far-reaching enclosure of the commons throughout England between 1700 and 1840 drew borders around countryside whose collective use for farming, grazing, and natural resources had for centuries

sustained village economies.[17] This dispossession of the peasantry was deeply contested and has been described by some historians as an 'internal colonisation' operating in tandem with the British imperialist project abroad.[18] Within this context, continued access to public footpaths was variously litigated as an exception within enclosure laws or fought out in court.[19] These walkways, then, inconspicuously testify to a heritage of plural ownership that made room for overlapping claims to the same property and a less discrete boundary between public and private.

Forster begins his essay by explaining that he purchased his wood with the royalties from his book, *A Passage to India*. However we might assess Forster's decolonial politics, there is an irony in the fact that Forster's book criticising the English colonial project should have allowed him to purchase land, and especially a piece of land bearing this particular legacy.

All this, perhaps, fuels Forster's self-ironising conclusion:

> 'I shall wall in and fence out until I really taste the sweets of property. Enormously stout, endlessly avaricious, pseudo-creative, intensely selfish, I shall weave upon my forehead the quadruple crown of possession until those nasty Bolshies come and take it off again and thrust me aside into the outer darkness.'[20]

Thrust into the outer darkness. Forster offers a fever-dream of total privacy and its violent breakdown, a fantasy of his own death in which pursuing the logic of privacy to the furthest extreme leads to revolutionary overthrow. What could a less self-invalidating death scene look like? This impasse, I think, points to the queer potential hiding in inheritance: the possibility, at the moment of its transfer, of stepping to one side of the closet of private property in favor of an alternative that would overwhelm our boundaries of private and public.

The other day I visited Forster's wood. I took the train from London to Gomshall station, then walked along a country road until I found the footpath leading into the property. The edges of the forest are thick with brambles and ferns, but at its centre is a cluster of large trees with almost nothing growing under them, so that they look like columns in an otherwise empty room. The land slopes downward on all sides from this enclosure.

I ate my lunch sitting on a dead tree trunk, and imagined downloading Grindr so I could say I'd had anonymous sex in Forster's wood. After scoping out the far ends of the wood, I climbed up an old tree with large, evenly-spaced branches almost like a spiral staircase. Somewhere up in the tree I found a remarkably snug saddle of branches to sit in. When this eventually became uncomfortable I climbed down and lay at the base of the tree. Several hours passed by.

Momentarily forgetting that I couldn't just call him, I wondered what Harry – who had a deep knowledge of Russian culture – thought about the Soviet dissident artists known as the Collective Actions Group. From about 1976 onward, these

artists would often take the train from Moscow into the countryside and stage performative actions in forests or snowy fields.

Because a will is like a musical score, I had been thinking about performances that are organised by instructional texts or that corral a group of participants to share in some predetermined activity. One or several members of the Collective Actions Group would have prepared such a scenario, which would prescribe a mundane but specific action for the group to carry out. This might involve each person unraveling a length of thread by walking in opposite directions into the forest from a central point, or simply waiting in an agreed upon location while the organisers walked towards them to deliver a certificate for having attended the event.

These esoteric actions were often so simple or 'empty' as to raise questions about what actually constituted the event. Returning home by train, participants would write reflections on their experiences which would then become subject matter for further debate. Contrary to the dominant impulse in Western participatory art towards 'unified collective presence and immediacy', art historian Claire Bishop argues that the Collective Actions Group aimed instead at giving rise to 'a space of privatised experience.'[21] 'Given the omnipresent surveillance and demands for political adherence under state socialism,' the goal was to produce 'a privileged liberal space that existed in covert parallel to official social structures.'[22]

What strikes me about this work is how it stages the co-creation of privacy: a self-determined group of artists working together not to produce a shared experience but to construct, for one another, the space to think one's own thoughts. This is not unlike the legal space generated by the wills queer people make. Exploiting the discretion that law traditionally affords to the testator, queer wills often trace alternative, non-biological kinship structures.[23] They have been inscribing these families into the law long before the law began to explicitly recognise or protect queer identities.

Contrasting Collective Action Group's work to the 'tunnel vision' involved in engaging with official artwork in the Stalin or Brezhnev eras, the artist Andrei Monastyrsky observed: 'but when it comes to a field – when one comes there, moreover, with no sense of obligation but for private reasons of one's own—a vast flexible space is created, in which one can look at whatever one likes.'[24]

Heading home from Forster's wood, I wrote out a draft of a letter I'll send to an extended group of other queer artists, one for each picture in Harry's collection:

Dear friend,

I'm writing to ask if you would take care of a photograph my friend Harry Carson gave me when he died. There are forty-six other photographs in this collection, which he assembled over a number of years as a way to describe his sexual desire and elaborate an erotic life. I'm hoping each will be taken by someone else who's also preoccupied with the queer erotic body, desire or pleasure.

The photo would be yours to keep, but if you accept it, comes freighted with a few requests. If someone contacts you about the picture, please invite them over to come see it. If the collection is ever reassembled for exhibition, please lend the picture – or better yet, send something else you've chosen. Lastly, when you die or get tired of owning the picture, give it to someone else on these same terms.

Is this something you'd be up for? No worries of course if not. I'm grateful to you for considering it.

Yours truly,
Russell

Endnotes

1 For a detailed account of testation's expressive potentials, see Sneddon (2013) 355.
2 Forster's will only refers indirectly to *Maurice*, assigning beneficiaries to copyrights and royalties of books 'unpublished at the date of my death'. For greater discussion and a reading of Forster's will 'against' Maurice, see Monk, (2013) 581. Conversations with Monk have also greatly informed this chapter and the art project it describes.
3 Monk (2013) 581.
4 Last Will and Testament of Edward Morgan Forster, 7 March 1967.
5 For an extended reflection on generational sexualities, see Plummer (2010).
6 The concept of a 'shaping presence' comes from Sedgwick (1990) 68.
7 Iowa Code § 216.6(1)(a).
8 Sedgwick (1990) 72.
9 ibid, 67.
10 ibid, 70.
11 Forster (1950) 23.
12 ibid, 23.
13 Sedgwick (2003) 37. Also see Munt (2007).
14 Sedgwick (2003) 36.
15 ibid, 38.
16 This is true at least of the UK and the US, where it applies to all wills filed with a probate court.
17 Anderson (2007).
18 Boyce (2020) 127.
19 Anderson (2007) 390.
20 Forster (1950) 26.
21 Bishop (2011) 8.
22 ibid, 9.
23 Monk (2011) 232.
24 Quoted in Bishop (2011) 9.

References

Anderson, J, 'Britain's Right to Roam: Redefining the Landowner's Bundle of Sticks' (2007) 19 *Georgetown International Environmental Law Review* 375.

Bishop, C, 'Zones of Indistinguishability: Collective Actions Group and Participatory Art.' (2011) 29 *e-flux journal* 1.

Boyce, J, *Imperial Mud: The Fight for the Fens* (London, Icon Books, 2020).

Forster, EM, 'My Wood' in *Abinger Harvest* (Boston, Mariner Books, 1950).

Monk, D, 'Sexuality and Succession Law' (2011) 19 *Feminist Legal Studies* 19 231.

— 'EM Forster's Will: An Overlooked Posthumous Publication' (2013) 33 *Legal Studies* 572.

Munt, S, *Queer Attachments: The Cultural Politics of Shame* (London, Routledge, 2007).

Plummer, K, 'Generational Sexualities, Subterranean Traditions and the Hauntings of the Sexual World: Some Preliminary Remarks' (2010) 33 *Symbolic Interaction* 163.

Sedgwick, E, *Epistemology of the Closet* (Berkeley: University of California Press, 1990).

— *Touching Feeling: Affect, Pedagogy, Performativity* (Durham, Duke University Press, 1990).

Sneddon, K, 'The Will As Personal Narrative' (2013) 20 *Elder Law Journal* 355.

9

Sentimental Value

Keeping Inheritance in the Family

SARAH GILMARTIN AND ANITA PUREWAL

I. Introduction

Inheritance laws predominantly prioritise familial beneficiaries.[1] Qualitative research using will samples has also found that the majority of testators leave property 'exclusively to kin … [with] will-makers in England … favour[ing] family members in their bequeathing decisions despite the [law providing] considerable freedom to bequeath'.[2] Keeping property in the family is therefore an important consideration in law and for some testators, with will-making permitting a person greater control over the disposition and division of their estate.

Property, both real and personal, may be imbued with monetary and sentimental value. Many will be sentimentally attached to property that they own, even that which carries little to no monetary value. Sentimental attachments to property, and particularly to inherited property, are recognised across international socio-legal scholarship and within the common law of England and Wales.[3] The influence sentimental attachments have on guiding decisions when will-making is consequently recognised and inferred. Will-making, in particular, is a means of extending sentimentality into the future, of passing property to those who testators know, or at least hope, will treasure it most or understand best the meaning of the property transferred. Some property transferring on death will be sentimental only, such as photographs of loved ones. Other property will have mixed value, such as jewellery, and there may be property which, to an objective observer, seems worthless, but to those inheriting the same will be worth more than money or gold.

Although sentimental attachments to property are recognised, inheritance laws have largely leaned in favour of monetary considerations when assessing

[1] For example, see the intestacy rules in the Administration of Estates Act 1925 (AEA 1925) s 46, and the Inheritance (Provision for Family and Dependants) Act 1975 (1975 Act) s 1.

[2] Finch et al (1996) 73.

[3] Some cases of relevance from Northern Ireland will also be considered.

inheritance rights. Key to inheritance law is that dependants of, and those closest to, the deceased are not suddenly without essential support as a result only of that person's death. The intestacy rules developed from earlier tripartite rules governing distribution of personal chattels to those closest to the deceased, namely the spouse and heir. The right of dower also subsequently provided the surviving widow with a life interest in her husband's realty, so as to prevent her from becoming homeless.[4] As homogenous family norms changed, similar considerations fuelled amendments to financial provision and maintenance legislation, expanding to include a broader category of relationships likely to be dependent on the deceased and in need of financial protection on their death.[5] Many beneficiaries, however, particularly those who inherit personal chattels, will have no intention of selling on their inheritance to realise its value, the monetary value of the property being of little to no consequence. They will instead keep the same as a token or memento of the deceased, of their life together or their shared family heritage. Monetary valuations can help for insurance purposes during estate administration, or to determine an even split of the estate between entitled beneficiaries, but the loss of assets of irreplaceable sentimental worth can arguably never be wholly insured against, and their loss on inheritance may be equally tough to bear, because of the sentimental attachment individuals form towards such property.

As inheritance cases most often concern questions of monetary division and financial support, relatively few refer to sentimental attachments to property. Items of pure sentimental value, that is property with little to no monetary value, cannot satisfy a debt, pay a tax liability, or achieve reasonable financial provision for a beneficiary or a dependant. Disputes over such property therefore rarely ever trouble the courts and yet their 'worth' will be at the heart of many a private family dispute. The expense of litigation, and the rule that costs generally follow the event,[6] deters legal action where the property in dispute has minimal monetary value. The law also provides limited legal resolutions for disputes over such property and beneficiaries are, therefore, largely left to negotiate the distribution between themselves, with assistance perhaps from the estate's personal representatives. This is why solicitors recommend testators include clauses in their wills to mitigate these situations.[7] In the absence of agreement between beneficiaries the law can simply offer a monetary means of resolution; that items within the estate be valued and sold, and the proceeds distributed in accordance with the will or intestacy.

Inheritance law's deference to financial support of beneficiaries and financial resolutions, however, harbours an understated and oft-ignored aspect of

[4] For it was introduced to protect a widow rather than a widower. See Simpson (1986).

[5] 1975 Act, s 1(1). See also additions made by the Civil Partnership Act 2004, Marriage (Same Sex Couples) Act 2013, and The Civil Partnership (Opposite-sex Couples) Regulations 2019.

[6] Civil Procedure Rules, r 44.2(2)(a).

[7] Practical Law, 'Will clause: personal possessions gift, category of items to divide by agreement or equally by value' Thomson Reuters, Private Client, available at uk.practicallaw.thomsonreuters.com/4-506-4235.

inheritance: the transfer of property carrying sentimental value to those who were close to the deceased, and who can appreciate best the meanings attached to the property. Whilst the transfer of a home or sufficient funds to prevent hardship after the death of a provider or contributor to finances is important, the transfer of irreplaceable sentimental property is an additional consideration, and for some will be a fundamental aspect of inheritance and will-making. It is therefore an issue that the courts must sometimes address. This chapter will first consider the definition of 'sentimental attachment', garnered from both social-legal scholarship and case law, and then turn to consider evidence of its impact on will-making decisions.

II. What is Sentimental Attachment?

Case law and socio-legal scholarship collectively offer a multi-faceted and shared definition of the concept of 'sentimental attachment'. The concept is comprised of the following elements: 1) length of property ownership;[8] 2) subjective associations and involvements with the property;[9] 3) objection to sale of the property;[10] and 4) emotional harm upon the property's loss.[11] The concept's application in case law particularly demonstrates its significance as a recognised value of ownership. Even though inheritance disputes most often concern items holding monetary value, such property may also carry great sentimental value, and this has proved influential to judicial reasoning. Sentimental attachment to property is also recognised in cases concerning property loss, disposal or division, such as divorce proceedings or trust law cases, especially where the property concerned has itself been inherited. Application of each characteristic of the concept assists to demonstrate an accepted definition of sentimental attachment and highlights a shared understanding.

A. Length of Property Ownership

Sociological scholarship has emphasised the development of sentimental attachment based on length of ownership. For example, Cuba and Hummon explain that long-term residence encourages the development of sentimental attachments and a sense of 'home', imbuing the property with personal meanings, which arise over

[8] For example: *Urry v Williams & James* (Fam, 1 March 1991); *Y v Y* [2013] 2 FLR 924; Cuba and Hummon (1993); Ulen in Mercuro (1992); and Grubbström (2011).

[9] For example: *Butler v Butler* [2016] EWHC 1793; *Sharp v Adam* [2005] EWHC 1806; and Conway and Stannard (2016a).

[10] For example: *Abbey National Plc v Moss* [1994] 1 FLR 307; *WS v WS* [2015] EWHC 3941; Nadler and Diamond (2008); and Grubbström (2011).

[11] For example: *WS* (n 10); Erikson (1976) in Cuba and Hummon (1993); and Svašek (2006).

time with the accomplishment of life experiences;[12] the longer the residence, the more life events associated with the home, and the stronger the emotional bonds to the property.[13] Ulen and Grubbström similarly found that an emotional bond arises from the historical family connections associated with property,[14] demonstrating the significance of length of ownership to the development of sentimental attachments. Case law also highlights this characteristic as an underlying factor. As noted, these cases do not always relate to inherited property, but they evidence a consistent consideration of sentimental attachment, applicable in all cases.

In *Urry v Williams & James*, a case concerning professional negligence arising from earlier divorce proceedings, the plaintiff wished to have the home she had lived in for 35 years transferred into her name.[15] The judge noted that this seemed 'irrational because the house was … in a poor state of repair and costly to maintain', but acknowledged the reason was that she held 'a great sentimental attachment to the house in which her two children grew up'.[16] Similar recognition of sentimental attachment to property in light of the length of ownership was given in *Englefield & Cohn v Steinberg*, which concerned a reversionary interest in a home.[17] The settlor accepted the property had to be sold, 'albeit reluctantly, because of her emotional attachment to the property which ha[d] been her home for … forty years'.[18] Although recognising that length of ownership can create sentimental attachments, the judges in both cases reverted to practical non-sentimental judgments. Sentimental attachments were, however, acknowledged and used as explanations for the decisions taken by the parties in these cases, and, as will be seen, recognition of sentimental attachments can prove influential in other judgments.

Length of ownership is also cited in family and divorce cases concerning inherited property. The case of *Y v Y (Financial Orders: Inherited Wealth)* concerned a financial order following the parties' marriage breakdown and included inherited assets.[19] In determining the division of property, the court noted the 'Obvious … sentimental value' that attaches to personal property such as family antiques, which the owner considers 'sacrosanct' given the length of time such assets have been in the family.[20]

Recognition of this kind of sentimental attachment is particularly highlighted in divorce settlement cases that involve agricultural property, which is particularly renowned for its generational ownership.[21] An example of this is *P v P (Inherited Property)*, which concerned a claim for ancillary relief by a divorcing wife for a

[12] Cuba and Hummon (1993).
[13] ibid.
[14] Ulen in Mercuro (1992); Grubbström (2011).
[15] *Urry* (n 8).
[16] ibid (Rattee J).
[17] [2005] EWHC 943. See also *Fusco v Georgiou, Georgiou and Homecircle* [1994] CLY 1527.
[18] *Englefield & Cohn* (n 17), [7] (Smith J).
[19] *Y v Y* (n 8).
[20] ibid, 929–30.
[21] Conway and Stannard (2016b).

40 per cent share in the husband's inherited farm, now in the fourth generation of the family.[22] To grant a 40 per cent share the farm would have to be sold, which would have been 'devastating for the husband'.[23] The court made an alternative award of 25 per cent, which was achievable without the need to sell.[24] Although the award was held to have been based 'on the wife's reasonable needs for accommodation and income',[25] prominence was also placed on the farm's inherited nature, with the court holding that, although 'the fact that certain property [is] inherited will [often] count for little … [o]n other occasions [it] may be of the greatest significance.'[26] The court acknowledged here that generational estates may be treated differently from other assets in this context, so as to provide the inheritor with the greater share of such property,[27] and thereby giving weight to sentimental attachments based on length of ownership within a family line. That property is inherited, however, is just one factor for the court to consider, and it 'can be expected to carry little weight, if any, in a case where the claimant's financial needs cannot be met without recourse to [the inherited] property.'[28]

The Northern Ireland case of *Donnelly v Donnelly* further highlights that although sentimental attachment may be influential, it may not protect the inherited property.[29] *Donnelly* also concerned ancillary relief in which the inheritor of a family farm had 'a strong emotional attachment' to it, and which he 'hoped … could be retained for future generations'.[30] The judge found this to be 'wishful thinking', as no future generation had shown an interest in taking over the farm.[31] Further, sentiment alone would not prevent the distribution of inherited property in 'a needs-based case where the needs' of one party, as here, could only be met by 'recourse to the inherited property'.[32] The case highlights again, however, that sentimental attachment accruing through length of ownership is at least a factor to be considered, as too is retaining property intact for future generations, even if it is not always possible to wholly protect the same.

Sentimental attachment accrued through length of ownership may, however, be effective where financial needs can be met from other sources. *Y v Y* similarly held that a factor to consider when determining equal division is how long property has been held in the family,[33] but noted that inherited property can be categorised as 'non-matrimonial … [placing] it in a special category … [which] the court should be slow to invade … without good reason'.[34] This demonstrates the recognition of

[22] [2005] 1 FLR 576.
[23] ibid, [44] (Munby J).
[24] ibid, [48].
[25] ibid, [44].
[26] ibid, [37].
[27] ibid; and see *White v White* [2001] 1 All ER 1.
[28] *White* (n 27) 14 (Lord Nicholls).
[29] [2010] NImaster 5 (Northern Ireland).
[30] ibid, [14] (Master Bell).
[31] ibid, [32].
[32] ibid, [42].
[33] *Y v Y* (n 8) 933 (Baron J).
[34] ibid, 931.

inherited property's sentimental value. It also recognises something deeply rooted historically within inheritance laws more generally; the orchestration of property transfer so as 'to keep it in the family'. This was also highlighted in *P v P* in which it was said that:

> Fairness may require quite a different approach if the inheritance is a pecuniary legacy that accrues during the marriage than if the inheritance is a landed estate that has been within one spouse's family for generations and has been brought into the marriage with an expectation that it will be retained *in specie* for future generations.[35]

The court therefore acknowledges intentions, even historic testators' intentions, to pass property through different generations so as to 'keep it in the family'.

These intentions are reminiscent of primogeniture, and also of the common law's development of entails utilised by landed families to keep estates together for the benefit of the settlor's family, and resettled to suit a family's needs, as well as to keep property out of the hands of unsuitable marriage prospects.[36] Whilst these sought to protect generational property predominantly for the benefit of male family members, especially in regard to aristocratic landed estates,[37] inheritance laws today are less gendered, but the historic notion of retaining property for future generations remains a prevalent undercurrent in judicial decision-making, as well as will-making, today.[38] Length of ownership by individuals, and particularly across generations, is clearly recognised by the courts as giving rise to sentimental attachments.

B. Subjective Associations and Involvement with Property

The second accepted characteristic of sentimental attachment to property is the memories of, and an individual or family's association and involvement with, property. Memories associated with property have been upheld as a factor indicative of a property's sentimental value, particularly demonstrated in judgments concerning inheritance. For example, in the cases of *Butler v Butler* and *Sharp v Adam*, considered further below, when determining the division of items left in a will, the court recognised sentimental attachments given the memories associated with the property.[39] Sentimental attachments formed through familial involvement with property have also been deemed by the court to be 'genuine and rational'.[40]

Significant milestone events and memories shared within the home are also upheld by the courts as an identifying feature of property's sentimental value. For example, the seminal events of marriage and the growth of a family are recognised

[35] *P v P* (n 22), [37].
[36] Simpson (1986); Spring (1964); and Probert (2009).
[37] For example, see the below discussion of *Re Bathurst* [2018] EWHC 21 (Ch).
[38] See section III below. Consider also the continued inclusion and upholding of conditional gifts.
[39] *Butler* (n 9); *Sharp* (n 9). See section III.B below for further discussion of these cases.
[40] *Butler* (n 9), [78] (Barker HHJ, QC).

as attributing sentimental importance to property.[41] In *R v Franks (Steven John Joseph) & Ors* a home burglary resulted in items of 'high sentimental value' being stolen,[42] including wedding rings, an action the court said caused a 'significant degree of loss to the victim and greater harm',[43] which 'may be more relevant to the issue of culpability'.[44] Case law therefore acknowledges that emotional attachments arise from memories associated with property.[45]

Memories are also a recognised definitional characteristic of sentimental attachment in socio-legal scholarship. For example, Conway and Stannard affirm sentimental attachment to inherited property, noting that desires to retain ownership within the family are motivated by the ongoing association with the decedent when sentimentally valued property is left to family members through a will; the property is now deemed to symbolise the deceased and holds a repository of memories for those to whom it is gifted.[46] Furthermore, media reports also endorse this definitional characteristic, for example, noting that property becomes imbued with sentimental value given the memories and legacy associated with it,[47] particularly if the property has been passed down by a family member.[48]

The actions of individuals towards their property are also recognised by the courts as giving rise to a sentimental attachment since, if one has built the property or is actively undertaking its maintenance and improvement, such actions reflect care and effort. For example, in *MacDonald and another v Frost* the claimants sought to rely on proprietary estoppel to establish an interest in their late father's estate, in the course of which it was recognised that *inter vivos* financial arrangements between the claimants and the deceased had been designed so that the deceased and the claimants' mother could remain in the home they had 'built … [as] it had sentimental value'.[49] Thus, the time and effort expended in a property's development, and the distinct memories and involvement associated with it, can be used to signify its sentimental value.

Subjective associations and involvement with property is therefore a recognised characteristic of sentimental attachment. Inherited and familial property particularly holds memories associated with the deceased and emotional connections are created over time by mutual involvement with the property or because of its association with the deceased.

[41] [2012] EWCA Crim 1491; *Urry* (n 8).

[42] *Franks* (ibid) [17] (Hambledon J).

[43] ibid, [10].

[44] ibid, [17].

[45] See also *Vajpeyi v Yusaf* [2003] All ER 128, [38] and [41].

[46] Conway and Stannard (2016a).

[47] J Moorhead, 'Marie Kondo: How to Clear Out Sentimental Clutter' *The Guardian* (14 January 2017), available at www.theguardian.com/lifeandstyle/2017/jan/14/how-to-declutter-your-life-marie-kondo-spark-joy.

[48] M Gardner, 'A Tempest Brews in Heirloom Teacups' *Christian Science Monitor* (14 April 2004), available at jsh.christianscience.com.

[49] [2009] EWHC 2276, [93] (Andrews QC).

C. Objection to the Sale of Property

Another defining feature of sentimental attachment to property recognised in case law is that the owner or beneficiary who has formed a sentimental attachment will not want to part with such property given its irreplaceable value. Property loss cases arising out of family disputes particularly highlight objections to the sale of sentimentally valued property. For example, in *Abbey National Plc v Moss* the family home was placed into the joint names of a mother and her daughter to ensure it would not be sold in the mother's lifetime, an action the court deemed to be motivated by the property's sentimental value; 'It was [the mother's] only home and she had a strong sentimental attachment to it and particularly to the memory of her husband … [an] almost painful attachment'.[50] This connection between sentimental attachments and a reluctance to sell, or a need to protect from sale, was further noted in *WS v WS*, in which the court had to determine which items were to be sold during divorce proceedings.[51] The court noted that the husband's actions 'seemed … largely motivated by an emotional attachment to the property … and by a wish to give the children a chance to retain' the property.[52] This attachment guided determinations as to which items should be sold, and which should remain in the ownership of those who sentimentally valued them.[53]

Scholars further note how the reluctance to sell property is informed by attachments developed over years, and so can be dependent on another characteristic of sentimental attachment: length of ownership.[54] Nadler and Diamond's study reveals that the longer property is held, the more likely a person was to refuse its sale.[55] Grubbström also found that the implication of developing a strong attachment to land is the reluctance to sell it, since emotions act as a constraint against sale.[56] This has been supported in media reports of individuals who, due to their sentimental attachment, refused to sell their property. Examples include widows who refused to sell the home because of the memories it held and despite it being an 'eyesore',[57] to articles noting that sold homes are examples of property to which the owner did not possess an emotional attachment;[58] the sale of the home inferred that a sentimental attachment did not exist since the owners were instead happy to part with it and felt no great pain on its loss. This is demonstrative of a more widely

[50] *Abbey National Plc* (n 10) 309 (Gibson LJ).
[51] *WS* (n 10).
[52] ibid, [22] (Meston HHJ, QC).
[53] ibid.
[54] See section II.A above.
[55] Nadler and Diamond (2008).
[56] Grubbström (2011).
[57] J Barbanel, 'Sale of "Eyesore" to end Nightmare on West 76th' *Wall Street Journal* (6 September 2014), available at www.wsj.com.
[58] 'Inside Pregnant Cheryl's Mansion with Liam' *Mail Online* (3 March 2017), available at www.dailymail.co.uk/tvshowbiz/article-4278076/Cheryl-puts-Hertfordshire-home-market-19k-month.html; S Horne, 'Debt Levels Force More Landowners to Sell up' *Farmers Weekly* (26 July 2013), available at www.fwi.co.uk.

shared understanding of this key characteristic of sentimental attachment, beyond academia and outside the court.

D. Emotional Harm on Property Loss

Another recognised characteristic of sentimental attachment to property, tied also to a reluctance to sell property imbued with the same, is the emotional harm that accompanies the property's loss. Recognition of the harm caused arises in all cases, as already demonstrated in cases concerning both voluntary and involuntary loss and division of property. The judicial language utilised within *WS v WS*, *Donnelly v Donnelly* and *R v Franks (Steven John Joseph) & Ors* particularly emphasises the emotional impact of losing property of sentimental value,[59] highlighting the greater loss and 'devastat[ion]' that can arise where, and should, such loss occur.[60] Emotional harm is a logical consequence of the loss since sentimental property is identified by the courts as that which the owner will not want to lose given its emotional importance, with any loss thereby being significantly felt by those affected.

This characteristic of sentimental attachment is also evidenced in media reports, which highlight the strong emotional reactions that follow the loss of sentimentally valued property. Such loss is described as 'heart wrenching' given the significant emotional weight afforded to the property,[61] and the distress caused has been deemed 'unimaginable'.[62] Given the memories and life events associated with sentimentally valued property,[63] a profound sense of grief is also felt when such property is lost or acquired by another.[64]

On the death of an individual, emotional harm felt at the loss of property associated with the deceased is conflated with the emotion of grief arising from the death and loss of the person themselves. Some will have a stronger attachment to property as of right, based on their ties to the deceased, as well as their own emotional and/or monetary investment in the deceased's property, and possibly also a shared history of generational investment in the same. Emotions may therefore play a pivotal role in decisions concerning how, and to whom, such property is to be distributed when will-making.[65] These psychological and emotional dynamics render wills highly emotive documents.[66]

59 *WS* (n 10); *Donnelly* (n 29); and *Franks* (n 41).

60 *Donnelly* (n 29), [30].

61 'Jewellery's Value Lies in its Emotional or Sentimental Worth' *The Guardian* (12 February 2014), available at www.theguardian.com/fashion/fashion-blog/2014/feb/12/jewellerys-value-emotional-sentimental-worth.

62 'War Medals Taken in Aberdeen House Break-In' *BBC* (23 June 2017), available at www.bbc.co.uk/news/uk-scotland-north-east-orkney-shetland-40381090.

63 Twigg (2006).

64 Erikson [1976] in Cuba and Hummon (1993); Svašek (2006).

65 Conway and Stannard (2016b).

66 ibid.

III. Will-Making and Sentimental Attachments

Wills permit testators to make specific bequests that are tailored and unique to an individual or family's circumstances. These tell us most about sentimental attachments to property transferring on death, and the importance to testators and families that treasured items pass to those who also attach sentimental value to the same.

A. The Meaning of Bequests

Bequests in wills are often emotionally charged with meaning and the property transferred imbued with sentimental attachments. Research undertaken by Finch et al revealed, from a sample of 800 wills across four probate years, that:

> 4 per cent … named specific household items, 2 per cent bequeathed clothing, 8 per cent jewellery, and 4 per cent included items [that the researchers] … categorised as being potentially valuable or possible family heirlooms. These included items of silverware, paintings, medals, and furniture … described as antique or … a 'family piece' in the will.[67]

Whilst this seems a low percentage, most items will transfer in any event to those who have a shared history and attachment to property, either under the will as part of the residuary estate, or by survivorship where property was already jointly owned. What is most telling as regards sentimentality in this research, however, was the discovery concerning the nomination of substitute beneficiaries.

Whilst in most cases it is essential to name substitute beneficiaries to prevent lapse, except now for gifts to a testator's lineal descendants,[68] Finch et al's research found that around three-quarters of those leaving gifts to non-family members failed to provide a substitute, whereas gifts to family members tended to provide for substitute beneficiaries within the same family.[69] It is agreed that this is indicative of two things. First, there is a desire to keep certain property with certain members of one's family and they are those of the deceased's choosing. Second, in other circumstances, with regard to gifts made to those outside the family, allowing lapse to occur indicates that 'If that beneficiary dies before the testator, the gift itself loses its meaning'.[70] The idea of providing a substitute beneficiary highlights that the property itself and its retention is important to the testator and presumably to those to whom the gift is given. The failure to name a substitute beneficiary suggests some gifts lose meaning on a beneficiary's predecease, evidencing that sentimental attachments to certain property comes only from a connection

[67] Finch and Hayes (1994) 417, fn 6.
[68] Wills Act 1837 (WA 1837), s 33 (introduced by the Administration of Justice Act 1982, s 19).
[69] Finch et al (1996).
[70] ibid, 149–50.

between the testator, that specific beneficiary, and perhaps from the gift itself.[71] As Banks et al note,

> the same object can carry with it different meanings for different people, and … can become more or less significant as our relationships to others change over time. This is true even through bereavement, where artifacts can take on new meaning as they shift to become objects of historical legacy.[72]

Sentimentality is therefore both personal and transient.

Given that most testators provide for those whom the intestacy rules include in any event,[73] albeit with the flexibility to distribute an estate in differing proportions, one reason for making a will is to secure the transfer of certain items of property, particularly those of sentimental value, to those without whom the property will lose all meaning. If property was not imbued with sentimentality then gift-giving on death would be less important.

The importance of will-making and of gift-giving on death has been highlighted most recently during the coronavirus pandemic, as the demand for wills increased significantly.[74] This may be explained by people having more time to focus on their financial affairs during lockdowns, or perhaps because of the increased awareness of one's mortality during such a global health crisis. Despite tight socialising restrictions there was still a need for people to have a say over the distribution of their estates, to write their last wishes, and to make specific gifts. So important was the ability of people to still be able to make a will during the pandemic that in regard to England and Wales the Government introduced The Wills Act 1837 (Electronic Communications) (Amendment) (Coronavirus) Order 2020 to overcome witnessing formalities,[75] by permitting the electronic witnessing of wills for the first time. Introduced on 28 September 2020 as a temporary two-year measure, it can apply retrospectively from 31 January 2020, and has now been extended until 31 January 2024.

Changes in the forms of property have also prompted increased scholarly and media interest[76] in the inheritance of chattels once tangible, but now intangible, and created and stored often only digitally. Harbinja and Edwards', and Conway and Grattan's respective work into the challenges surrounding digital inheritance highlights this as an area that particularly invokes sentimentality and a greater need for

[71] See also Odom et al (2010).

[72] Banks, Kirk and Sellen (2012) 65.

[73] Finch et al (1996).

[74] J Slingo, 'Will making on the rise in wake of coronavirus' *Law Gazette* (2 December 2020), available at www.lawgazette.co.uk/news/will-making-on-the-rise-in-wake-of-coronavirus-/5106639.article.

[75] WA 1837, s 9.

[76] 'Father asks Apple head Tim Cook to unblock dead son's iPhone' *The Guardian* (31 March 2016), available at www.theguardian.com/technology/2016/mar/31/father-apple-tim-cook-unblock-dead-son-iphone-leonardo-fabbretti; B Griffiths, 'Access Denied: Grieving parents blast Facebook's "cruel" social media rules for denying them access to their dead children's accounts' *The Sun* (22 June 2019), available at www.thesun.co.uk/news/9354138/facebook-blocks-dead-childrens-accounts.

will-making to assist in the distribution of digital property.[77] Data storage companies such as cloud services, email and social media require at least the deceased's authority, if not also court approval, to permit relatives access to a deceased's digital property, and even then they cannot guarantee access to devices.[78] Loss of access, particularly to photographs, it is argued, causes emotional harm.[79] These were items that once would have transferred tangibly in boxes or albums, and without great restriction. Legal professional bodies increasingly encourage their members to record testators' digital access information, highlighting the importance of such to administration of estates, but also the sentimental importance of a person's digital property.[80] The Law Society notes that 'Digital assets with sentimental value can be the most difficult to sort out, but can be the most important for those left behind.'[81] Photographs and messages will rarely be worth anything to anyone other than those connected to the deceased, but may be more valuable to them than monetary assets.

B. A Case of Keeping it in the Family

Case law sheds light on will contents, highlighting the types of gifts testators make and to whom. In *Shelley v Shelley* the testator left various items of jewellery to her nephew 'to go and be held as heir-looms by him, and by his eldest son on his decease … and so on, to the eldest son of his descendants'.[82] The court decided that a valid trust had been created in favour of the nephew's sons and so he was not free to leave them in his own estate to his wife, thus keeping the items in the testator's direct family line. *Shelley* was followed in *Re Steele's Will Trusts*, which contained a similar trust of jewellery, specifically a diamond necklace, which the testator requested be held on trust for her son 'as an heirloom' and to pass thereafter to his descendants.[83]

It is possible that sentimentality and monetary worth played their part in the testators' motives, but both cases highlight a desire to keep certain items within

[77] See, for example, Edwards and Harbinja in Maciel and Carvalho Pereira (2013); Harbinja (2019); and Conway and Grattan in Conway and Hickey (2017).

[78] Microsoft 365 Support, 'Accessing Outlook.com, OneDrive and other Microsoft services when someone has died', available at support.microsoft.com/en-us/office/accessing-outlook-com-onedrive-and-other-microsoft-services-when-someone-has-died-ebbd2860-917e-4b39-9913–212362da6b2f; Apple Support, 'How to request access to a deceased family member's Apple account' (April 2022), available at support.apple.com/en-gb/HT208510; and Google Account Help, 'Submit a request regarding a deceased user's account', available at support.google.com/accounts/troubleshooter/6357590?hl=en.

[79] See (n 76).

[80] G Rycroft, 'Protecting your online assets' *The Law Society* (12 May 2016), available at www.lawsociety.org.uk/topics/blogs/protecting-your-online-assets; and The Society of Trust and Estate Practitioners, 'Digital Assets', available at www.step.org/digital-assets.

[81] Rycroft (ibid).

[82] (1868) LR 6 Eq 540, 540.

[83] [1948] Ch 603, 603–04.

the family. There is no indication though, in either case, that the jewellery had previously held any sentimental value before coming into the testators' possession, though both class their gifts as 'heirlooms'. Neither case, and indeed no case law, truly address what is meant by an 'heirloom', though it is commonly understood to be a term synonymous with items of family heritage and importance. Odom et al noted that participants in their study regarded

> objects of historical legacy … as heirlooms in the classic sense and ownership had been retained within the family for many decades … These objects owed to the broader family line, rather than the life of the loved one that had recently bequeathed them.[84]

This suggests that heirlooms have broader and longer lasting sentimentality, spanning generations as opposed to just two individuals.

Whilst the cases considered highlight the sentimentality testators themselves attach to specific gifts in the way that they are gifted, and also in to whom they are gifted, the courts, often indirectly or as a subsidiary issue, have to navigate sentimentality in inheritance disputes. Often this is because the property's value is attached to a person or place and judges, as seen earlier in this chapter, have shown sympathy for those concerned in disputes over, sometimes quite literally, the family china.[85] Judges are faced with witness beneficiaries, the real people who hold sentimental attachments to items of property in dispute and so their recognition of sentimentality and their empathy is unsurprising.

In the case of *Butler v Butler*, the court recognised the sentimental attachment that two beneficiaries held for their father's '502 items of 17th century Chinese porcelain'.[86] In dividing up the assets between four beneficiaries, sentimentality was influential in the judge's decision to permit each beneficiary to choose in turn an item of their choice until all assets had depleted. The judge found 'that a 1-2-3-4 selection process would [not] produce an unjust result whether by reference to value or otherwise',[87] thereby allowing each beneficiary to choose at least some items holding the most sentimental value to them. Whilst the court recognised that selection may turn on sentimental as well as monetary value,[88] it was also dismissive of sentimentality in advising that where an uneven number of items fell to be distributed of equal monetary and sentimental value, the undistributed items would be ordered sold and the proceeds distributed equally.[89] This wholly ignores sentimentality and the emotional loss associated with such action, but would, as the court put it, 'break the deadlock'.[90] A principal concern for the court is always to resolve financial and family disputes practically and completely for the benefit of the parties concerned, litigation being the final resort and end to the matter.

[84] Odom et al (2010) 1834.
[85] *Butler* (n 9), and see below.
[86] ibid [1]–[2] (Barker HHJ, QC).
[87] ibid, [98].
[88] ibid, [76].
[89] ibid, [72]–[73].
[90] ibid, [72].

One way, and arguably the only way they can do this, without making orders that beneficiaries share property and thereby potentially perpetuate disputes for years to come, is to resort to a financial resolution to try and achieve equitable fairness.

The courts have also recognised that once detached from a person or place an item can lose sentimental value, or at least significance. In *Re Bathurst*, heard by the same judge as *Butler*, HHJ Barker QC, the court acknowledged that the large landed estate at the centre of the case was historic.[91] It was noted that the deceased Eighth Earl of Bathurst had tried to satisfy 'both his duty to his children and his desire to provide for Lady Bathurst', who was his second wife and stepmother to his heir.[92] Among other matters, the case concerned the construction of a trust created by statutory codicil to protect chattels within the deceased's estate, and referred to as heirlooms,[93] from passing out of the family on his wife's death. She was a US citizen at the date of the codicil, as a result of which there would have been tax implications for the estate and a potential loss of important assets inextricably linked to the same. By amending the testator's will, the court upheld what it deemed to be the testator's wish to keep property within the family line, and in doing so it also kept any tax benefit within the UK. The case indirectly highlighted that property that is often inherited, particularly in aristocratic and landed families, carries historic significance, and arguably with it a broader sentimentality, the loss of which could be of concern to more people than just the family involved, potentially being relevant to a country's historic or cultural heritage.

Another issue in the case relevant to sentimental attachment to property was whether the deceased's widow would be 'required to part with the use and enjoyment of the chattels … which have an important non-monetary significance to her'.[94] The court acknowledged that although the chattels were 'less valuable in monetary terms … monetary value [was] not the only consideration.'[95] Whilst the court decided against the widow on the point of construction, it was found unlikely that she would have to give up property that she had enjoyed use of for the past 30 years, as for the heir to require her to do this would be capricious.[96] Furthermore, there was evidence of 'an understanding between the Eighth Earl and Lady Bathurst … that upon Lady Bathurst's death [certain chattels] would be kept in the Bathurst family.'[97] In other words, whilst she would likely continue to enjoy them in her lifetime, she had no legal right to do so and the terms of the settlement meant they would ultimately revert to the deceased's heir. Sentimentality was engrained throughout the court's considerations in its efforts to uphold what it deemed the deceased would have wanted; to keep the property within his family,

[91] *Bathurst* (n 37).
[92] ibid, [20] (Barker HHJ, QC).
[93] ibid, [17].
[94] ibid, [32].
[95] ibid, [44].
[96] ibid, [101].
[97] ibid, [10].

but to preserve use in the wife's lifetime to property to which she was attached. This was not, however, a case about anyone parting with property on a permanent basis, which may explain the more prominent role of sentimental attachment in the judgment.

The courts have also recognised that a testator's sudden lack of demonstrable sentimentality can be indicative of a loss of testamentary capacity. In *Sharp v Adam* the testator had made repeated gifts to his daughters of furniture and paintings in both an earlier will and several codicils, and 'he had specifically asked them to keep [these items] in the family'.[98] In his last will and testament, however, he had excluded his daughters completely. The court found that although the financial value of these specific gifts was not significant, they carried 'sentimental value' for his daughters.[99] This was influential in the court's finding that the testator lacked testamentary capacity to make his purported last will. The testator's sudden ignorance of sentimentality, as well as inconsistency with his earlier testamentary dispositions, demonstrated irrationality.

As these cases evidence, testators consider sentimental attachments to property, particularly in relation to those items that they consider to be 'heirlooms', which although they may hold monetary value, are not intended to be sold, but to pass to future generations. A demonstrable lack of recognition of sentimental value, as in *Sharp*, can also raise questions as to testamentary capacity, particularly where no other reason could 'explain the decision' to ignore sentimental attachment.[100] No reason proffered in the case came 'anywhere near providing a rational explanation' for the testator's failure to pass sentimental property to his daughters.[101] The courts cannot avoid considering sentimental value where items mean so much more to the parties involved than just financial worth. Sentimentality factors into the court's considerations and can be influential and persuasive in the conclusions reached.

C. Negative Emotions Arising from Sentimental Attachments

It has been noted that heirlooms, seen 'through the lens of the life of a deceased member of a family, or a friend' 'have rich connections with memory'.[102] Bequests, however, may not always be well received. Beneficiaries may disclaim an inheritance.[103] Further, the sentimental attachment the testator had to the gifted

[98] *Sharp* (n 9), [247] (Strauss QC).
[99] ibid, [250].
[100] ibid.
[101] ibid, [252].
[102] Banks, Kirk and Seller (2012) 64.
[103] WA 1837, s 33A (1)(a); and AEA 1925, s 46A (1)(a).

property may not resonate the same with the beneficiary and could be a painful reminder of the past or of what has been lost.[104]

Research has highlighted the negative impact of inheritance arising when one inherits something so associated with the deceased that it can never feel as if it is theirs or serve the testator's intended purpose.[105] This is not necessarily due to a dislike of the property inherited or of the deceased, but the opposite; it is often rooted in the love beneficiaries had for the deceased and their grief, the emotional toil and strain of reminders of the person lost. It is

> a key peculiarity of this relationship [of bequeathing] … that it is *asymmetric* – the bereaved are left to come to grips with the things passed to them, which leaves them, sometimes, to grapple with understanding why they were chosen to be the bearer of particular things.[106]

Inherited property can be too emotionally charged with sentimentality.

The deceased may also have wished the beneficiary to use the property in a way in which the beneficiary is reluctant to do so. Finch and Hayes highlighted this in their research regarding the transfer of a family home.[107] One participant beneficiary did not want to live in the home she inherited from her father as he had intended. The participant's 'own views of what was appropriate were completely at odds with her father's expressed wishes, yet she found it difficult to ignore them with equanimity' and felt 'guilt … at not complying with her father's wishes'.[108] This may be because beneficiaries do not have the same sentimentality to the property transferred, or perhaps have too much sentimental attachment to the same to consider it their own home. It may also be that the beneficiary has their own sentimental attachment to another property which competes and outweighs any sentimentality held for the inherited property.

Positive and negative emotions associated with sentimental attachments to property can therefore influence what a beneficiary would like to inherit from the deceased and how they perceive and treat their inheritance. Testators who make gifts in wills based on their own perceived understandings of others' sentimental attachments may be misguided. As Banks et al have highlighted, sentimental attachments are personal.[109] Testators may therefore hold a different sentimental attachment to property than their beneficiaries or may perceive a beneficiary to hold a sentimental attachment that they do not, leaving beneficiaries, perhaps wracked with emotional guilt, to make a decision on what is to happen to property they have inherited and which holds negative sentimental attachments for them.

[104] Finch and Hayes (1994); and Odom et al (2010).
[105] ibid.
[106] Odom et al (2010) 1834.
[107] Finch and Hayes (1994).
[108] ibid, 425.
[109] Banks, Kirk and Sellen (2012).

IV. Conclusion

Sentimental attachments to property are real and can be established using the four criteria: length of ownership; subjective associations and involvement; objection to sale; and emotional harm. Sentimental attachments are recognised across socio-legal scholarship and by the judiciary, as well as more widely within society, as evidenced by the content of wills and media reports. Inherited property is particularly imbued with sentimentality and whilst the same may financially support family or dependants, will-making serves a whole other purpose: to transfer property of meaning to those to whom it means something to, regardless of whether it holds monetary value. The law, however, does not provide a 'sentimental solution' to disputes over inherited property, leaving beneficiaries and their representatives to navigate the same at times of often great emotional upset. The emotional toil and costs associated with making a claim, and of defending one, means that most people will not pursue litigation. This does not mean, however, that family disputes go away. The death of a loved one can cause seismic shifts in family relationships years after they have died.

The courts are at least sensitive to sentimentality and recognise a right of inheritance for some to keep property they have inherited, protecting the same where possible in disposal and division cases, and finding solutions to try and reflect a fair distribution of assets on death based on sentimental attachment. 'Keeping it in the family' is something the courts have always worked towards to uphold family finances and peace of relations, including recognising property's attachment to people, but also to places and history. Practically, the court's role is to ensure the expedient resolution of disputes and the administration of estates, and often the only way to achieve this is to see beyond emotion and sentimental attachment, and instead to apply monetary division as a remedy to any stalemate. In this way sentimental attachment, whilst recognised, can often be ignored, the law missing the 'true' value of the property in dispute. It is therefore incumbent on testators to make sure that they specify to whom property of sentimental value is to pass, and to recognise also the idiosyncrasies of beneficiaries' wishes in regard to the same, so a smooth property transition can take place on death that reflects a fair distribution of monetary and sentimental value acceptable to all. Inheritance is inherently imbued with sentimentality, an immeasurable value unique to the property and to the individuals who form such attachments to the same.

References

Banks, R, Kirk, D and Sellen, A, 'A Design Perspective on Three Technology Heirlooms' (2012) 27 *Human-Computer Interaction* 63.

Conway, H and Grattan, S, 'The "New" New Property: Dealing with Digital Assets on Death' in H Conway and R Hickey (eds), *Modern Studies in Property Law: Volume 9* (Oxford, Hart Publishing, 2017).

Conway, H and Stannard, J, 'Property and Emotions' (2016a) 8 *Emotion Review* 38.

—— *The Emotional Dynamics of Law and Legal Discourse* (London, Bloomsbury Publishing, 2016b).

Cuba, L and Hummon, D, 'A Place to Call Home: Identification with Dwelling, Community, and Region' (1993) 34 *The Sociological Quarterly* 111.

Edwards, L and Harbinja, E, '"What Happens to My Facebook Profile When I Die?": Legal Issues Around Transmission of Digital Assets on Death' in C Maciel and V Carvalho Pereira (eds), *Digital Legacy and Interaction: Post-Mortem Issues* (Springer International Publishing, 2013).

Finch, J and Hayes, L, 'Inheritance, Death and the Concept of the Home' (1994) 28 *Sociology* 417.

Finch J, et al, *Wills, Inheritance, and Families* (Oxford, Oxford University Press, 1996).

Grubbström, A, 'Emotional Bonds as Obstacles to Land Sale - Attitudes to Land Among Local and Absentee Landowners in Northwest Estonia' (2011) 99 *Landscape and Urban Planning* 31.

Harbinja, E 'Emails and Death: Legal Issues Surrounding Post-Mortem Transmission of Emails' (2019) 43 *Death Studies* 435.

Nadler J, and Diamond, S, 'Eminent Domain and the Psychology of Property Rights: Proposed Use, Subjective Attachment, and Taker Identity' (2008) 5 *Journal of Empirical Legal Studies* 713.

Odom W, et al, 'Passing On & Putting to Rest: Understanding Bereavement in the Context of Interactive Technologies' Association for Computing Machinery's Conference on Human Factors in Computing Systems (2010).

Probert, R, 'Control over Marriage in England and Wales, 1753–1823: The Clandestine Marriages Act of 1753 in Context' (2009) 27 *Law and History Review* 413.

Simpson, AWB, *A History of the Land Law*, 2nd edn (Oxford, Oxford University Press, 1986).

Spring, E, 'The Settlement of Land in Nineteenth-Century England' (1964) 8 *American Journal of Legal History* 209.

Svašek, M, *Postsocialism: Politics and Emotions in Central and Eastern Europe* (New York and Oxford, Berghahn Books, 2006).

Twigg, J, *The Body in Health and Social Care* (New York, Palgrave Macmillan, 2006).

Ulen, T, 'The Public Use of Private Property: A Dual-Constraint Theory of Efficient Government Takings' in N Mercuro (ed), *Taking Property and Just Compensation: Law and Economics Perspectives of the Takings Issue* (Boston, Kluwer Academic Publishers, 1992).

PART 4

Adjudicating Inheritance/ Adjudicating 'Family'

10

How Social Norms and Values Influence the Balance between Wills Variation Claimants and Testators

ALLISON A CARTIER

I. Introduction

Tension develops in the context of wills and inheritance in many common law jurisdictions, especially in circumstances where a person has died leaving a potential beneficiary disappointed or altogether disinherited. Legislative regimes exist in the Canadian provinces and territories, as well as in other common law jurisdictions, which allow a person to make a claim for provision or an award from a deceased person's estate. Wills variation claimants seek to ameliorate 'unfair' or 'inadequate' dispositions made by testators,[1] and depending on the governing legislation, a court may order that provision be made for the claimant.

Social and cultural values influence how we interpret the terms of testators' wills. Do we expect the right to dispose of our assets and worldly possessions on our own terms, absolutely, and without interference of legislative provisions imposed by the judiciary? Or do we sympathise with claimants for whom a testator did not provide under the terms of their will? If we sympathise with a claimant, do we ascribe different values to the claim of an infant child of the testator, an adult child of a testator with disabilities inhibiting their own independence, or an independent child of a testator of their own means? What factors persuade us that a testator failed to 'adequately provide': a claimant's contribution to the testator's estate; their age; gender; health status; or the historical conduct of the testator? What factors dissuade us from sympathising with a claimant: their means, independently attained; their treatment of the testator; or other claims upon the testator's bounty?

[1] A deceased person leaving a will is referred to as a testator, or on occasion testatrix if the deceased will-maker identifies as female. For the purposes of this chapter, a deceased person leaving a will shall be referred to as a testator and includes all genders.

In the Supreme Court of Canada's 1994 landmark decision of *Tataryn v Tataryn Estate*, Justice McLaughlin (as she then was) acknowledged the tension between the social and public policy interests of will variation claims and a testator's right to freely dispose of their assets pursuant to their wishes.[2] In *Tataryn*, McLaughlin J referred to the 'modern values and expectations' of society with respect to inheritance, and noted the fluidity in what is considered 'adequate, just and equitable' throughout the passage of time.[3]

This chapter explores how social and cultural values influence the weight we ascribe to either testamentary autonomy or 'just and equitable' relief proffered to wills variation claimants. It should be noted that there is much more legislation, case law, and commentary on this subject, particularly in other jurisdictions outside Canada, and that this chapter by no means explores this topic exhaustively. By reviewing current and historical legislation and case law on the subject, we attain a glimpse of 'modern values and expectations', 'contemporary standards', and where the pendulum falls between the interests of wills variation claimants and the individual autonomy of testators.

II. Values, Philosophies, and Inconsistencies

A. History and Origins

Between the mid-seventeenth century and the introduction of dependants' relief (wills variation) legislation, a testator had complete testamentary freedom, meaning the capacity to dispose of their assets pursuant to the terms of their will without interference.[4] In *Banks v Goodfellow*, a case of seminal importance, Cockburn CJ noted that 'English law leaves everything to the unfettered discretion of the testator'.[5] However, Cockburn CJ then referred to the expectations of a testator's family in the event they had not been provided for under the terms of the will: 'Hence arises a reasonable and well warranted expectation on the part of a man's kindred surviving him that on his death his effects shall become theirs, instead of being given to strangers'.[6] Of note, while there is discussion on the legitimacy of certain heirs in the *Banks* case, the case also serves as precedent for principles including testamentary capacity and undue influence.

The first common law jurisdiction to consider the validity of absolute testamentary freedom was New Zealand when, during Parliamentary Debates in 1895, members discussed occasions in which a widow and her children had been

[2] *Tataryn v Tataryn Estate* [1994] 2 SCR 807, 1994 CanLII 51 (SCC).
[3] ibid, 814–15.
[4] Amighetti (1991).
[5] *Banks v Goodfellow* [1861–73] All ER Rep 47 (QB) 55.
[6] ibid, 55.

left destitute by the will of a deceased husband and father.[7] By 9 October 1900, New Zealand had enacted the Testator's Family Maintenance Act.[8] This legislative regime, referred to as 'an independent creation of New Zealand's legislative genius', allowed widows and children to challenge the wills of deceased testators in circumstances where they had been inadequately provided for.[9]

The Province of British Columbia followed suit on 17 April 1920, when it enacted its own Testator's Family Maintenance Act. Over time, each of the Canadian provinces and territories enacted similar legislation, albeit with some subtle differences, discussed in further detail below.

England introduced a similar court-based discretionary application system for claimants in 1938,[10] which was later amended to the present-day Inheritance (Provision for Family and Dependants) Act 1975.[11] The delay in introducing legislation permitting claimants to seek relief from a testator's estate might have been due in part to the historical tradition that English testators had absolute and unfettered power in their testation.[12]

B. Legislative Schemes

While many common law jurisdictions have enacted dependants' relief or wills variation legislation, only legislative schemes within Canada's common law provinces and territories will be referred to in this chapter.[13] There are differences in the legislation between provinces, with perhaps the most significant distinctions being the individuals entitled to apply to seek relief or vary a testator's will. When these provisions are compared side by side, a spectrum as to who is entitled to seek relief appears.[14] On one end of the spectrum, widows, widowers, and/or children under age 16 are entitled to apply. On the other end, there is a broader inclusion of relatives or dependants of the testator, including: adult children; stepchildren; brothers and sisters; parents; grandparents; and cohabitating partners.

Perhaps the most expansive legislative regime is in British Columbia, which allows spouses and children of a testator to commence a proceeding for provision under the will that is 'adequate, just and equitable in the circumstances'.[15] Unlike most of the other provinces, British Columbia's wills variation legislation does not include the caveat that any child or children of the testator be under a certain age, unable to live independently due to a mental or physical disability, or dependent

[7] Amighetti (1991) 6–7; 102 New Zealand Parliamentary Debates (1898) 422–23.
[8] Testator's Family Maintenance Act SNZ 1900 No 20.
[9] Amighetti (1991) 10.
[10] Inheritance (Family Provision) Act 1938.
[11] Inheritance (Provision for Family and Dependants) Act 1975.
[12] Roggendorf (2018) 219.
[13] Québec's Civil Code CQLR c CCQ 1991, is not referred to in this chapter.
[14] Amighetti (1991) 24–25.
[15] Wills, Estates and Succession Act SBC 2009, c 13, s 60.

upon the testator at the time of the testator's death. An independent adult child of a testator may therefore make a claim pursuant to British Columbia's Wills, Estates and Succession Act, even if they are independently wealthy and have been independent of the testator for decades. The Provision for Dependants Act of New Brunswick allows a spouse, child, or other dependant of the deceased to apply for relief.[16] In Nova Scotia and Newfoundland and Labrador, their respective legislative regimes provide that a dependant means the widow, widower, or child of the deceased.[17]

Under Alberta's Wills and Succession Act, a 'family member' in relation to the testator means: a spouse or adult interdependent partner; a child under the age of 18 years; a child unable to earn a livelihood by reason of mental or physical disability; a child between the ages of 18 and 22 and who is a full-time student; or a grandchild or great-grandchild under the age of 18 years and in respect of whom the testator stood in place of a parent.[18]

Saskatchewan's legislation provides that a 'dependant' in relation to the deceased means: a wife or husband; a child under the age of 18 years; a child who is 18 years or older who by reason of mental or physical disability is unable to earn a livelihood or by reason of need or other circumstance alleges greater entitlement under the will; or a person who cohabitated as a spouse continuously for at least two years or was in a relationship of permanence and sharing a child with the deceased.[19] The legislation of the Northwest Territories and Nunavut is very similar to that of Saskatchewan, providing that a 'dependant' in relation to the deceased means: a spouse; a child under the age of 19 years; a child who is 19 years or older who by reason of mental or physical disability is unable to earn a livelihood; a person cohabitating with the deceased for one year or more, or with whom the deceased shared a child or children; or a foster-parent of the deceased's children.[20] Yukon's Dependants Relief Act differs, providing that a 'dependant' in relation to the deceased means: a common law partner; a child under the age of 16 years; a child over the age of 16 years who is unable because of a mental or physical disability to earn a livelihood; or a grandparent, parent, descendant, or divorced spouse of the deceased who was a dependant of the deceased for maintenance and support for a period of no less than three years immediately prior to the date of death of the deceased.[21]

The definition of a 'dependant' under The Dependants Relief Act of Manitoba is considerably more robust than the definitions in its neighbouring jurisdictions and makes it a requirement for certain claimants to have been 'substantially

[16] Provision for Dependants Act RSNB 2012, c 111, s 1.

[17] Testators' Family Maintenance Act RSNS 1989, c 465, s 2(b); Family Relief Act RSNL 1990, c F-3, s 2(c).

[18] Wills and Succession Act SA 2010, c W-12, s 72.

[19] The Dependants' Relief Act SS 1996, c D-25.01, s 2.

[20] Dependants Relief Act RSNWT 1988, c D-4, s 1; Dependants Relief Act RSNWT (Nu) 1988, c D-4, s 1.

[21] Dependants Relief Act RSY 2002, c 56, s 1.

dependant on the deceased at the time of the deceased's death'.[22] Such claimants include adult able-bodied children, grandchildren, parents, grandparents, brothers, or sisters of the testator.[23] Similarly, while the Succession Law Reform Act of Ontario includes spouses, parents, children, grandchildren, and siblings as potential claimants, the deceased must have been providing support to the claimant, or was under a legal obligation to provide support to the claimant, at the deceased's date of death.[24] Therefore, unlike in British Columbia, an independent adult child of the deceased would not have standing to make a claim for provision from the testator's estate.

Besides differences in the classes of individuals entitled to apply to seek relief or vary a testator's will, there are also differences with respect to how the courts may assess a claim. For example, Manitoba's Act provides that the court may order that reasonable provision be made out of the estate of the deceased, 'If it appears to the court that a dependant is in financial need'.[25] The Act further provides an extensive list of circumstances that the court shall consider in making an award, including: the measures available for a dependant to become financially independent; provision made to the dependant by the deceased during the deceased's lifetime; and in the case of a child, their aptitude for a reasonable prospect of obtaining an education.[26] Under the Dependants of Deceased Person Relief Act of Prince Edward Island, there is a provision for the court to contemplate any written statements made by the deceased person that offers reasons for not making provision for a dependant.[27]

The diversity in the legislation among the Canadian provinces and territories demonstrates that there are differences in social, moral and familial values represented by legislatures respecting dependants' relief and wills variation. The differences as to which individuals are entitled to seek relief suggests that some legislatures are more sympathetic to the claims of adult children of testators, without caveats, whereas others restrict the class of claimants to individuals to whom a testator was legally obligated to support. Comparisons between legislative schemes between jurisdictions shows that 'modern expectations' regarding wills variation, dependants' relief, and testamentary autonomy are apparent not only through the caselaw, but also by the legislation enacted by elected lawmakers.

C. 'Just and Equitable Provision'

Returning to the origins of dependants' relief or wills variation legislation, the guiding principles were to ameliorate unfairness perpetrated by a testator upon

[22] The Dependants Relief Act CCSM, c D37, s 1.
[23] ibid.
[24] Succession Law Reform Act RSO 1990, c S26, s 57(1).
[25] See n 22, CCSM, c D37s 2(1).
[26] ibid, s 8(1)(c), (i) and (j).
[27] Dependants of a Deceased Person Relief Act RSPEI 1988, c D-7, s 5.

his dependants and to relieve those dependants from becoming a burden on the state.[28] However, there has been much discussion about the extent to which provision is 'necessary', 'just', 'equitable' or 'fair'. The often-cited case of *Walker v McDermott* contemplated what constitutes 'proper maintenance and support'.[29] Duff J, writing for the majority, opined that numerous circumstances must be referenced when considering what constitutes 'proper maintenance and support', including claimant's personal situation, their standard of living, as well as any other relevant circumstances.[30] According to Duff J, 'proper maintenance and support' cannot be limited to 'the bare necessities of existence'.[31]

In *Pontifical Society for the Propagation of the Faith v Scales*, Dixon CJ considered the meaning of 'adequate provision for proper maintenance and support' in depth:

> It has often been pointed out that very important words in the statute are 'adequate provision for the proper maintenance and support' and that each of these words must be given its value. 'Adequate' and 'proper' in particular must be considered as words which must always be relative. The 'proper' maintenance and support of a son claiming a statutory provision must be relative to his age, sex, condition and mode of life and situation generally. What is 'adequate' must be relative not only to his needs but to his own capacity and resources for meeting them. There is then a relation to be considered between these matters on the one hand, and on the other, the nature, extent and character of the estate and the other demands upon it, and also what the testator regarded as superior claims or preferable dispositions.[32]

In *Pontifical Society*, a 1962 decision of the High Court of Australia, the testator separated from his wife when their son was four years of age, with no contact between the testator and son for the decades then on until the testator's death, 46 years later. The son supported his mother throughout his life and established himself in a comfortable position with a career and family. But for a modest monthly annuity made for his estranged wife, the testator left the residue of his estate to 10 charities. The testator left no provision for his son, resulting in the son applying for and obtaining provision from the testator's estate. On appeal by the charities named by the testator in the will, the Court was charged with considering the son's 'station in life' and its impact on what provision ought to be made for him from the testator's estate. Dixon CJ, writing for the majority, stated, 'One consideration here is that the son has made his way in life and though, like most people, he would find more money an advantage, he is not in need'.[33] Dissenting with the Court's outcome, Taylor J suggested that it was 'beside the point' that the son was not destitute; the son had a reasonable expectation that the testator was

[28] Franke (1988) 352.
[29] *Walker v McDermott* [1931] SCR 91, 1930 CanLII 1 (SCC).
[30] ibid, 96.
[31] ibid.
[32] *Pontifical Society for the Propagation of the Faith v Scales* (1962) 107 CLR 9, 19.
[33] ibid.

not 'morally free' to dispose of his estate without regard for the son.[34] The result, as per Dixon CJ's findings, was that the charities were allowed to appeal the prior order that made provision for the son.

The Manitoba Court of Appeal grappled between what was 'just and equitable' and the testator's freedom in the case of *Barr v Barr*.[35] Dickson JA, writing for the majority, noted that the claimant's case rested not on need, but rather on the moral ground that he had contributed his efforts to the family farm with the expectation that he would one day inherit it.[36] Like the son in *Pontifical Society*, the claimant in the *Barr* case was not destitute or in financial need. The Court concluded that, 'There can be a moral obligation to a son, even if that son is comfortably situated financially'.[37]

In 1987, the Court of Appeal of British Columbia explicitly referenced how 'just and equitable provision' ought to be evaluated within the confines of the province's wills variation legislation.[38] Esson J stated that:

> A long line of binding decisions has held that the question of whether the testator had made adequate provision for the proper maintenance and support of a claimant is to be determined by deciding whether he has discharged his 'moral duty' to them, and that need is not an essential element in a claim.[39]

The Manitoba Court of Appeal made it clear that its legislative scheme is different from that of other provinces in the case of *McAuley v Genaille*, and that indeed a claimant's 'need' is a necessary threshold requirement to proceed with a claim to vary a testator's will.[40] The Court noted that the history and language of Manitoba's Act clearly reflected a needs-maintenance approach to dependants' relief, in contrast to the legislation in British Columbia and other Canadian jurisdictions.[41] While other Canadian jurisdictions were found to contemplate financial need 'as one of a list of factors used to determine adequate provision', the Court explained that Manitoba was unique in the sense that if a claimant was unable to show financial need, they would be disqualified from proceeding with a claim for relief.[42]

The above-referenced cases, among others, demonstrate that a claimant need not provide evidence of financial need or 'destitution' in all jurisdictions to successfully seek provision from an estate. However, the financial circumstances of a claimant are frequently considered in the context of what might have been 'just and equitable provision' from the testator's estate, and factor to the relative strength of any such claim, discussed in greater length below.

[34] ibid.
[35] *Barr v Barr* [1971] MJ No 61, (1972) 25 DLR (3d) 401 (MBCA).
[36] ibid, para 3.
[37] ibid, para 19.
[38] *Price v Lychuk Estate* 1987 CanLII 165 (BCCA).
[39] ibid, 2.
[40] *McAuley v Genaille* 2017 MBCA 69.
[41] ibid, [54].
[42] ibid, [58].

D. Testamentary Freedom

The implementation of dependants' relief or wills variation legislation has not been without criticism. Staunch advocates of testamentary freedom and autonomy take the position that a testator ought to have the right to dispose of their assets as they see fit. In 1873 in *Boughton v Knight*, Sir Hannen observed that:

> It is thought better to risk the chance of an abuse of the power arising from such liberty [testamentary freedom] than to deprive men of the right to make such a selection as their knowledge of character, of the past history, and future prospects of their children or other relatives may demand.[43]

During the Parliamentary Debates of 1895 in New Zealand, one member of Parliament remarked that any legislative regime restricting testamentary autonomy was a 'lawyer's bill', as 'it simply made food for lawyers, and afforded opportunities for lawyers to go and contest wills'.[44]

The British Columbia Court of Appeal contemplated its new wills variation legislation in 1926, after a trial judge ordered that the entire residue of the testator's estate pass to his widow, contrary to the terms of his will, which specified a modest bequest of $10 to his wife and the residue to his nephew.[45] On appeal, Martin JA stated that the case dealt 'with a matter which is something wholly unknown to our former law, and the whole object of the new statute is to defeat the wishes of the testator'.[46] While MacDonald CJA dissented with the outcome of the majority of the Court of Appeal, his comments regarding the order of the trial judge were: 'It wholly disregards the testator's intention and disposes of his whole estate contrary to his wishes'.[47] In the 1942 case of *In Re Styler*,[48] some 40 years after the advent of New Zealand's Testator's Family Maintenance Act, Morton J of the English Court of Chancery opined:

> I do not think a judge should interfere with a testator's dispositions merely because he thinks that he would have been inclined, if he had been in a position of the testator, to make provision for some particular person.[49]

In the *Pontifical Society* case of 1962, the facts of which are referred to above, Dixon CJ described the lengthy period of estrangement between the testator and his son, then stating:

> If one really considers the situation of this old man in the closing stages of a long life in which his son has played no part at all, a son to whom his father has meant nothing and

[43] *Boughton v Knight* (1873) LR 3 P & D 64, cited in *Banks v Goodfellow* [1861–73] All ER Rep 47 (QB) 2–3.

[44] New Zealand Parliamentary Debates (1898) 422–23.

[45] *Brighten v Smith* (1926) 37 BCLT 518 (BCCA).

[46] ibid, 520.

[47] ibid, 519.

[48] *In Re Styler* [1942] Ch 387, [1942] 2 All ER 201.

[49] ibid, 389.

> who did not even know him, it is hard to see why the testator, in the interest of his son, should be deprived of his complete freedom of testamentary disposition.[50]

After thoroughly considering the unique factual circumstances of the *Barr* case, in which the claimant did not have a 'need' for maintenance or provision, but rather a moral claim on the grounds that he worked on the family farm, the Manitoba Court of Appeal concluded that: 'the court must not trample upon testamentary rights. The Court may alter a testator's disposition to the extent necessary to recognise a moral obligation to provide proper maintenance and support, but no further. The pendulum must not go too far'.[51]

A recent criticism of interference of a person's testamentary autonomy arose in the context of estate litigation in Nova Scotia. In *Lawen Estate v Nova Scotia (Attorney General)*,[52] two of the testator's daughters commenced wills variation proceedings, alleging the testator failed to make adequate provision for them. On behalf of the deceased testator, the executor sought declarations that portions of the Testators' Family Maintenance Act (TFMA)[53] violated ss 2(a) (freedom of conscience and religion) and 7 (right to life, liberty and security of the person) of the Canadian Charter of Rights and Freedoms.[54] The applicant executor was a public-interest litigant challenging the constitutionality of the TFMA. The applicant executor suggested that s 2(a) of the Charter is not limited to religious practices and beliefs, but also extends to non-theistic systems of belief and morality, asserting that the TFMA interferes with an individual's 'profoundly personal beliefs that govern one's perception of oneself and the moral choices which one makes'.[55] The Court rejected this argument, finding an insufficient basis for a testator's 'moral decision' to be regarded as 'a matter of conscience'.[56] However, Bodurtha J found that there was no dispute that dependants' relief legislation detracts from a testator's autonomy, and accordingly declared that the impugned provisions of the Act did violate the right to liberty guaranteed by s 7 of the Charter.[57] According to Bodurtha J, it was not 'an absurd argument' that disposing of one's estate is a fundamental personal choice, and one that is undermined by wills variation provisions allowing an independent adult child to challenge a testator's will.[58] The Nova Scotia Court of Appeal later found that by making no findings of fact to support his reasoning, Bodurtha J failed to undertake a proper analysis of s 7 in reaching the conclusion that the testator's liberty rights were infringed upon.[59] As s 7 of the

[50] *Pontifical Society* (n 32) 20.
[51] *Barr v Barr* [1971] MJ No 61, (1972) 25 DLR (3d) 401 (MBCA) [50].
[52] *Lawen Estate v Nova Scotia (Attorney General)* 2019 NSSC 162.
[53] Testators' Family Maintenance Act RSNS 1989, c 465.
[54] Canadian Charter of Rights and Freedoms Part 1 of the Constitution Act 1982, being Sch B to the Canada Act 1982 (UK) 1982, c 11.
[55] *Lawen Estate* (n 52).
[56] ibid, [75].
[57] ibid, [60] and [134].
[58] ibid, [60].
[59] *Nova Scotia (Attorney General) v Lawen Estate* 2021 NSCA 39.

Charter protects the personal autonomy of an individual in respect of their inherently private choices, it is not unfathomable that another Charter challenge will be brought in respect of wills variation legislation, especially if there is a more robust factual record of a testator's reasoning and decision-making process.

Critiques of dependants' relief or wills variation legislation have been prevalent from the time such legislation was introduced, demonstrating that considerable value is ascribed to a testator's autonomy to make their will according to their wishes. The laissez-faire attitude of some, and the outrage by others when a testator's freedom is infringed upon, indicates that the complete freedom to dispose of one's assets without interference is believed to be valuable.

E. Interpretations by Courts and the Exercise of Discretion

A prevailing and reasonable criticism of dependants' relief and wills variation legislation is the wide birth for judicial discretion, giving way to a wide array of potential outcomes conditional on how the legislation is interpreted. Despite efforts by lawmakers and the judiciary alike to maintain objectivity in these types of claims, evaluating claims by disappointed family members seeking to alter the terms of a testator's will is an inherently subjective exercise. While the framework to consider such claims is set out by the legislation, and *stare decisis* provides some certainty respecting how the legislation has been interpreted in prior cases, the innate characteristics of these cases gives rise to uncertainty. In each case, there is a unique set of circumstances contributing to that distinctive factual matrix: the testator; the claimant; the family structure, including the testator's other dependants; the familial history between the testator and the claimant; the testator and claimants' respective financial circumstances, life history, and other relevant events.

Essentially, there is no limitation to what unique circumstances might be relevant to a wills variation case, as each case will differ from cases before it. Circumstances that have been or could be pertinent to wills variation claims include: family illness, including substance use or abuse; disability; discord among family members, and the source of such discord; dynamics of a blended family; cultural values with respect to inheritance pertaining to gender; religious values; or recollections of promises or commitments made between family members. Not unlike a snowflake, each case will have unique traits, and depending on how those traits are manifested through the evidence and interpreted by the courts, there can be a vast array of outcomes. In particular, the 'moral claims' of independent adult children can be uncertain, as 'there being no clear legal standard by which to judge moral duties, these obligations are admittedly more susceptible of being viewed differently by different people'.[60]

[60] *Tataryn Tataryn v Tataryn Estate* [1994] 2 SCR 807, 1994 CanLII 51 (SCC) 822.

With respect to judicial interpretation of those circumstances and application to the law, the Court in the *Barr* case stated that 'The attitude of the Court has been one of great flexibility. Every case must, of course, be decided upon its own facts and circumstances'.[61] In Amighetti's comprehensive record of the law of dependants' relief in British Columbia, he opined that:

> The case of *Price v. Lypchuk Estate* is a recent illustration of the need for serious and urgent consideration of the *Act*. Both the majority and dissenting judgements purported to apply the principle enunciated in *Walker v. McDermott* and both came to opposite conclusions; it is clear the law is in need of clarification.[62]

In the *Price* case, Esson J noted that:

> The law developed in those cases is in a state of disarray such that is it all but impossible to predict with any confidence what result will flow from any given state of facts, and unduly difficult to decide what that result should be.[63]

As the Court in *Barr* pointed out, it is necessary for any court to consider the facts and circumstances of each case before it and ascribe weight as it sees fit.[64] Naturally, this will give rise to a wide range of possible outcomes, depending on how the court interprets how those facts and circumstances apply to the law framed by both the legislation and the case law before it. The uncertainty and range of potential outcomes will draw criticism, from the legal community and the public alike. As pointed out by Arthur Close KC of the Law Reform Commission of British Columbia, so long as wills variation legislation undertakes a subjective approach, 'there can never be absolute certainty. Somewhat divergent views on what constitutes proper maintenance and support is inevitable'.[65]

III. Categories of Claimants and the Strengths of their Claims

As above, there are differences between jurisdictions as to who may be entitled to recover relief from a testator's estate. Pursuant to the relevant legislation, a claimant's relationship to the testator either qualifies them to pursue a claim or disentitles them from having standing to make a claim. In the event the claimant has standing, the facts and circumstances of their claim will be considered in light of relevant caselaw in that jurisdiction. The case law that has emerged since the introduction of dependants' relief or wills variation legislation shows that certain claims are stronger than others. For example, it is well established that an infant

[61] *Barr v Barr* [1971] MJ No 61, (1972) 25 DLR (3d) 401 (MBCA) [11].
[62] Amighetti (1991) 48.
[63] *Price v Lychuk Estate* 1987 CanLII 165 (BCCA) 2.
[64] *Barr v Barr* [1971] MJ No 61, (1972) 25 DLR (3d) 401 (MBCA).
[65] Law Reform Commission of British Columbia (1983) 93.

child of the testator has a stronger claim against the testator's estate than an independent adult who was estranged from the testator. The factors or circumstances either contributing to or diminishing from the strength of a claim are briefly reviewed in categories below.

A. Infant Children

The least controversial class of claimants on a testator's bounty are a testator's infant children. In every Canadian province and territory, children under the age of majority may make a claim for dependants' relief if they were inadequately provided for under the terms of the testator's will. In *Tataryn*, McLaughlin J described two types of societal norms that wills variation legislation aims to address. The first sort of norms are 'legal obligations', which can be characterised as 'the obligations which the law would impose on a person during his or her life'.[66] With respect to children under the age of majority, any parent of that child would be expected, and legally obligated, to provide for that child. A person's obligation to provide for their child or children during their lifetime may be asserted against their estate after their death to provide 'adequate, just and equitable' provision.[67] With respect to infant children of testators, the consistency in the legislation among all Canadian jurisdictions clearly demonstrates an 'unequivocal' social expectation that a child under the age of majority is entitled to seek provision from their parent's estate. Accordingly, it is generally straightforward for an infant child of a testator to establish that they are entitled to relief.[68]

B. Women

When dependants' relief or wills variation legislation was initially introduced, women were in a far more tenuous position, with fewer protections under the law and sparse opportunities to become independent of their father or husband. In her review of the genesis of New Zealand's 1990 *Testators Family Maintenance Act*, Atherton opined that:

> Through a woman's eyes testamentary freedom came to be seen as a power that could be used against women; as a power not to bestow, but to take away; and a power which largely was one possessed by a husband and exercisable by him over his wife and children.[69]

Women could and would be left destitute and were themselves under legal disability by virtue of being disentitled to the same rights as their male counterparts.

[66] *Tataryn Tataryn v Tataryn Estate* [1994] 2 SCR 807, 1994 CanLII 51 (SCC) 820.
[67] ibid, 821.
[68] Renwick (2013) 170.
[69] Atherton (1990) 202.

Absolute testamentary freedom was recognised as 'another weapon in the armoury of patriarchal control to which wives were hostage', and the move by New Zealand's Parliament to limit testamentary freedom demonstrated 'greater recognition of women's legal disabilities'.[70]

In the early case of *Allardice v Allardice* in New Zealand, gender was a clear factor that was relevant to the outcome, where a testator's three daughters were awarded a greater share of the testator's estate than the testator's two sons.[71] The Appeal Court concluded that:

> The three daughters had married persons in a humble station of life with a very small and precarious incomes, and the two sons were able-bodied men, capable of maintaining themselves in the future as they had done for some years before their father's death.[72]

In *Walker*, the position of the claimant was considered by Rinfret J (dissenting), which shed light on the status of women in society in the early 1930s:

> She has never been since then and is not now in need of maintenance and support out of the estate and is adequately maintained and supported by her husband, who is a young man with a good income, a permanent employment, a reasonable opportunity of advancement and fully capable of supporting her in the future.[73]

While Rinfret J's opinion was dissenting from that of the Court, his comments suggest that it was more relevant that the claimant was 'maintained and supported' by her husband than whether she was capable of independence. This seems to indicate that during this period, at least some held the view that the responsibility to 'maintain' a woman shifted from her father to her husband upon marriage, and that as such, women 'adequately maintained' by their husbands might have more tenuous claims on the estate of their fathers than by women without a husband who could provide for them.

By 1973, another judgment in British Columbia illustrated what the contemporary standards were with respect to female claimants. The claimant in this case was the daughter of the testator, a woman in her 50s, who was married to a 'successful radiologist', and who independently controlled significant assets of her own. The court ordered that the testator's will be varied to make some provision for the claimant, although it was noted that the success of her claim was due only to the testator breaching his moral duty to his only daughter, as it was 'obvious that [she] is not now nor ever likely to be in any financial need'.[74]

In the 1987 *Price* decision, Justice Lambert distinguished it from the 1930 decision of *Walker*,[75] noting that due to changes in social circumstances, the

[70] ibid, 205–06.
[71] *Allardice v Allardice* 1911 AC 730, affirming (1910) 29 NZLR 959.
[72] ibid, 2.
[73] *Walker* (n 29) 100–01.
[74] *Re Michalson* [1973] 1 WWR 560 (BCSC) 563.
[75] *Walker v McDermott* [1931] SCR 91, 1930 CanLII 1 (SCC).

application of the facts and principles of *Walker* could have produced a different result if decided in 1987.[76] Lambert J stated that:

> Women now have a valued position in the workplace; everyone is entitled to rely on a widespread network of state financial support; the nuclear family is far from universal; and family relations legislation contemplates and promotes the financial independence of spouses from each other and children from their parents.[77]

When exercising discretion under wills variation legislation, courts have regularly reviewed the historical underpinnings of the legislation, noting that 'the original remedial purpose of the legislation was to prevent destitute dependants becoming a charge on the state where an estate existed from which adequate provision could have been made by the testator'.[78] When wills variation legislation was introduced, women were not generally seen as being capable to independently support themselves or their families; their position more akin to children than as equals to their adult male counterparts. By reviewing the case law over the decades, it becomes clear that there was a shift by which women were considered capable of independence and self-sufficiency.

In *Price*, Justice Lambert acknowledged that determining whether a testator has discharged his marital and parental duties depends on the contemporary view of marital and parental obligations during the material time, and that as a result, if the facts of a 1930 decision were contemplated in 1987 (or 2022, for that matter), the results could be different.[79] The differences between decisions reached in 1930 versus 1987 would not violate the principles of stare decisis,[80] however, on the basis that cases are determined by the application of 'contemporary views of marital and parental obligations', which in essence, are ever evolving and fluid concepts.

C. Able-Bodied and Independent Adults

As referred to in the discussion of legislative schemes, some Canadian jurisdictions allow for an able-bodied and independent child of a testator to make a claim for dependants' relief (British Columbia, Nova Scotia, Newfoundland, New Brunswick and Manitoba). In the *Barr* case, the Court noted that the claimant was not disbarred from relief just by reason of being an able-bodied adult son.[81] However, the order made by the trial judge awarding the family farm to the claimant, to the detriment of the claimant's other siblings, was found to be overly generous by the Court of Appeal.[82]

[76] *Price v Lychuk Estate* 1987 CanLII 165 (BCCA) 9.
[77] ibid.
[78] *Bell v Roy Estate* 1993 CanLII 1262 (BCCA).
[79] *Price v Lychuk Estate* 1987 CanLII 165 (BCCA) 9.
[80] ibid.
[81] *Barr v Barr* [1971] MJ No 61, (1972) 25 DLR (3d) 401 (MBCA) [32].
[82] ibid, [35], [47] and [52].

In *Price*, the Court pointed out that in the case of able-bodied adult children, there was no objective criterion, such as financial need, in determining the strength of a claim.[83] Instead, consideration of whether a testator made adequate provision is 'almost entirely subjective' and is based on the judge's evaluation of the unique facts and circumstances of the case.[84] In the *Tataryn* case, McLaughlin J noted that claims of adult independent children were more tenuous than that of infant children or children with disabilities, but that provision may be made in cases where the size of the estate permits.[85]

D. Adults with Disabilities or Adults with Special Circumstances

Like with infant children of testators, adult children with mental or physical disabilities are another uncontroversial class of claimants. This is demonstrated by the legislation throughout Canadian jurisdictions, referred to above, with each providing that dependant adult children with disabilities of testators are entitled to seek relief or vary the will.

In the case of *Clucas v Royal Trust Corporation et al*, the claimant was a 53-year-old son of the testator who, by reason of Parkinson's disease, was unable to support himself.[86] The testator had made some provision for her son under her will, but the claimant sought to vary the will for a greater share of the testator's estate than what she had left him. The testator left her reasons in writing, suggesting that she believed that she had 'amply' provided for her son and that she had discharged her moral obligation to him. The Court found that the provision left for the claimant was not ample in the circumstances, and that a 'reasonable judicious parent of a severely disabled son living as modestly' as the claimant would not interpret the testator's provision to be 'sufficient' enough to discharge their moral obligation.[87]

In a recent case, both of testator's children were adults with disabilities.[88] The testator's son sustained a brain injury but had continued to contribute to the testator's business. The testator's daughter, who had two able-bodied sons herself, struggled with alcoholism. The testator's will provided a one-half share of the residue to his son, with his daughter and two grandsons sharing the remaining one-half share in equal parts (ie, one-sixth of the residue to each of the daughter and her two sons). The Court of Appeal found that the daughter's need for assistance was real, and that given the testator had a significant estate, the testator did not discharge his moral obligation to his daughter. Accordingly, it was ordered that

[83] *Price v Lychuk Estate* 1987 CanLII 165 (BCCA) 3.
[84] ibid.
[85] *Tataryn v Tataryn Estate* [1994] 2 SCR 807, 1994 CanLII 51 (SCC) 823.
[86] *Clucas v Royal Trust Corporation et al* 1999 CanLII 5519 (BCSC).
[87] ibid, [15]–[16].
[88] *Scurek v Scurek* 2021 BCCA 178.

each of the testator's grandsons were to receive a one-twelfth share of the residue, with the remainder to be split between the testator's son and daughter equally.[89]

Provision for disabled adult children of testators from their respective estates appears to be universally accepted in Canada upon a review of both the Canadian caselaw and legislation. The consistency between Canadian legislative regimes allowing disabled adult children to claim relief under a testator's will demonstrates that 'adequate provision' for these claimants is universally held to be fair and reasonable.

E. Factors Influencing the Strength of Claims

In some wills variation cases, certain factual circumstances will be considered during the determination of whether a claimant made out their case for provision under the will. In 1938, Bora Laskin (as he then was) commented on dependants' relief legislation, noting that other factors to be considered included: any other dependants of the testator; any past, present, or future income of the claimant from other sources; and any statement by the testator that indicates the testator's reasoning.[90]

Beyond the objective considerations of whether the testator had any other dependants, or whether the claimant has means outside their claim, other factors that are more subjective will require the courts to exercise discretion. Some circumstances that have been accepted as relevant to the strength of claims by adult independent children include: the nature of the relationship between the testator and the claimant, including whether there was abandonment, neglect or estrangement; contributions by the claimant to the testator's estate; reasonably held expectations by the claimant; the standard of living of both the testator and the claimant; and gifts or benefit made by the testator outside the will.[91] Ontario's legislature has codified a very thorough list of factors in the Succession Law Reform Act, which lists what the courts ought consider in determining appropriate awards of maintenance to claimants.[92]

Certain 'positive' attributes or conduct of the claimant can factor into the determination of a claim to dependants' relief or wills variation, such as in *Pontifical Society*, where the claimant was said to have 'early devotion to his mother, steady advancement in the Public Service, marriage, the birth of children, and the proper discharge of all the obligations of family life and a praiseworthy career'.[93] The claimant's 'praiseworthy' conduct throughout his life, despite the estrangement from his father since infancy, was clearly a factor that militated in favour of his successful challenge of the testator's will. A common factor favouring the success

[89] ibid.
[90] Laskin (1939) 184–185.
[91] *Dunsdon v Dunsdon* 2012 BCSC 1274, [134].
[92] Succession Law Reform Act RSO 1990, c S26, s 62(1)(a)–(s).
[93] *Pontifical Society for the Propagation of the Faith v Scales* (1962) 107 CLR 9, 17.

of an independent adult's claim is when a claimant has worked in the family business or on a family farm, thereby contributing to the testator's estate as a result.[94]

Courts may 'refuse maintenance to persons exhibiting disentitling character of conduct'.[95] Some examples of such 'disentitling conduct' considered in relation to a claimant include: financial abuse of or manipulation against the testator by the claimant;[96] evidence that the claimant interfered with or meddled with the testator's property or assets;[97] and causing hurt and embarrassment to the testator and thereafter deliberately perpetuating a lengthy estrangement.[98] In such cases, testators must have 'valid and rational' reasons for disinheritance, which must be based on true facts that are logically connected to the act of disinheritance.[99] Nevertheless, a thorough review of the conduct of the claimant and the testator, and a determination of who was right or wrong, is not the proper test; rather, 'it is to look at the situation at the time of the death of the testator and determine whether, at that time, the children can show a special need or other special claim to establish that they are eligible "dependants" under the Act'.[100] In cases where a testator does not have a 'valid and rational' reason for disinheriting, the testator therefore fails to negate their moral obligation to the claimant and provision may be accordingly be ordered.

Separate and apart entirely from 'persons exhibiting disentitling character of conduct', there is a body of case law whereby testators have discriminatory motives in disinheriting. In such cases, a testator disinherits based on a beneficiary's choice of spouse, their religious affiliation, gender identity or expression, religion, sexual orientation, or lifestyle choices that the testator does not consider 'respectable'. Of note, this niche issue falls outside the purview of this chapter and is referred to only to acknowledge that such cases exist.

The examples above suggest that there is a plethora of facts that can be relevant to a wills variation or dependants' relief claim, and that some of these factors are highly subjective. Courts are required to weigh these factors when assessing claims, which undoubtedly must be a difficult exercise, especially when the factors are of an abstract or personal nature. The factors at play dictate how challenging evaluation of the claim may be. As Renwick notes:

> It is easy to understand the logic behind the claims of adult children who have made non-financial contributions to a family business of family farm, or who have suffered a 'disaster' of some sort, such as the early death of a spouse, injury and bankruptcy. It is harder to see why an able-bodied adult child, who is not financially dependent on the deceased and has not been for some time, should be granted provision.[101]

[94] Renwick (2013) 174.

[95] Franke (1988) 351; *Currie v Currie Estate* (1995) 166 NBR (2d) 144, 1995 CanLII 16592 (NBCA), 157.

[96] *Webb v Webb Estate* 1995 CanLII 9299 (ABKB).

[97] *Williams v Williams Estate* 2018 BCSC 711.

[98] *Brown v Pearce Estate* 2014 BCSC 1402.

[99] *Clucas v Royal Trust Corporation et al* 1999 CanLII 5519 (BCSC) [12].

[100] *Currie v Currie Estate* (1995) 166 NBR (2d) 144, 1995 CanLII 16592 (NBCA) 158.

[101] Renwick (2013) 175.

Clearly, there are innumerable factors that may make a claimant more or less 'deserving' or 'worthy' for provision out of a testator's estate. Given the highly subjective nature of what factors might either favour or disentitle a claimant from provision, there is bound to be inconsistency in the weight ascribed to such factors, as well as the results ultimately reached. The factors that make a claimant sympathetic depend on the contemporary social values and norms where the claim is made, as well as how those factors fit within the unique factual circumstances of the claimant's case. For example, an independent able-bodied adult claimant might have a greater chance of success if the testator left the entirety of their estate to charities due to an estrangement caused by events outside the claimant's control. Alternatively, if an identically situated claimant were seeking a greater share of the testator's estate after it had largely been left to the claimant's two dependant disabled siblings, the claimant might have a greater challenge in gaining the court's sympathy and making a compelling argument that they are more 'deserving'. The merits or moral implications of certain individual factors and how they may or may not influence the success of a claim are outside the scope of this chapter, but nevertheless the existence of these factors deserves acknowledgement when contemplating wills variation claims.

IV. Conclusion

Wills variation and dependants' relief legislation has evolved in both time and space, and will continue to as social, cultural, economic and moral values shift. So long as legislative frameworks exist allowing for wills variation, so too will the tension between a testator's right to liberty and autonomy, and dependants' rights to maintenance. There is a delicate balancing act between these two ideologies; one that we may visualise as being on a spectrum or pendulum. Further complicating this balancing act is the ways in which values and social norms are constantly evolving. In *Tataryn*, McLaughlin J stated that:

> The Act must be read in light of modern values and expectations. What was thought to be adequate, just and equitable in the 1920s may be different from what is considered adequate, just and equitable in the 1990s. This narrows the inquiry. Courts are not necessarily bound by the views and awards made in earlier times. The search is for contemporary justice.[102]

In *Lawen Estate*, we have seen a criticism of dependants' relief legislation and how it may infringe on a person's testamentary freedom and autonomy.[103] This case may be indicative of the pendulum swinging away from dependants' relief and towards testamentary freedom, but only time will tell. Another critique of wills

[102] *Tataryn v Tataryn Estate* [1994] 2 SCR 807, 1994 CanLII 51 (SCC) 814–15.
[103] *Lawen Estate v Nova Scotia (Attorney General)* 2019 NSSC 162 [59].

variation legislation is how it can render inconsistent or unexpected results, which is understandable given that it requires interpretation and the exercise of discretion on unique sets of facts. Furthermore, provision that is 'just and equitable' can be interpreted differently too, as this concept is relatively abstract.

On testamentary freedom, Dickson JA stated in *Barr* that:

> The Court was never intended to rewrite the will of a testator and in discharging its difficult task of correcting a breach of morality on a testator's part the Court must not, except in plain and definite cases, restrain a man's right to dispose of his estate as he pleases. But, equally, it is fair to say that the legislation has by and large received a very liberal interpretation. The attitude of the Court has been one of great flexibility. Every case must, of course, be decided upon its own facts and circumstances.[104]

The legislation, case law, and other sources referenced in this chapter suggest that social and cultural values influence how testators wills are interpreted and characterised; by the parties, their lawyers, the judiciary, and public at large, as well as the importance we ascribe to claims to vary wills or seek relief. Through reviewing the case law since the advent of dependants' relief legislation, we are proffered a window through which to see the social, cultural, economic, and family values commonly held in that time and space.

References

Alberta Institute of Law Research and Reform, 'Family Relief' Law Com No 29 (1978).

Amighetti, L, *The Law of Dependants' Relief in British Columbia* (Ontario, Carswell, 1991).

Atherton, R, 'New Zealand's Testator's Family Maintenance Act of 1900 – The Stouts, the Women's Movement and Political Compromise' (1990) 7 *Otago Law Review* 202.

Davern Wright, RJ, *Testators' Family Maintenance in Australia and New Zealand*, 3rd edn (Ontario, Carswell, 1974).

Franke, NA, 'Loosing the Bonds of Tradition: A Call for a More Liberal Family Maintenance System' (1988) 66 *Washington University Law Quarterly* 347.

Gray, VE, 'Dependants' Relief Legislation' (1939) 17 *Canadian Bar Review* 233.

Laskin, B, 'Dependants' Relief Legislation' (1939) 17 *Canadian Bar Review* 181.

Laufer, J 'Flexible Restraints on Testamentary Freedom – A Report on Decedents' Family Maintenance Legislation' (1955) 69 *Harvard Law Review* 277.

Law Reform Commission of British Columbia, 'Report on Statutory Succession Rights' Law Com No 70 (1983).

Renwick, S, 'Responsibility to Provide: Family Provision Claims in Victoria' (2013) 18 *Deakin Law Review* 159.

Roggendorf, H, 'Indefeasible Family Rights: A Comparative View on the Restrictions of Testamentary Freedom' (2018) 22 *Edinburgh Law Review* 211.

[104] *Barr v Barr* [1971] MJ No 61, (1972) 25 DLR (3d) 401 (MBCA) [11].

11

Testamentary Freedom in Debate

The Prerequisite of the Notary to Pass Down and to Inherit

CORINNE DELMAS

I. Introduction

Inheritance, which is polysemous and at the heart of relations between generations, was first thought of in religious terms and historically refers to the social relationships that organise the transmission of a concrete object by way of inheritance, a public distribution of wealth, and a political institution for the recirculation of property that will meet the requirements of rising capitalism.[1] In the current vocabulary, 'inheritance' refers to both the object of the transfer and the ownership of this object, and the fact that it has been transferred by a series of laws governing the transmission of property upon death. In this respect, the question of the transmission of the deceased's 'patrimony' or property arises, but also that of the order in which this transfer takes place. Succession specifies this order, which is both contiguous and creates continuity between classes of kinship or individual proximity. The history of inheritance in France is full of legal cases attesting to the specificities of French law in this area and the tension between two contradictory principles: on the one hand, that of the freedom of the testator to organizse, during his or her lifetime, the transmission of his or her property and, on the other hand, that of the interest of the children preserved by the 'hereditary reserve' ('*réserve héréditaire*' in French), by virtue of which a part of the patrimony is reserved for them; thus, they inherit part of the property of their parents following the death of the latter, who cannot, during their lifetime, disinherit their children, at least without their consent. Testamentary freedom is preserved with the notion of the 'available portion' ('*quotité disponible*' in French), ie the part of their estate not reserved for the children which can be freely transmitted by the parents.

[1] Gotman (2006) 29.

The evolution of morals and family forms, and the rise of international successions,[2] have contributed to calling this rule of available portion into question and to exacerbating tensions between the testator's freedom and the preservation of the interests of the children, but also of other family members: ascendants, who until recently enjoyed a right to the 'reserve', the surviving spouse, etc. In addition, there is the question of equality between all children, whatever their status (so-called 'legitimate' children, 'recognised' by the father, or not, etc) in a context marked by the multiplication of recomposed families, the decline of marriage and the remarkable increase in the divorce rate. The questioning and even reform of the 'hereditary reserve' and, more broadly, the resulting debates and projects concerning testamentary freedom, are valuable indicators of the contestations and transformations of the notions of 'kinship' and 'family' in France. Examining these debates will enable us to understand these changes, including the individualisation of family relations and the growing concern for equality between its members.

Testamentary freedom must also be considered in the light of inheritance practices themselves and their evolution. The methods of devolution of inheritance, the recognition and limits imposed on the freedom to dispose of one's property in France (with the hereditary 'reserve'), but also the way in which the will of testators can, or even must, be expressed (for example through the various forms of 'will') constitute particularly heuristic entry points for analysing what is at stake within families, provided that we take an interest in their most pragmatic and routine dimensions. Inheritance is, in France, primarily a matter for notaries, family and wealth, which, like most private matters, is duly informed by the action of the state and regulated by legislative provisions. In this respect, I have chosen to focus on the profession of notary, which in France is a quasi-obligatory step in matters of succession.

In France, the estate must be settled by the notary when the deceased's assets include real estate, or when the amount of the estate is equal to or greater than €5,000; it must also be settled by him or her if there is a will or if the deceased made a gift during his or her lifetime, such as a spousal gift.[3] Once appointed by the relatives of the deceased, the notary in charge of the succession must, among other things: identify all the heirs of the deceased; check in the central file of last

[2] It is becoming increasingly common to have to settle estates involving people of several nationalities or assets spread over several states. International succession is the succession of a person who dies either in a country other than that of his or her nationality or residence or by leaving property, movable and/or immovable, in a country other than that of his or her nationality or residence. To settle an international succession, it is necessary to determine the law that will be applicable to the succession. A European regulation was adopted on 4 July 2012 and entered into force in France on 17 August 2015. This regulation is applicable throughout the EU, with the exception of the UK (pre-Brexit), Ireland and Denmark. By application of this regulation, the law that determines the heirs is the law of the last residence of the deceased.

[3] In other cases, the notary's intervention is only optional and the estate can be settled directly with the banks and organisations.

wills (*Fichier central des dernières volontés*, FCDDV) whether a will has been written[4] and whether there is a gift to the surviving spouse. The notary also has to list the gifts made by the deceased during his or her lifetime and draw up several things such as the deeds enabling the heirs to justify their rights to the estate,[5] and a complete balance sheet of the deceased's assets (evaluation of the estate's assets and possible debts). The notary writes the declaration of inheritance, calculates the amount of inheritance tax, paying it to the Treasury within six months of the death and divides the inheritance. The settlement of an inheritance consists of four main steps: the notary draws up the deed of notoriety, establishes a complete inventory of the deceased's assets, carries out the mortgage and tax formalities related to the death and, finally, draws up a deed of partition of the inheritance. The deadline for settling the estate is limited by the payment of inheritance tax within six months of the death (one year for a deceased person who died outside France).

As such, notaries argue that they have expertise and a mandate in this area, with the public authorities, public opinion and their clients. While these professionals are defenders of the order and uniqueness of the family patrimony, as well as of a rather conservative vision of the family, for the last 10 years or so they have been demanding greater testamentary freedom through a relaxation of the hereditary 'reserve'. Their position with regard to this provision, which is very old in France but absent from Anglo-Saxon law, and which prohibits a parent from disinheriting his or her child or children and requires that a share of the family patrimony be paid to the descendants, attests to the multiple issues at stake in its liberalisation.

This chapter will examine both the positions taken by this profession on the subject and the activities that its members carry out on a daily basis in the field of successions. The study of these activities of notaries in matters of succession shows the contrasting expectations of clients as to how these professionals adapt their advice and contribute in practice to this relaxation, or not. Based on a long-term survey of French notaries conducted since 2013 (Delmas, 2019), this chapter will draw on several types of data: documentary (professional and legal journals, reports), archival (notarial and press), statistical (aggregated INED and INSEE data on successions), observational (from meetings with clients, congresses, training courses), and interviews (with 200 people, mainly notaries and employees of the notary's office, but also partners including lawyers and magistrates, as well as clients). These data highlight the ambivalence, reality and limits of testamentary

[4] This file, created in 1971 by the notaries and managed by them, centralises at national level the information relating to the existence and the place of deposit of the wills that the notaries have received at their office. The wills registered in the FCDDV are both authentic wills drawn up before a notary and holographic wills drawn up at home in secret and then entrusted to a notary. Knowing that it is not obligatory to file a will with a notary.

[5] In particular, the notarial deed listing the persons called upon to receive the estate as well as their respective rights, and the real estate ownership certificate noting the transfer of the deceased's property to his or her heirs.

freedom in France and the way it is expressed, according to the economic, social and gender profile of clients and professionals.

The history of testamentary freedom in France allows us to understand the importance given to the hereditary reserve. These limits to testamentary freedom are due both to a revolutionary heritage and to the weight of certain patriarchal representations of the couple and the family (section II). However, several developments have contributed to the aspiration for greater testamentary freedom and a relaxation of the regime of the reserve, both in law and in practice (section III), and notaries have played a leading role in this respect, both as practitioners assisting their clients in matters of succession and as lawyers specialising in family property law advising the legislature (section III). This liberalisation of testamentary freedom must be reconciled with the rights of the child, which remain very important in France.

II. The Weight of Patriarchal Representations of the Family

In France, the institution of the 'reserved portion of the estate' is the result of a compromise between testamentary freedom and a family conception of property (section A below). Established by a revolutionary egalitarian civil law (section B), it can nevertheless contribute to situations of inequality (section C).

A. A Compromise between Testamentary Freedom and a Family Conception of Property: The Hereditary Reserve

In France, one is free to dispose of one's property, which can be bequeathed by virtue of a will, in the absence of which the inheritance is governed by the law. If there are children, one can only dispose freely of the 'available portion' and on the condition that the children's inheritance reserve, ie the share reserved for them, is not affected. Although the reserve portion of the estate is a tradition in the law of about half of the countries in the world and in most Western countries (Germany, Italy, Spain, Switzerland, Greece, etc), the percentages applied and the methods used vary from country to country. In France, since the Civil Code of 1804, when there is only one child, 50 per cent of the estate must be reserved for that child, 66 per cent for two children and 75 per cent for three or more children. The available portion of the estate, of which the settlor may do as he or she wishes, is therefore at least 25 per cent and at most 50 per cent; a child or an heir entitled to the inheritance cannot be disinherited unless he or she is unworthy. However, the applicable rules are less clear when the deceased resides elsewhere than in France, for example in the US, as in the case of the French singer Johnny Hallyday, who completely disinherited two of his children by a will made in the US and by the creation of a trust within the framework of a significant and international patrimony including assets in France, in particular royalties, and abroad, in particular real estate in California.

B. A System of Egalitarian Civil Law Resulting from the Revolution

In France, the revolutionaries made an egalitarian choice, with the main target being the family of the Ancien Régime, modelled on the relationship between the King and his subjects; the aim was to put an end to the power and the bond of dependence in which the father held his children. It was also a question of eradicating the old nobility and preventing the reconstitution of ecclesiastical property. After having freed the property from all its charges and seigniorial rights, having abolished the substitutions (donations obliging the beneficiary to transmit, at his death, the given or bequeathed goods to third parties designated by the donor) and the rules of primogeniture which constituted the privilege of the aristocracy, the revolutionaries attacked the last bastion of paternal despotism: the freedom of the will. Children are given irreducible and equal shares in their fathers' inheritance. Freedom is reconciled with the egalitarian rights of children established by law. The radicalisation of the will at the time of the French Revolution thus implies a modification corresponding to the available share and to the reversion.[6]

The equality advocated by the Conventionalists was certainly fiercely opposed, in particular by the deputies from the south of France from 1791 onwards; the latter pleaded in favour of freedom of the will and criticised the demolition of paternal authority which, according to them, resulted from the new succession legislation, legislation which did not, moreover, constitute a radical break with the Ancien Régime, in which many customs were already very egalitarian.[7]

The revolutionary basis of French inheritance law remained unshaken, and was even strengthened in the nineteenth century by the accentuation of republican ideas of equality, the acceleration of economic development, the growing importance of capital to the detriment of property, and the emergence of an individualised conception of property rights. The egalitarian division in direct line introduced in 1793 was confirmed in the Civil Code of 1804, with the aim of multiplying the number of owners 'who are the firmest supporters of the security and tranquility of the States', according to the First Consul, Bonaparte. If, 10 years later, under the censal monarchy, the royalists insisted on the contrary that the infinite division of property was opposed to the principle of monarchic government, it was without being able to return to the pre-Revolutionary system; the

[6] Beckert (2009).
[7] Burguière (2001); Peguera Poch (2009).

terms of the debate, however, became more socio-economic in the years following Louis Napoleon Bonaparte's *coup d'état* in December 1851,[8] and again at the beginning of the twentieth century, following the introduction of a progressive inheritance tax.[9]

The supporters of testamentary freedom struggled in vain until about 1870 to restore a measure demanded by both liberals in favour of free enterprise and supporters of the patriarchal family. The inalienability of the hereditary reserve of children (and ascendants) and the almost absolute equality of their treatment, have hardly been shaken until today, even though they can, in their application, give rise to situations of inequality.

C. The De Facto Maintenance of Inequality

Although the reserve system frees children (sons and daughters[10]) from dependence on the head of the family, equal access to the inheritance of the family patrimony has long been limited to the so-called 'legitimate' family, resulting from marriage, and to the parental line. Until 2001, civil law ignored the spouse, and inequalities existed between children in a legal system that enshrined marriage as a true institution thereby concealing 'illegitimate' children born 'out of wedlock' (then called 'natural' and 'adulterine') who could not inherit from both parents;[11] only 'legitimate' children, born during the marriage and deemed to have the husband as their father, could inherit as heirs from both parents,[12] including from their father.

Even today, the hereditary reserve does not prevent the persistence of situations of inequality between heirs. Some heirs may have an advantage in the context of family arrangements aimed, for example, at avoiding the fragmentation of the inherited estate (in particular in the case of the presence of a business or a family home) and at arbitrating between several priorities (favouring an heir, preserving the business, avoiding undivided ownership) at the time of the distribution of the estate. In this respect, inheritance rules may contribute to reinforcing highly gendered inequalities in inheritance and family arrangements may be to the

[8] On the debates of the time, see Steiner (2008); Audren (2014).

[9] Steiner (2008) 76. On this tax and the question of high incomes in France in the 20th century, see Piketti (2018).

[10] Although gender inequalities persist in practice; in the 18th century, it is more difficult for girls to assert their inheritance rights. See Daumas (2003). The civil code, without calling into question the equality of the sexes in matters of inheritance, enshrined the inferiority of women, under the control of their husbands or fathers until the age of 21. Until 1965, women married without a contract could not manage their own property or engage in any activity without their husband's consent.

[11] 'Natural' children were born to unmarried women; 'adulterous' children conceived outside a marriage in which at least one of the two parents was already involved.

[12] According to the presumption of paternity stated in Art 312 of the civil code: 'The child conceived or born during the marriage has for father the husband'.

detriment of women,[13] given the weight of certain patriarchal representations and social roles that are still highly gendered.

III. Passing On and Inheriting: A Double Tension between Egalitarian Aspirations and Greater Testamentary Freedom

The controversies surrounding inheritance and the ways in which it is shared are indicative of the changes affecting society, property and the family. They are recurrent and have contributed to several reforms, past and present, aimed at strengthening both testamentary freedom and equality between different categories of heirs. It is to this that the chapter now turns.

A. Recurrent Controversies Surrounding Inheritance

Controversies around inheritance are recurrent and inheritance and tax laws can reinforce or reduce inequalities that depend on the modes of circulation of capital and goods (remuneration of capital, work, speculation, goods transmitted by donation, inheritance, etc) that are more or less favourable to the concentration of fortunes. At the individual and family level, inheritance allocates shares according to legally or freely established places and puts the members of the collective in competition. These are sensitive issues that are fiercely discussed and debated in national parliaments, in academic circles and in the secrecy of families, not to mention the media attention that a subject conducive to 'scandal' generates.[14]

Inheritance is particularly criticised in France as a structural factor of social inequality. It remains an important advantage for those who benefit from it, even in a society driven by a meritocratic ideal where social position depends mainly on diplomas.[15] Moreover, the weight of the wealth factor has increased in societies marked by a deepening of economic inequalities[16] and by the growing importance of the inherited share of wealth; disparities are strong in terms of the amount of inheritance[17] and inequalities are cumulative.[18] Moreover, certain actors and families with high economic wealth are similar to 'repeat players',[19] benefiting from legal and asset management support enabling them to optimise their wealth and its transmission, in particular by opting for the best investments, methods of

[13] Bessière and Gollac (2023).
[14] Gotman (2006) 7.
[15] ibid, 15.
[16] Piketti (2017).
[17] Gotman (2006) 18.
[18] ibid, 19.
[19] Galanter (1974).

sharing, and the most optimal family arrangements in tax and asset management terms. In this respect, legal and wealth advisory professionals, first and foremost notaries, play a key role.

Inheritance is also criticised, more discreetly in France where an egalitarian credo prevails, and more by the theorists of neoclassical micro-economics and certain liberal thinkers, as being counterproductive on the economic level. Thus, it would distort the development of free competition and competitiveness expected in a market economy. The long-standing distrust of the dynastic perpetuation of large fortunes[20] and the attachment to a liberal egalitarian conception of society persist and are debated in France. Inheritance is also considered to be counterproductive in that it discourages individual ambition and, consequently, economic dynamism, as a potential heir has nothing left to prove or undertake; conversely, a liberalism that claims absolute freedom of property rights asserts that the free transmission of assets, as a right attached to property, would be likely to spur and stimulate the entrepreneurial spirit.[21]

While the tensions inherent in liberalism are thus at the forefront, legislators have contributed to increasing testamentary freedom not so much in the name of individual freedom as in order to adapt the law to socio-demographic changes.

B. Testamentary Freedom at the Heart of the Reforms Adapting the Law to Societal and Demographic Changes

The transmission of family wealth is today a weaker practice than it was in the nineteenth and early twentieth centuries, given socio-demographic changes, in particular the lengthening of life expectancy, the generalisation of salaried work and the collective assumption of individual risks, in particular family, health and old age. The value of the contemporary family has thus become at least as much relational as patrimonial; it is measured as much by the quality of relationships as by the transmission of a heritage or know-how. However, if inheritance no

[20] Even today, while the family origin of France's great fortunes is regularly the subject of studies and journalistic commentary to explain the persistent social inequalities linked to the weight of inheritance in relation to work and qualifications. According to the economist Thomas Piketti (2017, 2018), inheritance could represent 80% of French wealth in 2050. Inequalities would also be gendered; even within families with several heirs and the need to share, family arrangements may favour a successor for the takeover of the family business or the family home (on these arrangements and their consequences in terms of gender inequalities, see Bessière and Gollac, 2023). This weight of inherited capital in France also motivates journalistic comments on 'the low share of fortunes built by entrepreneurs starting from nothing' (40% according to a ranking by *Forbes* magazine) compared to the US (70%) or Great Britain (80%). V Beaufils, 'Le poids de l'héritage dans l'origine des grandes fortunes françaises' Challenges (8 July 2015), available at www.challenges.fr/challenges-soir/le-poids-de-l-heritage-dans-l-origine-des-grandes-fortunes-francaises_61533.

[21] For neoclassical microeconomic theorists, intergenerational transfers represent another challenge. Indeed, they contradict the so-called 'life-cycle' model of consumption and savings, which aims to model the behaviour of the middle classes who have accumulated a wealth of 'enjoyment' and 'security' linked to the spread of home ownership since 1920 and especially 1950. See Gotman (2006) 20.

longer plays the decisive role in the social position of individuals that it did in the nineteenth and early twentieth centuries, it nevertheless remains an important, and even growing, vector of social reproduction in a French society marked today by strong inequalities in terms of the distribution of wealth; the share of inheritance in total wealth has increased steadily since the 1980s and now accounts for the majority of wealth,[22] reinforcing these inequalities. At the individual level, the financial support of parents or grandparents remains a determining factor in maintaining or strengthening the social position of individuals. This support has been facilitated by the adaptation of the methods of transmission of assets by legal professionals and the French state; we are witnessing a boom in prior real estate arrangements, gifts to children and grandchildren and shared gifts (a practice initially instituted by notaries), which enjoy tax advantages.

In France, the legislator has taken into account these societal changes by reinforcing the protection of the surviving spouse and by abolishing inequalities between children. A law of 3 December 2001 'relating to the rights of the surviving spouse and illegitimate children and modernizing various provisions of inheritance law' establishes a principle of equality between 'adulterous' and 'legitimate' children, ensuring that the interests of the children now take precedence over the institution of marriage.[23] This law also provides greater protection for the surviving spouse since, without making him or her a reserved heir, it grants him or her a two-tiered right to housing for the surviving spouse. Firstly, the widow or widower enjoys, for a period of one year from the death of his or her spouse, a free right to use the marital home and its furniture. This measure concerns the home inhabited as the couple's main residence, either belonging to them or to the estate. If this accommodation was rented, the rents will be paid by the other heirs. 'This is a provision of public order, which replaces the former obligation to provide assistance, which has been abolished,' explains a notary. It cannot be changed by will and is not subject to inheritance tax. Similarly, if the surviving spouses are in need, Article 767 of the new Civil Code obliges the heirs to pay them a pension, which must be claimed within one year of the death. After one year, another type of housing right, this time of a lifetime nature, takes over. Surviving spouses will have the right to use and live in the marital home until their death (provided it is a principal residence, owned by the couple or the estate). The surviving spouses have one year to decide whether or not they want this right. However, this right can be challenged by the testator, who can freely cancel or limit it, but with the help of a notary; such a provision must be included in an authentic will (dictated to a notary).[24]

[22] Piketti (2017, 2018).

[23] In 1972, the equality of legitimate and natural filiations have been proclaimed, the law of succession of 2001 strenghen it in this matter.

[24] Another element to be taken into account is that this right, unlike the previous one, is not of public order but of succession; it therefore has a cost equivalent to 60% of the usufructuary value of the dwelling in question (approximately 80% of its basic value); this cost will be passed on to the other rights that the surviving spouse has in the estate. Once assessed, the value of this right is deducted from the surviving spouse's other inheritance rights.

The reform of inheritance and gifts of 23 June 2006[25] extends the rights of grandchildren who, after having benefited from a tax advantage, are now legally entitled to benefit from a shared donation[26] previously reserved exclusively for children; this tool is now open to all presumptive heirs (brothers and sisters, nephews and nieces, etc). This extension introduces an increased degree of testamentary freedom; it should also 'stimulate the economy by accelerating the 'descent' of property to the younger generations' and constitute 'a means of circulating wealth'.[27] This law also introduces the 'inheritance pact' by means of which the heir with rights of succession can renounce in advance and of their own free will to contest gifts which would infringe their reserve in favour of one of their coheirs (a device known as the early renunciation of action in reduction, or RAAR), which is particularly intended to facilitate the endowment of a disabled child and the designation of a successor to the family business. It marks a shift in the code towards increased testamentary freedom, albeit surrounded by explicit precautions and guarantees. In particular, the agreement of the participants and the compulsory mention of the beneficiary in whose favour the will is made are required. This inheritance pact encourages disposants and presumptive heirs to choose a preferred successor together.[28]

C. Freedom of Wills and Successions as Sources of Emotional Conflict

While the socio-economic stakes of inheritance have diminished for some families with the increase in life expectancy, wage-earners and changes in relations between the generations, the emotional stakes have become more pronounced. The contemporary family depends more on the vagaries of relationships than on statutory obligations. Any inheritance division will therefore be interpreted in terms of law and emotional choice, and any share will be related to a particular bond. The framework provided by the law and the egalitarian principle do not protect against potential conflicts, which they may also exacerbate. The sharing may be equal in value and in kind, but this neutrality may be considered as the negation of individualised or even preferential relationships. The indexation, even relative, of inheritance on emotional relationships thus contributes to structuring conflicts between heirs on the dual economic and identity value of the share received, as reported by professionals involved in inheritances; thus notaries systematically report, in interviews, the acuteness of family conflicts surrounding inheritances.

[25] Loi n° 2006-728 du 23 juin 2006 portant réforme des successions et des libéralités.

[26] A shared donation is both a donation and a division, which allows the assets of one's future estate to be passed on and divided up during one's lifetime. It is made by notarial act. Unlike a will, the distribution of the estate is therefore made before death.

[27] Huygue (2006); Gotman (2006) 78.

[28] Gotman (2006) 79.

The notaries, confronted with multiple interactions which, in some cases, are beyond their control, systematically mention inheritance as an example of conflictual relations and cases that 'drag on' due to a lack of agreement between the members of the sibling group, whatever the family and the volume of assets involved. A notary who set up an individual office in a town of 55,000 inhabitants said:

> It's so complicated! Or else people, the typical things, you find a lot of them in the complaints. 'Ah, but I don't understand why you haven't settled my father's estate!' Do you get on with your sister? 'No.' Did the notary try to reunite you? 'Yes! But it didn't go well!' And the notary, what is he going to do now? 'Yes, but it's been going on for months'.[29]

A notary specialising in family law said that she was confronted, both in divorce and inheritance cases, with situations where 'we are taken to task by one person and everyone wants us to defend them, which is not our primary objective'.

Perceived as a source of disputes and delays, inheritance cases also exacerbate the stress inherent in a time of both mourning and transmission. An assistant in the succession department of a notary's office said:

> I have to manage the client's stress, I act as an intermediary between the client and the boss, I am there to try to manage this stress as best I can, to advise the client as best I can, because generally they tell me their life story, they cry on the phone.[30]

The slowness of succession procedures is a source of disputes. An interview with the president of an Interdepartmental Chamber of Notaries observed,

> We all have files that we let drag on because, well, it's … A sale goes ahead by itself. … Succession … you have to pull it … So, often, it's also because there are problems between heirs and they kindly blame it on the notary. Because it's true that it takes time to solve these problems. Time, patience, psychology.[31]

Similarly, another notary chamber president remarked,

> Often, there are cases that can last and then cases with also problems between heirs … the notary in the middle … he has tried, but he has not been able to put people in agreement … often it is a lack of communication.[32]

Inheritance conflicts pit individuals against each other, but also everyone against 'the family', a collective entity that has certainly changed in nature and weight in history. In this respect, the notary has a form of culpable knowledge[33] about certain facets of the human personality that are difficult to admit. 'Bad faith' is a recurring theme in support of certain forms of disenchantment and weariness

[29] Interview, 19 April 2016.
[30] Field Notes, Université du Notariat, Lyon, 2014.
[31] Interview, 28 May 2015.
[32] Interview, September 2014.
[33] Hughes (1958).

among these professionals. For example, an individual notary practising in a small town, who was at the end of his career, emphasised:

> The clients weighed on me in the end .... There is a certain amount of bad faith, there is a greed for money and then they are liars, they don't tell us everything, especially in the case of successions.[34]

When it comes to inheritance, conflicts arise less between parents and children than between brothers and sisters of the same lineage or between step-parents and children of different lineages.[35] Professionals often mention the manifestation of old resentments and jealousies during these successions. These conflicts also attest to the persistent and even growing financial stakes of inheritance. The rise of blended families is one of the many sources of conflict in the settlement of inheritances; it also raises the question of the status and possibilities of transmission of the new spouse to the children of a previous marriage, a question often raised during interviews and which is at the heart of clients' requests to notaries.

Succession is a time of stress and conflict for some clients, who are also confronted with 'the complexity of succession … they always have to be decided for them. The surviving spouse has to have the usufruct, the thing, explained to him in drawings'.[36] The notary's advice is often required, and may even be insisted upon, judging by an observed succession meeting where the person insists on being guided. During an appointment to organise an inheritance and gifts to children, where tax issues were central ('taxation is a big problem', 'you can't cheat?', 'because if you don't, taxes …'), the client repeatedly asked the notary for his opinion: 'What do you think? 'What should I do?', 'What do you think?', insisting on her need for advice: 'I need to be advised, sincerely', 'Yes, I need to be advised too'. During an absence of the notary, who had gone to get copies, she said: 'Oh, inheritance is always a big worry. And what should I do? I'm completely helpless. And yet I expected it, but you can't believe it when it happens'.[37]

Notaries occupy a key position in these family arbitrations as practitioners; they also play an important role as reformers, arguing that their prerogatives and competences in family property law as well as their privileged position would allow them to have a detailed knowledge of the evolution and needs of families. This is what we will now see in the next section.

IV. The Key Role and Position of Notaries as Legal Practitioners and Reformers

Among the stakeholders in the debate on testamentary freedom, notaries are leading professionals both as practitioners with a central and growing role in matters

[34] Interview, 24 October 2014.
[35] Gotman (2006) 13.
[36] Interview/field notes, 19 February 2016.
[37] Observation notes, 13 May 2016.

of succession and, correlatively, as experts. This profession, which collectively produces reports and positions and is listened to by public authorities, and defends the reconciliation of testamentary reserve and freedom in the form of a 'virtuous transmission regime'.

A. An Increasingly Obligatory Step in Inheritance Matters

In France, notaries are practitioners specialising in property and family law. These two branches of law constitute the core of their activities, even though they tend to be involved in other areas, particularly corporate law. The notary is a necessary step in any succession involving property or real estate rights. This particularity may also explain certain vocations, as shown by this extract from an interview with a notary:

> My uncle was a notary … In fact, I became interested in the notary's profession when I was doing my Master's degree because I had a teacher who was extraordinary and who connected me with inheritance law, and so I said to myself, 'the profession most closely related to inheritance is the notary's profession', and that's how I embarked on the adventure of becoming a public notary.[38]

Inheritances account for a large proportion of the activity and turnover of notaries, who appear to be specialists in this field; this proportion has even increased since 2019, due the COVID-19 crisis, as an accountant working in a notary's office in a medium-sized town pointed out:

> It's enormous and constant compared to the heatwave [in 2003]. During the heatwave, we had deaths over three weeks;… here, the deaths were spread out over months; … before the confinement, we had, to tell you the truth, two people in succession, today we have four people in succession …. we hired someone in January and my boss, looking at the succession files that had opened, said 'we have work for her for a year'. So even though we're not in a very big city, well, anyway, the retirement homes are empty …. one of my bosses … told me 'We can't take any more estates! I spend my time having appointments for estates …. In terms of volume, it has been multiplied … Maybe by two! … Moreover, we saw a lot on Facebook in the recruitment section that the office was looking for people in family law, so it appeared a lot … we feel it a lot. This helps to explain … that when you say succession, you might be saying sale. So there's also real estate behind it.[39]

This central role of notaries has been constantly recognised and extended. Thus, the aforementioned 2006 reform of successions, 'the result of work carried out by the profession in collaboration with the Chancellery', strengthens the notary's role and responsibility in the settlement of inheritances and in the advice he or she can give to his or her clients. It also introduces the 'mandate with posthumous effect' which,

[38] Interview, 26 November 2014.
[39] Interview, 7 May 2021.

to be executed before a notary, allows a person to designate during his or her lifetime one or more agents, natural or legal persons who will be responsible after his or her death for administering all or part of the estate on behalf of and in the interest of one or more identified heirs. The agent may be an heir. At the 102nd congress of notaries in Strasbourg in 2006, Jean-Paul Delevoye hoped for 'the trivialization of the notary in all acts of life, to protect against anything that might create a potential for vulnerability'. The President of the CSN was able to conclude in 2008 that the activity of the offices, due to the growth of the property market on the one hand, and the contribution of the new texts on family law on the other, is improving.

The notary's remit was also extended by the reforms to the justice system. The notarial profession proposed to relieve judges by taking over some of their responsibilities, even if it meant intervening in exchange for a mediocre level of remuneration. In line with this proposal, the law of 18 November 2016, known as the '21st century justice modernisation law', refocuses the courts on their missions and extends the powers of notaries to three measures which, until then, were of a judicial nature: the procedures for sending a person into possession, renouncing the estate and accepting the net assets. 'Sending in possession' is a procedure which until then obliged the 'universal legatee' designated by a sealed or holographic will (therefore not dictated to a notary) to have the President of the Tribunal de Grande Instance check the apparent validity of the will, as long as there is no reserved heir. This procedure could lengthen the processing of inheritance files and prove costly for the litigant, as representation by a lawyer was compulsory. It is now up to the notary to check that the universal legatee is indeed entitled to receive the entire estate and that there are no heirs with rights of retention, and automatic recourse to the judge is abolished. Furthermore, an heir designated by law or by will may accept or renounce the succession. The renunciation of an estate, which was also reformed in 2016, can now be made before a judge. For example, the heir can send it either to the court in whose jurisdiction the estate has been opened or to the notary, who will then send it to the court. 'Acceptance of the estate up to the amount of the net assets' (formerly under benefit of inventory) provided for by law (Article 787ff of the Civil Code) means that the debts of the succession are to be paid only up to the limit of the deceased's assets by the heir, whose personal assets are thus protected from the deceased's creditors. The heir may simply accept his or her estate if it is found that it is surplus to requirements, ie that there are more assets than debts to be repaid. If the declaration of acceptance of the succession up to the amount of the net assets is made at the registry of the Tribunal de Grande Instance of the place where the succession was opened, the notary may now, with this reform, receive this declaration and provide advice to the heirs, if they so wish, before taking a decision that may present risks, particularly if the extent of the deceased's assets has been wrongly assessed. The notary can then take care of the formalities of the declaration.

The issue of international successions and the adoption of a new regulation on successions within the EU in 2012 has also contributed to the profession's interest in this area and the introduction of training for its members. As a member of the board of the Conseil Supérieur du Notariat (CSN), the representative and decision-making body of notaries, points out:

> We found that there was unfortunately a lack of approach by colleagues to all aspects of private international law, so we are going to place a little emphasis on this, especially since, with the new regulation on successions, it is absolutely necessary for notaries to be at the top of their game in this area, hence the numerous training courses … our colleagues must take on board the dimensions of this essential subject nowadays.[40]

The essential nature of these legal professionals in matters of family assets and succession makes them experts who are recognised and listened to by the public authorities. The following sub-section will present the expert role played by notaries.

B. Notaries as Inheritance 'Experts'

Notaries are consulted by the public authorities as experts on various subjects relating to real estate, family, tax and inheritance law, corresponding to their specialities. Individually, they argue that their competence and high level of technicality stem from their daily practice but also from the means made available to them by the profession: research and documentation centre (CRIDON), support from professional bodies, training, etc. 'Deeds of sale are becoming increasingly complicated; inheritance files are becoming increasingly complicated. We have knowledge, we have fantastic training,' a notary practising in a small town emphasised in an interview.[41]

The intellectual dimension of the profession is strongly emphasised by the profession, which has set up several legal research structures and is developing numerous collaborations with law professors who contribute their theoretical knowledge and intellectual backing (via notarial training courses and journals that bring together practitioners and legal scholars, such as the *JCP Notariat*, or by participating in the profession's publications and reports, particularly those produced at notaries' congresses). The profession and its members have also created labels attesting to their skills in a specific field, namely, for family law – which includes inheritance law – '*notaire conseil aux familles*' (NCF) (notary advice to families). In September 2018, notaries who hold this label, issued by the CSN, and which attests to the completion of a training course specialising in family law, have, in a context of liberalisation and increased competition, created a professional network. This network, 'Notaries at the heart of families' ('*Notaires au Coeur des familles*'), aims to support the development of family advice,

> to make the expertise of our members known to the general public, which is often ill-informed and poorly protected legally, thanks to a national brand, to help our members

[40] Interview, 6 January 2016.

[41] Interview, 24 October 2014, notary, town of less than 10,000 inhabitants, Haute-Saône.

> to remain at the highest level thanks to continuous training courses, exchanges of good practice and shared tools, to promote the development of family advice activities in notarial offices.[42]

The profession has also set up research and training structures, in particular, within the CSN, the Institute of Legal Studies (*Institut d'études juridiques*, IEJ) and the Institute of Family Law and Patrimony (*Institut du droit de la famille et du patrimoine*, IDFP) which 'aims to be a force for reflection and proposals on all issues relating to family law and patrimony'.[43] This research and training institute is dedicated to the exchange and dissemination of knowledge and to the progress of legal techniques through training courses for notaries and lawyers but also through information and communication actions for public authorities and the media. In addition, each year, a legal issue is the subject of a report and proposals are submitted to the Ministry of Justice at the end of the annual national congress of notaries, which brings together part of the profession (nearly 2,000, ie more than 10 per cent) who vote on these proposals. The family has been at the heart of many congresses, in particular the 116th, held in Paris in 2020 on the theme 'Protecting. The vulnerable, relatives, housing, rights'.

Finally, notaries explicitly present themselves as experts on the family and, more broadly, on society, or even as 'sociologists' (a term sometimes used in interviews), which would justify a broad competence and generalist expertise among these professionals who, like priests in the past or doctors today, claim a legal, moral and intellectual 'mandate'[44] on many questions of society: 'Every year, notaries meet with almost twenty million clients. This enables them to gauge the changing attitudes and lifestyles of our fellow citizens, their expectations and the limits of the rules that govern us'.[45] Intervening in the media, in public debates, or even with candidates during the presidential elections, submitting to the public authorities their wishes or proposals for reforms on legal and social subjects, notaries are also solicited within the framework of the reforms. For example, they recently took part in the working group on hereditary reserve set up at the request of the Minister of Justice Nicole Belloubet, led by Cécile Pérès and Philippe Potentier.[46] In the context of this working group report, the profession reaffirms its attachment to the hereditary reserve and its concern to reconcile it with greater testamentary freedom.

[42] 'La vocation du réseau NCF', available at notaires-ncf.fr/qui-sommes-nous.

[43] www.institut-dfp.com/presentation.htm.

[44] Hughes (1958).

[45] Prohaszka et al, 'Contributions du 116e Congrès des notaires de France' in Pérès and Potentier (2020) 630.

[46] Cécile Pérès is a professor of private law at the University of Paris 2 and the author of two books on inheritance law, and Philippe Potentier is a notary in Louviers (Eure) since 1983, president of the CSN's Institute for Legal Studies (Institut des Etudes juridiques), and general rapporteur of the 108nd congress of notaries, in 2012, which was devoted to transmission.

C. For a 'Virtuous Transmission Regime' and a Balance between Freedom and Protection: Reconciling the Reserved Portion of an Estate with Testamentary Freedom

The transmission of property is at the heart of the activities of the notary defending the hereditary reserve, which would enable a balance to be struck between protection, family solidarity and testamentary freedom, as these remarks by the notary Philippe Potentier attest:

> Are we free to test or to give to whomever we wish? To dispose of our property as we wish? The answer is yes. This is a fundamental freedom, which represents a continuation of the inalienable right of ownership. But to what extent? As with all freedoms, there are limits to it. Reservation of inheritance is one such limit, but it does not mean confiscation of the estate. It is always partial and calls for its complement, the available portion, where the freedom to give and bequeath can be fully expressed in order to give to someone else, one's spouse or a philanthropic work …. Parents cannot freely give or test their entire estate when they have children. This is normal, isn't it?[47]

The notaries' defense of the hereditary reserve is made in the name of intra-family solidarity but also of the supposed attachment of the French to this system. These legal professionals, defenders of the autonomy of the will, the right of ownership and individual freedoms, promote the freedom to dispose of one's assets and to pass them on to third parties, for example to finance a cause, via foundations (charitable, animal protection, defense of causes, the fight against certain scourges, disease, etc), with which they maintain close links and to which they can direct their clients for bequests or donations.

Promoters of the right to property and of the freedom to dispose of one's assets as one wishes, notaries defend the reserved portion of an estate but also its possible reduction; thus, they proposed to the candidates in the 2012 presidential election to

> reduce the reserved portion of an estate without abolishing it in order to relax the rigor of this system, to which the majority of French people remain very attached. This measure would aim to respect more fully the autonomy of the will.[48]

This possibility, aimed at the largest estates, is included in the report submitted to the minister in 2021, because, as its co-author, the notary Philippe Potentier, points out:

> The question, asked most of the time by a very well-to-do minority, was the following: is this available quarter sufficient in the presence of three or more children? In most cases it is. We meet very few parents who want to give more to third parties. But we have

[47] 'Philippe Potentier: La réserve héréditaire n'est pas une confiscation de patrimoine', Interview with Chloé Rossignol, *Journal du dimanche* (29 March 2020), available at www.lejdd.fr/Economie/philippe-potentier-la-reserve-hereditaire-nest-pas-une-confiscation-du-patrimoine-3958551.

[48] CSN (2012).

> taken into account this recurrent and well-publicized request from wealthy people to give or bequeath more, and have proposed to extend the available share to a third party from two or more children.

Far from calling the reserve into question, the notaries are proposing to adjust its 'operation'. That is:

> It seems to us that the reserve must evolve in its operation but not in its principle. This evolution must be carried out while respecting the security of third party legatees, a balance between freedom and protection, but also between the rights of the individual and those of the family.[49]

The hereditary reserve is all the less questioned in principle since it is a formally egalitarian right preventing the disinheritance of one's children and imposing the transmission of quasi-equal shares to them. This does not prevent, in practice, situations of inequality being created, in particular between sons, who inherit more structural property, such as a business or the family home, considered to be economically and symbolically the most valuable, and daughters, who receive financial compensation, often under-valued by notary offices. This contributes to a sort of hidden inequality between sons and daughters, who are not equal in the face of inheritance.[50] In addition, there is also inequality between men and women within the couple, linked to persistent gender inequalities in terms of salaries, property and the home. The surviving spouse (most often the woman) is not in competition with the children who have the right to inherit and only benefits from a sort of reserve on the spouse's property in the absence of children, a provision that notaries are proposing to abolish, as it is considered 'unusual'.[51]

The legal changes proposed by the profession in 2020[52] are congruent with notarial practice, which emphasises the importance of consent, consensual decisions and family arrangements, even if it means lifting the hereditary reserve with the agreement of its beneficiaries, in particular by means of the advance waiver of the action for reduction instituted by the legislator in 2006. Jean-Pierre Prohaszka, notary and president of the 116th Congress of French notaries, which is proposing to reform the reserved portion of an estate, explains:

> Our proposal would be to extend it [the hereditary reserve] to a 'family pact' in which the future deceased and the heirs consult each other and increase the available portion together, by mutual agreement. This is in line with the idea of a calmer law rather than a contentious law, a consensual law rather than an arbitrary and totally free one. We believe that this pact would be very useful in many cases of blended families and that it would respond well to the new family sociology.

The rapporteur for the 116th Congress of Notaries in 2020 proposed going even further in this contractualisation, that is, in this increase in the power of

[49] Prohaszka et al (n 45) 630.

[50] Bessière and Gollac (2023).

[51] See Pérès and Potentier (2020).

[52] In the context of the 116th Congress of Notaries in 2020, and the hearing included in the above-mentioned working group report (Pérès and Potentier, 2020).

agreements; he stresses, with regard to the reform of successions of 23 June 2006, which opened the way to the early renunciation of the action in reduction, that

> Persons holding a right of reserve may thus, during the lifetime of the depositor, consent to a gift made to a third party or to one of them encroaching on their hereditary share and renounce any compensation in this respect. The increasing contractualization of family law may invite us to continue along this path and to imagine, as is the case in the German-speaking countries, pacts of succession with an even broader scope and leading more or less to an agreement on the rights of each of the heirs as to the respective amount of their rights, or even on the distribution of the property.[53]

This contractual succession has been favoured elsewhere, for example in Belgium, with the introduction in 2017 of a global inheritance pact. In France, such a pact, which must be drawn up in the form of an authenticated deed, ie before a notary, is in line with the trend to promote anticipation of inheritance and inheritance arrangements for which notaries are the essential intermediaries.

V. Conclusion

In France, notaries are essential actors in the inheritance process, particularly to draw up and/or keep a will, to 'liquidate' an estate or to divide the deceased's assets between the heirs. The legislator has constantly increased their role, in particular by creating inheritance schemes, some of which are proposed by notaries and involve notarial assistance.

These professionals promote their role as peacemakers, custodians of family secrets and acting in the interests of all stakeholders. If they defend testamentary freedom and its increase, it is in a measured way and through the promotion of a consensual right. In the name of reconciling freedom, equality and protection, they believe that the hereditary reserve can only be infringed on the basis of a family consensus, in the form of inheritance pacts for which they would be both the inspirers and the masters of the works, such pacts being concluded before them.

References

108th Congrès des Notaires de France, 'La transmission' (2012).

116th Congrès des Notaires de France, 'Protéger. Les vulnérables, les proches, le logement, les droits' (2020).

Audren, F, 'Le légiste, l'économiste et la liberté testamentaire sous le Second Empire' (2014) 28 *Revue d'histoire du XIXe siècle* 47.

Beckert, J, *Inherited Wealth* (Princeton, Princeton University Press, 2009).

[53] Prohaszka et al (n 45) 632.

Bessière, C and Gollac, S, *The Gender of Capital: How Families Perpetuate Wealth Inequality* (Cambridge, Mass, Harvard University Press, 2023).
Burguière, A, 'L'Etat monarchique et la famille. XVIe–XVIIIe siècles' (2001) 56 *Annales ESC* 313.
CSN 'Propositions notariales pour les élections présidentielles' (2012).
Daumas, P, 'Familles en Révolution. Vie et relations familiales en Ile-de-France, changements et conflictualités (1775–1825)' (Rennes, Presses universitaires de Rennes, 2003).
Delmas, C, *Les notaires en France. Entre héritage et modernité* (Rennes, Presses Universitaires de Rennes, 2019).
Galanter, M, 'Why the Haves Come Out Ahead: Speculations on the Limits of Social Change' (1974) 9 *Law and Society Review* 95.
Gotman, A, *L'héritage* (Paris, PUF, 2006).
Hughes, E, *Men and their Work*, (Glencoe, Free Press, 1958).
Huygue, S, 'Rapport n° 2850 déposé le 8 février 2006, Successions et libéralités' (2006).
Peguera Poch, M, 'Aux origines de la réserve héréditaire du code civil, la légitime en Pays de Coutume (XVIe–XVIIIe siècles)' (Aix-en-Provence, Presses universitaires d'Aix-Marseille, 2009).
Pérès, C and Potentier, P (eds), *La réserve héréditaire* (Paris, Panthéon Assas éditeur, 2020).
Piketti, T, *Capital in the Twenty-First Century* (Cambridge, Mass, Harvard University Press, 2017).
—— *Top Incomes in France in the Twentieth Century. Inequality and Redistribution, 1901–1998* (Cambridge, Mass, Harvard University Press, 2018).
Steiner, P, 'L'héritage au XIXe siècle en France. Loi, intérêt de sentiment et intérêts économiques' (2008) 59 *Revue économique* 75.

12

Children in Need and the Great Intergenerational Wealth Transfer

Squaring the Impossible Circle of Testamentary Freedom, Family Obligations and the Role of the State

HEATHER CONWAY AND SHEENA GRATTAN

I. Introduction

It is a trite observation that every human society, both ancient and modern, has developed a corpus of rules to govern the reallocation of objects that once belonged to its now deceased members. These have ranged from the interment of said property with the deceased's mortal remains at one end of the spectrum, to its confiscation by the state at the other. Most societies have opted for something in between these two extremes – what might best be described as inheritance 'by rule' and inheritance 'by election'. Under the former, a person's property is distributed in accordance with a rigid and inviolable scheme that defines both the beneficiaries (usually spouses, children and other close relatives) and the extent of their benefit. By far the most prevalent historically, inheritance by rule still dominates in developing countries, Islamic states and much of the civil law systems of continental Europe.[1]

In contrast, common law[2] jurisdictions such as England and Wales favour inheritance 'by election' whereby an individual is given the right to designate who

[1] The term 'civil law' is explained in n 2.

[2] Common law countries have a combination of judge-made law and statutes. Originating in England in the Middle Ages, the common law system was exported to various other countries including America, Australia, Canada, New Zealand and Ireland; see generally Dainow (1966). In contrast, civil law countries have comprehensive and continually updated codes, which cover all areas of law; shaped by Roman law tradition, this particular system dominates throughout continental Europe and South America – and also in Scotland (though Scots law is a hybrid of both common and civil law). It is worth noting, however, that wills still feature in civil law countries, just as they did in the Roman tradition. See eg Champlin (1991).

succeeds to their property after death. That right is exercised by making a will in the manner prescribed by law, and is available to all adult citizens who satisfy a minimum capacity threshold (commonly encapsulated in the phrase 'of sound disposing mind'). A person who has exercised the right to make a will is still generally known by the Latin-derived term 'testator',[3] and is said to enjoy 'testamentary freedom'. We explore this concept in detail later,[4] but at this juncture two points can usefully be made. The first is that testamentary freedom is a right, not a duty; and rather surprisingly, many individuals choose not to exercise it.[5] Secondly, and fundamental to the subject matter of this chapter, testamentary freedom is not an absolute right. Most common law succession regimes incorporate a mechanism for redistributing property on death following a judicial arbitration process.[6] Adult citizens remain free to make a will benefiting those whom they choose. However, courts have discretionary powers to set that distribution aside in favour of specific individuals who claim a (larger) share of the deceased's estate.[7]

This system of inheritance 'by arbitration' should not be viewed as some sort of legally endorsed 'free-for-all'. Only certain individuals – usually surviving spouses/civil partners, eligible cohabitants, children and certain dependants – can apply to court, and must seize this particular initiative. More fundamentally, perhaps, success is never guaranteed: *if* an award is made to a particular 'applicant' or 'claimant',[8] its size and nature is also at the discretion of the court. In England and Wales, the system is known as the 'family provision' jurisdiction and has its legislative basis in the Inheritance (Provision for Family and Dependants) Act 1975. It is this system, and how it applies to one particular member of the deceased's family, that are the focus of this chapter.[9]

[3] While 'testator' traditionally denoted a male will-maker with 'testatrix' the female equivalent, the former is used in a gender neutral sense throughout this chapter.

[4] See section IV.

[5] It is generally accepted that approximately two in three adults in England die without a valid will – see Law Commission of England and Wales, 'Intestacy and Family Provision Claims on Death' Law Com No 331 (2011) [1.3]. A parallel system of inheritance by rule therefore remains an essential component of any common law inheritance system. Persons who die without a valid will are said to die 'intestate' and the law prescribes how their property is to be distributed as between a surviving spouse or civil partner, children or other close relatives.

[6] With the exception of America, other countries have similar legal frameworks – most notably family maintenance statutes in Australia and New Zealand, and dependants' relief legislation in Canada.

[7] A claim under the family provision legislation does not affect the validity of the will itself. Wills may be challenged on various grounds such as non-compliance with the strict formality requirements surrounding execution (eg that the document was not properly signed or witnessed) or lack of substantive validity (eg that the testator was of not of sound mind, or acting under duress or undue influence). These raise fundamentally different legal issues, which are not discussed here.

[8] These two terms appear in the relevant statutes and judgments, and denote exactly the same thing.

[9] The primary emphasis here is on England and Wales, which comprise one legal jurisdiction for succession law matters – including the 1975 Act. In this article, the term 'English law' is used (for convenience) to refer to the law of the legal jurisdiction that is England and Wales, though occasional reference will also be made to Northern Ireland. The latter jurisdiction generally follows England in all succession law contexts and has a substantively similar version of the 1975 Act under the Inheritance (Provision for Family and Dependants) (NI) Order 1979. However, Scotland's legislative

Family provision claims by adult children against a dead parent's estate have long been regarded as the 'sharp end'[10] of the jurisdiction and, accordingly, one of the most difficult categories to predict. As Herring notes, the law has 'plenty to say about the rights and responsibilities [that] parents owe their minor children, but once the child reaches the age of majority, the law generally falls silent'.[11] Between 2007 and 2017, one particular English case was the perfect embodiment of this sentiment when an estranged daughter challenged her mother's decision to exclude her from an estate worth around £486,000. This triggered a protracted and much-publicised legal dispute against the animal welfare charities who were the sole beneficiaries of the mother's estate. When *Ilott v The Blue Cross*[12] eventually reached the Supreme Court, the seven Justices of the Court unanimously reinstated an earlier award of £50,000 for the daughter in a verdict delivered by Lord Hughes. However, as part of a forceful supplemental judgment,[13] Lady Hale (with whom Lords Kerr and Wilson agreed) observed that the case raised 'some profound questions about the nature of family obligations, the relationship between family obligations and the state, and the relationship between the [testamentary] freedom of property owners … and their duty to fulfil their family obligations'.[14]

Using Lady Hale's comments as a staging post, this chapter interrogates these fundamental questions through the lens of family provision claims involving 'disinherited' adult children who – for whatever reason – received nothing under a dead parent's will.[15] It explores what these claims reveal about changing family dynamics and whether adult children are (still) regarded as the natural recipients of parental bounty; what legal obligations parents owe their 'independent'[16] adult children; the consequent limits on testamentary freedom; and the complex policy issues around the concept of 'state provision versus estate provision' where an adult child is dependent on welfare payments and there are sufficient funds in a dead parent's estate to relieve (or reduce) the burden on the state. The chapter concludes that there are probably still more questions than answers. What follows, however, is an important analytical reference point for the legal, familial, social and policy issues at play in contemporary succession law narratives involving parents and their adult children.[17]

framework is different, because of the country's civil law influence, and is not discussed here. As a general observation, there has been an unfortunate tendency for international commentators to refer to UK law, when the correct reference should be English law; see eg Croucher and Vines (2019).

[10] Green (1988) 196.

[11] Herring (2016) 41, 41–42.

[12] [2017] UKSC 17, [2017] 2 WLR 979. The case was formerly listed as *Ilott v Mitson*.

[13] Namely, a short addendum judgment that agrees with the other members of the court but raises further considerations. In English law, this type of judgment is very unusual in a unanimous decision – on most occasions any non-binding guidance ('obiter dicta') is found within the main judgment.

[14] [2017] UKSC 17 [49].

[15] Though the term 'disinherited' is something of a misnomer: testamentary freedom means that parents are not legally obliged to provide for their children (or anyone else) on death.

[16] As defined in section III.

[17] While the chapter focuses largely on the English position, the discussion extends beyond this jurisdictional remit as other common law jurisdictions grapple with the same problems. For a flavour, see eg Peart and Sutton (2001); Villios and Williams (2018).

II. The Family Provision Framework and the *Ilott* Litigation: A Summary

The jurisdictional basis for all claims under the Inheritance (Provision for Family and Dependants) Act 1975 is that the testator's will[18] has failed to make 'reasonable financial provision'[19] for the applicant. In assessing this, judges pose two interrelated questions: (1) did the will make reasonable financial provision for the applicant; and (2) if not, what reasonable financial provision should be made?[20] Like other similar statutory regimes, the 1975 Act lists a range of relationships that trigger a potential claim against an estate, and a child of the deceased – regardless of age – is one such category.[21] However, for children, reasonable financial provision is limited to what is required for their 'maintenance'.[22] This sets English law apart from most other common law schemes, which tend to have a more generous basis for intervention.[23]

The concept of maintenance is not defined in the Act; it has been flexibly interpreted by judges as meaning something beyond the subsistence level, but not 'any or every thing which it would be desirable for the claimant to have'.[24] However, the 1975 Act does list certain criteria that judges must use to determine the success of each claim (question 1) and any consequent award (question 2). General factors automatically apply, and include things like the financial resources and future needs of the applicant and any estate beneficiaries, the size of the estate, and any obligations and responsibilities the deceased had towards any applicant or beneficiary.[25] Specific factors differ for each category of applicant; for claims by children, however, courts must only look at the 'manner in which the applicant was being, or … might expect to be, educated or trained'.[26]

[18] The 1975 Act (and most other equivalent statutory regimes throughout the common law world) also permit courts to alter an intestacy distribution where the deceased died without a (valid) will in place. However, this chapter focuses solely on will-making practices.

[19] 1975 Act, s 1(1).

[20] The range of potential orders is listed in s 2 of the 1975 Act, and includes periodical or lump sum payments of money, as well as property transfers.

[21] 1975 Act, s 1(1)(c). A 'child' includes an adopted child of the deceased, persons who would have been classed as an illegitimate child in the past, unborn children (a child *en ventre sa mere*) and children born by assisted reproduction techniques who are the legal child of the deceased. Step-children, foster children and other 'de facto children' fall outside s 1(1)(c), but may be able to apply under s 1(1)(d) if they were treated as a child of the family. Other categories of applicant under the 1975 Act include surviving spouses and civil partners, cohabitants of two or more years' standing, and a person who was being maintained by the deceased immediately before death.

[22] For all categories of applicant (other than a surviving spouse or registered civil partner), reasonable financial provision is limited to receipt of 'maintenance' – 1975 Act, s 1(2)(b).

[23] In the Republic of Ireland (which is a separate legal jurisdiction from Northern Ireland) the basis of a claim by an adult child is that the testator failed in their 'moral duty to make proper provision' for their child (Succession Act 1965, s 117(1)). In New Zealand it is that the testator did not make 'adequate provision' for 'proper maintenance and support' (Family Protection Act 1955, s 4(1)).

[24] *Ilott v The Blue Cross* [2017] UKSC 17 [14] (Lord Hughes).

[25] 1975 Act, s 3(1).

[26] 1975 Act, s 3(3).

Turning to the *Ilott* litigation, the facts are fairly well-known.[27] Melita Jackson had been widowed in 1960, while pregnant with her only child, Heather. In 1978 and aged 17, Heather left home to live with a man her mother disapproved of, causing a permanent family rift.[28] The daughter married her partner and had five children with him; Heather Ilott (as she now was) subsequently chose not to work in order to be a stay-at-home mother. When Melita died in 2004, her will left a £486,000 estate to three animal charities that she had no lifetime connection to, and nothing to her only child. Heather was then aged 44, had not worked since the birth of her first child in 1983, and was living with her husband and three of the couple's children in a three-bedroom property rented from a Housing Association.[29] The husband worked part-time, and the family were dependent on state benefits to meet basic living expenses.

Heather applied under the 1975 Act. An initial award of £50,000 in her favour by the court of first hearing was increased to £143,000 (with an option to draw upon a further £20,000) by the Court of Appeal[30] as part of a series of complex appeals. The charities lodged a final appeal to the Supreme Court, accepting that the mother's will had failed to make reasonable financial provision for her daughter (under question 1) but contesting the amount awarded (under question 2). Ruling for the charities, the Supreme Court reinstated the earlier award of £50,000 as being the proper sum for Heather's maintenance. The deceased's testamentary freedom was also an important aspect of the case, as was the position of the charities – both as the chosen beneficiaries of Melita's estate and because charities are heavily reliant on gifts in wills to carry out their work.[31]

Much of the febrile publicity generated by *Ilott* stemmed from the fact that it was the first family provision case – of any kind – to reach the highest appellate court in the UK. On calmer reflection, expectations among academics and practitioners as to what the Supreme Court might achieve were always entirely unrealistic, not least because the appeal was only on the issue of quantum.[32] In other words, the affirmative answer to question 1 was not challenged in the Supreme Court. The family provision jurisdiction is a highly fact-specific one,[33] and it was always going to be questionable how far any particular family provision case could meaningfully inform future litigation.[34] Just as it has been famously said that 'no will has

[27] For a more detailed analysis of the factual background and the entire *Ilott* saga, see Sloan (2019); Conway (2017).

[28] Several abortive reconciliations had been attempted over the years.

[29] Housing associations are non-profit organisations tasked with providing, constructing and managing affordable housing accommodation. See eg s 1(1) of the Housing Association Act 1985 in England and Wales.

[30] *Ilott v Mitson* [2015] EWCA Civ 797, [2016] 1 All ER 932.

[31] All charities rely heavily on legacy income to survive. For some statistics in the UK, see Smee & Ford, 'Charitable estate values on track to reach £20bn in 2022', available at https://smeeandford.com/articles/charitable-estate-values-on-track-to-reach-20bn-in-2022.

[32] Kerridge (2020) 384, 401.

[33] The outcome is heavily influenced by the specific facts of the individual claim.

[34] These cases remain an effective lottery – see Douglas (2014) 222, 225. We return to this point later.

a twin brother'[35] (in the context of dissuading lawyers from putting reliance on the meaning given to the same words in an earlier will), no family provision case has a twin sister. Moreover, *Ilott* was a particularly unusual combination of facts in terms of both the enduring estrangement between mother and daughter and the entire estate passing to charities. Arguably the singularly most important 'take away' point is a reminder of just how difficult it is to appeal the exercise of judicial discretion.[36] After a decade of litigation, a plethora of judgments, eye-watering legal bills and the inevitable emotional cost, the decision of the original judge was held to be correct. Nonetheless, the points raised by Lady Hale speak to core issues beyond the unique factual matrix and inheritance practices of the case itself, as the following sections illustrate.

III. Adult Children, Parental Wealth and the Problem of the 'Independent' Adult Child

Despite being an ostensibly private decision, inheritance is a 'public event with symbolic messages about normative property distribution, individual freedom, and familial or other collective obligations'.[37] It plays a pivotal role in family relations and intergenerational wealth distribution, and is underpinned by complex social and psychological issues.[38] This is especially true in posthumous transfers of wealth between parents and their adult children. Empirical and academic studies tend to emphasise the emotional and psychological impact of parental disinheritance, or a child getting significantly less than was anticipated.[39] However, the economic implications also create something of a harsh reality.

The post-war generation, the so-called 'Baby Boomers', are estimated to control 80 per cent of private wealth in the UK today,[40] thanks to a 'perfect' combination of free university education, final salary pensions and – most significantly of all – an exponential increase in the value of family homes during their working lives. All but the youngest of this richest generation in history are now pensioners, but they are not immortal. Over the next 20–30 years it has been estimated that £1.2 trillion in assets will transfer to the next generation (or elsewhere) in what has been dubbed 'the Great Wealth Transfer'. Without parental assistance, the reality is that a large portion of so-called 'Generation Rent' will never get on the housing

[35] *Matter of King* 200 NY 189, 192 (1910) (Werner J).

[36] Judicial discretion can only be appealed where the original judge misinterpreted the law or failed to consider all relevant facts of the case – not because the appellate court would have reached a different conclusion.

[37] Hacker (2010) 323.

[38] See eg Stum (1999).

[39] See eg Conway (2016); Izuhara and Koppe (2019).

[40] The statistics referenced in this section were taken from M Deacon, 'The Demise of the Baby Boomers Will Change Britain Forever' *The Telegraph* (1 September 2022). They are reflective of the many quoted by financial advisers and found on a weekly basis in the British financial press.

ladder. It is perhaps no coincidence that the first signs that English courts were 'softening' to claims by adult children[41] coincided with the time when house prices made it difficult even for graduates in secure, professional employment to buy their first home without parental assistance. At the time of writing, the shortage of affordable housing is more acute than it has ever been, with many adult children living at home for longer (the 'Boomerang Generation').[42] Such a financial climate is likely to fuel family provision claims.

More generally, there are also misplaced assumptions around inheritance: many adult children mistakenly believe that they have a financial interest in parental wealth, and, as a consequence of what they see as the 'dynastic' function of inheritance law, that this wealth will almost certainly pass to them. A system of family provision can broadly promote one of three functions: a mere support function (providing maintenance to those in economic need, either generally or restricted to those who were being maintained by the parent prior to death); a 'contribution' or 'reward' function (providing recompense for 'good deeds' such as caring for an ageing parent or working in a family business); or a purely dynastic function whereby an award is made simply because it is 'family' property. As we have seen, in contrast to other common law countries, adult children in England are limited to a claim for maintenance, a concept which connotes a support function, rather than reward or familial entitlement.

With adult heirs, much of the contemporary debate involves 'independent'[43] adult children – in other words, an able-bodied adult son or daughter who is economically self-sufficient (or, at least, has earning potential), and was not financially dependent on a deceased parent before death (even if in financial need). Such individuals can find themselves disinherited for all sorts of reasons.[44] Long-term estrangements and disapproval of children's lifestyle choices or romantic relationships both feature strongly in the case law.[45] Less censorious motives include passing wealth elsewhere if the parent leaves a surviving spouse/partner, or feels that their offspring have already benefited from substantial lifetime gifts.[46] Whatever the explanation, an independent adult child may be minded to challenge their exclusion from a validly executed will – and these types of family provision claims are some of the most 'contentious and complex' that English courts have had to deal with.[47]

[41] See eg *Espinosa v Bourke* [1999] 1 FLR 747.

[42] The COVID-19 pandemic increased further the number of adult children returning to live with their parents.

[43] Or, to borrow another descriptor, 'self-supportive' – Villios and Williams (2018) 253.

[44] The focus is on what we might term 'deliberate' disinheritance, where the parent makes a very conscious choice to leave nothing to an adult son or daughter. Contrast this with 'circumstantial' disinheritance, where there is nothing to pass on to adult children because the parent has exhausted their own capital through, eg funding their living costs and/or social care in advancing years, or by splurging accumulated wealth rather than saving it to pass on (often referring to as 'SKI-ing' or 'spending the kids' inheritance').

[45] As well as *Ilott*, see *Re Nahajec (Deceased)* County Court (Leeds) [2017] 7 WLUK 399.

[46] See eg *Ames v Jones* [2016] 8 WLUK 256 and *Re H (Deceased)* [2020] EWHC 1134 (Fam).

[47] Monk (2018) 198.

Goodnow and Lawrence note that inheritance practices engender certain expectations around what individuals will receive, both across and within generations.[48] This is especially true of adult children, who tend to be viewed as the natural recipients of parental bounty once a surviving spouse (and any minor dependants) have been provided for.[49] Familial and social assumptions, however, do not accord with legal realities. Living parents have few financial obligations to their adult children once they pass the age of majority,[50] with isolated exceptions linked to disability and ongoing full-time education or vocational training.[51] Where parents are now deceased, it is more difficult to see why an adult son or daughter with some earning capacity, who was not financially dependent on their parent(s) – and had not been for some time – should acquire a portion of the estate. As Douglas explains, any resultant family provision application calls into question

> the claim of the child, based on his or her individual needs, to be supported beyond the death of the deceased. Such 'children' challenge the usual assumption in English law that, once they reach adulthood, financial responsibility (as distinct from the tie of affection) towards one's children terminates.[52]

Before the *Ilott* litigation, independent adult children who used the 1975 Act to challenge a deceased parent's will usually faced something of an uphill struggle, even if they were in dire financial circumstances.[53] As Peart and Borkowski observed, English courts adopted a somewhat 'parsimonious' approach to these claims.[54] When *Ilott* reached the Court of Appeal for the second time[55] and Heather was awarded up to £163,000, the legal landscape seemed to shift dramatically. Delivering the leading judgment, Arden LJ was strongly influenced by Heather's very limited financial resources, noting that they were at 'such a basic level that they outweigh[ed] the importance that would normally be attached to the fact that [Heather was] … an adult child who had been living independently for so many years'.[56] Though also acutely aware of Heather's financial circumstances, the Supreme Court lowered the award significantly. Lord Hughes stressed that financial need in itself was 'not always enough'[57] to merit financial provision. As for the reasonableness (or otherwise) of the deceased's actions in disinheriting someone, this could be taken into account,[58] but a family provision claim would not succeed just because the deceased acted unreasonably or spitefully.

[48] Goodnow and Lawrence (2008) 98.
[49] Finch and Mason (2000) as well as the public attitudes' surveys listed at n 80.
[50] Under English law, this is 18 years of age.
[51] See Herring (2016) 43–44.
[52] Douglas (2014) 225.
[53] For an overview of the cases, see Conway (2015) 118.
[54] Peart and Borkowski (2000) 333.
[55] [2015] EWCA Civ 797.
[56] [2015] EWCA Civ 797 [57].
[57] [2017] UKSC 17 [19].
[58] Because courts are obliged to consider conduct under s 3(1)(g) of the 1975 Act, and the deceased's obligations and responsibilities towards the applicant under s 3(1)(d).

The Supreme Court judgment regrettably lacked any clear statement of principle about family provision claims brought by independent adult children,[59] and post-*Ilott* cases have done little to clarify what (posthumous) parental obligations exist here.[60] Yet, while the outcome of every case depends on its own facts, some general observations can be made. The mere existence of the parent–child relationship will not suffice, since there is 'no legal obligation on a parent to maintain an adult child'.[61] Being in financial need is not enough in itself, but might tip the balance where the parent has, for example, unfairly rejected an adult child's numerous attempts to reconcile where the parties were estranged,[62] or left their son or daughter nothing in the mistaken belief that they were capable of supporting themselves financially.[63] However, the composition and size of the estate, and the other demands on it, are important – especially where the parent leaves everything to a surviving spouse with a serious medical condition and/or long-term care needs.[64] In contrast, an illness that impedes an adult son or daughter's ability to work might generate a favourable outcome[65] and, within the factual matrix, certain factors can trigger some sort of moral obligation for a deceased parent to maintain their otherwise independent offspring.[66] Otherwise, where an adult child is self-reliant, no provision can be deemed reasonable financial provision under the 1975 Act; and courts look disapprovingly on financially secure children who are seeking a (larger) slice of the financial pie to fund an affluent lifestyle or climb the higher rungs of the housing ladder.[67] Finally, family provision cannot be used to 'correct' an unequal division where a parent leaves more of their wealth to one child.[68]

Overall, an air of unpredictability still lingers around family provision claims involving independent adult children.[69] Judges can set aside the deceased's autonomous choices and retrospectively impose financial obligations based on presumptive notions of parental responsibility – even where no such obligations were owed, or assumed, by the parent in life. However, inheriting parental wealth is *not* an entitlement, and independent adult children should not see a

[59] In this respect, it has been labelled a 'serious disappointment' – Kerridge (2020) 401.

[60] For a detailed analysis of these cases, see Conway (2023).

[61] *Miles v Shearer* [2021] EWHC 1000 (Ch) [102].

[62] *Ilott* demonstrates that long-term estrangement is not fatal, nor is the fact that the adult child never expected to inherit anything.

[63] *Nahajec* (n 45).

[64] An independent adult child is much less likely to succeed here – see *Shapton v Seviour* [2020] WTLR 1047.

[65] *H (Deceased)* (n 46).

[66] This might include things like an adult child leaving work to care for an elderly parent.

[67] See respectively *Miles v Shearer* (n 61) and *Shapton v Seviour* (n 64).

[68] *Ball v Ball* [2017] EWHC 1750 (Ch) and *Re Mohammed (Deceased)* [2021] EWHC 2532 (Ch). Here, the deceased's will runs contrary to the so-called equality norm – ie that parents treat all their children equally on death.

[69] As it does with most other types of application, with the exception of surviving spouses or civil partners and infant children – both of whom have a strong chance of success under the family provision system.

family provision claim as an immutable means of undoing what they undoubtedly perceived as the unjust and unfair actions of a now deceased parent.

IV. Testamentary Freedom and Family Obligation

Every family provision system must strike a balance between testamentary freedom and the perceived public policy of a testator providing for certain relatives and dependants on death. *Ilott* was a perfect – if somewhat extreme – illustration of the competing tensions at play here, but where does the balance lie?

Defined as the 'right to distribute property upon death solely according to the dictates of one's own desires, unfettered by the constraints of society's moral code or the claims of others',[70] testamentary freedom is regarded as a human and personal right in common law legal systems. Beckhert, for instance, describes it as an 'integral component of private autonomy, and thus as an individual right of freedom',[71] while Friedman likens it to something that 'is felt psychologically to constitute an essential element of power over property'.[72] Yet, from a family perspective, this freedom has always been tempered by obligations towards certain relatives and dependants.[73] Complete freedom of testation only existed for a comparatively short period in the history of the English common law,[74] from the early years of the twentieth century until the introduction of the family provision system in 1939.[75] And, while other restraints on testamentary freedom exist today,[76] the modern system of family provision under the 1975 Act remains the most significant.

Of course, its very existence means that wills – as individualised statements of property transmission – are open to challenge. It would, however, be wrong to suggest that family provision drives a proverbial coach and horses through one of the common law's most cherished values, or that it has ever done so. The system operates within clearly defined parameters. Only certain individuals can apply

[70] Leslie (1996) 235.

[71] Beckert (2008) 21; see also Gold et al (1938).

[72] Friedman (1966) 355.

[73] Croucher (2012).

[74] Kerridge (2020) 389–90. See also Hedlund (2021). For the landed aristocracy testamentary freedom was always rather illusory because of the so-called 'strict settlement', a finely tuned legal mechanism that defined with precision from birth the share of the patrimony every family member would take – see Habakkuk (1994).

[75] Under the then Inheritance (Family Provision) Act 1938. The Act was not without controversy. Brook describes it as 'the culmination of a decade of parliamentary consideration of the extent to which a limitation should be placed upon testamentary freedom, with the focus throughout being on the conflict between the need for the testator to leave his family with sufficient property for their maintenance, whilst maintaining individual liberty and keeping the courts out of private family matters' – Brook (2018) 493.

[76] The growth of certain forms of co-ownership, where property passes automatically to the surviving owner on death (regardless of the deceased's will) is one example. Brook (2018) also cites inheritance tax regimes as another– if somewhat subtler – influence on modern patterns of testamentary giving.

and not simply because they feel 'hard done by'; there must have been a failure to make reasonable financial provision (assessed against the statutory criteria), and the court's function is not to decide whether the testator acted unreasonably or to rewrite the impugned will.[77] The more pertinent question, as Croucher notes, is the '*degree* of interference in will-making'.[78] The Supreme Court judgment in *Ilott* seems to tip the scales more towards testamentary freedom and attaching significant weight to the testator's wishes where a valid will is challenged under the 1975 Act. This much is apparent from Lord Hughes' opening statement that 'English law recognises the freedom of individuals to dispose of their assets by will … in whatever manner they wish'.[79] Public opinion surveys show strong support for testamentary freedom,[80] and the *Ilott* rhetoric reasserts the idea that a testator's personal choices should have more prominence in family provision claims.[81]

For independent adult children, the case nevertheless demonstrates that they can still get *something* under the 1975 Act, and notwithstanding the parent's unequivocal reasons for excluding their son or daughter.[82] Perhaps we should not read too much into this. Melita Jackson's wishes were taken into account as a relevant factor, but endorsing freedom of choice must still leave sufficient room for judicial manoeuvre where reasonable financial provision has not been made. In this sense, the *Ilott* saga – like every other case involving an independent adult child – is simply a paradigmatic illustration of the persistent tensions between testamentary freedom and familial obligation, and judicial efforts to square this particular circle within the complex factual matrices of individual family provision claims.

V. State Provision versus Estate Provision?

The fact that Heather Ilott and her family were heavily reliant on state benefits was a central feature of the narrative in *Ilott*. Heather and her husband had a joint annual income of around £15,000, the bulk of which came from tax credits, plus housing and council tax benefits. The family lived within their means and had a very modest lifestyle: there was never any surplus money for family holidays or outings, and various household appliances and home furnishings needed replacing.

77 Something that the Supreme Court reaffirmed in *Ilott*.

78 Croucher (2012) 20 (emphasis supplied).

79 [2017] UKSC 17 [1]. In her supplementary judgment, Lady Hale described testamentary freedom as 'the default position …, subject to the courts' limited discretionary powers'; [2017] UKSC 17 [52].

80 Though not absolute testamentary freedom: see eg Conway and Glennon (2010); Douglas et al (2011).

81 The previous award of up to £163,000 to Heather Ilott, with its seemingly blatant disregard for her mother's wishes, attracted negative media headlines. See eg T Whitehead, 'Your Will Can be Ignored Say Judges' *The Telegraph* (27 July 2015).

82 Heather Ilott received almost one-tenth of her mother's estate.

When the case came before the Court of Appeal for the second time,[83] the only issue was how much to award Heather.[84] From the outset, the court's decision was shaped by one overarching theme: what reasonable financial provision could be made for Heather's maintenance which 'relieve[d] her everyday living expenses without affecting her state benefits'?[85] On this specific point, the Court of Appeal concluded that District Judge Million (who gave the very first judgment in *Ilott*)[86] had taken the wrong approach, in failing to consider what impact his award would have on Heather's state benefit entitlement since any sum over £16,000 would result in a loss of housing benefit.[87] The Court of Appeal instead opted for £143,000 as the amount that Heather would need to purchase her rented home at a discounted price under the Right to Buy scheme;[88] an additional £20,000 was also made available, to give her a 'very small additional sum to supplement her state benefits'.[89] These were a significant part of the family's net annual income, and had to be preserved.

The Supreme Court reduced this amount to £50,000:[90] District Judge Million's approach was not flawed, and therefore the lower sum was justifiable on the facts. While legally correct, the legacy of *Ilott* is one in which an estate worth nearly half a million pounds passed to animal charities while the deceased's daughter and her family survived almost exclusively on state benefits. In this respect, *Ilott* raises important public policy questions around the interplay between family obligation, inherited wealth and the welfare state.

The tensions between intergenerational support in families and financial demands on the welfare state are a fertile source of debate in contemporary societies where the state plays an integral role in the social and economic well-being of its citizens. The challenges posed by an ageing society and the costs of funding long-term social care raise all sorts of pressing questions; and while English law does not compel younger generations to contribute towards the costs of supporting their older relatives, such legal obligations do exist under certain civil law regimes.[91]

[83] *Ilott v Mitson* (n 30).

[84] In other words, the answer to question (2) above. The first hearing in the Court of Appeal had focused solely on question (1), ie whether the deceased's will had failed to make reasonable financial provision for her daughter.

[85] *Ilott v Mitson* (n 30) [1].

[86] *Ilott v Mitson*, High Court (unreported, 7 August 2007). The sum awarded had been confirmed by Parker J in an earlier appeal ([2014] EWHC (Fam), [2015] 1 FLR 201).

[87] Housing benefit is 'means-tested', and cannot be claimed if the individual has eg savings over £16,000 or is paying a mortgage on their home.

[88] Right to Buy is a government-backed scheme operated throughout the UK that allows council and local authority housing tenants to purchase their homes for a discounted rate, subject to certain eligibility tests. See generally Murie (2016). By putting the £143,000 towards her home, Heather's housing benefits would not be affected.

[89] *Ilott v Mitson* (n 30) [63].

[90] The consequence was that Heather lost her benefits. However, it was noted that several essential household items needed to be replaced including white goods, carpets and broken beds. Replacing these items would 'put the household onto a much sounder financial footing without for long retaining capital beyond the £16,000 [capital threshold]': [2017] UKSC 17 [41].

[91] See generally Twigg and Grand (1998).

Writing in 1998, Twigg and Grand counselled that any UK government should be extremely cautious about making adult children responsible for funding parental social care: from an English perspective, such policy would 'smack … of undue interference by the state in the autonomy of the individual and the privacy of the family'.[92] A quarter of a century later, one suspects that little has changed in this respect.[93] One also suspects that a similar response would greet any attempt to shift the burden of maintaining independent adult children away from the state and onto the estates of their (now deceased) parents, though the issues are more complex here.

The dichotomy of 'state provision versus estate provision' is, of course, part of a much wider debate about the functions of modern inheritance laws in balancing the interests of not only the individual and the family, but also of wider society. A number of questions arise. To what extent should a deceased person's estate be used to relieve the increasing and well-documented pressures placed on the public purse? With increased longevity, childlessness, fragile family and social relationships, and the acknowledgment throughout the western world that public funds will not be sufficient to care for an elderly population, who will be expected to care and what part, if any, should inheritance play in the equation?[94] To what extent should first generation home-owners, once promised 'cradle-to-grave' health provision, have to sell that home to fund nursing care? One can expect policy-makers to grapple with these very large questions for decades – and the long-promised 'national conversation' on the provision of social care in the UK has once again been placed on the back-burner.

The interplay of state benefits and the family provision jurisdiction is but one aspect of this debate. Before *Ilott*, the leading case was the lesser-known decision in *Hanbury v Hanbury*,[95] which imposed a trust on part of the deceased's estate with the prime objective of maximising state benefits for an adult child, albeit not an 'independent' one. Ultimately, *Ilott* does not change this: as in *Hanbury*, the core theme throughout *Ilott* was preserving Heather's state benefits if she received part of her mother's estate. As the leading practitioner text now observes, there is 'no settled approach to the questions whether, and, if so, to what extent, state benefits which are available to the applicant should be taken into account in deciding whether reasonable financial provision has been made'.[96]

[92] Twigg and Grand (1998) 143.

[93] Though it is worth pointing out that a key strategy of the Johnson-led Conservative Government (announced in 2021) has been to fund rising social care costs by increasing national insurance payments and capping overall care costs, while continuing to recoup these from an older person's capital assets. For an overview of the challenges, see Dalley (2022) 187–217.

[94] There has been relatively little scholarship which focuses on the relationship between caring and private (as opposed to public) law, a notable exception being Sloan (2013).

[95] [1999] 2 FLR 255. The *Hanbury* approach was also followed in *Challinor* v *Challinor* [2009] WTLR 931.

[96] Ross (2017) 126.

Of course, the bigger question is still unanswered – namely, whether a generous parental estate should be used to relieve the welfare purse. As Lady Hale pointed out in *Ilott*, our succession law 'has not, or not yet, recognised a public interest in expecting or obliging parents to support their adult children so as to save the public money'.[97] In some ways, this statement is unsurprising, though one could also make the point that – in making Heather ineligible for housing benefit by virtue of a capital sum of £50,000 (and until that sum was exhausted, whether on essential household goods or otherwise) – this was also saving the state money. In addressing the bigger question, there are significant policy issues at play that are beyond the judicial remit: any move from the public purse of general taxation to one of private parental support would be a major change in ideology, that requires parliamentary intervention. As emphasised earlier, living parents are not obliged to maintain their adult children; likewise, parental assets are not generally relevant when an adult child is claiming state benefits. One might argue that the death of a parent changes things, in the sense that death unlocks the capital value of an estate (though in many cases, there will be competing claims on it from other close family members and any financial dependants). By its very nature, a successful claim under the family provision system by an independent adult child interferes with the autonomous choices of the testator, and retrospectively imposes different legal obligations based on presumptive notions of parental responsibility that did not exist in the past. From a succession law perspective, replacing state financial support with parental wealth is nothing short of foisting a system of fixed inheritance on certain citizens, which is anathema to the common law.

VI. Conclusion: Still More Questions than Answers?

Family provision is typically viewed as a form of individualised justice. As McDonnell describes it, 'the 1975 Act is more of a surgeon's scalpel than a blunt instrument' and can be used 'to tailor relief in a very precise way to reflect the detailed facts of the case'.[98] This makes it, as we have argued, a very fact-specific exercise, and one from which it is difficult to distill a set of principles. The many succession lawyers who had hoped that the judgment of a seven judge Supreme Court would bring clarity to the multifarious questions raised by modern inheritance law have been sorely disappointed. It might have been ambitious to expect a full discourse on the outworkings of the 1975 Act, but even the more modest ambition – that the Supreme Court would make a clear statement of principle around adult children – has not been met.

Our overall assessment is that the *Ilott* saga has generated more uncertainty rather than less, and created a more fertile territory for expensive litigation. At the

[97] [2017] UKSC 17 [65].
[98] McDonnell (2017) 2.

very least, it has done little to discourage claims by independent adult children, even if eventual success translates to a more modest award than it might have done prior to the Supreme Court ruling in *Ilott*. Also, reported cases – by definition – only record those disputes that reach trial and are actually decided by a judge. In practice, a large number of these cases (and even palpably weak ones) will settle or compromise at various stages before a final hearing, with the estate making a 'nuisance payment' to avoid the expense and uncertainty of a full trial. As noted earlier, claimants must take the initiative and apply to court under the 1975 Act; and while certain types of applicants that the legislation was designed to facilitate may not know to make a claim,[99] it is evident that there are many sharp-elbowed adult children who are very much aware of their right to make an application (and the potential for an out-of-court compromise).[100]

The issues raised in this chapter are part of a much broader debate about the position that children ought to occupy in contemporary common law inheritance systems, which have to balance the interests of the individual, the family and wider society. One of these is which, if any, circumstances, duties or responsibilities relating to an adult child should be translated into a claim against a deceased parent's estate. The 1975 Act itself is a relatively short piece of legislation, and has little to say about how judges should exercise their discretion beyond listing the general and specific factors that must be evaluated; and for children, there is only one specific factor which has little relevance for independent adult children.[101] As Lady Hale noted in *Ilott*, 'The problem with the present law is that it gives [judges] … virtually no help in deciding how to evaluate [claims by independent adult children] … or balance them with other claims on the estate'.[102] One suspects that the purpose of Lady Hale's supplemental judgment was to nudge law reform bodies[103] and the legislature towards revisiting the family provision jurisdiction, with a view to providing 'guidance as to the factors to be taken into account in deciding whether an adult child is deserving or undeserving of reasonable maintenance'.[104]

[99] Such as non-financially aware elderly widows and those who are otherwise vulnerable, although legally capable. In England and Wales, unlike some Commonwealth jurisdictions, there is no obligation on executors to advise potential applicants that they have the right to make a claim.

[100] There has been a dearth of empirical research on the impact of the family provision jurisdiction at the stage of will-drafting and in claims that are compromised without a court hearing. In one of the authors' professional experience, based on the practice of the courts in Northern Ireland, virtually all adult child claims settle before final hearing – and are afforded every opportunity to do so by the judiciary. It is unusual for any such applicant to leave entirely 'empty-handed', and rarer still for an applicant to agree to bear the estate's legal costs, even if the applicant is seeking to discontinue. Accordingly, even a very weak claim which is eventually withdrawn generally reduces the estate which is passing to the beneficiaries named in the will.

[101] Though see *Nahajec* (n 45).

[102] [2017] UKSC 17 [58].

[103] In practice the Law Commission of England and Wales. More than one commentator (see Kerridge (2020) and Sloan (2017)) has made the point that this is somewhat ironic, in view of the fact that Lady Hale (then Professor Brenda Hoggett) was a member of the said Law Commission from 1984 to 1993, during which time it considered the reform of various inheritance laws.

[104] [2017] UKSC 17 [66].

However, it is questionable whether any such change, in itself, would constitute little more than legislative tinkering while the theoretical basis on which adult children should succeed in family provision claims is still a major point of discussion. The bigger questions posed in Lady Hale's judgment, as articulated at the outset of this chapter, are similar to those first posed in 1983 by the then Professor Brenda Hoggett in the first edition of her co-authored seminal text on family law which included the law of succession.[105] Some four decades later, there are still more questions than answers.

References

Beckert, J, *Inherited Wealth* (Princeton, Princeton University Press, 2008).

Brook, J, 'Testamentary Freedom – Myth or Reality' (2018) 82 *Conveyancer and Property Lawyer* 19, 20 citing S Cretney, *Family Law in the Twentieth Century: A History* (Oxford, Oxford University Press, 2005).

Champlin, E, *Final Judgments: Duty and Emotion in Roman Wills, 200 BC–AD 250* (Berkeley, University of California Press, 1991).

Conway, H, 'Do Parents Always Know Best: Posthumous Provision and Adult Children' in W Barr (ed), *Modern Studies in Property Law, Volume 8* (Oxford, Hart Publishing, 2015).

—— '"Where There's a Will": Law and Emotion in Sibling Inheritance Disputes' in H Conway and J Stannard (eds), *The Emotional Dynamics of Law and Legal Discourse* (Oxford, Hart Publishing, 2016).

—— 'Testamentary Freedom, Family Obligation and the *Ilott* Legacy' (2017) 81 *Conveyancer and Property Lawyer* 372.

—— 'More in Hope than in Expectation: The Legal Limits of Disinheriting Adult Children' in A Nair, L Rostill and N Mrockova (eds), *Modern Studies in Property Law, Volume 12* (Oxford, Hart Publishing, 2023, forthcoming).

Conway, H and Glennon, L, '"To Give Or Not To Give?": The Transmission of Wealth on Death by Older Persons' Report for the Changing Ageing Partnership, School of Law, Queen's University Belfast (September 2010).

Croucher, RF, 'How Free Is Free: Testamentary Freedom and the Battle between Family and Property' (2012) 37 *Australian Journal of Legal Philosophy* 9.

Croucher, RF and Vines, P, *Succession: Families, Property and Death, Text and Materials*, 5th edn (Sydney, LexisNexis Butterworths, 2019).

Dainow, J, 'The Civil Law and the Common Law: Some Points of Comparison' (1966) 15 *American Journal of Comparative Law* 419.

Dalley, D, *Caring in Crisis* (London, Palgrave Macmillan, 2022).

Douglas, G (2014) 'Family Provision and Family Practices– The Discretionary Regime of the Inheritance Act of England and Wales' 4 *Oñati Socio-Legal Series* 222.

Douglas, G et al, 'Enduring Love: Attitudes to Family and Inheritance Law in England and Wales' (2011) 38 *Journal of Law and Society* 245.

[105] Hoggett and Pearl (1983). At that time, succession law was very much in the academic doldrums in the UK.

Finch, J and Mason, J, *Passing On: Kinship and Inheritance in England* (Abingdon, Routledge, 2000).
Friedman, L, 'The Law of the Living, the Law of the Dead; Property, Succession, and Society' (1966) *Wisconsin Law Review* 341, 355.
Gold, J et al, 'Freedom of Testation' (1938) 1 *Modern Law Review* 296.
Goodnow, JJ and Lawrence, JA, 'How Should People Act in Inheritance Situations? Specifying Difference in Expectations' (2008) 32 *International Journal of Behavioural Development* 98.
Green, K, 'The Englishwoman's Castle- Inheritance and Private Property Today' (1988) 51 *Modern Law Review* 187.
Habakkuk, J, *Marriage, Debt and the Estates System: English Land Ownership 1650–1950* (Oxford, Clarendon Press, 1994).
Hacker, D, 'The Gendered Dimensions of Inheritance: Empirical Food for Legal Thought' (2010) 7 *Journal of Empirical Legal Studies* 322, 323.
Hedlund, R, 'The End to Testamentary Freedom' (2021) 41 *Legal Studies* 55.
Herring, J, 'Together Forever? The Rights and Responsibilities of Adult Children and their Parents' in H Keating, J Bridgeman and C Lind (eds), *Responsibility, Law and the Family* (Abingdon, Routledge, 2016).
Hoggett, B and Pearl, D, *The Family Law & Society: Cases and Materials*, 1st edn (London, Butterworths, 1983).
Izuhara, M and Koppe, S, 'Inheritance and Family Conflicts: Exploring Asset Transfers Shaping Intergenerational Relations' (2019) 8 *Families, Relationships and Societies* 53.
Kerridge, R, 'Family Provision in England and Wales' in KGC Reid, MJ de Waal and Re Zimmerman (eds), *Comparative Succession Law, Volume III: Mandatory Family Protection* (Oxford, Oxford University Press, 2020).
Leslie, M, 'The Myth of Testamentary Freedom' (1996) 38 *Arizona Law Review* 235, 235.
McDonnell, C, 'Blurring the Focus: The Supreme Court's Decision in *Ilott v The Blue Cross*' (2017) 23 *Trusts & Trustees* 1, 2.
Monk, D, 'Inheritance Law Matters' in B Clough and J Herring (eds), *Ageing, Gender and Family Law* (Abingdon, Routledge, 2018).
Murie, A, *The Right to Buy?: Selling Off Public and Social Housing* (Bristol, Policy Press, 2016).
Peart, N and Sutton, R, 'Testamentary Claims by Adult Children – The Agony of the "Wise and Just Testator"' (2001) 10 *Otago Law Review* 385.
Peart, N and A Borkowski, 'Provision for Adult Children on Death – The Lesson from New Zealand' (2000) 12 *Child and Family Law Quarterly* 333, 333.
Ross, S, *Inheritance Act Claims*, 4th edn (London, Sweet & Maxwell, 2017).
Sloan, B, *Informal Carers and Private Law* (Oxford, Hart Publishing, 2013).
—— '*Ilott v The Blue Cross* (2017): Testing the Limits of Testamentary Freedom' in B Sloan (ed), *Landmark Cases in Succession Law* (Oxford, Hart Publishing, 2019).
Stum, MS, '"I Just Want to Be Fair": Interpersonal Justice in Intergenerational Transfers of Non-Titled Property' (1999) 48 *Family Relations* 159.
Twigg T and Grand, A, 'Contrasting Legal Conceptions of Family Obligation and Financial Reciprocity in the Support of Older People: France and England' (1998) 18 *Ageing & Society* 131.
Villios, S and Williams, N, 'Family Provision Law, Adult Children and the Age of Entitlement' (2018) 39 *Adelaide Law Review* 249.

PART 5

Looking Backwards into the Future

13

The Power of Blood

How Succession Law's Reliance on DNA Reinvigorates White Supremacy and the Politics of Biological Privilege

DANAYA C WRIGHT

I. Introduction

In February, 2007, model and reality TV star Anna Nicole Smith died of a drug overdose in a Florida hotel room, leaving her five-month old daughter Danielynn as her sole legal heir.[1] Smith's 20-year old son, Daniel, had died just three days after the birth of his sister, also from a drug overdose. The lengthy litigation surrounding Anna Nicole's claim to a portion of her deceased octogenarian husband's fortune and the paternity suit over Danielynn occupied the tabloids for years.[2] Smith listed her long-time intimate partner and lawyer, Howard K Stern, as the father on Danielynn's birth certificate[3] and they participated in an informal commitment ceremony just weeks after Danielynn's birth. Upon Anna Nicole's death, however, multiple men came forward claiming to be the father of Danielynn, including entertainment photographer Larry Birkhead, Zsa Zsa Gabor's husband, Frédéric Prinz von Anhalt, and Alexander Denk, a former bodyguard. Despite being listed on the birth certificate, and Anna Nicole granting her daughter Stern's surname, Danielynn's custody was transferred from Stern to Larry Birkhead after a DNA test concluded that he was indeed Danielynn's biological father.[4] Although Birkhead had had no contact with

[1] A Goodnough and M Fox, 'Anna Nicole Smith Dies at 39' *New York Times* (8 February 2007).

[2] J Kever and C Feldman, 'Anna Nicole Smith's Life, and death, is a Tabloid Tale' *Houston Chronicle* (9 February 2007), available at www.buffalo.edu/content/dam/www/news/imported/pdf/February07/HoustonChronicleRappingSmith.pdf.

[3] Birth Certificate for Anna Nicole-Smith's Baby (16 October 2010), available at www.tmz.com/2006/10/16/birth-certificate-for-anna-nicoles-baby.

[4] P Turnquest, 'Birkhead is Father of Anna Nicole's Baby' Reuters (10 April 2007), available at www.reuters.com/article/topNews/idUSN1040771120070410.

Danielynn since her birth as Anna Nicole had cut off contact with Birkhead, Stern did not challenge Birkhead's right to claim parentage of Danielynn and he accepted the finding of the DNA test as the end of the matter.

For centuries, the Anglo-American law of property, inheritance, and family have relied on biological – or blood – relationships to guide the succession of status, wealth and power from one generation to the next. Biological kinship, albeit a narrow form of biology mediated by marital legitimacy, has been normalised as the logical basis of legal rights for so long that few question the logic and equity of property rights being based on family kinship relations. Yet today, over 50 per cent of children in the US are being raised in non-traditional families, including blended, same-sex, single-parent, and multi-generational families where primary parenting is being done less and less by the biologically related, married, cis-gendered, heterosexual parents and more and more by adults who have no biological connection to the children in their lives.[5] More than any time in history, people are rejecting the imperative of biology in favour of functional families, legal adoption, artificial reproductive technologies (ART), and testamentary freedom to create their own families and relationships.[6] With more liberal moral norms and greater social freedom, biology has become less important in determining family status, identity, and belonging than at any time in the past millennium.

At the same time, like Stern and Birkhead, millions of people have turned to genetic testing to gain a sense of certainty in their ancestral connections and to find their place in our complex globalised world.[7] They have relied on the apparent *truth* of science to provide them with a sense of identity based not on ephemeral cultural and personal ties, but on the seemingly solid ground of blood and biology. Ironically, despite recent efforts to weaken the supremacy of blood in succession law, the sense of certainty provided by science and DNA has in fact reinforced the primacy of biology in determining family membership, and with it the wealth of kinship.[8]

In the US, the 2008 amendments to the Uniform Probate Code and the 2017 amendments to the Uniform Parentage Act show that, in many respects, the law of

[5] G Livingston, 'Fewer than Half of US Kids Today Live in a 'Traditional Family' Pew Research Center (22 December 2014), available at www.pewresearch.org/fact-tank/2014/12/22/less-than-half-of-u-s-kids-today-live-in-a-traditional-family.

[6] Admittedly, these freedoms are generally limited to privileged, white people who can afford the ART, who have sufficient wealth to even exercise their rights to testamentary freedom, and who can reject their natal families because they are financially independent. See Houghton-Larsen (2019). See also Khanna and Killian (2015).

[7] 'World Consumer DNA (Genetic) Testing Market Report 2021' (28 June 2021) available at ww.globenewswire.com/news-release/2021/06/28/2253793/28124/en/World-Consumer-DNA-Geneti c-Testing-Market-Report-2021.html; A Regalado, 'More than 26 Million People have taken an at-home Ancestry Test' *MIT Technology Review* (11 February 2019), available at www.technologyreview.com/2019/02/11/103446/more-than-26-million-people-have-taken-an-at-home-ancestry-test. See also Nelson (2016) 8, noting that 'we have zealously (and often uncritically) seized upon DNA as a master key that unlocks many secrets'.

[8] DNA testing in criminal cases and later in paternity cases became available in 1986 and 1988 respectively in the which was a period of profound change in traditional family structures and relationships. See Adams (2008).

inheritance has become more dependent on blood in order to keep wealth within socially and legally acceptable families,[9] as succession law has become more disaggregated from family law and the intentional new families that are possible through ART, fostering, adoption, and parenting within same-sex couples.[10] As family law has come to accept the informal or functional family, protects the best interests of children, rejects marriage as critical to kinship, and seeks to nourish parent/child relationships and cultural expectations regardless of biological ties, the law of inheritance in many of the American states has rejected those functional relationships, strictly polices intestate succession, and narrowly defines family status for purposes of wealth transmission.[11] The court's rejection of Howard Stern's established physical and emotional relationship with Danielynn in favour of Birkhead's blood connection is just one example of the property law of inheritance trumping the family law of the functional parent–child relationship.

In this chapter, I trace a thread from the 1054 Peace Council of Narbonne to the white supremacy of Christian Nationalism to succession law's elevating of DNA by examining the meaning and power of blood in defining the channels through which wealth, legitimacy, and power are transmitted. Michel Foucault wrote that in the Middle Ages 'power spoke through blood … blood was a reality with a symbolic function.'[12] Today blood continues its symbolic function in the public imagination, from the blood of Christ that cleanses one's sins,[13] to the blood taint associated with HIV/AIDS,[14] to the tell-tale marker of truth provided by the DNA test in criminal law. We can trace the white supremacy of Christian Nationalism and the biological imperative of succession law to the social construct of blood purity in the political and legal structures of Christianity and the common law of inheritance. When millions of dollars rested on determining the biological *truth* of Danielynn's kinship, the science of blood came to the rescue.

In different ways, blood has become both more and less foundational to our sense of identity and belonging than in the past, in part because science has made blood certainty possible to within 99.9 per cent accuracy, but also because many people reject biology to prioritise intentional relationships. With genetic testing, blood has become a more potent carrier of legal rights to transmit wealth

[9] See Uniform Probate Code (2008) §§ 2-114 to 2-122; Uniform Parentage Act (2017) § 501 et seq. These laws unquestionably also help produce socially and legally acceptable families while rejecting the informal relationships of functional families or those who cannot afford legal assistance to cement their family ties.

[10] See Wright (2015) illustrating the myriad ways US succession law limits the rights of children in non-traditional families to inherit wealth their parents intend them to inherit including the very limited ways in which same-sex couples are permitted to adopt children.

[11] For instance, the 2012 US Supreme Court decision in *Astrue v Capato*, 566 US 541, denied federal social security benefits to twins born through ART 18 months after their father's death because federal law relied on state succession law for purposes of entitlements, and Florida law defined children for inheritance purposes as those born or in utero at the time of the parent's death.

[12] Foucault (1978) 147.

[13] 1 John 1:17.

[14] O Dryden, 'Blood out of Bounds' (undated), available at omisooredryden.com/?portfolio_page=blood-out-of-bounds.

and political power than marital status or public attribution. Yet as more LGBTQ couples and unmarried persons reject the heteronormative imperative of biological reproduction in favour of intentional relationships,[15] the power of blood to dictate and define community, family and belonging has been diluted. I would suggest that the tension between blood politics and intentional relationships in succession law mirrors the tension within racialised and gendered Christian Nationalism. With the culture wars hardening the power of blood in politics and the public imagination, the turn to DNA in succession law revives the violence and white supremacy inherent in a politics of blood.

II. 1054 – Blood and Christian Salvation

Christianity has treated blood as a crucial marker of belonging and as the conduit of racial and heteronormative privilege since the Middle Ages. We can see this by tracing the changing role of blood in Christianity as it dominated the political and social ordering of western Europe during the medieval and early modern periods. Christianity constructed white supremacy and patriarchy as biological imperatives, thus linking blood, religion and inheritance through unmitigated violence in ways that enabled biological kinship and blood purity to become the basis for maintaining wealth and political power. Christianity embraced white supremacy and racial purity as both a social construct and a legal order to protect wealth for the insider and deny it to the outsider. And to the extent the adherents of Christian Nationalism rising in the US, like the Proud Boys and the Oath Keepers, continue to deploy blood and ethnic purity in their claim to biological supremacy and entitlement, the power of blood continues to justify violence in protecting and embracing a social order in which power and privilege are rooted in biology and white supremacy.

Blood is both an object and a signifier – it is the life-giving elixir as well as the symbol of belonging and identity. It indicates humanity, Christian purity and family status. The spilling of blood has been a crime, a tort, a sin, a heroic act and a religious duty for centuries. Blood is the link to God and the symbol of His favour; it is a marker and a carrier of status and privilege as well as the marker of death and corruption.[16] For centuries the spilling of any human blood was a crime because it denigrated human dignity, fracturing the bond between people. But Gil Anidjar identifies a profound shift in the Christian attitude toward war, the bearing of arms, and the spilling of blood in the peace council of 1054 in which

[15] Ironically, many single and LGBTQ individuals retain a strong connection to blood as they use only a single gamete provider to mix with their own, thus perpetuating their blood line while rejecting the social imperative of marriage and coupling.

[16] The symbolic power of blood in the HIV/AIDs epidemic was often cast as God's punishment for the abomination of homosexuality.

Pope Gregory VII declared that it was not the shedding of human blood that was a sin, but rather the shedding of Christian blood, for such was shedding the blood of Christ.[17] The peace council in Narbonne hardened the schism between the Eastern and Western churches following the filioque controversy.[18] According to Anidjar, the distinction between the spilling of Christian blood and the spilling of human blood would have tremendous political impact as centuries of bloodshed and the Crusades marked Gregory's subtle distinction as an important theological and symbolic turning point.[19]

Blood purity, blood status and blood relationships came to be seen after 1054 as a fundamental signifier of Christian belonging and salvation as well as a boundary between the chosen and the damned. As Christianity became the dominant theology across the Latin and Greek worlds, the centrality of blood became a political marker of belonging and power in the medieval world.[20] And as Christ's blood marked those who were privileged and saved, the absence of Christ's blood damned the rest of humanity to the status of non-human animals, creatures who could be killed, owned, enslaved or sacrificed to serve the interests of the chosen.

Andijar concludes that the schism in the Church led to greater willingness to shed blood and the vilification of non-believers and heretics, which has been a marker of Christianity to this day.[21] The change in the Church's attitude toward bloodshed, from defining all shedding of any human blood as a sin, to defining only the shedding of Christian blood as a sin, is that:

> What would no longer be in doubt by then was that there was a difference between bloods, that there was a blood that was – shall we say, essentially? – a different and purer blood. It had undergone a first and gigantic transformation toward an asymmetric universality, a generalized hematology, and the establishment of blood, not as a concept but as an indubitable foundation of Western, which is to say Christian, politics.[22]

The centrality of blood in Christian ideology – as that which marks a person as deserving and nearly divine on the one hand, or impure and heretical on the other – became the fundamental basis of social order, and hence political power, in late medieval and early-modern Western society. Andijar equates the

[17] Anidjar (2018).

[18] The filioque controversy arose over the inclusion of language indicating that the Holy Spirit descended from both God the Father and the Son rather than just the Father, upending the doctrine of the Trinity. See Chadwick (2003).

[19] Anidjar (2018) 36 ('The church, which had long "considered bloodshed as a source of pollution now encouraged the shedding of blood – non-Christian blood – as a means to purification.').

[20] Bildhauer (2006) 21.

[21] We can trace Christianity's glorification of violence in the Crusades, colonisation, and the current violent rhetoric of Christian Nationalist groups as they dehumanise immigrants, police the border, and justify the armed insurrection of 6 January 2021. See, Southern Poverty Law Center, 'Proud Boys are still Violent, Despite Legal Woes' (25 August 2021) available at www.splcenter.org/hatewatch/2021/08/25/proud-boys-are-still-violent-despite-legal-woes.

[22] Anidjar (2018) 37.

elevation of the Christian doctrine of purity and Christian belonging, which of course is signified in the Eucharist as the blood of Christ himself, as crucial to the development of social hierarchy based on a rhetoric of blood. The purification of the soul through the Eucharist and through Christian sacrifice, including the shedding of heathen blood, thus became a marker of political power and social belonging which prevailed as a tenet of Christianity even after the Protestant Reformation.[23]

As a result of Christianity's spread, mass genocide of Indigenous peoples across the globe, the horrors of African slavery, and the atrocities of colonisation naturally followed. This is not to say, of course, that other religiously inspired zealots have not also committed similar atrocities. But the unique hemotology of Christianity, by elevating purification of blood in its theology and centering the symbol of blood in its faith, led to unparalleled violence and shedding of blood deemed impure. The distinction between the blood to be protected – Christian blood – and the blood to be shed – heathen blood – grounded biological relationships, where blood served as a conduit of political power and justified violence through the generations. Throughout the medieval and early modern periods, political power and religious institutions were symbiotically aligned as Church and state strengthened and legitimated each other.[24] Western politics based power on bloodlines and the righteousness of blood purity as the divine right of kings passed from father to son, family alliances and political power were amassed through marriage and kinship, wealth descended to legitimate (ie, pure) descendants and not to the corrupted blood of illegitimate children, and social ordering was maintained by violence.

This historical shift privileging Christian blood played out in the political sphere as well, where family dynasties used marriage and biological privilege to concentrate political power in successive generations of blood descendants strictly controlled by the Church courts' domination of marriage litigation. Ecclesiastical courts controlled entry and exit from marriage as well as the probate and succession of property, centering blood purity in the politics of family from the later Middle Ages until they were undermined in common law countries in the nineteenth century.[25] James Brundage has detailed how the Church systematically set out to control illicit sexuality, unregulated reproduction, and succession of property through sacramentalising marriage and regulating the religious marriage ceremony during the late medieval and early modern periods in an effort to control wealth and its connection to legitimacy.[26] Whether understood in a Foucauldian sense of discipline or a Hobbesian sense of sovereignty, the Church's control over marriage and succession, with its exegetical elevation of blood purity, linked wealth and political power to a biology of blood.

[23] ibid.
[24] Brundage and Eichbauer (2022).
[25] Brundage (1987) 195–96.
[26] ibid, 189–99.

By the Reformation, political and ecclesiastical forces cleaved even as blood came to play a greater role in succession law.[27] Henry VIII's struggle with the Catholic Church to have his marriage to Katherine of Aragon annulled, which would enable him to produce a legitimate male heir to provide a conduit for Tudor sovereignty and political power through succession in the male bloodline, highlighted the tension between political power and Papal supremacy. The Reformation continued the blood supremacy of Christianity generally and reinforced the primacy of blood, but from a Christian to a more biological form of purity that would govern sovereign politics in the western world for centuries. In one example, elective monarchies were replaced with strict hereditary succession in many European countries after the Reformation, and the power of dynastic families strengthened marital alliances and a robust form of male primogeniture as descent through the female line became a fate to be avoided at all costs.[28]

Of course, a pure blood politics could not survive, as homozygosity led to inbreeding and failure of the succession. Recognising the importance of 'fresh new blood' in a hemotology of succession and political power, however, meant strictly controlling the introduction of new blood throughout the medieval and early-modern periods. For Christians, this meant strict Church control over the Eucharist and entry into the chosen class. For the monarchies of Europe, this meant strict Church control over marriage and the dispensations necessary to keep monarchical marriage within the ruling class. For the average person, this meant strict Church control over the marriage rite and the jurisdiction of wealth succession and probate.[29] With the Protestant Reformation, the Catholic Church's iron grip eventually weakened as dissenting sects defined marriage rituals and succession rules in their own way. Alongside the plurality of religious views, however, a new form of control over blood purity arose to take its place: racial purity.

Richard Dyer explains that as Christianity became the religious export of Europe it relied on whiteness and racial superiority as central to its imperialising mission:

> [N]ot only did Christianity become the religion, and religious export, of Europe, indelibly marking its culture and consciousness, it has also been thought and felt in distinctly white ways for most of its history, seen in relation to, for instance, the following: the persistence of the Manichean dualism of black:white that could be mapped on to skin colour difference; the role of the Crusades in racialising the idea of Christendom

[27] For example, the elective monarchies of Poland (1790s), Bohemia (early 1600s), Iberia (1870s), Hungary (1687), Ireland (early 1600s), Scandinavia (1600s and 1800s), and the Dutch Republic (1700s) were gradually replaced in the 17th and 18th centuries with strict rules of succession based on legitimacy and bloodline.

[28] The hereditary monarchies of Europe generally limited succession through a female line, preferring agnatic succession over cognatic succession. This preference for male inheritance can be traced through centuries of English property and inheritance law where widow's rights to dower and the legal rights of female heirs were intentionally undermined and avoided. See Spring (1995).

[29] Brundage (1987) 189–99.

> (making national/geographic others into enemies of Christ); the gentilising and whitening of the image of Christ and the Virgin in painting; the ready appeal to the God of Christianity in the prosecution of doctrines of racial superiority and imperialism.[30]

The centrality of race in Christianity followed directly from its foregrounding blood in its theology. Just as Christians are defined by reference to their blood purity, race and white supremacy became central to Christian notions of succession, inclusion, and belonging. With colonisation came an entirely unprecedented and destructive ideology of blood as millions of Indigenous peoples across the globe were massacred and millions others enslaved and subjected to blood denigration in the name of Christian salvation and spiritual purity.[31]

Race became a biological trait that inhered in the bloodline so that the one-drop rule elevated biology as the marker of political power and inclusion which carried with it access to land and other resources. With blood quantum rules adopted in the colonial US, political power and the right to intermarry became dependent on a complex matrix of biological identifiers. Mulatto, quadroon, octoroon and other categories were developed in law to govern intermarriage and, by necessity, succession and inheritance of property and political rights.[32] By the twentieth century, antisemitism had become a core tenet of certain strands of Christian theology with the horrific consequences of the holocaust laid of the feet of white supremacists who viewed Christian identity in terms of blood purity.[33]

The logical consequence of Christianity's centering of blood purity and its reliance on white supremacy is the rise of DNA testing among Christian Nationalists. Two of the most violent US extremist groups – the Proud Boys and the Oath Keepers – view American history and American politics as the province of Christian evangelical blood right. Immigrants are characterised as impure, as polluting American identity and risking race suicide.[34] Hungary's far-right politicians have produced documents asserting their genetic purity by having no Jewish or Roma genetic markers.[35] White supremacists around the world are flooding Ancestry.com and 23andme with tests they hope will prove their 'white' heritage through DNA evidence.[36] Instead of using skull circumference,

[30] Dyer (1997) 17.

[31] See Harvey (2003) 13–27. See also ES Clark, 'Religion and Race in America' in Oxford Research Encyclopedias, available at oxfordre.com/americanhistory/display/10.1093/acrefore/9780199329175.001.0001/acrefore-9780199329175-e-322;jsessionid=361C44558CECB75EF3C97C63F83E1BAE.

[32] Prentiss (2003) 3.

[33] Cowan (2003) 112–23.

[34] Southern Poverty Law Center, 'Proud Boys' (undated) available at www.splcenter.org/fighting-hate/extremist-files/group/proud-boys.

[35] A Good, 'Genetic Testing of Far-Right Hungarian Politician Provokes an Uproar' *Foreign Policy* (15 June 2012), available at foreignpolicy.com/2012/06/15/genetic-testing-of-far-right-hungarian-politician-provokes-an-uproar.

[36] E Boodman, 'White Nationalists are Flocking to Genetic Ancestry Tests – with Surprising Results' *Scientific American* (16 August 2017), available at www.scientificamerican.com/article/white-nationalists-are-flocking-to-genetic-ancestry-tests-with-surprising-results. See also Panofsky and Donovan (2019).

phrenology or cultural heritage, white supremacists are using DNA tests and drinking milk to prove that they have a genetic, God-given blood purity.[37] The drinking milk is from the myth that white people are less prone to being lactose intolerant and therefore their bloodline is purer if they don't get nauseated from too much dairy.

The embrace of DNA testing, the validation of blood identity as a marker of Christian belonging, and the violence of Christian Nationalism have led to an unparalleled, if misunderstood, linking of blood and racial purity that has become even stickier than in the past, thanks to the normalising power of science. Acknowledging that the centralisation of blood in Christianity is a complex and contested dogma, and that this claim of the imbrication of Christianity and political power glosses over much theological doctrine, a turn to succession law's reliance on blood helps explain the stickiness of biology in inheritance and reveals its foundations in race supremacy. For as blood was being elevated in Christian politics, it was also being elevated in succession law as the two institutions mutually reinforced the insider/outsider duality of blood's signification.

III. 1066 – The Norman Invasion

The English common law of property profoundly changed when William, Duke of Normandy defeated King Harold at the battle of Hastings on 14 October 1066 and William imported his Norman feudalism into a country that had a variety of property and succession customs. William laid claim to sovereignty and ownership of all land within the dominion, which he then subdivided for his loyal supporters. Possession of large swaths of land were guaranteed to the Norman barons in exchange for their military and financial support of William's wars and his court. The Norman barons then proceeded to subdivide their possessions and granted lands to their own supporters in exchange for the same military and financial support, some of which the barons passed on to William. William's brand of feudalism was essentially a series of contractual agreements that guaranteed control over land and its income in exchange for military and financial support of William's right to the crown. And as his barons and mesne lords subinfeudated their landholdings, dividing possession into smaller and smaller pieces, the entire land tenure system of England became heavily dependent on personal relationships and contractual agreements to determine who would succeed to an estate upon the death of the current tenant. Most importantly, there was no guarantee that a tenant's eldest son would succeed to his father's lands as the tenant's lord had to accept the tenant's heir in the tenant's place and he would do so only if the heir

[37] A Harmon, 'Why White Supremacists are Chugging Milk (and Why Geneticists are Alarmed)' *New York Times* (17 October 2018), available at www.nytimes.com/2018/10/17/us/white-supremacists-science-dna.html.

could pay homage and perform the requisite duties of military service. The idea that the children of a tenant would succeed automatically to their father's estates was a vestige of Anglo-Saxon allodial tenancy that may have prevailed by custom among the lower classes, but was rejected by the Norman elites.[38]

After 1066 there existed two sets of succession laws: the law of military tenure that applied to the large landholders who supported William's right to the crown, and the law of socage tenure that recognised the rights of small landholders to have their property pass by custom automatically to their legal heirs. By 1200, however, the contractual character of military tenure had declined, although seizin remained key to entitlement and in the control of the lord who could choose a different heir.[39] Yet custom being applied in the feudal courts cemented the expectation that land as well as movables would pass to the owner's eldest son, or to his daughters jointly if he had no sons, by legal right through the writ of *mort d'ancestor*.[40] And as early as the 1130s it was common to insert language of inheritance in land charters.[41] The principal canon of descent became the parentelic scheme whereby lineal descendants were preferred over collateral heirs, and males were preferred to females in the same degree.[42] As a doctrine of legally binding heirship gradually developed in the common-law courts, Glanvill, in the mid-twelfth century, declared that 'heirs were made by God, not man': *solus Deus facit Haeredem*.[43] Succession and inheritance became matters of natural law, not human choice.

John Baker notes that the emerging universality of the common law in matters of inheritance rights was crucial to the stabilisation of land and aristocratic titles in the twelfth and thirteenth centuries:

> A grantor had no say in these rules; he could choose whether to use the words 'and his heirs', but he could not choose who those heirs would be. No doubt this was a major advance in securing good order. The uncertainty of discretion begat family squabbles, of which the Battle of Hastings and the war between Stephen and Matilda were extreme examples. The scope for such disputes was greatly reduced by the orderly application of legal principle to questions of inheritance.[44]

The adoption of the parentelic scheme for inheritance was simply one of numerous options available that privileged biology and blood relation.[45] But notably, the replacement of discretion with the writ of *mort d'ancestor* in the mid-twelfth century cemented blood over the contractual and personal choices of the earlier feudal law.

[38] Baker (2002) 223–29.
[39] ibid, 230.
[40] ibid, 234.
[41] ibid, 260.
[42] ibid, 266–67.
[43] Glanvill (1965) vii.1.
[44] Baker (2002) 266.
[45] Ultimogeniture and partible inheritance were customs used in different areas of England before primogeniture prevailed, but all involved heirship through blood relatives. Baker (2002) 267.

Legitimacy also played a key role in inheritance rights as nonmarital children were denied inheritance rights, even if they were biologically connected to a parent through the doctrine of *filius nullius*.[46] Throughout the early modern and modern periods, succession laws were based on a network of rights and responsibilities that privileged biology. Thus, adultery was criminalised and divorce was forbidden in order to maintain strict control over succession of property through biological ties. Adultery by a husband was deemed legally irrelevant because any children he fathered would not be entitled to inherit any family property. Adultery by a wife, however, was strictly forbidden and harshly punished on the grounds that her actions might potentially impose spurious offspring into a man's family.[47] Even when legal adoption became available in the US and the UK in the late nineteenth and early twentieth centuries, the law privileged biology through the stranger to the adoption rule which prohibited an adopted child from inheriting through an adoptive parent from other blood relatives.[48] An adopted child would inherit from the adopting parents who had intentionally chosen to legalise their relationship with the child but would not be entitled to inherit from other blood relatives of the adoptive parents who had not been parties to the adoption.[49]

For nearly 800 years the common law, which was imported to the English colonies, established strict rules of blood unity in succession law. Church courts in England and common law courts in the colonies maintained strict control over the rights of legal heirs to inherit through a variety of marital, bastardy and property doctrines. In many of England's colonies where slavery was permissible, anti-miscegenation laws as well as social norms about marrying within one's class helped to limit the mixing of blood and inheritance rights that might result from uncontrolled social interaction. In the US, *partus sequitur ventrum* laws dictating that a mother's slave status would be passed on to a child and not the father's free status allowed men to sexually exploit their slave women without risking the property rights of their legitimate white offspring.[50] By the late nineteenth century, eugenics doctrines and strict segregation laws were available tools to help police the negative social effects of intermingling bloodlines.[51] Even the ubiquitous blood test required for marriage in most US states, although originally aimed at detecting sexually transmitted diseases, was associated with fears of producing genetically disabled offspring as blood and marriage became indelibly linked in the public imagination.[52]

[46] *Filius nullius* proclaimed that an illegitimate child was the child of no one and therefore could not inherit from either parent. See Pettersen (1971) for a lengthy history of the *filius nullius* doctrine and its eventual abrogation under equal protection.

[47] Brundage (1987) 386.

[48] Tritt (2019) 383–86.

[49] See, eg, *Keegan v Geraghty*, 101 Ill 25 (1881); *Merritt v Morton*, 136 SW 133 (Ky 1911).

[50] Morris (1996) 44–45.

[51] McGregor (2002).

[52] Doroshow (2021) 141–69. The tie between blood tests, succession, and legitimacy continue today in the UK as veneral infections are grounds for an annulment of marriage. See Matrimonial Causes Act 1973 ch 18(I)(12)(e).

Until the late nineteenth century throughout much of Europe a man could not marry his deceased wife's sister because the Church considered marriage to create a prohibited blood relationship in which relations by affinity and consanguinity were treated equally.[53] By elevating the marital relationship to the same level of importance as the biological relationship, the Christian church cemented the sacramental character of marriage through the unity of person doctrine so eloquently articulated by William Blacksone in the eighteenth century.[54]

The primacy of biology gave way to pragmatics in the age before scientific certainty, however, as laws like the marital presumption – by which any child born to a wife during wedlock was deemed to be the child of the husband unless it was proven that the husband did not have sexual access to his wife – acknowledged that there was some wiggle room in the realm of biological certainty.[55] Similarly, laws on paternity were notoriously flexible when it was understood that proving paternity could not be an exact science. Men who held their wives' children out as their own, who participated in a marriage ceremony after the birth of a child, and men who simply acknowledged possible paternity would be deemed legal parents and the child would be given inheritance rights.[56] Prior to DNA testing, Howard Stern would have been deemed the legal parent of Danielynn Smith since he intentionally held himself out as the father and the mother had named him as such on the birth certificate; prior to the advent of DNA, the act of naming created truth.

Thus, although the common law of inheritance had grown to privilege biology and blood connection as early as the twelfth century, until the modern age of DNA parentage, and the property rights that accompany it, was an understandably imprecise legal conclusion. In the highly controversial 1989 case of *Michael H v Gerald D*, the US Supreme Court held that the husband of the mother of a child born during the marriage was the legal father, despite DNA evidence to the contrary.[57] The Court upheld California's irrebuttable presumption that the husband is the father of a child born into his family. By 2007, however, Howard Stern would relinquish his claim of paternity solely on the pervasive truth-making of the DNA test.

As with the blood purity central to Christianity, the blood primacy of inheritance law is essentially racist as well. Laws were adopted to protect the white male bloodline in the case of slave status following the mother, just as eugenics became juridically approved by the decree that 'three generations of imbeciles are enough'.[58]

[53] Brundage (1987) 355–57. In the UK, the Deceased Wife's Sister's Marriage Act 1907 finally abolished this rule which contradicted longstanding beliefs and practices under Islamic and Jewish law.

[54] Blackstone (1765) 442–45.

[55] The case of William Murray is instructive. Sir William Murray initially divorced his wife through a private Act of Parliament on the grounds of her adultery, which he proved by his wife's pregnancy at a time when he was absent from the country. He then laid claim to custody of the child on the grounds of the marital presumption.

[56] Uniform Parentage Act 1973, s 4.

[57] 491 US 110 (1989).

[58] *Buck v Bell*, 274 US 200 (1927).

Enslaved persons could own no property and could not participate in the wealth aggregation and inheritance protections that built the American economy and its government. Persons seen as defective were denied the ability to procreate and thus control the legal descent of their property.[59] Native Indians were denied the ability to own, devise or even reside on their own lands once it was held in trust as a result of the profoundly destructive allotment scheme and the fractionation of reservation trust lands.[60]

Today, blood quantum rules are becoming even more powerful as they are used in many North American Native tribes to determine membership and the resources that flow from inclusion in a racial category.[61] Few tribes today use family lineage without reference to blood quantum, thus continuing the primacy of blood in determining membership, inclusion and political power.[62] More notably, DNA tests have now replaced family records or enrollment status in determining inclusion in Native American tribes, replacing such traditional markers as living among the tribe, speaking the language or being married to an enrolled tribal member.[63]

Citizenship status also remains tied to blood as we saw in the 2019 case of Ethan and Aidan Dvash-Banks, twin brothers born of a surrogate in which one was the son of a US father and the other was the son of an Israeli father.[64] The son of the Israeli father was initially denied US citizenship based on the fact that the child was biologically not related to the US citizen father and he could not thereby pass his citizenship status on to someone who was not related to him by blood. Although the decision was overruled and the state department policy was eventually changed, the strength of blood primacy existed in citizenship determinations until just three years ago.

As the DNA test has become the gold standard for determining legal rights based on blood relationship, succession laws have moved even further from functional and intentional relationships to the seemingly truth-creating certainty of genetic relationships. In 2008, the Uniform Law Commission, which promulgates uniform laws recommended for adoption in states, amended the parent–child provisions of the Uniform Probate Code (UPC) to accommodate children conceived and born through artificial reproductive technologies. Dispensing

[59] A Stern, 'Forced Sterilization Policies in the US Targeted Minorities and those with Disabilities – and Lasted in the 21st Century' *The Conversation* (26 August 2020) available at theconversation.com/forced-sterilization-policies-in-the-us-targeted-minorities-and-those-with-disabilities-and-lasted-into-the-21st-century-143144.

[60] Tribal status continues today to be based on blood and biology which then translates to such a lack of property rights that 11 out of 13 million acres of land allotted to native Americans has been lost, while the remaining two million is so fractionated in title as to be incapable of being possessed by its owners. See Shoemaker (2015).

[61] Indian Act, Canada, RSC C I-5(5)(6) (1985). See also TallBear (2013); Shoemaker (ibid).

[62] Spruhan (2006) 'Legal History'. See also Spruhan (2006) 'Indian as Race'.

[63] Spruhan (2007–08) 9

[64] *Dvash-Banks v Pompeo*, 2019 WL 911799, CD Cal, 21 February 2019, affm'd 825 Fed Appx 479, 9th Cir, 9 October 2020.

with the term 'natural' parent in the earlier UPC, the 2008 amendments defined biological blood kinship in terms of 'genetic' relationship.[65] Furthermore, the 2008 amendments continued the primacy of marital status in determining whether presumptions of biological relationship would exist.[66] The 2017 Uniform Parentage Act also has a lengthy section dealing with when a court can order genetic testing to prove parentage and when it can be used to challenge parentage.[67] Although these provisions attempt to recognise and protect greater diversity of families and parent–child relationships, including intentional and functional relationships, the heavy reliance on genetic truth recreates the power of blood in the inheritance context. In other words, rather than rejecting biology outright in favour of intentional relationships, the ULC relies on the scientific certainty of DNA testing to reify inheritance rights in blood and to continue centering biology in succession law.

The danger of succession law's reliance on DNA and blood certainty is evident in the case of Danielynn Birkhead. Anna Nicole Smith had sexual relations with a number of men around the period Danielynn was conceived and yet, when the child was born, she explicitly declared Howard Stern to be the father. This declaration was based on the fact that they had a lengthy and stable relationship, that Stern was aware of the pregnancy and undertook the obligations of fatherhood, and that the two had engaged in a commitment ceremony just weeks after Danielynn's birth. Prior to DNA availability, those intentional acts would have protected Stern's rights to claim paternity and allowed Anna Nicole to control the family she sought to create.[68] Anna Nicole did not care who Danielynn's genetic father was as she asserted her desire that Stern be deemed the legal parent. Stern had developed an, albeit short, relationship with the infant, the kind of relationship that would normally take precedence over other claims. When the court upset the mother's asserted preference in reliance on a DNA test, it placed blood certainty over the intentional wishes of the mother who tried to form her own functional family, and it recreated the blood dominance of succession law by granting Birkhead, the biological father, control over the child's inheritance.

The role of blood primacy in determining property rights, citizenship status and inheritance has only increased with the law's reliance on the truth value of DNA testing. I would argue that the intractability of the blood rule has become even more powerful in the construction of insider/outsider status than at any time in human history because the illusion of scientific certainty provides a veneer of truth that rinses clean the old rule that was based in violence and white supremacy.

[65] Uniform Probate Code § 2-121(c)(2).
[66] Uniform Probate Code § 2-120(h)(1).
[67] Uniform Parentage Act (2017) § 501 et seq.
[68] Uniform Parentage Act (1973) § 4.

IV. Conclusion

Nearly 1,000 years after the Council of Narbonne and Christianity's turn to blood purity, and nearly 1,000 years after the Norman Conquest and the privileging of blood in succession and property law, blood remains the sticky conduit for inheritance and wealth transmission.[69] And although many have questioned the predominance of blood in succession law, especially as we are witnessing unprecedented rejection of biology in family formation, blood remains the standard against which all else is measured. Ironically, even as society has moved to recognise functional families and has critiqued the domination of biology, succession law has only strengthened the role of blood through privileging of DNA testing. While few are willing to challenge the hegemony of blood in inheritance, they often overlook its racialised and gendered qualities. Even as we decry the white supremacy of Christian Nationalism espoused by groups like the Proud Boys and the Oath Keepers, and we mock their pretension to blood purity through drinking milk and DNA testing for European ancestry, we elevate blood purity in law and politics. Although we have rejected phrenology and astrology as theories of social superiority, the strength of Christian Nationalism, the culture war attacks on LGBTQ families, and the espousing of traditional nuclear family values all reaffirm social and political privilege on the basis of biology. To the extent inheritance and succession law uncritically accept the dominance of blood in wealth entitlement, inheritance and succession law will further entrench the racialised and gendered omnipotence of biology in the social and political realm. To the extent succession laws remain mired in an ideology of blood connection, and not functional or even legal intent, it places biology at the center of wealth and the political power of family identity.

This matters, for it is not simply that those with wealth have unprecedented ability to affect the political sphere, although that is the case. And it is not simply that wealth is heavily concentrated in the hands of cis-gendered, heterosexual white men who can define the political and the legal to maintain their privilege, which is also the case. It is the stickiness of the politics of blood, that defines succession law, wealth, and political power into an ideology of white supremacy, that needs to be understood and guarded against. With an unprecedented racial wealth gap and the greatest concentration of wealth in the top one per cent of the population since the depression era, we need to think more critically about the social and political power of blood.[70] Since wealth translates into the ability to define and enforce laws that protect certain relationships and declare what relationships will be acceptable and what relationships are anathema, illegal or simply invisible, decentering

[69] Dare I say 'blood is thicker than water'?.

[70] Nelson's (2016) critique of DNA cautions us to think critically about the meaning and uses of DNA in constructing identity and belonging.

DNA in succession law could help ameliorate the way inheritance laws define what persons will be allowed to cash in on their blood status and who will be denied access to wealth and power because of their blood.

References

Adams, J, 'Paternity Testing: Blood Types and DNA; (2008) 1 *Nature Education* 146.
Anidjar, G, 'Blood' in JM Bernstein, A Ophir, and AL Stoler (eds), *Political Concepts: A Critical Lexicon* (New York, Fordham University Press, 2018).
Baker, JH, *An Introduction to English Legal History*, 4th edn (London, Butterworths, 2002).
Bildhauer, B, *Medieval Blood* (Chicago, University of Chicago Press, 2006).
Blackstone, W *Commentaries on the Laws of England*, Vol 1 (1765).
Brundage, J, *Law, Sex, and Christian Society in Medieval Europe* (Chicago, University of Chicago Press, 1987).
Brundage, J and Eichbauer, ME, *Medieval Canon Law*, 2nd edn (NY, Routledge, 2023).
Chadwick, H, 'East and West: The Making of a Rift in the Church' in *Oxford History of the Christian Church* (Oxford, Oxford University Press, 2003).
Cowan, D, (2003) 'Theologizing Race: The Construction of "Christian Identity"' in CR Prentiss (ed), *Religion and the Creation of Race and Ethnicity: An Introduction* (New York, New York University Press, 2003).
Doroshow, D, 'Wasserman before Wedding Bells: Premarital Examination Laws in the United States, 1937–1950' (2021) 34 *Social History of Medicine* 141.
Dyer, R, *White: Essays on Race and Culture* (New York, Routledge, 1997).
Foucault, M, *History of Sexuality, vol 1* (trans R Hurley) (New York, Vintage Books, [1978]1990).
Glanvill, R, *Treatise on the Laws and Customs of the Kingdom of England* (trans GDG Hall) (London, Thomas Nelson, 1965).
Harvey, P, '"A Servant of Servants Shall He Be:" The Construction of Race in American Religious Mythologies' in CR Prentiss (ed), *Religion and the Creation of Race and Ethnicity: An Introduction* (New York, New York University Press, 2003).
Houghton-Larsen, MA, 'Paid for a White Baby: How Assisted Reproductive Technologies Reproduce White Supremacy' (2019) 11 *Georgetown Law Journal* 161.
Khanna, N and Killian, C, '"We Didn't even Think About Adopting Domestically": The Role of Race and Other Factors in Shaping Parents' Decisions to Adopt Abroad' (2015) 58 *Sociological Perspective* 570.
McGregor, R, '"Breed Out the Colour" or the Importance of Being White' (2002) 33 *Australian Historical Studies* 286.
Morris, T, *Southern Slavery and the Law, 1619–1860* (Chapel Hill, University of North Carolina Press, 1996).
Nelson, A, *The Social Life of DNA* (Boston, Beacon Press, 2016).
Oxford Annotated Bible, Revised Standard Version (New York, Oxford University Press).
Panofsky, A and Donovan, J 'Genetic Ancestry Testing Among White Nationalists: From Identity Repair to Citizen Science' (2019) 49 *Social Studies of Science* 653.
Pettersen, J, 'A Return to Filius Nullius' (1971) 48 *North Dakota Law Review* 59.
Prentiss, C (2003) 'Introduction' in CR Prentiss (ed), *Religion and the Creation of Race and Ethnicity: An Introduction* (New York, New York University Press, 2003).

Shoemaker, J, 'No Sticks in my Bundle: Rethinking the American Indian Land Tenure Problem' (2015) 63 *University of Kansas Law Review* 383.

Spring, E, *Law, Land, and Family: Aristocratic Inheritance in England, 1300–1800* (Chapel Hill, University of North Carolina Press, 1995).

Spruhan, P, 'A Legal History of Blood Quantum in Federal Indian Law to 1935' (2006) 51 *South Dakota Law Review* 1.

—— 'Indian as Race/Indian as Political Status: Implementation of the Half-Blood Requirement under the Indian Reorganization Act, 1934–1945' (2006) 8 *Rutgers Race & Law Review* 27.

—— 'The Origins, Current Status, and Future Prospects of Blood Quantum as the Definition of Membership in the Navajo Nation' (2007–08) 8 *Tribal Law Journal* 1.

TallBear, K, *Native American DNA: Tribal Belonging and the False Promise of Genetic Science* (Minneapolis, University of Minnesota Press, 2013).

Tritt, L, 'The Stranger to the Marriage Doctrine: Judicial Construction Issues Post-Obergefell' (2019) *Wisconsin Law Review* 373.

Wright, D, 'Inheritance Equity: Reforming the Inheritance Penalties Facing Children In Non-Traditional Families' (2015) 25 *Cornell Journal of Law and Public Policy* 1.

14

Women, Property and Agency

Contours of Matrilineal Inheritance among the Nayars in Kerala, India

LEKHA N B AND ANTONY PALACKAL

I. Introduction

The southernmost Indian state, Kerala, is hailed for its high levels of political consciousness, activism, literacy, socio-political reforms, social development, material quality of life achievements, religious harmony, low infant mortality, high life expectancy and gender equality. Consequently, the state continues to be the focus of attention for both Indian and international scholarship on account of this unique pattern of development. Initially, Kerala gained renown owing to its unique political and socio-cultural history as the first elected communist government in the world. The matrilineal kinship organisation among the Nayar community, one of the dominant caste[1] groups in terms of demographic and electoral superiority, was yet another feature that brought Kerala to the limelight of academic interest among international scholars and development practitioners.

A matrilineal social structure and its features, such as the importance given to the girl child and women's rights to property, are considered key attributes for the so-called progressive 'status of women' in Kerala. 'Matriliny' refers to the practice of tracing descent and inheritance rights through the mother's line. It is a female-based kinship system wherein individuals are related only through women, and family structures are more strongly oriented around related women than related men.[2] Anthropologists in the nineteenth century postulated that in the grand scheme of socio-cultural evolution, a matrilineal descent system with matriarchal authority was the precursor to patrilineal societies. Added to this was the belief that matrilineal societies were matriarchal too, in the sense

[1] MN Srinivas defines 'dominant caste' as the particular caste economically, religiouslly, numerically and politically above any other castes in a given region.

[2] Fortunato (2012); Henn (1984); Mattison et al (2019).

that both the line of descent and the line of authority favoured females. Hence, Bachofen[3] claimed in *Das Mutterrecht* for 'mother right' in matrilineal societies. However, anthropologists later posited that matriarchy and matriliny are not equivalents, and that matriliny is subsumed within matriarchy. More importantly, anthropologists understood matriarchy as mythical and legendary, and matriliny as historical and real. Similarly, it was found that both matriliny and patriliny, though inherently distinct forms of authority structures, are not mirror images of each other.[4] Comparative studies by anthropologists of the succeeding generations[5] have endeavoured to delineate the salient features of matrilineal societies in contrast to patrilineal ones. These include matrilineal descent, that is, tracing the lineage through the mother or female member of the family; matrilocality, where women continue residing in their natal home even after marriage; and, property inheritance systems that favour women. Overall, a female-based kinship system is comprised of the norms regulating inheritance, succession to office, marital residence, authority within the family, and descent.

The 'Kerala model of development' has often been attributed to, among other things, its matrilineal past where women were considered to have enjoyed a greater degree of freedom than in areas where patriliny was the norm of social organisation.[6] The *marumakkatayam* (matrilineal system of inheritance) conferred certain special rights on women with regard to sexuality and property. However, changes in social conditions brought about by British colonisation and its notions of modernity and progress in the late nineteenth and early twentieth centuries cast these rights as 'immoral' and 'primitive'. This was accomplished by overturning inheritance and descent through the female line, kinship ties that revolved around women, women's property rights, and rights over children belonging to a mother's family.[7] Today, matriliny is no longer the organising principle of the Nayar community and other communities who followed matriliny. Nonetheless, a strong emotional attachment to the natal home and relatively greater importance to maternal relationships still exist in Nayar society.

Many researchers[8] have focused on women's high literacy rate and higher sex ratio, which is often attributed to its matrilineal past, while the relation between property and gender relations, which is a qualitative indicator for status of women, is ignored. This chapter focuses on the inheritance system of the Nayars that privileged women with the ownership of property. More specifically, it seeks to engage with two objectives: 1) understanding the position that women enjoyed in the Nayar matrilineal tradition in Kerala; and 2) using a longitudinal frame, mapping the changes that have occurred in the inheritance of property of Nayar women in Kerala vis-a-vis gender relations. We employ a narrative paradigm that draws on

[3] Bachofen (1861).
[4] Schneider (1961).
[5] Puthenkalam (1977).
[6] Jeffery (2005).
[7] Kodoth and Eapen (2005).
[8] Jeffery (2004); Kodoth and Eapen (2005).

empirical research findings gathered from an ethnographic field engagement with three generations of Nayar women in Kerala to argue that the changing property relations in the matrilineal Nayar tradition tend to determine gender relations, which render women's bargaining power within the household. We submit that the power that women enjoy in the private sphere, when translated into the public sphere, has the potential to bestow them with higher degrees of agency. Agency,[9] at the micro/household level, includes, but is not limited to, having freedom of mobility, managing household income and expenditures, and taking decisions regarding the everyday management of the household chores, which are extended at the macro/public level.

Paying special attention to the experience of gender relations of Nayar women within their household, coupled with the continuities in the rights that a woman retains in her natal house and the right to a share of the property, will help in understanding the complexities of gender relations vis-à-vis property relations. In this endeavour, the predominant question that this chapter addresses is how the changes that occurred in the inheritance of property of three generation of Nayar women in Kerala contributed to subsequent changes in gender relations within the household. It is argued that property, the primary matrilineal heritage of Nayar woman, seems to undergo a region-wide metaphoric transformation that essentially empowers Nayar women to bargain with patriarchy in the contemporary social milieu that continues to implicate gender relations.

II. Methodology

We undertook an intensive ethnographic field engagement among the Nayar women in three regions of Kerala that represented not only its geographical but also socio-cultural and political zones. The ethnographic field work was carried out for one and a half years between 2017 and 2019 in the Thiruvananthapuram, Palakkad and Kannur districts of Kerala that represent the south, central and north regions of the state respectively. Thiruvananthapuram, the southernmost district of Kerala where the princely state of Travancore (as the Central Kerala was known prior to the formation of the State of Kerala) had its headquarters and Nayars were closely associated with the royal family, was chosen because elements of matriliny still exist. The Central Zone, Palakkad, was chosen because prominent features of matriliny still exist and the literature describes that Palakkad had a 'pristine' form of matriliny.[10] Kannur, in the northern region, was selected because it is known as the Malabar area in Kerala, which was under the direct rule of the British and thus has a different socio economic and political background for the growth of Nayars.

[9] Vandsemb (2014) defines 'agency' as that which denotes individual's capability to make decisions on their own life and having the possession of and control over entitlements and resources.

[10] Mayadevi (2015).

Within the epistemological framework of narrative paradigm, we collected empirical data using a sequential exploratory method which prioritises qualitative data with quantitative inputs as supplementary. The narrative paradigm is founded on the principle of narrative rationality in contrast to the formal rationality of the positive sciences, which is hypothetico-deductive. From the perspective of narrative paradigm, social anthropologists perceive human beings as *Homo narrans*[11] and social life as 'enacted narrative'. In this sense, narratives are regarded as the fundamental mode of knowing.[12] The discussions and arguments of the chapter are built on a narrative epistemological and methodological framework.

The ethnography was carried out among three generations of women, classified according to their age group: 60-plus, 40–59, and 18–39 for the first, second and third generations respectively. The first generation (60–plus) were women who experienced *marumakkatayam* in their early life and were adults at the time of the enactment of Kerala Joint Hindu Family System (Abolition) Act of 1976.[13] The second generation (40–59) of women encountered the transition from the old system of matriliny to the present inheritance system. The third generation of women (18–39 age group) are those who have only a little knowledge about the matrilineal system. In total, 49 women were interviewed.

We used multi-stage purposive sampling for collecting quantitative data. As census data was not available for caste-wise distribution of population in Kerala, we relied on the survey conducted by Zacharia et al[14] to study caste wise demographic distribution in Kerala. We divided Kerala into three zones: south, central and north. It was found that Kollam in the south (17.8 per cent), Palakkad in the central region (7.4 per cent) and Kannur in the north, (13.1 per cent) had the highest population of Nayars. Using a sample size calculator, the sample size was fixed as 118, 107 and 112 for the south, central and north respectively, making a total of 337 Nayar women.

In what follows, we examine Nayar matriliny and the property relations of Nayar women in terms of inheritance of parental property, inheritance of *taravad*, the nature of the house, inheritance of land and finally the idea of barganing within matriliny.

III. Nayar Matriliny

Nayar, a dominant matrilineal community in Kerala, is at the middle layer of the hierarchical order of the Hindu caste system, and hence considered one of the

[11] Turner (1982); MacIntyre (1981/1990); Czarniawska (2002).
[12] Bruner (1987).
[13] An act to abolish the joint family system among Hindus in the State of Kerala.
[14] Zacharia et al (2003).

forward caste-communities.[15] To understand the different gender perspectives in matriliny, it is essential to analyse the salient features of Nayar matriliny. The most important element of the *Nayar* kinship system, based on the *marumakkatayam* law of inheritance, has been the matrilineal kin group called *taravad*. The *taravad*, consisting of all the matrilineal descendants of a female ancestress, holding property collectively which is managed by the senior-most male member known as the *karnavan* (headman).

It is often questioned whether matriliny signifies a higher status for women. Schlegel[16] noted that matrilineal societies differ with respect to the domestic autonomy women acquire. Furthermore, Friedl[17] has stated that it is men, traced through matriliny descent, who hold land and look after political and ritual affairs. Here, the position of women is analysed with reference to the specific and peculiar variables attributed to Nayar society. Rather than defining the status of Nayar women as high or low, we studied the interrelations between men and women in the traditional *marumakkatayam* system and the changes that have happened over a period of time.

Gough[18] and Fuller[19] studied the status of Nayar women in general while Murickan[20] and Saradamoni[21] noticed the changing status of women in Kerala with respect to their property and family. However, it was Nair[22] who pioneered the study of Nayar women and their social interactions. In *taravad*, the birth of a girl child was of considerable significance and more prized than a male child, and still is, because of the role she plays in carrying the name of the *taravad* and for continuing the legacy of the *matrilineal taravad*. Girls were taught to read and write, and families who could afford to sent their daughters to *kalaries* along with boys. It is also known that they were taught short poems to inculcate moral principles. Music was also an integral component in their curriculum. In short, Nayar society placed high importance on the overall education of girls.

In the matrilineal system, women played a pivotal role in family and property affairs. Married women were financially independent. They were safeguarded in their own *taravads*. However, Saradamoni[23] observed an organic relationship between these women and their land. Other studies have also cited the freedom, power and status enjoyed by women in *marumakkatayam* family. Gopal Panikkar notes that, 'The spirit of the law governing these *Taravads* is that while

[15] 'Forward caste' means those castes in the upper layers of the caste hierarchy and superior caste below them, economically, socially, politically and educationally.

[16] Schlegel (1972).

[17] Friedl (1975).

[18] Gough (1965).

[19] Fuller (1976).

[20] Murickan (1975).

[21] Saradamoni (1982).

[22] Nair (1969).

[23] Saradamoni (1982).

the joint property belongs to the females, their natural incapacity for family governance has made the eldest male member the life trustee of the joint estate'.[24] Further, he commented that women along with male counterparts were capable of acquiring and disposing property as per their will. Echoing this, Her Highness Sethu Parvati Bai stated that Travancore women independently bought and sold properties.[25] Fuller[26] also observed the high status held by Nayar women with regard to property inheritance. This is of paramount importance in the context of the paradoxical climate prevailing in Kerala today. As the primary role of a woman centres on family, to understand women and their position in society, it is a prerequisite to study their familial roles. Mothers played and still play a decisive role among Nayars. The eldest woman in traditional *taravad* is venerated and looked upon for decision-making and leadership.

IV. Property Relations of Nayar Women: A Historical Perspective

The most important unit in the *Nayar* kinship system based on the *marumakkatayam* law was the matrilineal kin group called *taravad*. As stated earlier, this group was a corporate unit consisting of all the matrilineal descendants of a female ancestress, holding property collectively and managed by the senior-most male member called the *karnavan*. According to MSA Rao,[27] the three main structural principles on which the *taravad* was based until the twentieth century were matrilineal descent, exogamy and impartibility.

The changes within the Nayar *taravad* are significant, such that the property group no longer exists. The first element which was lost was the co-residential domestic unit. When the residential unit became small, the *taravad* ceased to remain as a group which consisted of members of a matrilineage exclusively, and the co-habitation of spouses also meant that affinal kins came to live in this group. Land, which was the central part of the *taravad*, came to have two connotations. After the 1925 regulation land was divided into two categories: family property or *taravad* property; and individual property. Family property is that property inherited by a woman from any one of her matrilineal relatives. Family property is regarded as the property of not only the woman in whose name it is held, it is also meant for her children and daughter's children. Without the consent of all her adult matrilineal descendants, she cannot sell it or alienate it. If at the time of dividing it, there are minor matrilineal descendants, then provision must be made so that each receives a share at the time of becoming an adult. When partition takes place, family property

[24] Panikar (1983) 26.
[25] Pillai (1940).
[26] Fuller (1976).
[27] Rao (1957).

must be divided equally between all matrilineal descendants. Indeed, a pregnant daughter receives a share for her unborn child. Individual property is self-acquired property or property obtained by a person from any other source. Individual property can be sold or alienated without the consent of any person. The property inherited from a woman's father becomes individual property, since a father's property is not considered family property. This individual property is then handed down to her daughter, which becomes family property for the latter. Individual property is normally divided equally among all the children. However, with the implementation of the Kerala Joint Hindu Family System (Abolition) Act 1975, no property is considered family property on the matrilineal side. Thus today daughters do not receive an additional share for their children from the family property. Property is divided equally between all children, but the house invariably goes to the daughter by matrilineal custom, as the house is still considered as the seat of one's ancestry.

A. Inheritance of Parental Property

Division of property of Nayars started only in the late twentieth century. In our study most first-generation women had inherited their parental property and had *Alohari* (per capita) division of property. In earlier times, property was joint and it was an indissoluble unit. After the implementation of the Kerala Joint Hindu Family System (Abolition) Act 1975, division of property began. In the case of partition, individual members in the *taravad* were entitled to a share in the *taravad* properties on the basis of per capita (*Alohari*).[28]

Analysis of the quantitative data revealed regional variations in the inheritance of property. Most of the women (75.4 per cent) from the south had already inherited their property; but for 57 per cent from the central region and 54.5 per cent from the north, parental property was yet to be divided. In the south region, property division began as early as the 1930s and 1940s, from the first generation women's mothers' time onwards. *Alohari* division of property was the form of division of inheritance. Under this system, every woman from the first generation received a greater share than her male siblings.

Most of these women received a share even for their children who were born before 1975. The second-generation women had a clear idea about their property and some of them inherited their parental property just after marriage as a form of dowry. But, unlike those women from a non-matrilineal tradition, the property is inherited in her own name. Among the third generation in the south, only a few women inherited their parental property but all of them had a clear understanding of their inheritance of property. They became aware of

[28] Nambiar and Kumar (2006).

matters concerning the inheritance of property, particularly at the time of their marriage or their elder siblings' marriages. So the discussions regarding their property and about its division had already taken place in their families. Aruna, a 25-year-old unmarried Nayar woman, who was working as a senior software engineer at Techno Park, testified to this when she recounted,

> Normally property division took place only after the marriage. When my elder sister got married my parents gave her 17 cents of land and built a house near our house … and she is living there now. I think that my mother inherited 17 cents of land from my grandparents and she gave it to her. As my sister was already settled, this house is for me and I will inherit this. It is all our parents' decisions. As I have to stay here, we are looking for a good alliance from nearby places. My father has some properties, which he may divide equally between both of us.

In central Kerala, most of the individual property was divided but it was very difficult to divide the *taravad* property because of the many shareholders. Property division started only at the time of the first-generation women. The first-generation women were the last generation to experience 'joint family'. Compared to the south, property division in the central and the north regions was a slow process and the first-generation women inherited their property only in their 60s and 70s. Among the second-generation women in central and the north Kerala, only 31.6 per cent (12 out of 28) and 14.6 per cent (7 out of 48) respectively inherited their parental property; they were more inclined to acquire property by their own hard work and most of them acquired it jointly with their husbands. They knew that they would surely inherit their parents' property, but were reluctant to ask about it. Partition of property usually occurs only after the death of their parents. Saritha, a 50-year-old Nayar woman from North Kerala, explained it clearly:

> Our property is not divided yet. Most of the parents don't want to see the division when they are alive. Whatever amma (mother) decides about partition will be accepted by all of us. I think she has written her Will[29] but we don't ask anything about that. In most of the cases, female children will be given the *taravad* and brothers tend to give more property to their sisters.

B. Inheritance of *Taravad*

In contemporary times, the word *taravad* is used to refer to a house/property and kin group not necessarily organised on the principle of *marumakkatayam* or matriliny. Our respondents also referred to *taravad* as a house that used to be a joint family abode but had been partitioned and inherited as one person's share.

[29] A legal document in which a person states who should receive his or her possessions after he or she dies. The inheritor will have complete freedom on the property as per the will.

For a better understanding of inheritance, we regard the respondent's house – the one built by the parents and the place where she lived – as *taravad*.

Puthenkalam, in one of his studies (1977) in Travancore, reveals that the nuclear family is seen as the emerging type; parents staying with their married daughters, with or without their unmarried children, account for almost 25 per cent of the households. The reason could be that it is the daughters who inherit the house. If there are more than two daughters, the principal of ultimogeniture[30] is resorted to. Only in the absence of daughters is the house given to sons. However, we observed that the mandatory custom of giving *taravad* to daughters has changed and regional variation regarding this can also be noticed. Nayars from south Kerala are more inclined to this change compared to those in the north and the centre. Bhavani amma, who is 82 years old, from the South, and from an upper-middle-class background, has four sons and one daughter with whom she now lives, elaborated on the shifts in the transfer of the *taravad* and other properties from the traditional inheritance pattern to contemporary times:

> I gave my house to my younger son. My husband was an Ayurvedic doctor at Govt. Ayurvedic College and we also had a clinic, which was adjacent to our house. My daughter was a professor in Malayalam who worked in different universities. After her marriage, she went with her husband. Two of my sons chose their father's path and became Ayurvedic doctors. So we thought it would be easier for them to take up that clinic and continue it. So I gave our house and clinic to my younger son. But, now, that shop does not exist at all. I have not inherited that house but my husband built it after our marriage. I had to sell my land, which I inherited from my mother to support my husband to buy this land and build this house. So it is in my name itself. As the society changed daughters were married off and sons were with us and we think that they will look after us, so we have to give our house to our son; but that's not true in my case. Now I am living with my daughter. Even though *taravad* was not given to her, this house was built by my husband and given to her as a present. So I have all the right to live here also.

Rukmani, a retired professor aged 63 and the daughter of Bhavani amma, made this comment on the inheritance of her property from her parents.

> My *taravad* was given to my younger brother. My father was an Ayurvedic doctor (vaidyan). My elder and younger brothers were also ayurvedic doctors and near to my *taravad* they prepared all those ayurvedic medicines. As I am a retired College Professor, and not in the ayurvedic field my younger brother got the *taravad* along with the ayurvedic shop which is just near to the house. Now that shop does not exist at all. If I were in the Ayurvedic field I might have inherited it and preserved it. Now he (younger brother) ruined all of it. What to do? My father built a house for me at Vanchiyoour. In fact, he built house for all of his children. He gave all property equally to all of his five children.

[30] Ultimogeniture, also known as postremogeniture or junior right, is a system of inheritance whereby the youngest daughter gains the inheritance in the matrilineal system.

> My father didn't give more share to me even though I am the only daughter for them. They gave gold for my marriage and also for my daughter's marriage. He gave two lakhs for buying gold for her marriage.

Lakshmi Priya, daughter of Rukmani, a 40-year-old Nayar and an assistant professor, had the following remarks regarding the inheritance of natal home:

> Nowadays property is transmitted not based on gender. It is more based on the need of each one. For example, I got land from my father to build my house and not from my mother. … My father has two brothers and one sister. There is a lot of land in his native place and most of the land was given to 'appachi' i.e. father's sister. … The land where they lived and house was given to father's sister … My husband has two brothers and their parents built two houses for them and gave them. Both my husband and I had a sentimental attachment to this place. We thought we will build a house in Vanchiyoor because my father gave me this land.

Hence, property transfer in Nayar community is increasingly based on need and not on gender. The tradition of giving more property to women no longer exists; gender does not become a factor in inheriting property. Hence women are becoming increasingly marginalised. As Leela stated, for example,

> If I build a house in my husband's land I may not get this land from my father. My mother is living in the house which was built by my grandfather before 35 years and as my brother is staying with them mostly, that property will be given to him.

Analysis of these responses from three women from different generations shows that in the first generation itself, the importance of male children is clearly depicted and the idea of a son looking after the parents has already emerged. We consider this as one of the major reasons for not giving *taravad* (natal home) to women. Even the grandmother, who gave *taravad* to her son, is in old age staying with her daughter, who is looking after her. She does not have any feelings of guilt for staying with her, but she has full rights in her house because her husband built it. Regarding the second-generation women, that is, the mother, she has the feeling that if the *taravad* property and related adjacent production unit had been given to her daughter, it would have been maintained by her daughter. Moreover, women tend to preserve the property more than men do. Bina Agarwal[31] had also observed that access to and command over property by women will lead to efficiency in maintaining that property and will lead to the welfare of family. The daughter has clearly stated that gender is not a factor in present days in the division of property and more or less equal division is happening. Consequently, women are marginalised. This is because the importance given to daughters in the earlier Nayar *taravad* is diminishing. Lineage tracing through women has almost vanished. The importance of sons and the idea that 'the son should look after family' has emerged. This, coupled with the increase in dowry, has diminished women's rights in the inheritance of property.

[31] Agarwal (1994).

C. Nature of the House

The fallback position and bargaining power of women depends on the type of house they are living in. When *taravads* were broken down to nuclear households, they were built in the family property of women. Thus, they were mostly close to women's *taravad*. Our qualitiative data revealed that in the south region of Kerala, settling down in the husband's village was rare in the first generation; even if the men worked in cities, they preferred to spend holidays with the family at their in-laws' place. Upon retirement, couples, with or without their children, shift to the wife's house, if she inherited it, or build a house near to her natal house.

In the south region of Kerala, the first-generation women lived in the house built in their own name. As noted above, in the property division at the early stage of their marriage, women received either land with a home or land upon which they built a home. Slowly virilocal residence emerged, which was a characteristic of a patriarchal system. Under patriarchy, matrilocal residence was embarrassing to men and in the early phase of marriage most men hesitated to reside in their wife's home. However, by their 40s, they would not mind staying in homes owned or inherited by women and they would justify it on their own terms. Thus, for example, Radhakrishnan Nayar, who retired from the army, told us that while he had been away on duty, his wife and children had lived in her *taravad* house. When he retired and came back he said, 'there were no men there, so I lived there'. The absence of men in the household was seen as the rationale for staying in a wife's undivided *taravad*. This is one way in which residence in one's wife's house is justified, in order to counter the idea that a man living in his wife's house is powerless. Women's inheritance of property thus enables a flexibility in residence despite the strong norm of virilocal residence. 45-year-old, Rathi from the south, who is from an upper-middle-class background, testified to this:

> After marriage women have to stay in [their] husband's house itself. Chettan (husband) doesn't like to stay in my house. He is very particular about it. He feels that it is very shameful to stay continuously in my house. He used to say 'I won't stay in "achiveedu" (wife's house), if we stay there no one will respect us, If you want to live with me you have to stay in my house.' So I agreed. But when my children grew up and they started going to school, we found it very difficult as the school was far away from my husband's home, but it is nearer to my home. Travel has also become a problem for him, as he had to travel two hours a day for his office. At that time, my father gave me twenty cents of land near to my house and with the help of my father we started to build a new house there and shifted to that house.

Abraham[32] has rightly observed that there are certain exigencies that threaten this flexibility. In the case of migration to another town, a woman's share of property may be sold and a house bought elsewhere, which may not necessarily be in the woman's name. Similarly, when women inherit property, but do not have an

[32] Abraham (2017).

income that enables them to obtain a loan from a bank, the property may be registered jointly in the names of the couple so that the husband can avail a loan. Such a situation diminishes the security that a woman has with a house of her own. In fact, such instances point to the importance of not only women's right to property, but also to their earning capacity.

D. Inheritance of Land

In agrarian economies, land is considered an important item of property. Thus, families and communities which recognised women's inheritance rights in land ensured that the land stayed within the kin group.[33] Analysing the situation in central and north Kerala, the first generation women and a few from the second generation inherited agricultural land and they used to cultivate crops, whereas, in the south, women mostly inherited non-agricultural land. What follows is the experience shared by Saraswathy, a 73-year-old Nayar woman from central Kerala:

> In the past, agriculture was the main livelihood. Our *taravad* had lots of landholding, mainly paddy fields. In my childhood I remember all the festivals related to agricultural activities. My husband used to look after the agricultural activities of my *taravad* also. The karanavan of my *taravad* was very much fond of him. He used to discuss all the matter with him, the main reason for that was that he was the only person who got high education. When *taravad* was divided, our agricultural land was also divided and I got '100 para' (bushel) area of paddy field. We have been cultivating there and now my eldest son is looking after it, because others have no time as they have other jobs. It was his duty to give share to all his siblings after the cultivation. I partitioned my property and gave a portion of agricultural land to my daughter. Elder son, with the help of her husband, is managing the cultivation. But now they are saying that agriculture is not profitable these days as the cost of cultivation also is increasing. But still it is very prestigious to cultivate in our agricultural land. I told them that till my death I want to see the cultivation in our paddy land and after that, I don't care.

Coming to the second generation, Lalitha, daughter of Saraswathy, a 54-year-old working woman, explains how the importance of agricultural cultivation decreased in their lifetime:

> Earlier paddy cultivation was the main occupation of our area and now it became side business. Attention towards the agricultural activities is becoming less. Major reason is that we cannot solely depend on agriculture for livelihood or for a high standard of living. My husband is working in Co-operative bank and we are depending on that income. But still we are continuing it. But it is very difficult as the labour charges and other costs are increasing, but the return is too low. I don't think that in the next generation these agricultural activities will be maintained.

These narratives explain how most of the first-generation women from central Kerala inherited agricultural land and how they continue to cultive the land

[33] Agrawal (1994).

despite less profit. The second generation considers agriculture only as a non-profitable side business and hence do not have much interest in cultivation of the land that they inherit. They find it very difficult to cultivate the land, as labour costs are increasing. When the joint family system prevailed, lots of undivided land could be found and when individual based division began, land became fragmented and agricultural production became only nominal. Hence, the property-owners do not engage in serious agricultural activity. The second-generation women, who lived with their husbands away from their natal homes, tend to sell their share of property if it proves inconvenient or unprofitable. In the current economic climate, selling land is an attractive option for many, and the income accrued is used to buy property or build house elsewhere.

In the southern region, inheritance of agricultural land among second generation and third generation women was lower compared to those in the central region. In the South, the first generation was found to be the last generation to inherit agricultural land from their parents; for the second generation, the land became fragmented and their parents transferred much less agricultural land to them. This reflects the historical development in Travancore. During the nineteenth century, land became a readily saleable commodity due to the influence of colonial economy. Colonial economy concentrated on the trade economy as evidenced in the emergence of cash crops.[34] This led to two interrelated trends: the decline of agricultural activities, and the monetisation of land in the south.

V. Bargaining within Matriliny

The extent to which women can apply their control within the household depends on their bargaining power within the household. Sen,[35] Kathewera Banda et al[36] and Agarwal[37] have identified the effect of gendered institutions and social norms as a special form of bargaining power, which affects the bargaining processes. The female-friendly norms that provide the perception or even illusion, as Sen[38] refers to it, of the legitimacy of one's claims within the household can affect one's autonomy or decision-making behaviour. According to Rahman and Rao,[39] women's perceptions or experiences of their decision-making authority on a range of issues can actually influence their autonomy.

[34] Jeffrey (1992).

[35] Sen (1990).

[36] Kathewera Banda et al, 'Women's Access to Land and Household Bargaining Power: A Comparative Action Research Project in Patrilineal and Matrilineal Societies in Malawi Research Report for the Women's Legal Resouce Centre' (2011), available at landwise-production.s3.amazonaws.com/2022/03/Kathewera-Banda_Womens_access_to_land_and_household_bargaining_power_2011-1.pdf.

[37] Agarwal (1997).

[38] Sen (1990).

[39] Rahman and Rao (2004).

Agarwal's[40] theory relating to gender relation and bargaining power is useful in explaining this situation. She rightly observed that gender relations are not uniform as they are constructed socially and culturally. From the perspective of women, in the Nayar community we also find different types of gender relations which vary from generation to generation. As Agarwal argued, a woman's bargaining power lies in her fallback position on economic independence, which is gained through inheritance rights in property, and also control over it. Another element is employment. Combined, these factors gave women a great fallback position, which vested women with bargaining power in their gender relations. Social norms also influence bargaining power. The ethnographic approach here revealed that for first-generation women, the social norm of matriliny provided the main bargaining power in gender relations, as matriliny gave more importance to women. However, for the second and the third generations, changes in societal norms, which are more inclined to patriarchy, had adverse effects on women's bargaining power. Nonetheless, the women's right in their natal home was a good fallback position for Nayar women whereby they are able to better exercise their freedom and rights in an unequal gendered socio-cultural mileiue.

The irony is that, though similar large-scale transformations have already come about in the nature of social structure of Kerala from the times of matriliny, in the present day women are at a disadvantage. Pre-modern Kerala was characterised by a variety of special provisions granting women a certain amount of autonomy, at least among the matrilineal communities. Modern Kerala, on the other hand, has undermined most of those positions. As Arunima[41] puts it: 'women's right to property, authority, inheritance and residence were all affected by the vicissitudes of codified matrilineal law'. The resistance shown by the Nayar women for the shift to patrilineal families, with blatantly patriarchal authority structures, is probably a sign of their increasing insecurity within a changing matrilineal context. Even though legislation and laws[42] had adverse effects on Nayar women's property rights, with the help of matriliny, they are trying to cope with the situation. For the first-generation women, matriliny provided them with fallback positions and gave them bargaining power in gender relations. However, for the second and third generations, changes in matriliny, with the patriarchy gaining dominance, means that they experience adverse effects on their bargaining power. Women's right in their natal home became a good fallback position for second-generation Nayar women, which vested in them bargaining power in gender relations. Nevertheless, they retain some bargaining power as they can exercise control over property and other resources, including employment. Hence, they are bargaining within matriliny against patriarchy.

[40] Agarwal (1994).

[41] Arunima (2003) 135.

[42] The Kerala legislature passed subsequent land reform bills in 1960, 1963 and 1964. But the historical land reform act, the Kerala Land Reforms (Amendment) Act, 1969, brought an end to the existing feudal system and made sure that the tenants right on the land came into effect from 1970.

VI. Conclusion

Exploring the case of Nayar women and their property relations helps us understand the ways in which changing property relations determine the gender relations which shape women's bargaining power within the household. Our empirical journey with the Nayar women revealed that matriliny, especially the right to property, provided for them a fallback position, and accorded them bargaining power in gender relations in a patriarchal social milieu. However, more importantly, it was fascinating to observe that in the process, property seemed to gather different semiotic meanings in different regions. Accordingly, we argue that property, which is basically an economic entity, assumes metaphoric attributes according to the regional variations that conferred Nayar women autonomy and a say in gender relations within the household.

At this juncture, what is more important is that this favourable condition or potential agency of property be translated into actual women's agency in the public domain; that is, the macro field of power operations.[43] The power and authority that women enjoy in the household has to be converted into the empowerment of women in other fields in and through education, employment and control over resources. Until then, women's empowerment and identity questions may remain as a rhetoric.

References

Agarwal, B, *A Field of One's Own – Gender and Land Rights in South Asia* (Cambridge, Cambridge University Press, 1994a).

—— 'Gender and Command over Property: A Critical Gap in Economic Analysis and Policy in South Asia' (1994b) 22 *World Development* 1455.

—— '"Bargaining" and Gender Relations: Within and Beyond the Household' (1997) 3 *Feminist Economist* 1.

Arunima, G, *There Comes Papa: Colonialism and Transformation of Matrilinity in Kerala, Malabar c.1850–1940* (Hyderabad, India, Orient Longman, 2003).

Bachofen, JJ, *Mother Right: An Investigation of the Religious and Juridical Character of Matriarchy in the Ancient World* (trans D Partenheimer) (New York, Edwin Mellen Press, 1861).

Bruner, J, 'Life as Narrative' (1987) 54 *Social Research* 11.

Czarniawska, B, *Narratives in Social Science Research* (Thousand Oaks, Sage Publications, 2002).

Davison, J, *Gender, Lineage and Ethnicity in Southern Africa* (Boulder, CO, Westview Press, 1997).

Ehrenfels, UR, 'Matrilineal Joint Family Patterns in India' (1971) 2 *Journal of Comparative Family Studies* 54.

[43] Bourdieu (1986).

Fortunato, L, 'The Evolution of Matrilineal Kinship Organization' (2012) 279 *Proceedings of the Royal Society B: Biological Sciences* 4939.

Friedl, E, *Women and Men: An Anthropologist's View* (Holt, Rinehart and Winston, 1975).

Fuller, CJ, *The Nayars Today* (Cambridge, Cambridge University Press, 1976).

Gough, K, 'Nayar: Central Kerala; Nayar: North Kerala; Mappilas: North Kerala: The Modern Disintegration of Matrilineal Descent Groups' in DM Schneider and K Gough (eds), *Matrilineal Kinship* (Berkeley, University of California Press, 1961).

—— 'A Note on Nayar Marriage' (1965) 65 *Man* 8.

—— 'The Origin of the Family' (1971) 33 *Journal of Marriage and the Family* 760.

Henn, J, 'Women in The Rural Economy: Past, Present and Future' in M Hay and S Stichter (eds), *African Women South of the Sahara* (London, Longman, 1984).

Holden, CJ, Sear, R and Mace, R, 'Matriliny as a Daughter Biased Investment' (2003) 24 *Evolution and Human Behaviour* 99.

Jeffrey, R, *Politics, Women and Well-Being: How Kerala became 'a Model'* (London, Palgrave Macmillan, 1992).

—— 'Legacies of Matriliny: The Place of Women and the "Kerala Model"' (2004) 77 *Pacific Affairs* 647.

Joshi, R and Liddle, J, Daughters of Independence – Gender, Caste and Class in India (New Delhi, Kali for Women Press, 1986).

Kodoth, P and Eapen, M, 'Looking beyond Gender Parity: Gender Inequities of some Dimensions of Well-Being in Kerala' (2005) 40 *Economic and Political Weekly* 3278.

MacIntyre, A, *After Virtue: A Study in Moral Theory* (Indiana, University of Notre Dame Press, 1981).

Mattison, SM, Shenk, MK, Thompson, ME, Mulder, MB, and Fortunato, L 'The Evolution of Female-Biased Kinship in Humans and other Mammals.' (2019) 374 *Philosophical Transactions of the Royal Society B.*

Mayadevi, M, 'Women and Marriage in Marumakkathayam' (2015) 4 *International Research Journal of Social Sciences* 32.

Mencher, JP, 'Changing Familial Roles among South Malabar Nayars' in MF Nimkoff (ed), *Comparative Family Systems* (Boston, Houghton Mifflin, 1965).

Menon, SA, *Social and Cultural History of Kerala* (New York, Sterling Publishers Pvt Ltd, 1979).

Murdock, GP, *Ethnographic Atlas* (Pittsburg, University of Pittsburg Press, 1967).

Murickan, J, 'Women in Kerala: Changing Socio-Economic Status and Self-Image' in A De Souza (ed), *Women in Contemporary India* (New Delhi, Manohar Book Service, 1975).

Nair, PT, 'Malayalam Women: Their Past and Present' (1969) 10 *Folklore* 157.

Nambiar, K and Kumar, AAP (2006) *Hand Book on Joint Hindu Family System (Abolition) Act* (Ernakulam, Swamy Law House, 2006).

Parayil, G, *Kerala: The Development Experience: Reflections on Sustainability and Replicability* (London, Zed Books, 2000).

Pillai, TKV, *The Travancore State Manual*, Vol 4 (Ernakulam, Government Press, 1940).

Puthenkalam, SJ, *Marriage and Family in Kerala* (Calgary, University of Calgary, 1977).

Rahman, L and Rao, V, 'The Determinants of Gender Equity in India: Examining Dyson and Moore's Thesis with New Data' (2004) 30 *Population and Development Review*, 239.

Rao, MSA (1957) *Social Change in Malabar* (Mumbai, Popular Book Depot, 1957).

Saradamoni, K, 'Women's Status in Changing Agrarian Relations: A Kerala Experience' (1982) 17 *Economic and Political Weekly* 155.

Schlegel, A, *Male Dominance and Female Autonomy: Domestic Authority in Matrilineal Societies* (Yale, Human Relations Area Press, 1972).
Schneider, DM, 'The Distinctive Features of Matrilineal Descent Group' in DM Schneider and K Gough (eds), *Matrilineal Kinship* (Berkeley, University of California Press, 1961).
Sen, A, 'Gender and Cooperative Conflicts' in I Tinker (ed), *Persistent Inequalities: Women and World Development* (Oxford, Oxford University Press, 1990).
—— *The Idea of Justice* (Cambridge MA, Harvard University Press, 2009).
Turner, V, *From Ritual to Theatre: The Human Seriousness of Play* (Performing Arts Journal Publications, MIT Press, 1982).
Unny, G, Kinship Systems in South and South-East Asia (New Delhi, Vikas Publishing House, 1994).
Zachariah, KC, Mathew, ET, and Rajan, I, *Dynamics of Migration in Kerala: Dimensions, Differentials and Consequences* (London, Longman, 2003).

15

Egalitarianism or Just a Need for Revenues? Debates on Inheritance Taxation in Scandinavia

MARTIN DACKLING

> Our new Constitution is now established, and has an appearance that promises permanency; but in this world nothing can be said to be certain, except death and taxes.
>
> Benjamin Franklin, 1789

I. Introduction

Few things are as universal as inheritance. Everyone who dies leaves something behind. If the deceased owned any kind of property, it must be allocated to someone else. But who has the right to that property? The answer to that question varies through the ages and between societies. Property can be held together over generations; for example, if just one heir in each generation is entitled to take over the estate. But property can also be divided evenly, so that all heirs receive an equal share of the estate. A third possibility is to define the right of a testator to dispose of his or her property by will, with or without restrictions with respect to direct heirs. The ways in which property has historically been passed on through generations are many and varied. However, inheritance is not only a matter of family ties and making wills. Apart from family members and testamentary heirs, shares of inherited property have also been allocated to the state through taxation of inherited wealth. Thus, the question of how to divide and redistribute property – how to regulate wealth transmission – has been a question decided by governments.

Over time, the features of inheritance taxation have varied greatly, and governments have taxed inheritance in different ways. From a European perspective, the size of the share allocated to the state was quite low until the last two centuries. A sample of 19 European countries, presented by Kenneth Scheve and David

Stasavage, indicates that the highest rate in 1880 was 3.25 per cent, applied in the UK. In the first decades of the twentieth century a new era of progressive inheritance taxation was launched, and tax rates were raised in a way 'that would have seemed like outright expropriation just a few years prior'.[1] The tax rate reached its peak just after 1950, with an average maximum rate of just over 40 per cent; up to 80 per cent in some countries. The second part of the century instead saw decreasing rates all over Europe.[2] However, just as rates started to go down, there are indications that inherited wealth began to grow in importance. A key contention of Thomas Piketty's work is that inherited wealth has started to make a massive comeback. The high levels of inheritance flows make it more or less impossible for those who do not inherit to catch up with those who do.[3] From this perspective, it is even more surprising that some countries have gone so far as to abolish inheritance taxation completely. Two possibly surprising examples are Norway and Sweden. The Scandinavian countries (Sweden, Norway, and Denmark) – or, in a broader meaning, the Nordic countries (including Finland and Iceland) – have often been depicted as a distinct model of welfare states: a 'third way' between capitalism and socialism, characterised by a high degree of economic egalitarianism shaped by redistributive policy.[4] Sweden, in particular, has been viewed as 'a natural habitat for egalitarian ideals' with redistributive inheritance taxation as a natural element.[5] It has been commonplace to see this 'Scandinavian egalitarianism' as the result of a long historical trajectory. However, as Erik Bengtsson has recently argued, using Sweden as an example, this view misconstrues historical development. In fact, Sweden between 1850 and 1920 was one of the most unequal countries in Western Europe, in terms of, for example, wealth distribution and suffrage, and Bengtsson concludes that there is definitely 'no unbroken continuity of egalitarianism'.[6]

These opposite views of Sweden and Scandinavia – as significantly unequal or a home for egalitarianism – calls for further studies. Since the importance of inherited wealth was conceived and dealt with all over Europe from the late nineteenth century, it is especially interesting to analyse how Scandinavian countries handled the regulation of inheritance. How was inherited wealth regarded and regulated? Are traces of a 'Scandinavian egalitarianism' detectable in the discussion about inheritance tax? In this chapter I will examine the political debate on inheritance taxation in Sweden, Norway, and Denmark from the last decades of the nineteenth century to the time of the highest and most progressive rates in the early 1950s.

[1] Scheve and Stasavage (2016) 100–01.
[2] Scheve and Stasavage (2016) 101, 112.
[3] Piketty (2014).
[4] Esping-Andersen (1990); Kautto (2010).
[5] Halliday (2018) 2–3.
[6] Bengtsson (2019) 123–24.

II. Inheritance Taxation in Scandinavia: An Overview

The taxation of inheritance has a long history, much longer than, for example, comprehensive income taxation. An oft-mentioned example is Caesar Augustus' establishment of a tax of five per cent on inheritance in AD 6, aiming to fund soldiers' salaries.[7] There are early versions of inheritance taxation also in Scandinavian countries. During the Middle Ages, Danish law, for example, posed certain dues to the Crown on inheritance passed on to heirs abroad. In general terms the regulation of inheritance taxation was formalised from the seventeenth century onward through a flat stamp tax. The tax rate was very low – less than one per cent of the inherited wealth – and close relatives were entirely exempted from tax duty.[8]

At the turn of the nineteenth century, tax regulation was reformed in all three countries and the inheritance tax became progressive in two ways; the tax rate depended on both the size of the inherited wealth and the closeness of family relations. Close relatives inheriting small shares paid less (or nothing), while distant relatives with large inheritance and transfers by will between unrelated persons were subject to higher tax rates. Over time there was a gradual increase in tax level, just as in many European countries during that time. Even if the elevation of the tax rates continued over several decades, there was a clear boost in the 1930s, which initiated an era with very high tax rates. This period, with top rates up to 60 per cent, lasted until the 1980s. The last decades have been characterised by slowly decreasing tax rates. In the beginning of the 2000s, the inheritance tax was finally abolished in Sweden (2004) and Norway (2014), while Denmark still has a form of taxation of inherited wealth today (*boafgift*).[9] This follows a general European pattern; the tax has recently been abolished in several European countries – eg Portugal (2004), Austria (2008), and the Czech Republic (2013) – and are negligible for the total tax revenues in the remaining.[10]

The Scandinavian trajectory described above shares similarities with the development of inheritance taxation in other European countries, but how do the rates correspond? Scheve and Stasavage show that a few decades into the twentieth century, Scandinavian countries had tax levels on par with the rest of Europe.[11] In the latter part of the century, the inheritance taxation was on a level with the European average or even higher. Sweden, for example, had a marginal inheritance tax rate of 60 per cent in both 1950 and 1975, which was certainly lower than the UK (at 80 per cent) but higher than most other European countries.[12] However, a few centuries earlier the situation was quite different. Around 1900,

[7] Scheve and Stasavage (2016) 93.

[8] Eberstein (1956) 1–3; Tank (1973) 15–16; Munkholm Povlsen and Krog Thomsen (1982). See also Dübeck (1999).

[9] Du Rietz, Henrekson and Waldenström (2015); Arveafgiftsudvalget (2000) 20–24; Dübeck (1999).

[10] Drometer et al (2018) 48–51.

[11] Scheve and Stasavage (2012) 12–13.

[12] Scheve and Stasavage (2016) 107–12.

when the inheritance tax was reformed in Scandinavia, the Norwegian Parliament conducted a survey of inheritance tax rates in different European countries. From a comparison of 11 states, it showed that Sweden, Norway, and Denmark had among the lowest rates.[13]

III. Explaining Inheritance Taxation

The position of inheritance tax in a Scandinavian context thus seems to change over time: from comparably low to distinctively high. This reversal leads to questions about how changes in inheritance taxation have been legitimised. Scheve and Stasavage state that research on this subject has been neglected: there are just a few studies that have focused on why some governments have chosen to introduce a high progressive tax on inheritance and others have not.[14] However, some relationships have been discussed. One relates to the wealth inequality in society and poses a connection between increased tax rates and high wealth inequality.[15] Another explanation has been the case of the introduction of universal suffrage: when large masses with little or no wealth were given the right to vote, it appeared logical to establish a high tax on property, especially inherited property.[16] Scheve and Stasavage instead put forward inheritance tax as an instrument for mass mobilisation in relation to World War I and World War II, based both on an economic need and ideological motives about the distribution of financial burdens in war time.[17] In their analysis, they find significantly stronger support for their mass mobilisation thesis than for their thesis on suffrage. Despite this, there are complicating factors. The Scandinavian countries did not take any great part in the World Wars – Sweden was non-aligned in both – but still they had a high tax rate. As Scheve and Stasavage themselves note in relation to Sweden, it is clear that 'war mobilisation was not the only way to progressive taxation in modern states'.[18] In an analysis of the inheritance tax in Sweden, Magnus Henrekson and Daniel Waldenström have placed the emphasis on ideological motives, especially from the 1930s onwards. In particular, social democracy is seen as driving a redistribution policy with high taxes on large fortunes.[19]

One conclusion of the above accounts is that tax on inheritance could be legitimised in different ways. However, the described analyses are primarily based on data on tax scales and revenues. Undeniably, these are sources that provide important information, but they do not offer further information about *how* the political debate was conducted and which value conflicts were at stake. The importance

[13] Stortingsforhandlinger (1900/1901); Dokument 58.
[14] Scheve and Stasavage (2012) 1.
[15] Scheve and Stasavage (2016) 103–08.
[16] *cf* Acemoglu and Robinson (2006).
[17] Scheve and Stasavage (2012) 2–11.
[18] Scheve and Stasavage (2012) 18.
[19] Henrekson and Waldenström (2016) 1251–52.

of Scandinavian egalitarianism is thus hard to deduce from tax schemes alone. The transition from low to high inheritance taxation in Scandinavia took place through successive parliamentary decisions, which makes it possible to analyse how the development was politically justified. In a study of political debate in France, Germany, and the US during the nineteenth and twentieth centuries, Jens Beckert has investigated how a particular inheritance tax discourse developed. He shows how the discourse in the investigated countries had common features, but also reveals clear differences and arguments that were specific to each country. In the US, inheritance tax has been mainly discussed as a way to achieve equal opportunities for all and prevent the concentration of capital across generational boundaries.[20] In Germany, inheritance tax has been seen as a way to finance the state's commitments, but at the same time is seen as a threat to family property.[21] The debates illustrate several value conflicts that are often related to the transfer of inheritance: family property is pitted against meritocratic ideals, and freedom to dispose of property is pitted against a social responsibility for all citizens, as is diligence and frugality against economic inequality.[22]

Based on his research, Beckert introduced a model with four value principles used to justify inheritance taxation.[23] The *family principle* assumes that property primarily belongs to the family; inheritance tax is therefore seen as an intrusion into family affairs. The *equality of opportunity principle* instead focuses on strongly redistributive taxation to promote equal opportunities for everyone. The intention is to create similar conditions for everyone within the same generation. Closely related to this is *the principle of social justice*. This also aims at redistribution, but not with the goal of giving everyone the same conditions, but instead through state welfare to create security for those who need it. Finally, the *community principle*, assumes that neither heirs nor the state should dispose of the estate, instead the testator himself should distribute the funds for the public good (for example through foundations or wills). Analytically, egalitarianism can be associated with both equality of opportunity and the social justice principle; Beckert sees them as closely tied to each other but claims that the first one is input-oriented (equal start conditions) while the principle of social justice is output-oriented (thereby correcting the unequal success one has in life).

Beckert's model will provide an analytical instrument in the following examination of the political debate surrounding inheritance tax in Sweden, Norway, and Denmark. The analysis stretches from around 1880 up until the 1950s, from the modernisation and introduction of progressive inheritance taxation to the years with the highest tax rates. This period corresponds well with the problem discussed: if egalitarianism played any great part in the formation of inheritance taxation in Scandinavia, it seems reasonable to find supporting evidence during

[20] See also Graetz and Shapiro (2005).
[21] Beckert (2007); Beckert (2008a) 167–274.
[22] *cf* Halliday (2018) 1–73.
[23] Beckert (2008b).

these years. For each impact, inheritance tax discourse is examined through an analysis of the parliamentary material: bills, propositions, committee reports, and debate. Up to 1905, Norway was in a personal union with Sweden, but had a separate parliament with supremacy in, for example, issues of taxation. Even if Scandinavia is the starting point, the intention is not to consider the countries as a unit; an important question is rather to discover what differences exist between the countries. As Jürgen Kocka points out, a comparative perspective involves a method of exposing themes and facts that are otherwise unnoticed by drawing attention to both similarities and differences.[24] Even if the chronology of inheritance taxation was the same in all three countries, it is therefore of interest to find out whether the political debate looked the same.[25]

IV. The Introduction of Double Progression

A flat tax on inheritance existed in all three countries at the end of the nineteenth century, but there were sharp differences in how the tax was framed. In Sweden, it was essentially an estate tax, collected as a fee paid as the estate was probated. The tax level was modest: half a per cent of the estate and an additional tenth of a per cent if inheritance did not go to direct heirs.[26] Danish inheritance taxation was sharper, both in terms of tax rate and in terms of progressivity based on kin relations. Heirs were arranged into three classes based on their relationship to the deceased. The tax rate was one per cent for the first inheritance class (direct heirs) and up to seven per cent for distant relatives and non-relatives in the third inheritance class.[27] In Norway, the tax was as high as four per cent, but one's closest relatives (direct heirs, parents, and spouses) were completely exempt.[28] From the end of the nineteenth century, inheritance taxation was reformed in all three countries by the introduction of double progression and slightly increased fees (Sweden in 1894, Norway in 1901, and Denmark in 1907–08).

At a basic level, the reformation of inheritance taxation in Scandinavian countries was built on the same principle: they were essentially aimed at increasing revenue. However, the context differed between Denmark and Sweden on the one hand, and Norway on the other. In the former the question was linked to reforms of the customs duties. It aimed, among other things, to lower taxation on consumer goods. To finance these reforms, new sources of income were required. The sharpened inheritance taxation was, as Finance Minister Vilhelm Lassen

[24] Kocka (1996) 197–99.

[25] For a similar approach, see Bradley (1998).

[26] Eberstein (1956) 5.

[27] Munkholm Povlsen and Krog Thomsen (1982) 71–72.

[28] Tank (1973) 15–16; Arveafvigtsudvaltage (2000) 20–21.

admitted in the Danish Parliament, a 'compensation law'.[29] In practice, the rate was made progressive within all three inheritance classes and the percentage rate was substantially increased. The highest rate was set to six per cent in the first inheritance class and 15 per cent in the third. Even in Sweden, legal changes were partly linked to customs issues, but even more to the reform of the Swedish national defence. Traditionally, defence expenses had been related to land rent, meaning that it was basically freeholding farmers that contributed to the armed forces. As the farmers' proportion of the population decreased considerably in the 1900s, a prolonged debate about the economic and moral responsibilities of financing national defence took place in Parliament. A modernisation of defence and the establishment of a conscript army was considered a priority. However, since the farmers' representatives dominated Parliament, their political support was needed, and they demanded an abolition of the old land rent.[30] An expanded inheritance tax thus became an important piece of the puzzle to solve the financing of the national defence forces. Just as in Denmark, increased inheritance taxation took place to compensate for the loss of previous revenues. In Norway, in contrast, inheritance taxation was not linked to any major economic reform. When tax rates were increased, a general need for the state to increase its revenues was in the foreground.

The difference between the countries repeats itself in the structure of the debate. In Sweden and Denmark there was general political support for modernising and expanding inheritance taxation. The parliamentary discussions contain very little opposition against the principles of inheritance taxation, rather, it was emphasised that the tax was 'very appropriate and fair' and that 'inheritance in general was a tax basis that could bear a greater burden'.[31] In Sweden, the political agreement was almost total, while in Denmark there were advocates for both higher and lower progressivity. The principal debate concerned the level of taxation. It was stated that 'an inheritance tax should not be of such a size that it can be feared to decrease people's wish and desire to practice thrift', as this was seen as necessary for a desirable development of society.[32] This disagreement was manifested in the fact that the two chambers of the Danish Parliament disagreed on how strongly direct heirs should be taxed: the lower chamber voted for a progression up to six per cent, while the upper stayed at three per cent, which ultimately became the decision. Thereby, the effects of the reform were mitigated for large fortunes. This was met by strong criticism from liberal members of parliament, who argued that the Conservatives had endeavoured to create 'protection for millionaires'.[33]

[29] Rigsdagstidende (1906/07): FT, 4702. The main sources for this chapter are minutes from the parliamentary debates (covering the period 1880–1950) for Sweden (Riksdagens protokoll), Denmark (Rigsdagstidende), and Norway (Stortingsforhandlinger). All translations are by the author.

[30] Stråth (2012) 166–69.

[31] Riksdagens protokoll (1894): AK nr 38: 18, 25, 29, 35; Rigsdagstidende (1906/07): FT, 56, 4670, 4676.

[32] Rigsdagstidende (1907/08): LT, 1988.

[33] Rigsdagstidende (1907/08): FT, 8449.

Although not legitimised as a compensation for other reforms, the Norwegian debate was much sharper. The need to increase tax revenues was repeatedly debated, but the Parliament opposed taxing inheritance in general and direct heirs in particular[34] In 1901, a proposal to introduce a tax on direct heirs, ranging from one to four per cent, generated an extensive debate and ended with a vote where nearly 40 per cent of the members of the Parliament voted against. The proponents emphasised – as had been the case in Denmark and Sweden – that this was a tax characterised by fairness: it only hit once, and it was demanded at a time when the recipient was in a significantly improved economic position. In addition, it was pointed out that inheritance no longer had the same importance for heirs' living conditions. While inheritance in former times had gone to younger children in need of support, modern heirs were depicted as adults that already had established an independent position.[35] Whereas inheritance tax in the Danish and Swedish debates was highlighted as a very appropriate and fair tax, the Norwegian debate contained repeated statements about how the tax was contrary to thrift and counteracted the natural desire to improve one's position; of all thinkable taxes, it was 'the very last one that should be used'.[36]

The opposition against inheritance tax for direct heirs in Norway was essentially based on two arguments: the tax's effects on the agricultural industry, and its consequences for the accumulation of capital. In the Norwegian debate, property was mainly conceived of as farmland. The proposal was therefore considered extremely damaging to the farming population, who were also said to lack the capital needed to pay the tax. It was predicted that more people would try to circumvent the tax by prematurely handing over the farm in exchange for retirement contracts, ensuring them care and support from the new owner. Such transactions were said to place heavy burdens on the younger generation, and they were predicted also to occur in industry.[37] These objections were partly linked to different kinds of property. Land and other immovable property were difficult to hide and were therefore more easily affected by taxes, while movable property and capital could be disposed of in such a way that it was withheld from taxation.[38] The argument about the risk of weak capital accumulation put particular focus on Norway's economic structure. Of course, it was said, the tax could work in financially strong countries – like England and France – where fortunes were many and large, but in countries 'that like Norway are poor in capital' all obstacles for sound wealth accumulation should be avoided.[39] This self-image of a country lacking capital was the single argument that was cited the most times in Parliament; the state should not limit the accumulation of capital; on the contrary, attempts to 'accumulate capital should be rewarded'.[40]

[34] For example, Stortingsforhandlinger (1866): Prop S 13; Stortingsforhandlinger (1880): Prop X.
[35] Stortingsforhandlinger (1901/02): Prop 7, 4.
[36] Stortingsforhandlinger (1901/02): Stortingstidende 1589.
[37] Stortingsforhandlinger (1901/02): Stortingstidende, 1585, 1590, and Indst S XXXB.
[38] Stortingsforhandlinger (1901/02): Stortingstidende, 1620.
[39] Stortingsforhandlinger (1909): Indst S XXX.
[40] Stortingsforhandlinger (1901/02): Stortingstidende, 1611.

The Norwegian opposition against inheritance tax bore close resemblance to other debates involving family property. When, for example, the Norwegian Parliament had debated the practice of *odelsrett*, a kind of redemption right that gave family members a right to reclaim land that had been sold outside the family, similar arguments were central.[41] Basically, this stance was founded on what Beckert calls 'the family principle'. Ownership was not solely an individual matter and the same could be said about inheritance tax; it was a fee on 'fortunes created by the toil and moil of ancestors'.[42] This argument could also be connected to the future, as ownership could be linked to the next generation. Children, particularly those on farms, were not only future heirs; their work multiplied the family capital. Taxation therefore meant that the state seized the fruit of *their* work, as well.[43]

Even if lack of capital was sometimes put forward as an argument in Denmark and Sweden, it was of much lesser importance compared to the Norwegian debate.[44] Rather, it was stressed how 'millionaires now are formed much easier than in the old days'.[45] In a similar way, it was emphasised how inheritance was 'created with help of the institutions of society and under the protection of society', which reinforced that society therefore also had the expectation to receive a share of the accumulated capital.[46] The family principle did not have a prominent place in either the Danish or Swedish discourse, and arguments based on that principle were depicted as outdated. An important motive for increased taxation was related to the changing social conditions; in the *past*, it was said, capital and wealth were more a matter for families and individuals, while now 'society, more than in the old days, becomes involved in the creation of great fortunes'.[47] This argument was also occasionally mentioned in the Norwegian debate.[48]

The state's right to inheritance and the need for increased revenue were thus prominent themes in all three countries. However, it is not easy to link the debate to Beckert's principles. As mentioned, the family principle was actualised only in Norway and the community principle played no role at all. But arguments about the state's right to, or demand for, inheritance were not explicitly supported by arguments about equal opportunities or social justice. Altogether, the debates seldom focused on how the funds should be used; inheritance tax was highlighted as a reasonable and possible source of revenue, rather than a redistributive tool. Admittedly, the introduction of a progressive scale – which generally meant that larger amounts of capital were taxed more heavily while small inheritance lots were exempt from tax – could, on paper, be linked to the principle of meritocracy.

[41] *cf* Dackling (2020a) 11–15.
[42] Stortingsforhandlinger (1901/02): Stortingstidende, 1608.
[43] Stortingsforhandlinger (1901/02): Stortingstidende, 1613.
[44] Riksdagens protokoll (1892): Bevillingsutskottets report 19, 10; Rigsdagstidende (1907/08): LT, 1986.
[45] Rigsdagstidende (1906/07): FT, 4702, and 1907/08, 8381.
[46] Rigsdagstidende (1907/08): LT, 1993; Riksdagens protokoll (1894): FK 29, 17.
[47] Rigsdagstidende (1906/07): FT, 4680.
[48] Stortingsforhandlinger (1909): Stortingstidende, 2093–94.

After all, by taking a fraction of the estates of the deceased, governments put limits on the concentration of wealth. In the Norwegian debate, there were speakers that argued this way, but they were in fact *opponents* to the tax, accusing it of 'equalising wealth conditions'. Interestingly, the instigators of an increased tax rate even denied that this was the purpose. The intention was to use progression only to 'adjust the burden to the small conditions of the country'; certainly not to create economic equality.[49]

Ideals about redistribution and economic equality thus did not play any significant role in the debates at the turn of the century. However, that does not mean that they were completely absent. There were a few occasions when such thoughts and arguments were mentioned. In Sweden, the equalisation argument had a prelude in a private bill from the writer Richard Gustafsson, who was a member of the lower chamber of Parliament in the 1880s. Gustafsson argued explicitly from a redistribution ideal, advocated considerable higher progression, and emphasised the advantages of inheritance taxation. Inheritance was not a result of saved salaries, entrepreneurial spirit or diligence, and he believed that a stronger inheritance taxation would prevent wealth accumulation and enable 'the desirable aim: a more even distribution of wealth'.[50] However, such a meritocratic rationale won almost no support in Parliament at that time; the proposals were rejected on the grounds that revenues did not need to be strengthened.

V. From Low to High Rates

After the inheritance tax adopted a similar structure in all three countries around the turn of the century, successive increases in the tax rate followed during the subsequent decades. The highest tax level for the first inheritance class (direct heirs) was raised; for example, in Sweden in 1909 (four per cent) and 1915 (4.5 per cent), while the rates were revised in Denmark in 1915 (five per cent) and 1918 (eight per cent), and in Norway in 1909 (five per cent) and 1915 (eight per cent).[51] However, before the end of World War I, the increases were modest in relation to the greatly increased rates that occurred during the 1920s and 1930s. Sweden more than quadrupled the highest rate in 1933, Denmark raised its rate to 13 per cent in 1922, and in 1933 significantly increased the levels for all but the first inheritance class, while Norway reached 30 per cent by 1924 and went on to strengthen the progression by adjusting the thresholds between different rates. For large fortunes, Norway thus went from zero to a 30 per cent tax rate in the first inheritance class in less than a generation. However, the increase for more distant heirs was sharpened to an even greater extent. After 1934, the maximum rate in the highest inheritance

[49] Stortingsforhandlinger (1901/02): Stortingstidende, 1595, 1606.

[50] Riksdagens protokoll (1886): AK bills No 10, 25.

[51] Du Rietz, Henrekson and Waldenström (2015); Rigsdagsårsbok (1914/15) and (1918/19); Tank (1973) 15–16.

class in Sweden was 35 per cent, in Denmark 45 per cent, and in Norway as much as 60 per cent. The progression was also of different intensities. The Swedish rate rose faster and was constantly above the Danish scale. The Norwegian rate closely followed the Danish for smaller estates but increased rapidly for larger capitals. An inheritance of SEK 50,000 was taxed, for example, at 3.3 per cent in Denmark, four per cent in Norway, and 4.8 per cent in Sweden. For shares up to a million, the figures were around nine per cent in Denmark, 17 per cent in Sweden, and 25 per cent in Norway.[52]

The successive increase in tax rates was consistently motivated by the increased financial need of the state. It is clear that, for example, the economic crisis of the 1930s – when unemployment in all three countries quickly rose to between 24 and 32 per cent and government expenditures followed the same pattern – was a triggering factor for the sharp increases during 1933–34.[53] The vulnerable economic situation was probably the reason why the increases were carried out under considerable political agreement. In Denmark, the higher tax level was in fact decided in a kind of consensus. It was generally stated that 'the finances of the state require this increase', especially based on the economic consequences of the crisis in the 1930s.[54] Even principled opponents such as Emil Piper, leader of the Conservatives in the Danish upper house, stated that 'there is indeed the hard necessity that we need to get the state treasury more revenue' and believed that inheritance tax was at least preferable to wealth tax.[55] Part of this political agreement probably depended on the fact that the increase only fell upon the higher inheritance classes: while the tax for all others increased by 50 per cent, the tax rate for direct heirs was left untouched. There was no principled debate on the matter in Parliament, but the fact that inheritance to direct heirs was not affected can be indirectly linked to the family principle. If the proposal had meant a general increase for everyone, even direct heirs, it would probably have been much more controversial.

In Sweden, the sharp increase was a kind of compromise. The Social Democrats had formed a government in 1932 and the following year proposed the introduction of an estate tax alongside ordinary inheritance taxation. The proposal was justified by a need to cover costs for a rapid expansion of public works in the wake of the crisis.[56] The idea was to tax inheritance twice: first through a tax on the entire estate of the deceased, then through the usual inheritance tax on each heir's share. Basically, these taxations had different purposes and motivations: the latter focused on the heir's strengthened financial position, while the estate tax was seen as a fee caused by accumulation of wealth: it was a wealth tax recovered 'only after the owner of the wealth has died'.[57] However, the proposal for an estate tax was not

[52] Stortingsforhandlinger (1934): Budg-innst S no 150, 2.
[53] *cf* Gustafsson (1997) 225.
[54] Rigsdagstidende (1921/22): FT, 6048; 1932/33: FT, 5737–38.
[55] Rigsdagstidende (1921/22): LT, 1419.
[56] Riksdagens protokoll (1933): Prop no 34, 12.
[57] Riksdagens protokoll (1933): Prop no 34, 25.

approved by the Swedish Parliament. The refusal was economically motivated; it turned out that public finances did not require such a strong increase in revenues as had been feared.[58] Instead, inheritance tax rates were raised, with peak levels of 20 per cent in the first inheritance class and 35 per cent in the last. This solution seems to have been accepted by all members of parliament; the decision passed through both chambers without any debate. When a light version of the estate tax was introduced later in 1948, the same pattern was repeated, although there were anxious voices about how the tax would affect the farming population.[59]

It can be noted that not even the proposals for an estate tax were justified from a redistribution perspective. In the 1932 bill, the finance minister, Ernst Wigforss, mentioned in passing that the proposal *could* be motivated in this way, but contented himself with advocating for it from aspects on which 'everyone should be able to agree'; that is, the financial needs of the state.[60] However, there is no doubt that the Social Democrats in general, and Wigforss in particular, saw estate tax as an instrument of economic equalisation. A few years earlier, in 1928, Wigforss had been the main author of a private bill demanding a strongly progressive taxation of inheritance in order to achieve economic equality. Wigforss then argued, clearly based on the social justice principle, that an estate tax that ultimately expropriated larger fortunes was the only reasonable solution for future generations.[61]

The idea of redistribution was thus expressed in public political discussions at the end of the 1920s, but it was not used as argument in later proposals. In the Danish debate, redistribution arguments were completely missing. In Norway, however, arguments and statements about the use of inheritance tax for redistributive purposes appeared early. A peculiarity of the Norwegian debate was that rates for different classes of inheritance were decided annually, which meant that the inheritance tax was almost continuously under debate. It becomes clear that representatives of the Norwegian Labour Party were already arguing for significantly higher tax rates by the end of the 1910s. In the 1919 debate, the Government proposed a sharp tax increase, from eight to 20 per cent for direct heirs, but the Labour Party countered with a proposal demanding an increase to 40 per cent. That the Labour Party saw inheritance tax as a central instrument is apparent in these debates, and the proposal was justified both by arguments about how the state as a co-creator of capital should have the right to shares of inherited wealth, and statements that large inheritances made heirs idle and of no use to society.[62] Over time, the redistribution argument was gradually strengthened. In the 1925 debate, the inheritance tax was praised 'since it is an excellent instrument to even out old economic injustice'.[63] A further step was taken in 1931/32, when representatives of

[58] Riksdagens protokoll (1933): Special committee's report no 23, 36–37.
[59] Riksdagens protokoll (1948): AK nr 25, 39–40.
[60] Riksdagens protokoll (1933): Prop. no. 34, 25.
[61] Wigforss (1928).
[62] Stortingsforhandlinger (1919): Indst S L, 10.
[63] Stortingsforhandlinger (1925): Innst S no 108, 2.

the Labour Party suggested that the burden of inheritance tax should consider the heir's total wealth, not only the inherited wealth. Thus, the received inheritance should be added to the heir's private capital and the inheritance tax calculated based on this accumulated sum.[64] In a similar way, the debate highlighted the importance of society arranging itself 'so that the most possible equal conditions are given when it comes to life conditions and life opportunities'.[65] Christopher Hornsrud, the Labour Party's first prime minister in 1928, emphasised the importance of placing the heaviest taxes on those with the greatest wealth, 'because the start of life should be as even as possible for everyone'.[66] Taxing wealth and inheritance was not, Hornsrud stated, a question of reducing national wealth. Instead, it aimed to create 'a different distribution of national wealth'.[67] After World War II, when the Labour Party came into power, an additional inheritance tax for wealthy heirs was approved by Parliament.[68]

While the Norwegian debate shows the most obvious signs of the principle of equal opportunities and the need for a redistributive tax, it was also characterised by very sharp contradictions. While representatives from the Labour Party emphasised inheritance tax as 'the fairest tax we have', members from the Conservative and Farmers' parties considered it irrational and a form of 'serious wealth confiscation'.[69] In the debate, the family principle was again actualised: inheritance was a 'co-work', a collaboration between older and younger family members, and it was emphasised as essential that families were be able to preserve 'the wealth that they have created'.[70] Similarly, the argument about the importance of landed property resonated. The proposals from the Labour Party were criticised because they seemed to view inheritance as 'a dollar amount from a rich uncle in America', while in reality it was mainly transfers to direct heirs and often in the form of capital tied up in land and forest.[71] It can be stated, however, that the references to national conditions or national wealth were no longer cited as arguments in any of the three countries.

VI. Patterns, Differences and Value Conflicts

The debates on inheritance taxation in Scandinavian countries shows that inherited wealth could be problematic. The level of conflict varied, however, and was most clearly marked in Norway. In Norway, tax for direct heirs was introduced late and under great opposition, rates and progression have been debated repeatedly,

[64] Stortingsforhandlinger (1931): Budg-innst. S no 143, 1–4.
[65] Stortingsforhandlinger (1934): Stortingstidende, 1342.
[66] Stortingsforhandlinger (1934): Stortingstidende, 1349.
[67] Stortingsforhandlinger (1936): Stortingstidende, 1282.
[68] Stortingsforhandlinger (1947): Ot Prp 57.
[69] Stortingsforhandlinger (1934): Stortingstidende, 1343–44, 1347.
[70] Stortingsforhandlinger (1934): Stortingstidende, 1344, 1346–47, and (1936): Stortingstidende, 1278.
[71] Stortingsforhandlinger (1933): Stortingstidende, 1792.

and the exchange of opinions has been characterised by strong principled statements both for stronger taxation and against inheritance taxation, as such. In Sweden and Denmark, the same contradictions do not appear at all; the development from low to high inheritance taxation seems almost to have been taken under political consensus. Thus, in practice, two questions are actualised: how should the lack of controversy in the Swedish and Danish cases be explained; and why does the Norwegian debate stand out?

To answer these questions, there is reason to return to Beckert's four principles. That the Norwegian inheritance tax discourse involved sharper contradictions can be explained by the fact that two of Beckert's justification arguments – the family principle and the equal opportunity principle – appeared clearly in the political debates; in fact, the development can even be seen as a struggle between them. Throughout the period studied, there was an articulated political opposition to the inheritance tax, per se, of a kind not found in Sweden or Denmark. The idea that property belonged to the family and its members – both past and future – was represented during the entire period under study. During the 1920s, the principle of equal opportunities also gained in impact. The representatives of the Labour Party explicitly argued for equalisation as a way of promoting everyone's equal starting point in life. It should be emphasised that redistribution aimed at creating equal material *starting* position – to 'equalise the living conditions at the beginning of people's life'.[72] Up to 1950, the Norwegian Labour Party did not promote the output-oriented social justice principle, that is, an ideal to correct unequal structures later in life. The fact that Norwegian taxation was also designed with a significantly stronger progression confirms the importance of the meritocracy principle in a Norwegian context.

The Norwegian debate certainly involved tensions between different values. However, the main motives behind the successive tax increases in all three Scandinavian countries was the state's increased need for revenues. Arguments related to, for example, military rearmament and mass mobilisation, which appeared as explanatory grounds in international research, did not appear in the debates. The need to modernise defence was certainly the triggering factor in Sweden in 1894, but the revenues from inheritance tax played just a minor role in the financing. However, the fact that inheritance tax was justified with reference to the state's need for revenue and that society as a guarantor or co-creator of capital should be entitled to a share of inherited property does not, strictly speaking, correspond to any of Beckert's principles. Tax revenue was not related to a special state expenditure or specific task of the state, such as financial support for the vulnerable. With a growing welfare state, this may of course have been the result in practice, but it is important to note that this relationship was not articulated in political debates, at least not in Sweden or Denmark. Beckert's model, which primarily aims to illustrate differences between the US and Germany, thus fails to

[72] Stortingsforhandlinger (1920): Stortingstidende, 1310.

capture the Scandinavian discourse where inheritance tax was primarily justified as an adaptable alternative to adjust the state budget. For such a purpose, it is more reasonable to think of a fifth principle which, in short, states that the state has the right to adjust inheritance tax level if necessary, at least to a 'normal European' level. This *treasury principle* can be said to have been the dominant one in all three countries. Since it does not say anything explicit about the use of the funds, no sharp value contradictions were actualised; no one argued against growing the state budget.

VII. Conclusion

The egalitarian and redistributive Scandinavian welfare state is mainly dated to the post-war period, but the results of this survey show that the ideal of redistribution cannot be traced that far back in time. The strengthened position of Social Democracy changed the picture, but there is no clear correlation between high inheritance tax and Social Democracy.[73] In Norway, the Labour Party only came to power in 1935, when rates were already quite high. The successive increases up to 1933 were thus enforced by *other* governments. In Denmark, the opposite situation prevailed: the Social Democrats took power as early as the 1920s, but inheritance taxation nevertheless remained lower than the rates in either Sweden or Norway. It is also notable that the Swedish Social Democrats called for stronger inheritance taxation based on a redistribution perspective in 1928, but abstained from using that type of argumentation when they raised the tax in 1933. It is of course conceivable that the political consensus was due to a fear of more radical reforms, but the lack of opposition in that case was also due to the fact that reforms were not always pushed or justified as sharply.

It is apparent that the practice of taxing inherited wealth varied greatly during the twentieth century. Even if the need for revenues was the most prominent argument used up to 1950, it is at the same time obvious that inheritance taxation did not result in huge contributions to state's finances. The ineffectiveness of the tax has later been used as an argument to decrease or abolish it. Not even in the middle of the twentieth century, when the rates peaked, did the inheritance tax revenues represent more than one or two per cent of the annual revenues.[74] It has, so to speak, been a tax that has resulted in more debate than income. Thus, it is not possible to understand it just as an economic question. Support for the tax depends on different societal understandings of the nature of property, family relations and the role of the state. But public notions about inheritance and the amount of inherited wealth are also important. Recent findings indicate, for example, that the support for inheritance taxation is closely linked to perception of the

[73] In fact, inheritance taxation in Sweden was abolished by a Social Democratic government.
[74] Ohlsson (2011). For a contemporary picture, see Drometer et al (2018) 48–51.

societal importance of inherited wealth. Increased inequality more often leads to support for income taxation than wealth taxation, basically because a low salience of inherited wealth.[75]

In a historical perspective, the understanding of what inheritance is – and the nature of inherited wealth – can explain different strands in the political debates. That the family principle was articulated in Norway was based on the idea that the property structure mainly consisted of inherited farmland. It is a notion that, for the Norwegian part, stretches far back in time and differs from Sweden and Denmark. In the nineteenth-century land policy debates, there was also a clear difference between Sweden and Norway, based on a stronger Norwegian defence against market forces and an emphasis on the importance of keeping farmland within the family.[76] In other words, in contrast to the non-existing egalitarianism ideal, the discursive differences that emerged between the countries regarding inheritance taxation during the twentieth century had deep historical roots.[77]

References

Acemoglu, D and Robinson, JA, *Economic Origins of Dictatorship and Democracy* (Cambridge, Cambridge University Press, 2006).

Bastani, S and Waldenström, D, 'Perceptions of Inherited Wealth and the Support for Inheritance Taxation' (2021) 88 *Economica* 532.

Beckert, J, 'The Long Durée of Inheritance law. Discourses and Institutional Development in France, Germany, and the United States since 2008' (2007) 48 *European Journal of Sociology* 79.

—— *Inherited Wealth* (Princeton, NJ, Princeton University Press, 2008a).

—— 'Why is the Inheritance Tax so controversial?' The Foundation for Law, Justice and Society (2008b).

Bengtsson, E, 'The Swedish Sonderweg in Question: Democratization and inequality in comparative perspective, c. 1750–1920' (2019) 244 *Past & Present* 123.

Bradley, D, 'Politics, Culture and Family Law in Finland: Comparative Approaches to the Institution of Marriage' (1998) 12 *International Journal of Law* 288.

Dackling, M, 'Traditional or Modern Peasants? *Odelsrett* and *Bördsrätt* in Parliamentary Debates 1810–1860' (2020a) 46 *Scandinavian Journal of History* 63.

—— 'Staten som arvinge. Arvsskatt i politisk debatt i Skandinavien, ca 1890–1935' (2020b) 82 *Slagmark* 53.

Drometer, M, Frank, M, Hofbauer Péréz, M, Rhode, C, Schworm, S and Stittender, T 'Wealth and Inheritance Taxation: An Overview and Country Comparison' (2018) 16 *ifo DICE report* 45.

[75] Bastani and Waldenström (2021).

[76] Dackling (2020a) 14–15.

[77] This chapter draws on research carried out in the project 'The inherited problem: the politics of inheritance in Scandinavia 1800–2000', founded by *Vetenskapsrådet*. Some results have previously been published in Swedish (Dackling, 2020b).

Du Rietz, G, Henrekson, M and Waldenström, D, 'Swedish Inheritance and Gift Taxation (1885–2004)' in M Henrekson and M Stenkula (eds), *Swedish Taxation: Developments since 1862* (New York, Palgrave Macmillan, 2015).

Dubeck, I, 'Arveskifte og arveavgift I retshistorisk belysning' in L Dybdahl (ed), *Generationsskifte i ret og praksis: festskrift til Finn Taksøe- Jensen 19. mai 1999* (Copenhagen, Magnus, 1999).

Eberstein, G, *Den svenska arvslotts- och gåvobeskattningen* (Stockholm, Norstedts, 1956).

Esping-Andersen, G, *The Three Worlds of Welfare Capitalism* (Cambridge, Polity, 1990).

Graetz, M J and Shapiro, I, *Death by a Thousand Cuts: The fight over Taxing Inherited Wealth* (Oxford, Oxford University Press, 2005).

Gustafsson, H, *Nordens historia: en europeisk region under 1200 år* (Lund, Studentlitteratur, 1997).

Halliday, D, *The Inheritance of Wealth: Justice, Equality, and the Right to Bequeath* (Oxford, Oxford University Press, 2018).

Henrekson, M and Waldenström, D, 'Inheritance Taxation in Sweden, 1885–2004: The Role of Ideology, Family Firms, and Tax Avoidance' (2016) 69 *Economic History Review*, 1228.

Kananen, J, *The Nordic Welfare State in Three Eras: From Emancipation to Discipline* (Farnham, Ashgate, 2014).

Kautto, M, 'The Nordic Countries' in F Castles et al (ed), *The Oxford Handbook of the Welfare State* (Oxford, Oxford University Press, 2010).

Kocka, J, 'The Uses of Comparative History' in R Björk and K Molin (eds), *Societies Made up of History: Essays in Historiography, Intellectual History, Professionalisation, Historical Social Theory & Proto-industrialisation* (Stockholm, Akademitryckeriet, 1996).

Munkholm Povlsen, JB and Krog Thomsen, E 'Et bidrag til belysning af arveafgiftens historie' (1982) 5 *Justitia* 1.

Ohlsson, H, 'The Legacy of Swedish Gift and Inheritance Tax, 1884–2004' (2011) **15** *European Review of Economic History* 539.

Piketty, T, *Capital in the Twenty-First Century* (Cambridge, Mass, Belknap Press of Harvard University Press, 2014).

Scheve, K and Stasavage, D, 'Democracy, War, and Wealth: Lessons from Two Centuries of Inheritance Taxation' (2012) 106 *American Political Science Review* 81.

Scheve, K and Stasavage, D, *Taxing the Rich: A History of Fiscal Fairness in the United States and Europe* (Princeton, Princeton University Press, 2016).

Stråth, B, *Sveriges historia. 1830–1920* (Stockholm, Norstedts, 2012).

Tank, Y, *Arveavgiftslovgivningen: Lov om avgift på arv og visse gaver av 19. juni 1964 med senere endringer* (Oslo, Norsk skattebetalarförening, 1973).

Wigforss, E, *Egendomsutjämning och arvsskatt* (Stockholm, Tiden, 1928).

16

Émile Durkheim's Proposal to Abolish Inheritance*

MÉLANIE PLOUVIEZ

'Inheritance of wealth implies as its counterpart the inheritance of misery'[1]

I. Introduction

As demonstrated by Anthony B Atkinson for the UK, by Joseph Stiglitz for the US, and by Thomas Piketty for France and other European countries,[2] inherited wealth has been making a comeback since the 1970s. After decreasing in the first half of the twentieth century, the share of inherited wealth in the total resources of households has now reached a level comparable to the level it held in the nineteenth century. Far from benefiting everyone, this comeback is a strong factor of discrimination because it is highly concentrated.[3]

Despite this inheritance comeback, the contrast is striking between the nineteenth century's rich ideas and debates regarding inheritance, and the relative silence of today. First contrast: in the nineteenth century, the subject of inheritance was omnipresent. It was impossible to address the 'social question' without first questioning the legitimacy of inheritance itself. To give just one example, Charles Renouvier, a proponent of a republicanism inspired by

* This article was translated from the French with the help of Tracy Nuzzo.

[1] Durkheim (2009) 137.

[2] Atkinson (2018); Stiglitz (2019); Piketty (2011); Piketty (2014); Piketty, Alvaredo and Garbinti (2017).

[3] In 2010–11 in France, the 10% highest fortunes represented about 62% of the total wealth of the country, while the 50% lowest ones only corresponded to 4%. In the US, over the same period, the top decile owned 72% of US wealth, while the bottom half only 2%. See Piketty (2014) 257.

Kant, defended in his *Science de la morale* (1869) the total freedom to bequeath. However, this defence begins with a very radical assessment of the inheritance institution itself:

> But what is not so clear is that a person may legitimately dispose of what is possessed, at the time when, after death, it is no longer possessed. … Is not the right to bequeath an abuse derived from a fiction?[4]

Second contrast: in the nineteenth century, the range of positions held regarding inheritance was very wide. Some defended the complete freedom to bequeath, others were in favour of a cap on inheritances,[5] or a progressive taxation of inheritance,[6] or a distinction between first and second generation transfers.[7] Some suggested granting an equal endowment to all young adults[8] while others held still different abolitionist positions.[9] In contrast, our contemporary political imagination seems very meagre. Today we seem incapable of thinking about a reform of this institution in terms other than of levels of inheritance taxation. We seem incapable of seriously considering or even imagining the abolitionist position as a possibility. Third contrast: in the nineteenth century, inheritance reform targeted radical goals. The reform or abolition of inheritance was considered to be a favoured instrument for transforming society, introducing greater equality and extending the democracy of political rights acquired during the French Revolution and to new social and economic rights not yet acquired. This is illustrated by the abolitionist positions proposed at the time. Mikhail Bakunin, for example, suggested transferring the capital resulting from the abolition of inheritances to a fund to support education and public instruction with the intention of establishing education as a right for all.[10]

This chapter examines one of the abolitionist positions specific to the nineteenth century, namely that defended by Émile Durkheim (1858–1917), the founding father of French scientific sociology. Contrary to the conservative interpretations that are regularly made, Durkheim expressly and repeatedly speaks out in favour of the abolition of inheritance and its transfer to occupational groups. My purpose is to highlight the two ways in which the Durkheimian proposal is original compared with other abolitionist positions of the same period. First, Durkheim bases his abolitionist claims on sociology. Studying morphological evolutions of the family, Durkheim shows that inheritance is archaic, adapted to old forms of the family but unsuited to the modern, conjugal family. In the process, he sociologically denaturalises inheritance by historicising and de-essentialising its

[4] Renouvier (1908) 46 (my translation).

[5] John Stuart Mill, for example, in books 2 and 5 of his *Principles of Political Economy*: see Mill (2004).

[6] In the late writings of Charles Renouvier, for example.

[7] See Rignano (1901).

[8] Thomas Skidmore, François Huet or Hippolyte de Colins, for example.

[9] Babeuf, the Saint-Simonians, Bakunin, or even Durkheim.

[10] Bakunin (2009).

link to the family and to private property (section II). Second, Durkheim proposes that the capital resulting from the abolition of family inheritances be transferred, on the death of individuals, not to the state, but to the occupational group to which they belong. This is an unprecedented way of connecting the abolitionist position to the question of work, which goes against the common allegation that abolishing inheritances would remove the motivation to work. Above all, for Durkheim, this proposal offers the possibility of completely overhauling the organisation of work by introducing more social democracy and allowing workers to acquire new social rights (section III).

II. Family Inheritance as an Anachronism

Émile Durkheim unwaveringly supports the abolition of family inheritance. He deals with the question of inheritance in more than 20 texts written from 1886 to 1913. The corpus of literature that Durkheim devotes to inheritance shows that his normative proposal is not external to the new science of societies he founded, but is at its very heart. It stands at the crossroads between his sociology of family and his sociology of property rights. Based on the morphological evolution of the family from the clan family of totemic tribes to the modern conjugal family, and on the corresponding evolution of property rights, Durkheim advances this surprising thesis: inheritance is a vestige of primitive family communism, a remnant totally unsuited to the modern conjugal family and to the regime of individual property.

It is a little-known fact that the first branch of sociology on which Durkheim founded the new science of societies is the sociology of the family, to which Durkheim devoted 10 years of courses. This is often ignored because the Durkheimian corpus on the family is scattered: with the exception of the introductory lecture to his 1888–89 course, entitled 'Introduction à la sociologie de la famille',[11] and the last lecture of his 1891–92 course entitled 'La famille conjugale',[12] these teachings have not been published even in French. Besides these two lectures, the only details we have regarding their content is the summary written by Marcel Mauss and the more detailed presentation given by Georges Davy.[13] In this section, I will explore the Durkheimian sociology of family using an exceptional yet complementary source, rarely studied until now: the numerous book reviews on the family that Durkheim wrote in the 12 issues of the review he founded, *L'Année sociologique*, under the categories 'Family' and 'Marriage' in the 'Domestic organisation' section for which he was responsible.[14]

[11] Durkheim (1975) 9–34.
[12] Durkheim (1965).
[13] Mauss (1925); Davy (1925).
[14] In fact, Durkheim's scientific works are not limited to his books, articles and published courses one usually studies. From 1898 to his death, Durkheim wrote more than 500 book reviews, primarily for *L'Année sociologique*, which is a little-explored corpus.

In this scattered corpus – and this is even less known – Durkheim explains social evolution no longer according to the very general typology of mechanical and organic solidarity which dominates *The Division of Labour in Society*, but according to a precise classification of family types, based on a considerable amount of ethnographic material.[15] Durkheim describes the morphological evolution of family institutions in several stages: the amorphous exogamous clan; the differentiated clan composed of families, either matrilineal or patrilineal; the joint agnatic family (the *joint family* of Sumner Maine, the Slavic *zadruga*, etc); the Roman patriarchal family; the Germanic paternal family; and finally, the modern conjugal family. It is not my purpose here to detail each stage of this development. It may, however, be useful to compare its starting point to its end point. At the starting point, Durkheim places the clan family, whose first forms can be observed in the totemic Australian tribes (particularly in the Kamilaroi and the Kurnai studied by Fison and Howitt and in the Arunta studied by Spencer and Gillen), and to a lesser extent, because they correspond to an already more advanced stage, in the totemic tribes of North America (primarily the Haudenosaunee tribes studied by Morgan).[16] At the end point, Durkheim places the modern conjugal family. According to him, two morphological laws sum up this evolution from the clan family to the conjugal family.

The first law is called 'the law of contraction' and it applies to the size of the family group: the history of family institutions coincides with 'the reduction in the number of family members and the concentration of family ties'.[17] The ethnographic observation that caught Durkheim's attention is that the clan forms one and the same family. In other words, the clan family can include up to several thousand individuals. For Durkheim, this implies that kinship within the clan is not a natural kinship based on biological consanguinity. The clan is based on an artificial kinship, which Durkheim describes as totemic, in line with the work of Robertson Smith. Thus, the members of the clan consider themselves kin, not because they are fathers, mothers, sons, daughters, brothers and sisters, etc, but because they think they come from a common mythical ancestor: the totemic being. With the concept of clan kinship, Durkheim completely redefines kinship which he dissociates from the concept of generation with which it is usually assimilated. However, that does not mean that totemic kinship is unrelated to biological descent. The members of the clan maintain certain consanguinity relationships. Yet, within the clan, kinship is not proportional to the degree of

[15] The principal ethnographic works that Durkheim used to support his family sociology are those of Alexis Giraud-Teulon, Albert Hermann Post and Theodor Waitz on the most primitive forms of the family; of Johann Jakob Bachofen on the maternal family; of John Lubbock, John Ferguson McLennan, Lewis Henry Morgan, Lorimer Fison and Alfred William Howitt on the exogamous family; of August Rossbach, Numa Denis Fustel de Coulanges and Moritz Voigt on the Roman family; of Sumner Maine on the *joint family*; of Emil Friedberg, Rudolf Sohm and Hermann Habicht on the Germanic family; of Joseph Bergel, C von Vincenti and Johann Heinrich Plath on the oriental family.

[16] Fison and Howitt (1880); Spencer and Gillen (1899). Morgan (1877).

[17] Marcel Mauss, 'Note 15' in Durkheim (1965) 532.

consanguinity. On the one hand, the same kinship nomenclature can include different degrees of consanguinity.[18] On the other hand, ceremonial techniques are required not only for adoptions, but even for consanguineous relationships, in order to introduce totemic kinship. The child does not become a member of the clan by the mere fact of his or her birth. Consanguinity is not a sufficient condition for kinship. Thus, in the clan family, kinship is widely dissociated from descent. It is a social and not a natural regulation, which depends on the social institution of the family, rather than on the biological act of generation. Compared with the clan group comprising several thousand individuals, the modern nuclear family is very small: indeed, it is limited to the nucleus composed of the spouses and their immediate descendants, and this only until they come of age. Thus, we see the extent to which we naturalise and essentialise blood ties when we consider the conjugal family as the natural and universal form of the family.

The second law refers to the family property rules: 'The constitution of the family is modified as its volume contracts. From this point of view, the great change produced is the progressive destruction of familial communism.'[19] The clan family is organised by what Durkheim calls familial or domestic communism, with two axes: first, all the parents live together (community of life); and second, all the parents share their possessions (community of goods). The originality of Durkheim's position lies in the co-establishment of the family and of the family's things. First, because the clan family extends to all current and future members of the clan, it offers an extremely stable base for the family's assets, unshaken by the hazard of individual death. This is one of the main critiques that Durkheim wields against modern inheritance regime: the conjugal family cannot offer a sufficiently stable and lasting foundation for the family assets. Indeed, the conjugal family is contracted around a single conjugal nucleus which makes the family assets strongly dependent on individual death. Second, the clan family holds together by the possessions shared. According to Durkheim, in the clan family, the family attachment is more an attachment to the family things than to the family persons. The family is associated first and foremost with possessions that are held in common and that are sacred things: ritual objects such as the Australian *churinga* or land owned in common. Clan solidarity is a link between relatives, not because of their kinship but because of the possessions they share.

[18] In Lewis Henry Morgan's terminology, in exogamous clans with uterine filiation, the kinship system is not descriptive but classificatory. In *Ancient Society*, Morgan distinguishes two types of terms used for kinship: the descriptive type and the classificatory type. In the classificatory type, 'consanguinei are never described, but are classified into categories, irrespective of their nearness or remoteness in degree to *Ego*; and the same term of relationship is applied to all the persons in the same category'. In this type, direct and collateral kin are classified in the same category. In the descriptive type, 'consanguinei are described either by the primary terms of relationship or a combination of these terms, thus making the relationship of each person specific'. In this second type, the direct kin (father, mother, son, etc) are distinguished from collateral kin (brother of my father, son of my father's brother, etc); Morgan (1877) 403–04.

[19] Durkheim (1965) 532.

This co-establishment of the family and of the family's things can be seen more particularly in the inheritance customary rules. Durkheim notes that, in the most undifferentiated clans which he calls 'amorphous exogamous clans' (in which he detects the elementary form of the family), inheritance itself is collective and undifferentiated: 'Originally it [the right of succession] appertains indefeasibly to all relatives, even the most distant collaterals.[20] The family's assets are collective and inalienable: they belong to the family and remain in the family irrespective of the desires of one, several or even all of its members. Better still, kinship can be reversible, while the family's assets can never be. Because kinship is artificial, it can be broken by secession or acquired by adoption. But the family's assets remain non-transferable.[21] This inalienability of the family's things determines what individuals have to be and do, whatever their individual aspirations may be. To show that this 'possession of people by things' can become 'a real form of slavery', Durkheim studies the Athenian Epicleros:[22]

> This is what happened to the 'epicleros' daughter in Athens. If the father had as offspring a daughter only, she would inherit, but it was the status in law of the property which came to her that fixed her own status in law. Since the estate could not go out of the family, precisely because it was the very heart of it, the heiress was bound to marry her nearest male relative; if she was already married, she had either to break her marriage or renounce her heritage. The person followed the thing: it was a question of the daughter being inherited rather than inheriting.[23]

This submission of people to family possessions is another main critique that Durkheim wields against modern inheritance regime: as an heir, the individual does not determine himself, but is determined by the family's things. They possess the individual as much as the individual possesses them. The individual is inherited as much as he or she inherits.

It is within this framework that Durkheim identifies the modern inheritance institution as an anachronistic remnant of primitive domestic communism.[24] The second law shows how family communism progressively shrinks as the size of the domestic group decreases. Durkheim describes the correlative changes that occur in family, property rights, and inheritance rules: in the amorphous exogamous clan, ownership is fully collective, extended to all things and to all members of the clan, with inalienability of the family's asset; in the agnatic family,

[20] Durkheim (1965) 533.

[21] Durkheim (2003) 164.

[22] In Greek antiquity, the heiress, known as the 'epicleros', was the daughter who, in the absence of a brother, inherited her father's estate on his death. This heiress was obliged to marry her father's closest relative in order to have children with him who would inherit the estate of their maternal grandfather.

[23] Durkheim (2003) 164.

[24] 'The right of succession no longer has any basis. The right of succession has, in fact, become nothing more than family communism persisting under the regime of private property. If communism is retreating, then, disappearing from all the zones of the family, how can this right be maintained'. Durkheim (1965) 533. 'Inheritance is therefore bound up with archaic concepts and practices that have no part in our present-day ethics'. Durkheim (2003) 174.

the collective ownership is limited to agnates, excluding collateral kin, with patrimonial transmission limited to agnates; in the patriarchal family, individual property appears for the father, with emergence of a right to bequeath; in the conjugal family, individual property is extended and collective family property is reduced to the conjugal unit (conjugal community property regime). This second law subsumes two correlative processes. In the first process, family communism (community of life and community of goods) gradually contracts: from the clan as a whole to the group of agnates, to the patriarchal house, and finally to the conjugal nucleus. In the second process, along with this shrinking, individual property develops, with individuals progressively endowed with a right to individually enjoy collective family property.

This is where the ethnographic history of property rights proposed by Durkheim takes on a new dimension: the right of individual property, in its first forms, is only the right granted by the family by which the individual can use these goods during his life. But this right ceases on the death of the individual, when the individual goods become family possessions once again. According to Durkheim, this is the very origin of inheritance law:

> In this way the right of succession came to be established. For a long period the right of family joint ownership was so strong and respected that, although the family no longer lived as a community, this right stood opposed to any actual holder being able to dispose of his property through donation, testamentary or otherwise. He had only a right of life interest: it was the family who was the owner.[25]

In other words, according to Durkheim, individual property has historically developed as a right of individual use without any right of alienation in a context of collective family property. This individual right of use without any right to dispose is particularly clear upon the death of the individual. To mention only one of the examples studied by Durkheim, in the intermediary clan society of the Baganda, where families and individuals had begun to differentiate, individuals own personal goods and each new household builds its own house. But 'the clan keeps a right of eminent domain over the property of each individual, which is evident at the time of the inheritance': the clan, and not the individual owner, designates the heirs.[26] This kind of concession of collective family property to individual property is in no way primitive: it was still practiced, for example – and this is not one of Durkheim's examples – in the system of *substitution héréditaire* which was abolished in France only at the French Revolution, or in the entails of British law which lasted until 1925 (and which were beautifully described and condemned by Jane Austen in her various novels).

The current inheritance institution is a *vestige*, a *remnant* of ancestral family communism. For Durkheim, it is even the last form of hereditary transmission tolerated: 'For the hereditary transmission of property is but the last, and the

[25] Durkheim (2003) 174.
[26] Durkheim (1975) 307–08.

most tenuous, form of hereditary transmission'.[27] In earlier times, the family was the place where a profession, offices, dignities and even political power were hereditarily transmitted. Today, it is illegal to inherit a profession or political power. Yet, we continue to accept that economic wealth be transmitted hereditarily according to a biological lineage.[28] Durkheim suggests that the French Revolution did not go far enough: the arguments which led to the prohibition of the hereditary transmission of professions should equally have led to the prohibition of the hereditary transmission of economic wealth. The hereditary transmission of occupations confers on individuals a profession not by virtue of their individual merit, but by virtue of their family. The hereditary transmission of property equally allows individuals to be rich or poor by virtue of their birth, whatever their respective merits and efforts. If the hereditary transmission of occupations is unfair and illegal, the hereditary transmission of economic wealth is just as unfair, although it is not yet illegal – which, according to Durkheim, it should become thanks to the abolition of family inheritances.

Durkheim concludes from his ethnographic history of property and inheritance law, that the right to individual property is strictly limited by the chronological limits which are the birth and death of an individual. 'For individual property is property that begins and ends with the individual.'[29] Any extension of ownership beyond these individual boundaries is a form of collective ownership. The point, for Durkheim, is to replace family communism, unsuited to modern times, with another post-mortem form of collective property, which I will present in the following section and which can be called 'occupational communism'.

III. The Transfer of Family Inheritance to the Occupational Group

Supported by his sociology of the family and his ethnographic history of property and inheritance rights, Durkheim argues for abolishing family inheritance. The modern conjugal family is, because of its restricted size, morphologically unsuited to remain the basis of economic life. It is also illegitimate as it perpetuates birth inequalities. This points to the direction to follow: legally prohibit the transmission of hereditary assets. Thus, Durkheimian sociology proposes a modified right to property, which combines the right to individual property during one's lifetime with a form of collective, yet non-family property, after death.

It remains, however, to be understood what, in the Durkheimian proposal, should happen upon an individual's death to the capital accumulated during his or her lifetime. This is where the Durkheimian proposal stands out for its originality.

[27] Durkheim (1965) 534 (my translation).
[28] Durkheim (2003) 216–17.
[29] Durkheim (2003) 217.

Durkheim does not recommend that family inheritance be transferred to the state. If the conjugal family is morphologically unsuited to support economic life, so too is the modern state, according to Durkheim. The first is too limited, too ephemeral, too dependent on the random death of its members. The second is too far removed from economic activities. Durkheim therefore proposes to transfer the capital resulting from the abolition of family inheritances to the occupational group which, in his view, is the only social group morphologically capable of supporting modern economic life.

In doing so, Durkheim intends to overcome one of the recurring arguments against abolitionist projects: why would individuals continue to work if they no longer have the prospect of passing on the fruits of their labour to their children? Durkheim notes, on the one hand, that such an argument has validity only in the current organisation of private property and familial inheritance. Thus, he points to a vicious cycle of family inheritance: because hereditary transmission creates an initial inequality, we seek that our children are the least affected by this inequality, so we work to transmit to them the fruits of our labour and in doing so we increase the initial inequalities.[30] On the other hand, Durkheim intends to substitute a motivation to work driven by attachment to the occupational group for the motivation to work driven by family attachment. In this manner he proposes an unprecedented link between abolishing inheritance and rethinking work.

This original Durkheimian provision has largely been forgotten. On three occasions, in his 1892 course on the conjugal family,[31] between 1898 and 1900 in his course on *Professional Ethics and Civic Morals*,[32] and in the preface to the 1902 second edition of the *Division of Labour in Society*,[33] Durkheim argues that inheritance should no longer be passed on to descendants or legatees, or even to the state, but to occupational groups. Because of this provision, it is only possible to fully understand the Durkheimian inheritance abolitionist position by going into the details of his occupational group reform.[34]

[30] 'It is clear that at the present day the idea that we could be prevented from leaving our possessions to our children would meet with very lively resistance. For our work is done quite as much to ensure their happiness as our own. That does not mean that this state of mind does not derive very closely from the present structure of property. Let us grant that there is a transfer by inheritance and in consequence an initial inequality in the economic status of individuals at the time they enter the life of the society. We then attempt to make this inequality have as little disadvantage as possible for the human beings with whom we have the closest ties; we go further, and try to make it even a positive advantage. Hence our anxiety to work for them. But if equality were the rule, this need would be of far less concern to us. For the peril to them of facing life with no resources but their own would have disappeared. This peril comes solely from certain people being at present endowed with initial advantages, a fact that places those not so endowed in a position obviously inferior'. Durkheim (2003) 217.

[31] Durkheim (1965) 534–36.

[32] Durkheim (2003) 218.

[33] Durkheim (1960) 30–31.

[34] The Durkheim proposal for occupational group reform is often reduced to three works: the concluding chapter of the 1897 *Suicide* (Durkheim (2002) 328–59), the first three 1899–1900 lectures of *Professional Ethics and Civic Morals* dedicated to 'Professional Ethics' (Durkheim (2003) 1–41), and the preface to the 1902 second edition of the *Division of Labor in Society*, entitled 'Some Notes on Occupational Groups' (Durkheim (1960) 1–31). In doing so, one ignores that Durkheim has constantly returned to this proposal throughout his work and has detailed it in some 30 other texts (articles,

What is the situation of occupational groups at the time Durkheim writes? In France, under the *Ancien Régime*, the organisation of labour was structured by *corporations* and guilds which had two main characteristics: centered on the occupation, they grouped together all the members of the same profession; they thereby united, in the same organisation, the masters of the trade and the workers. Accused of perpetuating privileges, these *Ancien Régime corporations* were dismantled during the French Revolution by the D'Allarde Decree and the Le Chapelier Law of 1791. Thus, throughout the nineteenth century, all types of occupational group (*corporations*, guilds, but also trade unions, worker's associations, etc) were prohibited in the name of freedom of enterprise and trade. Even though the Waldeck-Rousseau Act of 1884 once again authorised trade unions and professional associations, their organisation remained, at the end of the nineteenth century, in its infancy. It is in this context of the disorganised occupational group that Durkheim makes the surprising, even unfortunate, choice to call for an overhauling of occupational *corporations*.[35]

But whatever the prejudices attached to the *corporation*, it is necessary to identify the reasons why Durkheim sought its renovation. Why is Durkheim calling for a reorganisation of the occupational group in the form of the *corporation* rather than as a trade union or worker association? For him, the *corporation's* first advantage is that it corresponds perfectly to the occupation, which was not the case of the nascent state of trade unions in France at the end of the nineteenth century. At the time, often there would be no union to defend an occupation, or there would be several competing unions defending a single occupation, or there would be one single union defending several occupations. In the Durkheimian plan, an occupation corresponds to a single *corporation*; and a *corporation* supervises a single occupation.

So, for Durkheim, the *corporation*, occupational group and occupation are all the same group. Thus, he considered the question of an obligation of affiliation to be of little relevance. There is, according to Durkheim, as little relevance to the question of whether membership in the *corporation* should be mandatory as there is to the question of whether an individual engaged in a particular occupation belongs to the occupational group that includes all members of the profession.[36]

book reviews, courses, debates). For the complete list of these texts, see Plouviez (2015) 62–63. From this little-used corpus, his project of occupational group reform proves not to be, as Raymond Aron asserted, the 'academic solution' of a professor of philosophy (Aron (2018) 47), but a relatively thorough plan, discussing the practical details of this institutional reorganisation and specifying the expected effects on professional and production relations.

[35] This choice of terminology has greatly hindered the reception of the Durkheimian proposal. Indeed, the *corporation* amasses the criticisms related to its *Ancien Régime* past (privilege of the masters, corporate selfishness, etc) and the criticisms related to its future, this institution having been largely misguided in the fascist experiments of the Corporate State.

[36] 'The occupation group, thus restored, … could it be mandatory? The question is of little importance. Because the individual couldn't remain outside of it. It is only prejudice that opposes this new obligation.' Durkheim (1975) 219 (my translation).

In short, the *corporation* that Durkheim calls for brings together, necessarily and at the national level, all the members of the same occupation, without considering other factors such as religion, political affiliation, or location.

For Durkheim, there is no question of restoring the former *corporations* of the *Ancien Régime* in the same forms. On the contrary, his reform project is a matter of profoundly transforming them through their democratisation. Indeed, the *corporation*'s second advantage, in Durkheim's eyes, is its social mix: *corporations* differ from unions in that they are made up of all employees and employers in the same occupation. Thus, one of the fundamental reasons that Durkheim chooses this professional institution, despite its bad reputation, is the *corporation's* social diversity. The characteristic separation of social classes, seen in trade unions, could not overcome the prevailing socio-economic inequalities and conflicts in the market.

> Finally, the syndicates of employers and the syndicates of employees are distinct from each other, which is *legitimate and necessary*, but with no regular contact between them. There exists no common organization for their union where they can develop a common authority, fixing their mutual relations and commanding obedience, without a consequent loss of individuality. Consequently, it is always the law of the strongest which settles conflicts, and the state of war is continuous. Save for those of their acts which arise from common ethics, employers and workmen are, in relation to each other, in the same situation as two autonomous states, but of unequal power. They can form contracts, but these contracts express the respective state of their military forces. They sanction a condition of fact; they cannot make it a condition of right.[37]

The relationship between employers' organisations and trade unions, when they remain separated into autonomous institutions, only reflects their respective strength in the labour market. In this way, labour relations are merely the recording of de facto inequalities. In Durkheim's view, the principle of trade union separation merely transfers the factual inequality that exists between the employer and the employee at the level of their respective professional organisations. It duplicates the inequalities characteristic of the economic world instead of imposing a standard of justice on them.

However, the social mix that characterised the *Ancien Régime corporations* did not make them fair. On the contrary, the *corporations* were run by the masters alone, and solely for their own interests. This is why Durkheim advocates democratisation of the *corporation* through election and democratic representation: the occupational group should be run not solely by the owners, but jointly by employers' and employees' elected representatives. So that this joint management does not degenerate into a monopolisation of decision-making power by the economically most powerful party, employers and employees must however remain, within the *corporation*, two separate and above all independent groups. The subgroup of employees and the subgroup of employers must constitute two separate and

[37] Durkheim (1960) 6.

independent electoral colleges, each responsible for electing representatives to the governing bodies of the occupation group. Each *corporation* must be run by what Durkheim calls an 'administrative council', which he conceives as a 'miniature parliament' composed of representatives of both the employees and employers of the occupation, in charge of all decisions concerning the occupation.[38] The Durkheimian renovated *corporation* does not constitute an anti-democratic institution. Rather, it is a democratically structured institution, governed by the elective principle and the deliberative procedure in its various bodies and in its various decisions.

One of the main functions that Durkheim assigns to the democratic *corporation*, which links his occupational group reform to his proposal to abolish inheritance, is to ensure 'occupational solidarity' between its members, in the form of social insurance funds, health insurance funds and retirement funds. These different funds are aimed at materially protecting members who are temporarily or permanently unable to work, because of disease, accidents, old age, etc.[39] What is most interesting about Durkheim's proposal is that this social solidarity must be financed bt the transfer of family inheritances to occupational groups.

How should individual property be transferred to *corporations*? On the death of an individual, his asset must be transferred to his occupational group. As for the management of the property which the *corporation* becomes the owner upon the death of its members, Durkheim imagines two possibilities: either the *corporation* 'possesses goods and exploits them itself', or it hands it over 'to some other individual holder to improve them.[40] In the first solution, it seems that the occupation group becomes a fully fledged player in economic life: it owns and operates the transferred goods; it employs, produces and sells on the market. In the second alternative, the *corporation* entrusts the operation of the transferred property to some individual holder. It would be a question of delegating the management of the assets received to private actors already existing in the professional sector concerned. Unfortunately, Durkheim does not specify the terms of this delegation (shareholding, concession, lease, etc) and its compensation.

Because of its very source of funding through family inheritance, Durkheim's occupational solidarity forms a largely innovative collective protection system. Occupational solidarity determines the social solidarity of workers not as a class consciousness, but as a set of social rights (right to healthcare, right to retirement, etc). Firstly, this occupational solidarity is compulsory. These social rights are not an optional private insurance but instead a compulsory social insurance, any individual necessarily bequeathing to his or her *corporation* his or her property, whatever it may be and whatever its importance. Secondly, these social rights are managed by all: the different occupational funds are democratically organised and jointly managed by employee and employer representatives, like

[38] Durkheim (2003) 37.

[39] If there is no mention in Durkheim's texts of unemployment funds, it is because involuntary unemployment is not yet a recognised occupational risk. Salais, Baverez and Reynaud (1999) 33–82.

[40] Durkheim (1960) 31.

the rest of the occupational bodies. Thirdly, these social rights are for the benefit of all: the resources of occupational solidarity are not reserved for the needy alone; they are for the benefit of all the members of the *corporation* in the form of new social protections. This system of collective protection differs from the mutualist protections imagined at the same time by Solidarists. Durkheim, unlike Charles Renouvier, Léon Bourgeois or Célestin Bouglé, theorises a social insurance whose contribution is compulsory for any member of the profession at his death, the benefit of which occurs at the occurrence of the risk whatever the amount of the *post-mortem* contribution, whose arithmetic thereby escapes the individual logic.

In this way, occupational solidarity, financed by the transfer of family inheritance to the democratic *corporation*, is kept away from any form of charity, even from public charity. In the Durkheimian proposal, occupational solidarity is not addressed to the 'poors', the 'miserables', the 'unfortunates' whose misery it would seek to 'alleviate' and 'soften' the painful fate, according to what Durkheim identifies in his course on *Socialism* as the communist logic of public charity.[41]

> To establish welfare projects alongside of economic life, is not to bind the latter to public life. The diffuse state in which industrial and commercial functions are found does not diminish because one creates welfare funds to ameliorate the fortunes of those who, temporarily or forever, have ceased to fulfill these functions. Socialism is essentially a movement to organize, but charity organizes nothing. It maintains the *status quo*; it can only attenuate the individual suffering that this lack of organization engenders.[42]

Instead, the transfer of family inheritance to a democratically organised occupational group should make it possible to move from a palliative treatment of the symptoms of social inequalities to a curative intervention on their causes. According to Durkheim, public charity is ineffective because it doesn't organise. Socialism can be effective because it aims to organise economic life. The reformed occupational group, with its social funds financed by family inheritance, is such a socialist organisation of economic, industrial and commercial sectors.

*

The hypothesis of this work is that there is, in past discourses on inheritance and inequalities, a possible source of profound renewal of our contemporary ways

[41] Émile Durkheim explains this in his course on *Socialism* through the different definitions he gives of communism and socialism. It is necessary at the outset to determine the specific meaning that Durkheim gives to these two doctrinal sets. 'Communism' refers to communitarian and collectivist utopias prior to the French Revolution that philosophically condemn private property. These are, on the one hand, the utopias of Plato, Thomas More or Tommaso Campanella which Durkheim groups under the name of 'ancient' communism. These are, on the other hand, those of Étienne-Gabriel Morelly, Gabriel de Mably or Jean-Jacques Rousseau which he places under the category of 'modern' communism. 'Socialism', for its part, refers to the set of post-revolutionary doctrines which propose an economic critique of large-scale industry. In the dichotomy established by Durkheim, the theory of Karl Marx, far from belonging to communism, therefore belongs to socialism.

[42] Durkheim (2009) 15.

of thinking about the problem of social justice. Even though the political and economic context of the nineteenth century is very different from ours today, the richness and radicality of the proposals made at that time regarding inheritance could contribute to fertilise our political imagination.

Returning to Durkheim allows us to consider firstly what our preconceived attachment to inheritance usually prevents us from thinking, namely the disjunction between inheritance, individual property and family. Durkheim challenges two pre-notional naturalisations to which we are constantly drawn when we think about inheritance. First naturalisation: we believe that the transmission of inherited wealth is an intrinsic property of the family. Durkheim shows instead that, although it is a characteristic of certain historical forms of the family, it is not characteristic of all of them, since the conjugal family is precisely the family form in which family attachment no longer passes through 'family things'. Second naturalisation: we believe that inheritance derives from individual property. Durkheim shows instead that inheritance is a survival of family communism which is precisely what makes it totally unsuited to the modern notion of private property.

But Durkheim's contribution to thinking about inheritance today is also in his proposal to transfer it to the occupational group, that is to say to a group close to the individual, in which the essential part of his or her life now takes place (as much, if not more, than in the family) and in which he or she can have active democratic participation. In this way, the wealth resulting from inheritance cease to be the source of original inequalities and instead become the instrument for acquiring new social rights. Such a proposal reopens theoretical possibilities which had ceased to exist for us: a path of reform of this institution, linked to the world of work, which makes it the ideal tool for extending democracy beyond the defence of political rights, through the acquisition of new social rights.

References

Aron, R, *Main currents in sociological thought. Volume 2 – Durkheim, Pareto, Weber* (London, Routledge, 2018).

Atkinson, AB, 'Wealth and inheritance in Britain from 1896 to the present' (2018) 16 *The Journal of Economic Inequality* 137.

Bakunin, M, *Le catéchisme révolutionnaire* (Paris, L'Herne, 2009).

Davy, G, 'Vues sociologiques sur la famille et la parenté d'après Durkheim' (1925) 100 *Revue philosophique de la France et de l'Étranger* 79.

Durkheim, É, *The Division of Labor in Society* (trans G Simpson) (Illinois, The Free Press of Glencoe, 1960).

—— 'A Durkheim Fragment: The Conjugal Family' (trans G Simpson) (1965) 70 *American Journal of Sociology* 527.

—— *Textes 3 – Fonctions sociales et institutions* (Paris, Éditions de Minuit, 1975).

—— *Suicide. A study in sociology* (trans JA Spaulding and G Simpson) (London and New York, Routledge, 2002).

—— *Professional Ethics and Civic Morals* (trans C Brookfield) (London and New York, Routledge, 2003).
—— *Socialism and Saint-Simon* (trans C Sattler) (London, Routledge & Kegan Paul LTD, 2009).
Fison, L and Howitt, AW, *Kamilaroi and Kurnai* (Melbourne, Robertson, 1880).
Mauss, M, 'In memoriam: l'œuvre inédite de Durkheim et de ses collaborateurs' (1925) 1 *Année sociologique* 13.
Mill, JS, *Principles of Political Economy* (New-York, Promotheous Books, 2004) (original work published 1848).
Morgan, LH, *Ancient Society, or Researches in the Lines of Human Progress from Savagery, through Barbarism to Civilization* (Chicago, Charles H Kerr and Co, 1877).
Piketty, T, 'On the Long-Run Evolution of Inheritance: France 1820–2050' (2011) 126 *The Quarterly Journal of Economics* 1071.
—— *Capital in the Twenty-First Century* (trans A Goldhammer) (Cambridge/London, Belknap Press, 2014).
Piketty, T, Alvaredo, F and Garbinti, B, 'On the Share of Inheritance in Aggregate Wealth: Europe and the USA, 1900–2010' (2017) 84 *Economica* 239-.
Plouviez, M, 'Le projet durkheimien de réforme corporative : droit professionnel et protection des travailleurs' (2015) 157–58 *Les Études Sociales* 57.
Renouvier, C, *La science de la morale*, vol 2 (Paris, Alcan, 1908) (original work published 1869).
Rignano, E, *Di un socialismo in accordo colla dottrina economica liberale* (Torino, Fratelli Bocca Editoria, 1901).
Salais, R, Baverez, N, and Reynaud, B, *L'invention du chômage* (Paris, Presses Universitaires de France, 1999).
Spencer, B and Gillen, FJ, *The Native Tribes of Central Australia* (London-New York, Macmillan and Co, 1899).
Stiglitz, J, *People, Power and Profits: Progressive Capitalism for an Age of Discontent* (New-York, WW Norton & Company, 2019).

INDEX

Printed in the USA
CPSIA information can be obtained
at www.ICGtesting.com
LVHW020334261023
762199LV00005B/48

9 781509 964819